Pakistan

Owen Bennett Jones was a BBC
1998 and 2001. He currently prese
Service.

Pakistan
Eye of the Storm

THIRD EDITION

Owen Bennett Jones

YALE UNIVERSITY PRESS
NEW HAVEN AND LONDON

For information about this and other Yale University Press publications, please contact:
U.S. Office: sales.press@yale.edu   www.yalebooks.com
Europe Office: sales@yaleup.co.uk   www.yaleup.co.uk

Set in Minion Pro by IDSUK (DataConnection) Ltd.
Printed in Great Britain by MPG Books Ltd, Bodmin, Cornwall

Library of Congress Cataloging-in-Publication Data
Bennett Jones, Owen.
   Pakistan: eye of the storm/Owen Bennett Jones.—3rd ed.
      p. cm.
Includes bibliographical references and index.
ISBN 978-0-300-15475-7 (ci: alk. paper)
   1. Pakistan—History.   I.   Title.
      DS382.J66 2009
      954.9105—dc22   2009020428

A catalogue record for this book is available from the British Library.
10 9 8 7 6 5 4 3 2 1

For my parents

Contents

Illustrations

Plates

Maps

designed with the help of the Army Press, Rawalpindi

Tables

Figures

Preface

I began the preface to the 2003 edition of this book with the remark that Pakistan is an easy place for a journalist to work. Sadly that is no longer true. Although most Pakistanis remain remarkably open and hospitable, the security risks now mean that it is difficult for Westerners to stay in major cities such as Peshawar and Quetta.

Many of those who helped with the earlier editions of this book have remained very help0ful. I repeat my thanks to Zaffar Abbas, Shahid Abbasi, Idrees Bakhtiar, Amit Baruah, Jaffar Bilgrami, Admiral (retd) Fasih Bokhari, Cecil Chaudhry, Paul Danahar, Karen Davies, Ms Ha, Hussain Haqqani, Mishal Husain, Abida Hussain, Mushahid Hussain, Talat Hussain, Fakhar Imam, Chris and Valerie Kaye, Michael and Kim Keating, Saleem Khan, Tanvir Ahmed Khan, Shahid Malik, Farooq Memon, Jugnu Mohsin, Niaz Naik, Abbas Nasir, Bob Nickelsberg, Richard Parrack, Brigadier (retd) Shaukat Qadir, Haroon Rashid, Brigadier Saulat Raza, Najam Sethi, Akhter Shah, Andrew Whitehead and S. Akbar Zaidi. Jaleel Akhtar did a tremendous job in responding to my ceaseless requests for books, figures and other documents.

This third edition of the book has benefited from the advice of Nicola Bennett Jones, James Brazier, Alexander Evans, Simon Henderson, Liliane Landor, Richard Lawson, Anatol Leiven, Barbara Plett, Farzana Sheikh, Sydney Sober and Andrew Whitehead. Graham Usher very kindly read all the chapters and although he disagrees with a fair amount of what I have written, he made many excellent suggestions. I would also like to acknowledge institutes and journals that have published my articles on Pakistan, some of which have formed the basis of the updated material in this book. They are the Royal Society for Asian Affairs, the *London Review of Books*, the Stanley Foundation and Chatham House.

Last, but by no means least, thanks to my wife Amanda and children Nic, Xara and Guy for their support and tolerance throughout the many hours I disappeared to my study.

Introduction

When the first and second editions of this book came out in 2002 and 2003 respectively, there was relatively little published about Pakistan. Since then, as the country has become one of the most important front lines in the US 'war on terror', there has been a profusion of material. As well as many new books there has been an even greater number of reports written by various think tanks around the world. As a result there is now a far better understanding of Pakistan than there used to be. Ideas such as the distinction between tribal and religious groups, the different agendas of the various militant outfits, the army's relationship with the militants and the relative merits of democratic and military rule have all become topics of debate on the front pages of major international newspapers. Because of its size, its location, its border disputes, its attitude to radical Islam and its nuclear weapons, Pakistan has long been a country that matters. And with the Pakistani state now engaged in a violent struggle with parts of its own population, it matters more than ever. This book, like the first and second editions, has the relatively limited ambition of providing a clear explanation of the history behind the many difficult issues that face Pakistan.

In December 2000 the CIA's National Intelligence Council produced a document that predicted what the world might look like in 2015. Its comments about Pakistan were especially controversial. The country, it declared, 'will not recover easily from decades of political and economic mismanagement, divisive politics, lawlessness, corruption and ethnic friction. Nascent democratic reforms will produce little change in the face of opposition from an entrenched political elite and radical Islamic parties. Further domestic decline would benefit Islamic political activists, who may significantly increase their role in national politics and alter the makeup and cohesion of the military, once Pakistan's most capable institution. In a climate of continuing domestic turmoil the central government's control will probably be reduced to the Punjabi heartland and the economic hub of Karachi'.[1]

The publication of the CIA report led to uproar in the Pakistani press. But even if the predictions seemed outlandish at the time, in retrospect they seem to have been remarkably well judged. By mid-2007, halfway into the 15-year period covered by the report, the government in Islamabad had lost control of the Federally Administered Tribal Areas on the border with Afghanistan, and significant parts of Balochistan and North West Frontier Province. The advance of the Taliban in both Afghanistan and Pakistan, and the evidence that the Pakistani establishment was, at the very least, protecting some of the militant groups, left the United States in a remarkable position. In March 2009 the chairman of the Joint Chiefs of Staff, Admiral Mike Mullen, and the head of US Central Command, General David Petraeus, both openly stated that the Pakistani state continued to maintain links with some elements of the Taliban. Off the record, US officials complained that Pakistan was providing military supplies to the Afghan Taliban.[2] Put more bluntly, the US was giving billions of dollars to a government that was actively helping jihadis to kill US troops.

This extraordinary situation could be explained in part by confusion about what the Taliban consisted of. The word 'taliban', which means religious students, came to prominence in the 1990s when a southern Afghan cleric, Mullah Omar, led a force of young ideologues to victory against the warlords in Afghanistan. Mullah Omar, like many of his adherents, had attended a madrasa, or Islamic seminary, in Pakistan: both his movement and his government became known as the Taliban. For all their Pakistani connections the Taliban were, before 9/11, active only in Afghanistan. But after the collapse of the Taliban government in late 2001 many of them, like some Al Qaeda members, fled to Pakistan.

The development of the Taliban since that time has been a complex process which has brought together many groups which have distinct histories, leaderships and funding arrangements. In this book I shall use the term Taliban to refer to the militant Islamists who have used jihadi ideology to seek power through violence in Pakistan and Afghanistan. But it has to be acknowledged at the outset that the Taliban movement is highly diverse and decentralised. Groups which are often included under the general term Taliban include Mullah Omar's fighters in Afghanistan, various radicalised tribal forces in Pakistan (including some young men from the diaspora whose corpses turned out to have tattoos of the emblems of British football clubs), advocates of sharia law, men devoted to sectarian violence, Uzbek and other foreign jihadis, former Kashmiri militant groups looking for new battlefields and Punjabi militant groups which used to fight in Kashmir. While all these groups share a vitriolic anti-Americanism and a willingness to use extreme violence, at various points in time elements of the Pakistani state have supported some groups and opposed others. Musharraf, for example, distinguished between sectarian groups (bad), Al Qaeda (bad, although not really Pakistan's problem), the Afghan Taliban (less than ideal, but engaged in a legitimate struggle and bound to win), the Pakistani Taliban (problematic, but acceptable as long as they stuck to helping the Afghan Taliban) and the Kashmiri groups (good, as long as they obeyed ISI instructions about where and when to fight).

The policy of treating parts of the Taliban in different ways gave Pakistan the possibility of denying Western accusations. Consequently, whenever General Musharraf was challenged with the complaint that elements of the state were working with the Taliban, he could respond by pointing out that in some places, the state was in fact fighting the Taliban. He could deflect claims that Pakistan was helping the Afghan Taliban, for example, by demanding recognition for his troops who had died fighting the Pakistani Taliban in the tribal area of Waziristan. The picture sometimes became even more convoluted because of the tendency of some Western observers to explain (sometimes with rather mischievous Pakistani encouragement) apparently inconsistent aspects of Pakistani policy by arguing that the main intelligence agency, the ISI, contained rogue elements who were acting without official sanction. I shall argue in chapter 6 that on all important policy areas the ISI in fact follows the orders of the senior military leadership.

For all these reasons it has never been easy to work out what attitude the army really has towards the Taliban. And yet, despite all the ambiguities, it is indisputable that in addition to his Waziri campaign, on two important occasions General Musharraf did order significant operations against Taliban fighters. The first was at the Lal Masjid – the Red Mosque – in Islamabad in July 2007. As I shall argue in chapter 1, the assault on the Red Mosque, which contained hundreds of armed militants, was a turning point. While the war currently being fought in Pakistan has many deep and long-standing causes, the Red Mosque assault was the trigger. For months Western governments had urged General Musharraf to take decisive action against the Red Mosque militants. Diplomats and officials, especially from the US and the UK, made the argument that the state could not afford to ignore such a direct challenge to its writ right in the heart of the capital city. Eventually that argument prevailed. But what General Musharraf feared, and what his Western interlocutors never understood, was how the militants would respond to the Red Mosque assault. Accustomed to decades of appeasement the militants were jolted into action and launched a ferocious campaign of suicide attacks and other bombings, targeting both security personnel and civilians. It was a moment when both the military and the militants began to understand that the only way they could resolve their differences was through violence.

The second major confrontation between the two sides came in 2008. Bajur, the smallest of the Federally Administered Tribal Areas, was remote and sparsely populated. The tribal areas had resisted control by the Pakistani state just as they had defied the British colonialists. By 2008, however, Bajur had come to be seen as the command and control centre for the Pakistani Taliban[3] and, under strong US pressure, the Pakistani military took a stand there. It also tried to widen the gap between the tribal leaders in Bajur and the religious militants. As well as being part of an international Islamic revival, the Taliban is a revolutionary movement enabling young tribal men to challenge the stifling authority of elders, or maliks. There is, in other words, a social as well as a religious aspect to the Taliban's appeal. Many maliks resent the militants who are trying to take control of their areas. Aware of these underlying tensions, the Pakistani army paid some of the maliks to form private armies or lashkars which, using their local knowledge, were better able to identify and punish Taliban elements in their society. By March 2009, the army could legitimately claim to have cleared Bajur of militants, but the victory came at a huge cost.

Hundreds of thousands of people, probably more than half of the population of Bajur, had been forced to flee their homes. Entire villages were so heavily bombarded that not one building remained standing.

The Bajur campaign was highly significant. Together with the assault on the Red Mosque in Islamabad, it marks one of the very few occasions in Pakistan's history when the state has decisively confronted the forces of radical Islam. But Bajur raised difficult questions. Was it the high-water mark of state resolve? Would Pakistan summon the will to mount similar campaigns in other jihadi-controlled tribal areas such as North and South Waziristan? And even if it did, would the campaigns work? Would the tribesmen displaced by the fighting blame the army, rather than the Taliban, for their desperate situation? Would the state manage to negotiate with the Taliban from a position of strength and exploit the opportunity to extend its writ? Or would it fail to capitalise on its military victories?

Some of those questions were answered in April 2009 when, in the Swat valley, the army launched its biggest offensive yet against the Taliban. Just a few hours' drive north from Islamabad, Swat was once Pakistan's most attractive tourist area. Honeymoon couples would go there to trek, fish for trout and even ski on the country's only piste. But the sense of serenity hid deep social fissures. The administration of justice in Swat had been an issue ever since the British first reached the valley in the nineteenth century. At that time it was a sparsely populated and remote place where the people lived under a mix of tribal and sharia law. Once the British established rudimentary military control of the North West Frontier Province, they set about extending their influence by working through the valley's most powerful family, the leading member of which was, in effect, the king of a mini-state and enjoyed the title of wali of Swat. The successive walis, descendants of a revered saint, were noted for their progressive ideas about education – opening girls' schools and sending the brightest and the best abroad to study. But their forward-looking policies were combined with some distinctly old-fashioned displays of ruthlessness.

Miangul Abdul Wadud Badshah, who ruled Swat between 1917 and 1949, described what happened after he brought the first car to the valley. The local children dared each other to dart out in front of it and on one occasion a small girl was accidently hit and killed. Reasoning that he might as well teach the other children a lesson, the wali had the girl's body tied to the car's back bumper. He then drove up and down the valley dragging the little corpse behind. It put an end to the children's games.[4] The paternalistic despotism of the walis remained in place until Pakistani independence in 1947, when Swat acceded to Pakistan, although it retained considerable autonomy. But in 1969 the last wali bowed to what he considered the inevitable, and Swat became fully integrated into Pakistan.

The Pakistani state, however, failed to fill the power vacuum created by the wali's departure. Swat was given the status of a Provincially Administered Tribal Area, a designation that led to considerable uncertainty as to which laws applied. It was unclear, for example, in the event of a conflict between the provincial and federal governments, which would prevail. And that left room for a local radical Islamist cleric, Sufi Mohammed, to make himself heard. A product of the anti-Soviet jihad, in 1988 Sufi Mohammed gave up fighting and returned to Pakistan to concentrate on preaching. Above all else he believed that the Pakistani legal system should be swept aside in favour of Quranic rulings. By 1993 Sufi Mohammed was directly confronting the state. In May of that year his organisation, the Tehrik e-Nifaz e-Shariat Mohammadi (TNSM), attracted an estimated 25,000 tribesmen to a rally. In 1994 the TNSM occupied the valley's main airport at Saidu Sharif, set up road blocks and kidnapped nearly 200 government functionaries including judges, civil servants, police officers and even three army captains.[5] It was a clear challenge to the authority of the state which, in time-honoured fashion, gave in without a fight. And the price it paid to regain nominal control of its territory and to get the hostages released was extraordinarily high: it agreed to the imposition of sharia law not only in Swat, but throughout the Malakand Division of which Swat is a part. The government justified its decision to cede so much of its authority by arguing that anyone going through the sharia system in Malakand would have a right of appeal to the regular provincial high court or the federal Supreme Court. Nevertheless, the Islamists had won a major concession. That is not to say that sharia law had no popular support in Swat: it did. Many Swatis not only looked back to the time of the walis when judicial hearings relied in part on Quranic principles, they also despaired of the regular courts ever delivering justice: it could take years to resolve the simplest of cases.

Sufi Mohammed next came to prominence after 9/11 and the US attack on the Taliban in Afghanistan, when he raised a force of 9,000 men to fight alongside the Taliban forces. 'Today, if we do not fight with the Muslims and for Islam,' he declared, 'tomorrow after Afghanistan, America will target another Muslim country . . .'[6] There were, however, a couple of significant flaws in his plan. First, even if his immediate target was the anti-Taliban Northern Alliance, he was effectively taking on America. Secondly, whilst the jihadis he led may have been zealous, they were ill-equipped: some went to fight the most advanced army on earth mounted on horseback and brandishing swords. Many of his followers were killed or captured and when he got back home he was imprisoned in Pakistan. So, too, was his son-in-law, Mullah Fazlullah, who had joined the private army, or lashkar, and gone to Afghanistan alongside Sufi Mohammed. In January 2002 Musharraf banned the TNSM.

While Sufi Mohammed stayed in prison, a disastrous decision was taken to release Fazlullah after just 17 months behind bars. He returned to Swat and assumed the leadership of his father-in-law's campaign there. Using a small FM radio station to broadcast his interpretation of Quranic readings, he became a master propagandist. His twice-daily broadcasts focused on the benefits of virtue, the perils of vice, the excellence of the Taliban and the perfidy of the Americans. His distrust of modernity even extended to the World Health Organization. He urged parents not to vaccinate their children against polio on the grounds that it was a conspiracy of the Jews and Christians to stunt the population growth of Muslims.[7]

Officials in the valley could see that Fazlullah was a menace. One ruefully remarked that he realised there was a problem when his wife put the TV on a bonfire.[8] 'Why can't the authorities deal firmly with Maulana Fazlullah,' the *Daily Times* asked with considerable prescience in 2007, 'who at this stage is still little more than a nuisance?'[9] Local officials, however, were too weak to act without central support. 'If I proceed against illegal FM radio stations the clerics accuse me of placing a ban on the Holy Quran. You tell me what I can do?' asked the

Swat district nazim, or mayor, Jamal Nasir Khan.[10] The problem was that Swati members of the National Assembly from the MMA religious alliance opposed any limits on Fazlullah.[11] Their stance was echoed by the MMA-controlled NWFP Provincial Assembly in Peshawar. Much as Musharraf may have disliked what was happening in Swat, he could hardly take on the MMA while they were part of his ruling coalition in the National Assembly. And whilst the MMA was defending Fazlullah, the authorities in Islamabad were not feeling any countervailing pressure: the cleric had not yet become a major issue for Washington. General Musharraf figured he could deal with Swat's militants in the future should the need arise, and in the meantime he saw little point in adding to his problems by creating another front.

It took the Red Mosque siege and a retaliatory suicide attack in Swat that killed 16 Pakistani soldiers and 3 civilians to change the military's thinking.[12] Two thousand Frontier Corps paramilitary troops were deployed to the valley in the hope that such a show of force would be enough to scare the militants off. But it was too little, too late. And in September 2007 Fazlullah made his move. His followers, enraged by the Red Mosque assault, took over towns and villages all over Swat. They encountered very little resistance. In many places the militants didn't even need to fire a shot; when they reached a town they would find that the police, fearing summary execution, had fled.[13]

With the security forces demoralised, the militants were a growing force. Realising that Swat had become an important battleground, former Kashmiri fighters, tribal militants and foreign jihadis all headed to the valley. Increasingly, outside elements came to dominate the TNSM. In October the militants mounted another devastating attack in which a suicide bomber blew up a military truck killing 17 members of the Frontier Corps. Within days Fazlullah's forces and their new allies had seized control of nearly 60 towns throughout the valley and declared the imposition of sharia law. They removed Pakistani national flags from all government buildings.[14] The militants wanted to terrify the local population, and they did so. In one incident they publicly decapitated six captured soldiers, a police officer and seven civilians, and paraded their heads in public. Music shops were torched, girls were barred from going to school, women were forced to wear burqas and men told to grow beards. In an attempt to emulate the Taliban across the border in Afghanistan, Fazlullah ordered his men to drill holes in the face of a massive 1,300-year-old statue of Buddha.

The poorly armed Frontier Corps was swept aside. In fact some of its members did not even want to fight their fellow Pukhtoons. For example, one member of the Frontier Corps, Wilyat, simply handed over his weapons to the militants: 'When I joined the paramilitary forces and we were sent to this area, we were told that non-Muslims had come into Pakistan and were fighting under the name of mujahideen giving Pakistan a bad name and creating lawlessness. But when our tour of duty came, we saw that these people were true Muslims and were fighting to implement sharia for the sake of Pakistan to stop the Hindus and the English coming. So we announced we were with them and would hand ourselves over to them.' One of his colleagues, Safraz, agreed. Asked about his military duty he replied: 'I have finished with that now. I am a Muslim and therefore I won't fight any more.'[15]

The militants also set about the task of enforcing their form of Islamic justice. An American academic, Nicholas Schmidle, was in Swat when Fazlullah first became dominant there and he witnessed a trial of three suspected kidnappers in front of 15,000 men and boys who were sitting on blankets and eating picnics. One of those due to be punished was a teenager:

He looked as if he might collapse, legs wobbling with fear as hundreds of heavily armed Taliban spread out around him. I stood among then waiting to see the boy receive 15 lashings ... Every time the whip crashed on the boy's back, the crowd called out the corresponding number of lashes as if counting down the final seconds of a baseball game. The teenager's body convulsed under the crack and thud of each lash. When he finally stood up he was shaking and drenched in tears. 'This punishment is permitted in Islam,' announced one of Fazlullah's deputies.[16]

Even the most relaxed of the generals in Rawalpindi could now see that they had a major problem: the Islamists were winning territory and taking over the functions of the state quite close to the capital. By having let things drift for so long, Musharraf had greatly complicated his task. Fazlullah and his Taliban backers had built up sufficient momentum to withstand a significant army operation. And whilst his men were confident, the population of Swat was terrified. At last, though, Musharraf acted and by November 2007 there were 20,000 troops in Swat. Equipped with artillery and helicopter gunships, they killed hundreds of militants, retook the towns and, on 29 November, captured Fazlullah's headquarters and arrested his brother. In a sense, then, the army prevailed. But total victory proved elusive: Fazlullah himself slipped away to fight another day.

Nonetheless the army had cleared militants from 90 per cent of the Swat valley. Fazlullah and his leadership team had been forced to take refuge high in the mountains. And when the people of Swat voted in the elections of February 2008, they revealed their feelings: by an overwhelming majority they rejected the Islamists and the violence they had brought to the valley, voting instead for the relatively secular Pukhtoon nationalists in the Awami National Party (ANP).

But there was a twist. The Pakistani state did not press home its advantage. In April 2008 General Ahmed Shuja Pasha (who a few months later became chief of the ISI) together with the ANP held talks to try to establish a lasting peace in Swat. As part of the deal the government released Sufi Mohammed from prison. In return, Islamabad won a TNSM statement that killing policemen was un-Islamic and an acceptance, as if any were needed, that the security forces had the right to act against any Islamic extremist who attacked the government. Fazlullah treated the peace initiative with contempt: 'We welcome the release of Sufi Mohammed,' he declared, 'but we will only lay down arms when the government will enforce sharia.'[17] Fazlullah demanded the release of all his men in detention, and an amnesty for all the clerics and madrasa students from the Red Mosque who had been captured and charged. To press home his demand he moved back into the valley. Eventually accepting that the peace talks had failed, in 2008 the army redeployed the soldiers to Swat.

The army would discover that its second battle for Swat was far tougher than the first. The recently elected ANP members of the National Assembly left the area for fear of being killed. Virtually everyone who could afford to do so followed their example. With a significant proportion of the valley under militant control and with intense conflict in the rest of it, local officials were quite unable to administer the area in any meaningful way. Policemen posted to Swat almost invariably left their jobs rather than accept what they thought would be a fatal assignment. Many of the militant fighters were impoverished local men who were motivated not only by the idea of jihad but also by a desire to kill the valley's leading families: it was a class struggle as well as a religious one. Young men burnt girls' schools throughout the valley. The military's response, often in the form of helicopter gunship assaults, inevitably led to civilian casualties resulting in increased militant recruitment.[18] Troops and civilians were once again killed in large numbers, sometimes as many as 50 a day: the events in the Swat valley could hardly have been more out of control.

In January 2009 the army chief, General Kiyani, on a visit to Swat, vowed to restore government control. 'The army has both the will and resolve to establish the writ of the government', he said.[19] Yet just two weeks after that statement the government in Islamabad, acting on military advice, signed a deal that recognised the writ of the Islamists and allowed them to impose sharia law in Swat with no right of appeal. It was a humiliating capitulation. The security personnel who died in Swat (and many of them had only fought with reluctance) had given their lives in vain. Not only would there now be Islamic law, but all the restrictions associated with Taliban rule would come into force: music, TV, clean-shaven male chins, girls' education and women's inheritance rights were all banned.

The main reason for the surrender in Swat was the army's misreading of public opinion in the valley. The victory of the Pukhtoon nationalist Awami National Party (ANP) in the 2008 elections had apparently shown that most Swatis rejected the militants and favoured a relatively secular, modernist approach. But the result was in some ways misleading because more than anything the Swatis wanted peace. Renewed fighting led the people to demand an end to the violence even if that meant accepting militant rule.

The fact that, when pushed to the brink, the people chose a few thousand militants over the army was highly significant. There were a number of factors behind the transmogrification of the demand for peace into an insistence that the army leave the valley. To some extent people were motivated by fear: the Taliban's public beheadings made many calculate that it was safer to support rather than oppose them. But there was more to it than that. The Swatis had long been known as highly devout, and by 2009 most of the wealthier and more moderate Swatis had fled the valley, leaving behind the poorer and more conservative elements in society. Even if most people remaining in the valley abhorred the militants' violence, at the same time they admired the depth of their faith and their willingness to risk their lives in defying the Pakistan army and its US backers. Furthermore, the jihadis offered some highly desirable policies such as quick (albeit rather rough) justice and a clampdown on anti-social elements such as drug dealers. The army, by contrast, represented successive governments in Islamabad which ever since 1969 had failed to rule Swat effectively. The wali of Swat may have been an anachronism but he offered better administration of justice and educational facilities than the Pakistani government ever managed.

The recent history of Swat is littered with missed opportunities. After 9/11 and their abortive lashkar to Afghanistan, both Sufi Mohammed and Mullah Fazlullah were behind bars. The valley would surely have benefited had they remained there. Fazlullah, the first to be released, was allowed to build a support base in Swat through his radio station which was never taken off-air. Despite these blunders, in 2007 the security forces did make potentially important gains, forcing the militants into the mountains. But even that victory was thrown away. The reluctance to consider radical Islamists as a genuine threat; the state's ambivalence about extending its writ; the desire to use negotiations rather than force; the constraints imposed by the very high levels of public antipathy towards the Americans, and by association the Pakistan army; and the arrogant belief that ultimately, in combat, the militants were no match for the army – all these factors contributed to the state's apathetic and disastrous response to the events in Swat.

And yet despite its track record, in April 2009 the state suddenly became serious. For the third time it sent troops into Swat, but this time was different: there was a greater will to win. Within two months the army was claiming to have killed over 1,200 militants in Swat alone. The violence forced another two million Pakistanis to flee their homes. A religious, social and political struggle was in full swing. The army campaign was the logical conclusion of the Red Mosque and Bajur operations, but the scale of the 2009 offensive led many to wonder why the state had changed its mind: what lay behind the new policy?

The key decisions were taken by the military and not political leadership. On paper President Asif Ali Zardari held all the power in Pakistan. He was not only legitimately elected but also had no civilian rivals for power. Other members of the government including the prime minister, Yusuf Raza Gilani, invariably deferred to Zardari. Given that a period of military rule had just ended and the army was reluctant to take over again so soon, Zardari could perhaps have asserted himself in the face of the generals. In fact, he never tried to. Instead, he followed the long-established Pakistani tradition of civilian politicians abdicating power to the military commanders. Indeed, Zardari's lack of interest in the army campaign of April 2009 was so marked that when it began he spent nearly two weeks abroad, some of it on a private holiday.

The army, by contrast, was hard at work. It moved into Swat for a number of reasons. First, public opinion had changed. During the 2007 assault of the Red Mosque, many Pakistanis had complained that the military had been too aggressive. Naturally inclined to respect and sympathise with devout young religious students, many believed that the army should have managed to negotiate a settlement rather than break into a mosque, all guns blazing. By 2009, however, the mood had changed. The first major blow to the jihadis' image came in early April in the form of a movie captured on a mobile phone showing a 17-year-old girl whimpering in pain as she was flogged by a Taliban official. Perhaps because of the obvious vulnerability of the victim, the pictures, which were repeatedly shown on the Pakistani news channels, had more of an impact than all the suicide attacks, beheadings and other much more serious acts of Taliban violence. Although it later claimed the movie was fake, the Taliban initially accepted that the incident had occurred and explained that the 17-year-old girl had been accused of an improper pre-marital relationship with a local electrician.[20]

Within days of the girl's flogging being broadcast, Pakistanis had another reason to worry about the Taliban. In breach of their ceasefire deal with the army, the militants moved from Swat and took over the adjoining area of Buner. This meant that they were now just 100 kilometres away from the capital, Islamabad. As they set about terrifying the locals and burning their TV sets, videos and music cassettes the rest of Pakistan began to wonder just what the Taliban's objectives were. Many Punjabis, with more than just a touch of condescension, had long taken the view that if the mountain people of the wild northwest wanted sharia law then they could have it. But it now seemed that the Taliban had rather greater ambitions and might be thinking of imposing their ideology on Pakistan as a whole. That impression became even more widespread when Sufi Mohammed, who had always said he was interested only in having sharia in Swat, apparently revealed his true intentions in a huge rally held to celebrate the government's decision to grant sharia to the valley. The ageing cleric, perhaps carried away by his success, revealed that he had a national agenda, declaring that democracy and Islam were incompatible and denouncing Pakistan's courts, not just in Swat but in the whole country.[21]

Together with the flogging video and the advance into Buner, the Pakistani public had received three wake-up calls in quick succession. General Kiyani, who had always argued that he could not fight the Taliban without broad public support, now calculated that he had the popular base he needed to mount a campaign. Whether he also felt compelled to go onto the offensive because of direct US pressure or threats is, for the moment, unclear.

Some officials tried to downplay the decision to fight in Swat, describing the military action as little more than a security operation against some troublemakers. But taken together with the army offensives which followed all over north-west Pakistan it was much more than that. The military was not just restoring law and order: it was engaged in a civil war.

The conflict between the army and the Taliban is brutal. While the militants have slaughtered their opponents and deployed child suicide bombers, the army has taken few prisoners. A few weeks into the Swat campaign the army claimed it had killed over 1,000 militants and wounded fewer than 50. When the military spoke of eliminating the Taliban it seems it meant just that. Both sides in the fight for Pakistan are formidable. Even if the military, with over half a million troops, succeeds in the short term, the militants have the strength and depth to keep fighting a guerrilla campaign for years to come. The militants may also show the capacity to open new fronts including in the Punjabi heartland. One of the crucial questions in the months and years ahead will be the resilience of Pakistani public opinion. The widespread criticism of the Taliban in early 2009 emerged so quickly that some believe it could equally rapidly revert to a more ambiguous position in which the government and the army would be under increasing pressure to bring an end to the violence by reaching some kind of negotiated settlement with the Taliban.

Some Pakistanis are predicting a Taliban victory. Mahboob Mahmood, for example, has concluded that the most likely outcome is the transformation of Pakistan into the world's first Sunni militant fascist state, which he calls Jihadistan. He fears that within a few years all or most of Afghanistan and Pakistan will fall to Pukhtoon groups such as the Taliban which can rely on their ideological fervour, command over an ethnically homogeneous territory, good funding arrangements (drugs and weapons sales as well as other mainstream businesses), the patience to fight a long war, well organised and highly motivated militant allies and finally, a revolutionary mood amongst Pakistan's impoverished youth. Jihadistan, he argues, could become a major international force and its creation 'will constitute one of the defining geo-political events of the 21st century' because its leaders will try to export their ideology and their militancy, via the Pakistani diaspora, all over the world. 'In addition to its sizeable revolutionary armies,' he writes, 'Jihadistan will possess a million man conventional military force, a nuclear missile arsenal, a nuclear weapons development capability, a substantial conventional weapons production capability and the world's largest informal weapons manufacturing industry. . . .'[22]

Such deep pessimism is by no means a mainstream view but few can doubt that the outcome of the battles (which could go on for years) in Swat and the tribal areas such as Bajur are critical. And yet these remote areas have in many ways never been fully integrated into the rest of the nation. The future of Pakistan, and it does hang in the balance, will ultimately depend on the battles yet to come in mainstream parts of the country. With remarkable speed, major cities such as Peshawar and Quetta have become insecure. In fact, neither is likely to 'fall' to the Taliban in a formal military sense, yet they are increasingly under Taliban influence. Many young Peshawarites, for example, already think of video shops selling Indian movies as immoral, and increasing numbers of women feel social pressure to cover themselves up. People who want local disputes resolved have started turning to Taliban leaders to arbitrate and enforce a settlement. Some see parallels with Soviet-occupied Afghanistan in which Moscow controlled the cities and the Mujahideen had the countryside. The Taliban is winning hearts and minds, and even if it has not yet managed fully to combine the ideologies of radical Islam and Pukhtoon nationalism, it is well on the way to doing so. Should Pukhtoon nationalists ever conclude that the best way for them to achieve an independent homeland would be to embrace radical Islam then Pakistan would face an existential threat.

Owen Bennett Jones
Oxford, June 2009

Note on Spellings

In transliterating words from Urdu and Pakistan's other languages, I have tried to strike a balance between reflecting the local pronunciation and finding a spelling that eases comprehension for a Western reader. To give an example, I favour the simpler spelling 'madrasa' over one possible alternative, 'madrassah'.

Names can be, and often are, spelt in several different ways. I have opted for the spelling preferred by the person being referred to, with one exception. In the interests of consistency I have used the standard 'Mohammed' even if the bearer of that name used a different spelling. I have not, however, standardised the spelling if it refers to an author of a printed book mentioned in my text or listed in the bibliography.

The word Baloch refers to the people, Balochi to the language. In line with official usage in contemporary Pakistan, I shall use Baloch and Balochi rather than the British Imperial versions, Baluch and Baluchi. Similarly, in line with official usage I prefer Sindh to Sind and Sindhi to Sindi.

Pathan, Pushtoon or Pukhtoon? I favour Pukhtoon on the grounds that it is closer to local pronunciation in North West Frontier Province. Similarly, Pukhto for the language. In line with contemporary usage in Pakistan, I shall refer to the dreamt-of Pukhtoon homeland as Pukhtoonkwa throughout the text.

All other place names are according to the *Times Atlas of the World*. In cases where I quote extracts from passages of text, I have stuck with the original spelling.

Chronology

1947   Independence of Pakistan

         Start of the first war in Kashmir

1948   Death of the founder of Pakistan, Mohammed Ali Jinnah

1952   Language riots in East Pakistan

1953   Anti-Ahmedi riots lead to the imposition of martial law in Lahore

1955   West Pakistan provinces are amalgamated into 'One Unit'

1956   Pakistan's first constitution is passed

1958   General Ayub Khan takes over in the first military coup

1959   The capital moves from Karachi to Islamabad

1965   Second war with India over Kashmir

1966   Bengali leader Mujibur Rahman publishes his Six Points

1969   General Yayha Khan takes over from General Ayub Khan

1970   First ever national elections are held in East and West Pakistan

1971   War in East Pakistan leads to the creation of Bangladesh

         Zulfikar Ali Bhutto comes to power

1972   Zulfikar Ali Bhutto signs the Simla Accord

         Zulfikar Ali Bhutto calls on Pakistani scientists to build a nuclear bomb

1973   Start of Baloch uprising demanding greater autonomy

1974   First Indian nuclear test

1977   General Zia ul Haq takes over in a coup

1979   Zulfikar Ali Bhutto hanged

         Soviet invasion of Afghanistan

1984 Siachin conflict begins

1986 MQM formally registered as a party

1988 General Zia killed in an air crash

Benazir Bhutto begins first administration

Start of Kashmir insurgency

Soviets withdraw from Afghanistan

1990 Benazir Bhutto's first administration is dismissed

Nawaz Sharif begins first administration

1993 Nawaz Sharif's first administration is dismissed

1994 Benazir Bhutto begins second administration

1996 Benazir Bhutto's second administration is dismissed

Taliban come to power in Afghanistan

1997 Nawaz Sharif begins second administration

1998 India and Pakistan conduct nuclear tests

1999 Kargil conflict in Kashmir

General Musharraf takes over from Nawaz Sharif in a coup

2001 General Musharraf abandons Taliban regime in Afghanistan

2002 Musharraf wins referendum allowing him to stay in power for a further five years

2004 A.Q. Khan makes his nuclear confession

2007 Siege of the Red Mosque in Islamabad

General Musharraf re-elected president after declaring a state of emergency

Benazir Bhutto and Nawaz Sharif return from exile to contest elections

Benazir Bhutto assassinated

2008 Musharraf resigns and Asif Ali Zardari becomes president

2009 A.Q. Khan released from house arrest

Government launches offensive against the Taliban

Pakistan, 2001

1

The Insurgency

The world is losing the war. I think at the moment they [the Taliban]
definitely have the upper hand.

—Asif Ali Zardari, 24 August 2008[1]

On 27 December 2007 Asif Ali Zardari, after more than a decade
in various Pakistani prisons, was at one of his homes, in Dubai,
enjoying his liberty, his children and his fabulous wealth. As a result of
some highly astute political manoeuvring by his wife, Benazir Bhutto,
most of the corruption cases against him had been dropped. His
friends said that, partly because his reputation for financial malpractice
made him something of a liability, he planned to keep a low profile
while his illustrious wife ran for a third term as prime minister. It didn't
work out like that. Within nine months Zardari was the legitimately
elected president of Pakistan. He found himself in charge of a country
that was not only the sixth most populous on earth but also a nearly
bankrupt nuclear power on the front line of the US 'war on terror'.

On that day in December when Zardari was in Dubai, Benazir
Bhutto was in Rawalpindi, Pakistan, holding a rally at the Liaquat
National Park, so called because in 1951 the then prime minister of
Pakistan, Liaquat Ali Khan, had been shot dead there. History was
about to be repeated.

Everyone attending the rally had been searched before entering the
park, and the speech passed without incident. Once she had spoken,
aware of the many threats against her, Bhutto moved straight from the
podium into an armoured Toyota land cruiser. But moving away was
difficult. Her supporters, keen as ever to get a closer look at their
leader, mobbed the vehicle, and as she moved her vulnerability
increased: none of the people outside the park had been screened. And

it was there she made a fatal decision: she put her head and shoulders through the sunroof of the vehicle to wave at the crowds. A few moments later she was dead. There was to be one more echo of the events 56 years before. When Bhutto's body was rushed to Rawalpindi General Hospital, one of the doctors who tried to revive her was Dr Sadiq Khan. Back in 1951 his father, also a doctor in the Rawalpindi General, had tried to do the same thing for Liaquat Ali Khan.

It is not clear what killed Bhutto and it probably never will be. The history of investigations into assassinations in Pakistan is filled with cover-ups and incompetence. But thanks to modern technology there was, in Bhutto's case, a fair amount of evidence in the public domain. Mobile-phone footage gathered by independent TV channels shows that a man aimed a gun at her at short range and fired. Seconds later a suicide bomber blew himself up. While there are many different explanations of what happened, they can be put into two broad camps: Bhutto's friends and supporters believe she was shot and that there were multiple attackers. The Pakistani authorities, by contrast, argued that she was killed by the explosion that smashed her head against the escape hatch or sunroof of her vehicle. The different views are to some extent informed by political considerations. Bhutto's supporters want to establish that there was a sophisticated, officially sponsored conspiracy to assassinate her. The Pakistani state, by contrast, maintained that it was a crude attack organised by Islamic militants and that nothing could have been done to stop it.

The evidence is contradictory. Certainly, there were shots followed by an explosion. The video footage shows a young man, clean shaven with dark glasses, aiming a gun at Benazir Bhutto and firing.[2] The pictures suggest that she was indeed hit and that she fell down heavily into the vehicle before the explosion went off. Her movements did not appear to be consistent with someone ducking from fire: it looked as if she was already dead, or at least seriously injured, when she fell. As the gunman fired at her, her head scarf moved away from her with a jerk.[3] Furthermore, Bhutto's aides, including those who bathed her body in preparation for its burial, insisted there was a bullet wound to her neck.[4]

The government, however, had a different version. It pointed to x-rays taken in the hospital which show a severe injury to Bhutto's skull.

Officials said that wound was the result of her head hitting the side of the escape hatch after the explosion went off and that there was no sign of a bullet entry or exit wound. The doctors at the hospital have given various different accounts of what they saw but their evidence is of limited use because they did not perform a proper autopsy. Whilst there are various conspiracy theories concerning that issue, there appear to be two good reasons for the lack of an autopsy. First, the authorities were afraid that if Benazir Bhutto's body remained in the hospital the angry crowd outside could have started a riot, broken in and destroyed some of the medical facilities. Secondly, her widower Asif Zardari was later offered an autopsy (before the burial), but he said it would not be necessary.

Aware of the growing controversy and the desire for a proper investigation, President Musharraf asked the British police in Scotland Yard to assist. It was another parallel with 1951: Scotland Yard had also been asked to look into Liaquat Ali Khan's case. On both occasions the idea was to create some consensus about what happened but when the report into the Bhutto case was published, it was met with a barrage of cynicism. Scotland Yard found that although gunshots were fired, they were not the cause of death and that one man had both a pistol and a suicide bomb.[5] The Scotland Yard report, in other words, completely backed the Pakistani government's version which was one reason why people were suspicious of it. But there was another: for some inexplicable reason the report failed even to discuss the mobile-phone images suggesting that she was shot. It was an omission that led many Pakistanis to conclude there had been a cover-up.

The precise cause of death, however, is of limited significance. Clearly someone tried to shoot Benazir Bhutto and someone (probably the same person) tried to blow her up. The important question is who was behind the assassin. Before her death Bhutto had written emails to journalists and friends saying Musharraf should be held responsible if she died. But she also wrote to Musharraf himself, naming four other people who she said were plotting to assassinate her.

She knew beyond doubt that someone was trying to kill her because on 18 October 2007 an assassination attempt had nearly succeeded. It was the day she returned to Pakistan after eight years in self-imposed exile in London and Dubai. She was moving through vast crowds of her supporters in Karachi when two explosions rocked her vehicle. Over 140 people were killed, but she walked away unharmed. The day after that attack she privately accepted that Musharraf was genuinely trying to protect her life and that he was dismayed by what had happened.[6] Many have speculated about the four names in the letter she sent to Musharraf: most lists name a rival politician, Chaudhry Pervez Elahi; the former head of Pakistan's main intelligence agency, Inter-Services Intelligence (ISI), and prominent radical Islamist, General (retired) Hamid Gul; the director general of the Intelligence Bureau, Ijaz Shah; and the former chief minister of Sindh, Arbab Ghulam Rahim.[7]

In her posthumously published book *Reconciliation* Bhutto mentioned another name. Having repeated her claim that government officials had been involved in trying to assassinate her, she went on to say that an Islamic radical, Qari Saifullah Akhtar, had helped procure the bombs that went off in Karachi.[8] Ever since 1995 Akhtar had been in and out of prison. He was first arrested for participating in an attempted Islamist coup against Benazir Bhutto's second government (see chapter 6), and had subsequently built a relationship with the Afghan Taliban leader Mullah Mohammed Omar who used to call Akhtar's fighters the 'Punjabi Taliban'.[9] Akhtar was the leader of Harakat-e-Jihad e-Islami (HEJI), which primarily focused its efforts on Kashmir but also had fighters in Bangladesh, Burma, Uzbekistan, Tajikistan and Chechnya. In 2004 he had been arrested in the United Arab Emirates and handed over to Pakistan, which held him for three years until the chief justice of Pakistan, much to President Musharraf's irritation, took up the cases of men like Akhtar, demanding that they be produced before the court. Rather than admitting their failure to give him due process, the authorities instead secretly released him. Two weeks after the publication of Bhutto's allegations in *Reconciliation* Akhtar was arrested again, but after three months of fruitless interrogation was released without charge in June 2008.[10]

Whilst Bhutto's supporters have accused establishment figures of using militants such as Qari Saifullah Akhtar to mount the attack in Rawalpindi, the Interior Ministry put out a different account. Shortly after her death it published what it claimed was a phone conversation, secretly recorded hours after the assassination, between a militant mullah and Baitullah Mehsud, a 34-year-old tribesman from the South Waziristan tribal area near the Afghan border. He had not long been a prominent figure in Pakistani politics. He emerged after 9/11 leading a new organisation: the Pakistani Taliban. Whilst Mullah Omar continued to lead the Afghan Taliban, Mehsud's Pakistani counterparts pioneered the use of suicide bombers in Pakistan. This is the transcript of the tape:

Mullah: Asalaam Aleikum [Peace be with you].

Baitullah Mehsud: Waaleikum Asalaam [And also with you].

M: Chief, how are you?

BM: I am fine.

M: Congratulations, I just got back during the night.

BM: Congratulations to you, were they our men?

M: Yes they were ours.

BM: Who were they?

M: There was Saeed, there was Bilal from Badar and Ikramullah.

BM: The three of them did it?

M: Ikramullah and Bilal did it.

BM: Then congratulations.

M: Where are you? I want to meet you.

BM: I am at Makeen [town in South Waziristan tribal area], come over, I am at Anwar Shah's house.

M: OK, I'll come.

BM: Don't inform their house for the time being.

M: OK.

BM: It was a tremendous effort. They were really brave boys who killed her.

M: Mashallah. When I come I will give you all the details.

BM: I will wait for you. Congratulations, once again congratulations.

M: Congratulations to you.

BM: Anything I can do for you?

M: Thank you very much.

BM: Asalaam Aleikum.

M: Waaleikum Asalaam.[11]

People who had met and spoken with Baitullah Mehsud confirmed that the voice on the tape was his,[12] and on the face of it this was strong evidence that Islamists were responsible. Certainly that was the view of the director of the CIA: in February Michael Hayden said, 'This was done by that network around Baitullah Mehsud. We have no reason to question that.'[13] Officials in Pakistan's Intelligence Bureau, however, are not so sure about the authenticity of the tape recording and have said their analysis suggests that the voice is not that of Baitullah Mehsud.[14]

The first man arrested in the Bhutto case was Aitzaz Shah, a 15-year-old school drop out who had ended up in a madrasa and, according to the police, was part of a five-strong squad of suicide bombers targeting Benazir Bhutto. He told investigators that he was next in line to kill her had the first attempt failed.[15] Aitzaz Shah named some of the others involved in the plot, including Hasnain Gul and Rafaqat. Gul was also a madrasa student and in 2007 he had persuaded his cousin, Rafaqat, to travel with him to North Waziristan in the hope of finding a militant group they could work for. There they were instructed to join the group trying to kill Bhutto: the militant leaders in North Waziristan feared she would move against them if she came to power. Aitzaz and Gul said the man who actually killed Bhutto was called Bilal and that he came from South Waziristan.[16] Gul confirmed Scotland Yard's view that one person was responsible for the shots and the explosion.[17] Then in April 2008, when the Pakistani ambassador to Afghanistan was kidnapped in the Khyber tribal area, the militants holding him (widely believed to be Baitullah Mehsud's men) demanded the release of Aitzaz Shah, Hasnain Gul and Rafaqat.[18]

The evidence that Islamic militants ordered and organised the assassination of Benazir Bhutto is strong. And they had a motive. After the government's assault on the Red Mosque in Islamabad in July 2007, the militants mounted revenge attacks all over Pakistan. Indeed, Hasnain Gul had first gone to North Waziristan because a friend of his was killed in the Red Mosque.[19] Some of these targets, such as President Musharraf and his interior minister, Aftab Sherpao, survived the revenge attacks. Others such as Benazir Bhutto did not.

Indeed, the biggest remaining mystery about the assassination of Benazir Bhutto is why the case against these men has made so little progress. Although Aitzaz Shah, Hasnain Gul and Rafaqat are all being held in prison, the legal cases against them have barely got under way. The government controlled by Benazir Bhutto's widower, Asif Zardari, has made very little effort to widen the investigation into her death, arguing that a UN enquiry would have more credibility. For many Pakistanis the failure of Benazir Bhutto's relatives and friends to use the power she bequeathed to them to investigate her murder is simply inexplicable.

The Red Mosque

Those close to Asif Zardari believe that his primary political objective is to encourage business and economic growth. Whilst Zardari's critics say that his interest in the economy is purely selfish and that he wants to make money for himself, his supporters see it differently. They argue that he sees trade as the route to peace with India, and investment at home as the surest way of delivering security and prosperity for Pakistan. Whatever the motivation, Zardari's desire to focus on economic policy was thwarted from the outset. The security situation, especially in the tribal areas and the North West Frontier Province (NWFP) was too dire to be ignored. By international standards Pakistan had experienced high levels of Islamist violence for decades, but the situation reached crisis levels a year before Zardari came to power with the assault on the Red Mosque in Islamabad.

The assault began the moment the former prime minister, Chaudhry Shujjaat, left the Red Mosque compound. It was 10 July 2007 and, after months of 'final' deadlines, Shujjaat and a delegation of clerics had made yet another attempt to get the leader of the militants who was holed up inside the mosque, Abdul Rashid Ghazi, to back down. Emerging grim-faced from the talks, Shujjaat announced by loud-speaker that his efforts had failed: 'We offered him a lot but he wasn't ready to come out on our terms.'[20] For the commandos from the Special Services Group (SSG) it was the signal to move. Within minutes the commandos broke through the perimeter wall, but they came under heavy fire from gunmen dug in behind sandbags and perched in the mosque's minarets. The soldiers rushed to the ground floor of the mosque, taking it quite easily. But as they advanced towards the women's madrasa beside the mosque, they started encountering serious resistance.

The madrasa building was so well protected because it was Ghazi's home. The Red Mosque was actually led by his brother Maulana Abdul Aziz, but after months of defiant statements he had, a few days before the assault, apparently lost his nerve and had fled from the compound disguised in a burqa. The authorities had spotted the ruse, arrested him and then humiliated him by putting him on state TV dressed in the burqa. That left his brother in charge. And in numerous TV interviews given over his mobile phone, Ghazi had said that if the army attacked, he wanted to die. As the soldiers closed in on his living quarters they met a wall of fire from militants hiding in a stairwell and armed with machine guns, fragmentation grenades and petrol bombs. It was here that the army suffered its heaviest casualties. In one room the SSG found six militants, one of whom detonated his suicide jacket as soon as the soldiers entered. Everyone in the room was killed.[21]

As the soldiers fought room by room, the militants retreated towards the building's basement. Abdul Rashid Ghazi was amongst them and it was from there he gave his last TV interview to Pakistan's most watched station, *Geo*: 'The Government is using full force,' he said. 'My martyrdom is now certain.' He was shot dead a few minutes later.

Operation SILENCE, as the army called the assault, had been a long time coming. For months militants inside the Red Mosque had been challenging the authorities with ever bolder outrages. Some of their provocations were just rhetorical, such as the calls for the government to be overthrown and for Musharraf to be killed. But they went much further than that. Female students at the madrasa, for example, had kidnapped some women whom they accused of being prostitutes, including seven Chinese nationals, and had taken them back to the seminary for 're-education'. Dubbed 'chicks with sticks' by the Pakistani media, the students set fire to the Ministry of the Environment and targeted the Capital Development Authority, accusing it of demolishing mosques that had been constructed illegally. At one place where an illegal mosque was due to be demolished, the female students occupied the site and refused to leave until the authorities backed down.

Eventually, President Musharraf concluded that he had to act. He was reluctant for a number of reasons. First, he knew it would mean great violence in the heart of the capital. According to the authorities (which many say deliberately underestimated the fatalities), the military operation resulted in the deaths of 11 soldiers and 73 militants. Secondly, Musharraf feared there would, in all likelihood, be reprisals. Even so, he may not have anticipated their scale. Just one day after the siege the Al Qaeda deputy Ayman al-Zawahiri issued a videotape entitled *The Aggression Against the Red Mosque*. 'Musharraf and his hunting dogs have rubbed your honour in the dirt in the service of the Crusaders and Jews,' he said. He called for revenge.[22] All over Pakistan militants heard his message and acted on it.

The Red Mosque siege was a turning point. It changed everything. Throughout the country militants finally concluded that the Pakistani state was their enemy. Ever since Pakistan had been created in 1947, successive governments had time and again given in to radical Islamist demands in return for short-term stability. Under intense international pressure, and with some reluctance, Musharraf had just decided that those days were over. For many Islamists the government's use of the lash came as a real shock and it was followed by a ferocious backlash. Within months Pakistan faced the biggest insurgency since East Pakistan had broken away to form Bangladesh in 1971. There was a humiliating incident in August 2007 when Baitullah Mehsud captured over 200 soldiers and held them hostage for over two months. The army was unable to respond even when three of the soldiers were beheaded. Eventually the surviving soldiers were released in exchange for 28 militants. For the first time, the army had been exposed as incapable of defending itself in the tribal areas.

Between the start of 2002 and the end of 2006 there were 22 suicide bombs in Pakistan – an average of just over four a year. In 2007 there were 45.[23] In one highly significant attack, over 30 ISI workers were killed as they travelled to work on a bus. In the 1990s, when the Pakistani state was supporting the insurgency in Kashmir and the establishment of the Taliban government in Afghanistan, the ISI staff used to work with the very same people who were now trying to kill them. It was blowback of the most vicious kind.

Pakistan's Schools of Islam

The militants inside the Red Mosque by no means represented Pakistani society as a whole. The defining characteristic of Pakistan's Islamic radicals is their view that the political systems that existed in the cities of Mecca and Medina fourteen hundred years ago should be emulated today in every detail. Their attitudes are backward-looking and regressive. Although some embrace computer technology, many shun modern scientific knowledge and favour a return to a medieval-style theocracy of the kind attempted by the Taliban regime in Afghanistan. The majority of Pakistanis does not agree with them and would prefer to live in a stable democracy with a good economy. That's not to say that the modernist majority is secular: it is not. Most Pakistanis believe that Islam should inform public policies in the country. Indeed, they believe that Islamic principles can make a positive contribution to contemporary democratic theory and practice. The modernists, in short, believe that ancient tenets of Islam sit easily with a progressive political outlook.

The conflicting views of the modernists and the radicals are reflected in different schools of Islamic thought. Some 75 per cent of the Pakistani population are Sunni Muslims, but there are important fissures within the Sunni community. Although the ultra-conservative Wahabis are gaining support in Pakistan, there are still two main broad groupings: Barelvis and Deobandis.

Deoband is a town 100 miles north of Delhi and a madrasa was established there in 1867. It brought together many Muslims who were not only fiercely hostile to British rule but also committed to a literalist and austere interpretation of Islam. The founders of the madrasa in Deoband saw modern technology as ßnothing more than a method by which the people of the West kept Muslims in subjugation. They argued that the Quran and Sunnah (the words and deeds of the Prophet) provided a complete guide for life that needed no human improvement. Despite the fact that most leading Deobandi clerics, who saw nation states as man-made, ungodly constructs, were opposed to Mohammed Ali Jinnah's call for the creation of Pakistan, many Deobandi teachers moved to the new country in 1947. They have been a vocal, and often militant, element of Pakistani society ever since.

It was talibs (religious students) from Deobandi madrasas who formed the backbone of the Taliban movement that swept to power in Afghanistan in 1996.[24] Some leading Deobandi clerics, such as Sami ul-Haq from the famous Haqqaniya madrasa at Akhora Khattak in NWFP, have freely admitted that whenever the Taliban movement in Afghanistan put out a call for fighters, they would close down their schools and send their talibs to help.[25] Deobandi talibs also tried to impose their views within Pakistan. As early as 1998, for example, there were the first indications of what would happen to whole swathes of Pakistan when Deobandis began a campaign to purge the Baloch capital Quetta of video-rental shops, video recorders and televisions. In late 2000 young religious students, encouraged by madrasa teachers and local mullahs, ordered the burning of television sets, video players and satellite dishes in a number of villages in NWFP. 'This is an ongoing process,' said one mullah who helped organise a TV bonfire. 'We will continue to burn TV sets, VCRs and other similar things to spread the message that their misuse is threatening our religion, society and family life.'[26] It was, indeed, an ongoing process. A few years later such incidents were commonplace.

The Deobandis, however, by no means constitute a majority. Although they have claimed that some Barelvis are switching over to them,[27] it's generally reckoned that 10–15 per cent of the Pakistani people are Deobandis and 60 per cent Barelvis or Sufis. Compared to the Deobandis, the Barelvis have a moderate, less austere interpretation of Islam. They trace their origins to pre-partition northern India where in the town of Bareilly a leading Muslim scholar, Mullah Ahmad Raza Khan Barelvi, developed a large following. Barelvi and his followers felt that there was no contradiction between practising Islam and drawing on the subcontinent's ancient religious practices. The Barelvis regularly offer prayers to holy men, or pirs, both dead and alive. To this day many Pakistanis believe that pirs and their direct descendants have supernatural powers, and each year millions visit shrines to the pirs so that they can participate in ceremonies replete with lavish supplies of cannabis and music. The Deobandis shun such practices as pagan, ungodly distractions.

Ever since Pakistan was created the Barelvis have been the Islamic radicals' most effective obstacle. In a fascinating study an American academic, Richard Kurin, illustrated why the radicals find most Pakistanis too passive.[28] Kurin went to live in a small Punjabi village so that he could assess the attitudes to Islam in a typical Barelvi community. He found that two men in the village were trying to propagate Islam: the local syed (descendant of the Prophet) and the mullah. The syed's chosen method was to commandeer the loudspeaker of the village mosque at dawn and deliver a lecture on the merits of following the ways of the Quran and the Prophet. He would speak for several hours at a time. Much to his frustration, however, the villagers failed to show much interest in his exhortations, and he regarded most of them as uneducated cheats. Privately the villagers would talk about the syed as a man who took life too seriously and who got worked up about issues that didn't really matter.

The second Islamic figure in the village, the mullah, was expected to preside over the daily prayers, teach the Quran to young boys and generally, as the villagers put it, 'do all the Allah stuff'. Like the syed, the mullah felt that he had to put up with a somewhat wayward flock. Only a handful of the villagers would say their prayers five times a day, and in the month of Ramadan most only managed to fast for five to ten days rather than the whole month. Worse still, around a dozen villagers were having adulterous affairs that were the subject of much idle gossip. The villagers did, however, show considerable enthusiasm for attending the many Sufi shrines in the area. Virtually every man in the village had a pir who would offer him spiritual guidance.

The picture presented by Kurin is true of many villages throughout Pakistan. Of course, his study was conducted over 20 years ago and the mood has changed. A similar study today would probably find greater numbers observing Ramadan and saying their prayers five times a day. There are many signs of Pakistan's growing religiosity. In 2008 the Pakistani novelist, Mohammed Hanif, moved back to the country after 12 years resident in the UK. The changes were striking:

Graffiti on walls in Karachi, my adopted home city, calls for jihad. Adverts for luxury Umrah pilgrimages are omnipresent. And for those who cannot afford to go all the way to Mecca, neighbourhood mosques offer a series of regular lectures and special prayer sessions. I went to a

Nike store, and it was no different from any such store in any part of the world: expensive shiny sneakers and branded football shirts. But in the background, instead of the expected pumping dance music, recitations from the Koran were being played. The multinational companies, sensing the mood of the people, have included religious messages in their marketing campaigns. Mobile phone companies offer calls to prayer as ringtones, and religious sermons as free downloads. During the month of Ramadan some international banks were giving their preferred clients fancy boxes containing rosaries, dates and miniature Korans.[29]

The public expression of piety in Pakistan is a post-9/11 development. But it is still the case that the majority of Pakistanis would not want to live under the Taliban, and many only give it a degree of tacit support because they share its ideas about Muslims being victimised by the United States. Pakistanis are relatively moderate. In most mosques in most villages the mullahs may denounce America each Friday, but they also speak against extremism and urge their flock not to get involved in militancy.

Because of this 'moderate majority', as General Musharraf used to call it, the religious parties have never come close to winning an election in Pakistan. Nonetheless it is worth noting that the divisions within Sunni Islam are reflected at a political level. The two most significant Deobandi political parties are Jamiat Ulema-e-Islami (JUI), which has its base in the Pukhtoon areas of Balochistan and NWFP and Jamaat-e-Islami. The JUI's leader, Fazl ur-Rehman, used to be known for his strong anti-American statements, and in the late 1990s the party offered moral and material support to the Taliban regime in Afghanistan. Historically, the party has depended on the madrasa network, the protection of which is one of its main objectives. It lost a lot of support as a result of its particI-pation in the six-party Muttahida Majlis-e-Amal (MMA) alliance[30] which backed General Musharraf and, by association, the Americans. The Taliban, accusing him of selling out, has tried to assassinate Fazl ur-Rehman. Whereas the JUI is a largely rural party, its urban counter-part is Jamaat-e-Islami (JI) which draws its strength from the urban middle classes and advocates sharia law, the redistribution of wealth and the banning of interest payments.[31] An ideological party, it was founded in 1941 by a leading Muslim intellectual, Abul A'la Maududi.[32] The best way to put Islam into practice, he believed, was to create a Leninist-style, highly organised party that would act as a vanguard for the Islamic revolution. Individual piety, he argued, could be achieved not so much through personal struggle as societal change and the power of the state. Jamaat's party discipline is tight. Party decisions are subject to internal consultation (and compared to most of Pakistan's political parties the process of consultation is genuine), but once a party line is agreed every member must follow it. Jamaat is the only Pakistani party to have computerised membership lists, a daily newspaper and its own academic journal. Jamaat's message may be backward-looking, but its methods are more advanced and contemporary than any other political party in the country.

The Barelvis have far less effective political representation. Their Jamaat Ulema-e-Pakistan (JUP) has never overcome the problem that most Barelvis vote for mainstream, non-religious political parties. Repeated electoral failures persuaded many in the JUP leadership that their organisation should give up electoral politics, and by the late 1990s the JUP had stopped standing in elections. Some of its leaders, though, did manage to secure seats by forming local alliances with mainstream parties such as the Muslim League.

Political Responses to Islamic Radicalism

The disputes between the Barelvis and the Deobandis, the modernists and the radicals, the Sufis and the puritans, even the democrats and the theocrats, predate Pakistan's creation. As he advanced the case for a separate Muslim state, Jinnah relied in part on an appeal to Islam. Indeed, religious identity provided the basis for his national demand. The argument that Jinnah presented to the British was that the Muslims and the Hindus of the subcontinent constituted two separate nations that could not live together. In 1947 his arguments prevailed and Pakistan was created as a Muslim homeland. But what did that mean? Was it simply a country for Muslims to live in or was it, in fact, a Muslim country? Was Jinnah the founding father of an Islamic state or merely a state in which Islam could be practised without fear of discrimination? Ever since 1947 these questions have been contested.

Many of the men who led the Muslim League, Jinnah included, never envisaged the creation of a state in which Islam would provide the framework for all political activity. Like most of his followers, Jinnah was a modernist. His educational background owed more to Oxbridge than Deoband. And his demand for Pakistan was opposed not only by Britain and the Congress leadership in India but also by many Islamic radical scholars. In pre-partition India the vast majority of the Islamic scholars, collectively known as the ulema, saw Jinnah as a Western-trained lawyer who had lost his religion. Jinnah meanwhile viewed most of the ulema as ignorant, power hungry and often corrupt. In 1946, for example, he dismissed their demand for the imposition of sharia law as laid down by the Quran and Sunnah. 'Whose Sharia?' Jinnah asked. 'I don't want to get involved. The moment I enter this field the ulema will take over for they claim to be the experts. I certainly don't propose to hand over the field to the ulema.'[33] Many of Jinnah's speeches clearly indicated his progressive attitude to Islam. The most famous passage of all was delivered to the Constituent Assembly of Pakistan on 11 August 1947:

> You are free; you are free to go to your temples, you are free to go to your mosques or to any other place of worship in this State of Pakistan. You may belong to any religion or caste or creed – that has nothing to do with the business of the State. . . . We are starting with this fundamental principle that we are all citizens and equal citizens of one State.[34]

The case for Jinnah as a modernist is compelling. But the Islamic radicals can also produce some evidence to back up their claim that Jinnah was on their side. When one leading cleric, Mullah Shabbir Ahmed Osmani, addressed the Constituent Assembly in 1949, he tried to counter the claim that Jinnah was a secularist:

> Islam has never accepted the view that religion is a private matter between man and his creator and as such has no bearing on the social or political relations of human beings. . . . The late Quaid-e-Azam made the following observations in the letter he wrote to Gandhiji in August 1944.

'The Quran is a complete code of life. It provides for all matters religious or social, civil or criminal, military or penal, economic or commercial.'[35]

Any fair-minded assessment of Jinnah would have to recognise that he did make some comments about the all-encompassing nature of the Quran. But it would also have to acknowledge that such remarks were few and far between, and that anyone studying Jinnah's speeches has to go through them with a toothcomb to find many examples. Furthermore, when he did make such comments Jinnah often had a pragmatic, short-term political reason for doing so. Jinnah's views, it is true, did change over time, and towards the end of his life he became increasingly religious and placed greater emphasis on the need to respect Islamic values. But one thing is clear. At no stage of his life would Mohammed Ali Jinnah have had any time whatsoever for the regressive prejudices of the Taliban regime in Afghanistan and their Islamic radical supporters in Pakistan.

After Jinnah's death in 1948 the arguments between the radicals and the modernists intensified. As the politicians debated the content of the Pakistani constitution, the Islamic-based parties pressed for a document that would establish Pakistan as an ideological state committed to Islam. Some even asked whether a constitution was necessary. The Quran and Sunnah, they maintained, set down all the rules necessary for life and there was no need for mere men to create political institutions that could only distort Allah's word. Throughout the 1950s the politicians charged with writing the first Pakistani constitution grappled with these issues, and when they produced the 1956 Constitution they came down firmly on the side of the modernists. As a sop to the radicals, the constitution's preamble did include a clause that recognised the sovereignty of Allah over the entire universe. But read as a whole, the document made it clear that, in practice, the people of Pakistan would be sovereign. As the prime minister, Liaquat Ali Khan, had said when proposing the Objectives Resolution that formed the basis of the constitution:

All authority is a sacred trust, entrusted to us by God for the purpose of being exercised in the service of man, so that it does not become an agency for tyranny or selfishness. I would, however, point out that this is not a resuscitation of the dead theory of divine right of kings or rulers because in accordance with the spirit of Islam the preamble fully recognises the truth that authority has been delegated to the people . . . this naturally eliminates any danger of the establishment of a theocracy.[36]

Even if the vast majority of Pakistan's first generation of politicians were firmly in the modernist camp, it is highly significant that they tried to avoid a direct confrontation with the Islamic radicals. On the contrary, they tried to exploit Islamic ideology to serve their own political objectives. Faced with growing challenges from Baloch, Sindhi, Pukhtoon and Bengali nationalists, even the most secular leaders found it was expedient to appeal to Islam so as to foster a sense of Pakistani unity. In doing so the politicians established a trend which has been a feature of Pakistani politics ever since. Pakistani politicians have never wanted to share power with the ulema. But they have also been reluctant to offend them. Few have wanted an Islamic state, but they have been hesitant to say so with any clarity.

Pakistan's first military ruler, General Ayub Khan, was an exception to this rule. From the moment he took power in 1958 he brought the dispute between the modernists and the Islamic radicals into the open. In his autobiography *Friends Not Masters* he complained about the 'obscurantists who frustrate all progress under the cover of religion'.[37] He recognised that Pakistan had witnessed a conflict between the ulema and the modernist elements in society, and he left no doubt whose side he was on. Many of the ulema, Ayub pointed out, had opposed Jinnah and the creation of Pakistan. And once Pakistan was established they tried to carve out a niche for themselves by denouncing the political leadership and calling for a more orthodox Islamic state. As Ayub put it, the ulema:

spread throughout the length and breadth of the country to convince the people of the misery of their existence and the failings of their government. They succeeded in converting an optimistic and enthusiastic people into a cynical and frustrated community.[38]

Ayub clearly opposed those who wanted to put Islam at the heart of the Pakistani state. And they opposed him. One of Jamaat-e-Islami's slogans during this period was 'Stop the innovations!'[39] The mutual antagonism between the military and the radicals at this time clearly contradicts the often-stated assertion that these two elements in Pakistani society always work together (because, the argument normally goes, they have a shared interest in thwarting democracy). The Ayub Khan period from 1958 to 1969 reveals that there is nothing inevitable about a close relationship between the military and the mosque.[40]

When Ayub proposed a new constitution in 1962 he tried to change the name of the country from 'The Islamic Republic of Pakistan' to 'Republic of Pakistan'. His Muslim Family Laws Ordinance of 1961 was in much the same vein. Amongst other things, the measure was intended to make it more difficult for Pakistani men to take more than one wife. Under the ordinance nobody could enter a second marriage without the consent of the first wife. 'A Muslim,' Ayub later wrote, 'is allowed by Islam to have more than one wife, under certain conditions. This permission has been used to practise indiscriminate polygamy causing immense misery to innumerable tongue-tied women and innocent children. Thousands of families have been ruined because of the degenerate manner in which men have misused this permission to suit their convenience.'[41]

In the event, for all his military strength, Ayub was unable to get these proposed reforms past the religious lobby. His Family Laws Ordinance, like his encouragement of family planning and his distaste for the burqa, all ran into deep-seated traditional cultural as well as religious objections. Ayub Khan, though, could at least say that he had attempted to confront the radicals. The next strong leader to emerge in Pakistan, Zulfikar Ali Bhutto, didn't even try.

Although he was one of the most modernist leaders Pakistan has ever had, Bhutto, who ruled from 1971 to 1977, consistently gave in to radical demands. He was cynical in his use of religion. A man of broad intellectual horizons, he repeatedly pandered to the Islamic radicals in the hope of securing short-term political advantage. This characteristic was apparent early in Bhutto's period of office. The first major religious issue to confront him concerned the Ahmedis or Qadianis – a sect that followed the teachings of a nineteenth-century Punjabi cleric, Mirza Ghulam Ahmed. Ahmed said he had revelations direct from Allah: he maintained, in other words, he was a prophet. Even though Ahmed considered himself subservient to Mohammed, his claim clashed with the basic Islamic tenet that Mohammed was the last and final prophet. In 1953, long before Bhutto came to power, radical Islamists had demanded that the Ahmedis be declared non-Muslims. The issue had led to rioting throughout Punjab. Many Ahmedis had their properties looted and burnt, and some of the riots became so violent that Ahmedis had been murdered. The central government, after some prevarication, decided to resist the rioters' demands and called out the army to restore law and order in Lahore.

Twenty years later, faced with renewed anti-Ahmedi demands, Bhutto caved in and gave the radicals what they wanted: the Ahmedis were declared non-Muslims. Bhutto followed a similar approach three years later when he was desperately trying to cling onto power after the 1977 elections. Up against sustained opposition protests, he again tried to appease the religious parties. He imposed a ban on drinking, gambling and nightclubs, and declared that Friday, not Sunday, would be the weekly holiday. It was a futile effort. Few of the religious leaders, who all knew that Bhutto himself was a regular drinker, were prepared to side with him. Bhutto's tilt to Islam convinced nobody.

For the first three decades of the country's history, then, no Pakistani leader had any real sympathy with the Islamists, even if they pandered to them. But then, after Bhutto was ousted in a coup in 1977, came General Zia ul-Haq. He was to rule for eleven years and throughout that period he consistently promoted the role of Islam in the state. Indeed, the moment he grasped power Zia made Islam the centrepiece of his administration: in his first address to the nation he clearly stated that he would try to create an Islamic state. In December 1979 a decision taken thousands of miles away, in Moscow, gave Zia the chance to advance his programme. The ailing secretary general of the Soviet Communist Party, Leonid Brezhnev, approved the invasion of Afghanistan. Brezhnev and his colleagues were chiefly motivated by their concern that instability in Afghanistan could spread across the Soviet Union's southern border. But their decision to move their tanks into Kabul had profound consequences for Pakistan. For General Zia, the invasion seemed like a gift from Allah. At a stroke he became a key cold war ally of the United States. Zia's support for America's anti-Soviet campaign not only provided him with enough foreign exchange to sustain his regime, but also gave him a free hand to ignore internationally accepted human rights norms. As Zia pressed on with his Islamicisation campaign, Washington turned a blind eye.

Zia's policies affected every aspect of the Pakistani state. His first measures concerned the legal system. In July 1977 he declared that theft could be punished by 'amputation from the wrist of the left hand of a right handed person and vice versa'. Some other crimes, he decreed, could be punished by public whippings.[42] The Hudood Ordinance of 1979 stated that punishments laid down in the Quran and Sunnah were now operative in Pakistan. Under the Zina Ordinance, rape was to be punished by the public flogging of the woman as well as the man. Zia also created a Federal Sharia Court. Its task was to 'examine and decide the question whether or not any law or provision of the law is repugnant to the provisions of Islam'.[43] Any law found to be repugnant would immediately become void. Potentially this was one of the most far-reaching of all Zia's reforms. Interestingly, though, he was quick to see its dangers and in a move that demonstrated the limits to Zia's Islamic radicalism, he declared that the Sharia Court could not challenge any martial law regulation or order. The military, it seemed, was above Islamic law.

Zia also tried to Islamicise the economy. In 1981 interest payments, explicitly banned in the Quran, were replaced by so-called 'profit and loss' accounts. In reality the profit accruing to a bank account was interest by another name, but Zia insisted that he had at least taken a first step towards an Islamic banking system. He also introduced Islamic fiscal measures in the form of a zakat tax. This meant a 2.5 per cent annual deduction from the money resting in someone's bank account on the first day of Ramadan. Zia justified zakat on the grounds that the Quran and Sunnah specifically mentioned it as one of the five pillars of Islam, and he decreed that the zakat revenues were to be used for poverty relief.

Zia also wanted Islam to be given greater status in the education system. Textbooks were overhauled to ensure their ideological purity and un-Islamic reading matter was removed from libraries and schools. Government officials were given the task of persuading people to pray five times a day and government offices were required to allow for prayer time in drawing up their schedules. Zia also insisted that the confidential annual assessments of civil servants should include a section in which staff were given marks for regularly attending prayers and for having a good knowledge of Islam.

Throughout his period in office Zia rewarded the only political party to offer him consistent support, Jamaat-e-Islami. Tens of thousands of Jamaat activists and sympathisers were given jobs in the judiciary, the civil service and other state institutions. These appointments meant that Zia's Islamic agenda lived on long after he died. The sustained campaigns for women to cover their heads, for shutting down restaurants during Ramadan and enforcing the Hudood and Zina Ordinances can all be ascribed to the fact that, after Zia, Islamic radicals held positions of authority.

General Zia's impact on Pakistan was so enduring in part because his civilian successors, Benazir Bhutto and Nawaz Sharif, did little to dismantle his legacy. Benazir Bhutto followed much the same policy as her father. Although she had no sympathy for the Islamic radicals, she consistently failed to confront them. Privately she made little secret of her modernist outlook. In public she repeatedly stressed the role of Islam in the state. To some extent Benazir Bhutto needed to overcome the criticism that, as a Western-educated woman, she was an inappropriate choice to lead Pakistan. Determined to prove the Islamists wrong, she felt the need to present herself as a prime minister who could be trusted to protect and even advance the role of Islam in the Pakistani state.

Her rival, Nawaz Sharif, had a different approach. As Zia's protégé, and coming from a religiously conservative family, he always felt more comfortable with the Islamic radicals. In October 1998 Sharif began a process that could have handed the radicals a massive victory. He managed to secure the passage of the 15th Constitutional Amendment through the National Assembly. Even if Sharif was motivated by political rather than religious considerations and saw the measure as a way of silencing his opponents, the Sharia Bill had huge implications: it stated that sharia law would become the supreme law in Pakistan. At a stroke the prime minister would have won the power to interpret the Quran and Sunnah in any way he pleased, and to act accordingly.

Sharif's efforts to introduce sharia law were interrupted by the 1999 coup of General Musharraf. In 2007, whilst in political exile, Nawaz Sharif said that should he ever return to power he would not revive the Sharia Bill.[44] Interestingly, a few months later, once he had returned to Pakistan, he would not repeat the same commitment, leaving the door open to some sort of sharia legislation in the future.[45]

Having removed Nawaz Sharif, General Musharraf adopted a very similar approach to that of Ayub Khan. Firmly in the modernist camp, he often denounced the Islamic radicals. But compared to Ayub's times, the issues for Musharraf were painted in much starker terms. After 9/11 the challenge posed by radical Islam was no longer just a matter for Pakistani leaders to worry about: it had become the most pressing of all global issues. Musharraf was the leader of a country on the front line. His attitude to religion, his understanding of the role of Islam in Pakistan and his relationship with the Taliban and other militants are issues fully discussed in chapter 8.

Pukhtoon Nationalism

Most of the Islamic militants have a strictly religious agenda; above all else they want sharia law. Many people living in North West Frontier Province, however, harbour a different dream. Whilst they are generally very devout, they are more interested in a nationalist demand – for an independent Pukhtoon homeland. The issue for Swat, the rest of NWFP and, for that matter, Pakistan as a whole, is whether in the future the Islamists making religious demands will join forces with Pukhtoons making the nationalist one. Should they ever become a united force then they could threaten the very integrity of Pakistan. The Pukhtoon nationalists have traditionally been represented by the ANP, which has remained a determinedly modernist party. The question now is whether the ANP can survive the current wave of Islamic radicalism or whether it might be tempted to shore up its electoral base by joining it.

The demand for an independent Pukhtoon homeland is over a century old and not without historical justification. When the British started taking over Pukhtoon areas in the nineteenth century, the Pukhtoon people were living as one Afghan nation. Their consistent and violent resistance against the British presence forced the imperial government in Delhi to devote tens of thousands of troops to control the Pukhtoons. In 1893 the British tried to stabilise the situation by creating the Durand Line which today constitutes the border between Afghanistan and Pakistan. The line cut the Pukhtoon people in two: roughly one half remained in Afghanistan but the other half ended up in the British empire. The situation was further complicated by the British decision to divide the Pukhtoons under their control. Although most found themselves in the NWFP, some ended up in the area that became Balochistan.

The British policies gave rise to two slightly different demands. The first, advanced by the Pukhtoons in NWFP, was that all Pukhtoon people should be reunited as they were before the British arrived. The second, championed by successive governments in Kabul, was for a Greater Afghanistan. Ever since partition, Kabul has argued that the Durand Line was never meant to be an international boundary and complained that it deprived Afghanistan of territory that had historically been under its control.

As the British prepared to leave the subcontinent, the most effective champion of Pukhtoon nationalism was the 'Frontier Ghandi', Abdul Ghaffar Khan. He argued that the creation of Pakistan would be a disaster because Muslims from elsewhere in India would come and take over the Pukhtoons. Ghaffar Khan's acumen and anti-imperialist rhetoric, backed by a quasi-military organisation known as the Red Shirts, resonated throughout NWFP. Of all the provinces that were to become part of Pakistan it was NWFP that had the strongest nationalist movement: Mohammed Ali Jinnah's Muslim League was no match for Ghaffar Khan.

As partition approached, the British announced there would be a referendum in NWFP. That decision brought matters to a head and

Ghaffar Khan insisted that as well as offering a choice between India and Pakistan, the British should allow the Pukhtoon voters another option: an independent state called Pukhtoonkhwa. The government in Kabul wanted the inclusion of a fourth option: union with Afghanistan.[46] Jinnah knew that he had to resist all such proposals. To achieve Pakistan he had to secure the Pukhtoons' support. Without NWFP his demand for a Muslim state would be fatally weakened. The crucial moment came on 15 August 1947 when the referendum took place. The viceroy of India, Lord Louis Mountbatten, declared that there would be just two choices: union with India or Pakistan. Since he wanted neither outcome, Ghaffar Khan boycotted the vote and the devout Pukhtoon electorate really had no choice. Of those who voted, 99 per cent opted for Pakistan.

Pukhtoon nationalist sentiment did not disappear after the 1947 referendum and Abdul Ghaffar Khan continued to campaign for Pukhtoonkhwa. Indeed, in 1948 Jinnah travelled to Peshawar in an attempt to win him over and get the Red Shirts disbanded. His mission failed, and although the nationalists were nervous about making their demands explicit, Jinnah left with the impression that the Red Shirts were still committed to some form of independence.[47] Setting a trend that characterises Pakistani politics to the present day, the Pakistani government responded to Ghaffar Khan's increasingly muted challenge by imprisoning him.

Both in Pakistan and Afghanistan, Pukhtoon nationalists have continued to harbour dreams of either Pukhtoonkhwa or a Greater Afghanistan. In 1955 Afghan objections to Pakistan's plans for One Unit were so strong that public demonstrations led to the ransacking of the Pakistani Embassy in Kabul and the consulate in Jalalabad. The two countries withdrew their ambassadors from each other's capitals. In 1956 an Afghan government spokesman said the Durand Line had no legitimacy and that it artificially divided the Pukhtoon people. The response from Pakistan was sharp. The foreign minister, Hamid ul-Haq Chaudhri, insisted that the Durand Line 'has been, is and will continue to be the international boundary between Afghanistan and Pakistan'.[48] But the Afghans have never given up their emotional attachment to the Pukhtoons in Pakistan. And again, in 1979, the

Afghan prime minister Hafizullah Amin explicitly stated Kabul's desire for a Greater Afghanistan. The Durand Line, he said, 'tore us apart'. He even suggested that a Greater Afghanistan would incorporate Balochistan:

> Our sincere and honest brotherhood with the Pukhtoons and Baloch has been sanctified by history. They have been one body in the course of history and have lived together like one brother. Now the waves of their love and brotherhood extend from the Oxus to Attock[49] and they want to live side by side, embrace each other and demonstrate this great love to the world at large.[50]

The Durand Line barely exists as a physical entity. It cuts through arid, mountainous, remote areas and is for the most part not demarcated on the ground. Villagers on both sides of the line take no notice of it and cross at will. After 9/11 that status quo became difficult to maintain. US and other foreign troops were based on the Afghan side of the line and complained that, while they could not cross, the militants were able to do so quite freely. Pakistan suggested in February 2006 that the line be mined and fenced. The proposal was intended to put the Afghan president, Hamid Karzai, in an awkward position and it succeeded. Despite his many complaints about the Taliban's cross-border movements, he rejected the idea outright saying he did not want to add obstacles in the way of Pukhtoons living near the line. He said a fence would create distances between what he called the brotherly people of Pakistan and Afghanistan.[51] Later that month he went further. At the funeral of Ghaffar Khan's son, Abdul Wali Khan, the Afghan president described the Durand Line as a 'line of hate' which had raised a wall between two brothers.[52]

The Tribal Areas

If Pukhtoon nationalism and Islamic radicalism ever mutate into one movement it will first happen in the tribal areas. Indeed, by the end of 2008 some believed that process was already under way. One of the reasons Pakistan has failed to persuade the Afghans to accept the

Durand Line is its inability to assert government control in the tribal areas located alongside Afghanistan. These have never been fully incorporated into Pakistan and the arrangements for governing them still date back to the days of the British empire. Having conquered most of South Asia, Britain's imperialists tried to accommodate the areas with the strongest Pukhtoon resistance by devising a special system of political administration under which the tribes were given a large degree of autonomy. Tribal elders, or maliks, were given cash and status by the British in return for which they were expected to keep the peace and, in particular, guarantee safe passage on key roads. The maliks were further controlled by the British (and later the Pakistanis) through the Frontier Crimes Regulation (FCR). Imposed in 1901, it had two crucial elements.[53] First, people could be held without charge, indefinitely. Secondly, it sanctioned collective punishment: whole communities could be punished for the crimes of an individual member.

The British and later the Pakistanis, in other words, accepted that the tribesmen lived according to their own customs and traditions, which together are known as Pashtunwali. It's an ancient code which to this day governs tribal life. To outsiders some of its requirements seem absurd. Guests, for example, are afforded such extraordinary levels of hospitality that there have been cases of hosts giving up their lives to protect that of an unknown visitor. Other central tenets include loyalty to the tribe, honour, revenge, self-reliance and adherence to the jirga system in which tribal elders gather to discuss issues and make decisions. Famously devout, and ever willing to rally to the slogan 'Islam is in danger', the tribesmen often proclaim their attachment to sharia law. In fact, the decisions made by jirgas tend to mix sharia law and tribal custom. The importance of tribal tradition is revealed by the relative strengths of the malik, who traditionally has been widely respected and deferred to, and the mullah, who until recently was more often than not treated as an uneducated functionary.

That is now changing. Radical Islam has posed a direct challenge to the power and authority of the maliks in the tribal areas. Indeed, Mullah Omar first came to pre-eminence in southern Afghanistan when he confronted the authority of a tribal chief near Kandahar who was raping a young boy. By responding to the complaints of the boy's mother, Mullah Omar began the populist campaign against the traditional power structures that eventually swept him to power. Today many young tribesmen see the glamour and heroism of the Islamist fighters as more appealing than the staid conservatism of their tribal elders. Furthermore, the tribal system has hardly delivered prosperity. At $250 a year, per capita income in the tribal areas is half the already low levels in the rest of Pakistan. Some 71 per cent of men and 97 per cent of women in the tribal areas are illiterate. There is one doctor for every 6,762 people in the tribal areas compared to one for every 1,359 people elsewhere in Pakistan.[54]

The tribal areas are divided into seven separate units or agencies: Khyber, Kurram, Orakzai, Mohmand, Bajur and North and South Waziristan. There are important differences between them. Because it has the main road leading to the famous pass and beyond to Afghanistan, Khyber has always been the most open of the tribal areas: its disputes are as likely to concern smuggling profits as religion. After 9/11 Orakzai became known as the most stable of the tribal agencies, and as a result, by 2009 it was being used as a safe haven for jihadis from which they launched attacks on the NATO supplies moving through the nearby Khyber Pass and into Afghanistan. Kurram has a large Shia population and most of its religious extremists devote themselves to sectarian violence. Three of the tribal areas in particular have a history of religious conservatism and hostility to non-Muslim outsiders: North and South Waziristan and Bajur. A young British captain, Francis Stockdale, was in Waziristan between 1917 and 1919 and recorded his impressions in the aptly named memoir, *Walk Warily in Waziristan*: 'We often used to ask ourselves,' he wrote, 'how could they survive so long living in a rocky area, with a film of earth capable of growing only scrub trees.' The British men lived in fear of capture: 'It would result in death by torture, an activity in which I was informed the tribal women folk used to luxuriate.' Captain Stockdale ended up serving two years in Waziristan and considered himself lucky to get out alive.[55] Ninety years later, Pakistani soldiers who survived a deployment in Waziristan felt much the same way.

Waziristan was lifted from obscurity by 9/11. After the Taliban fell, some of its supporters together with Al Qaeda fighters fled Afghanistan, crossed the mountain passes on the Durand Line and found refuge in

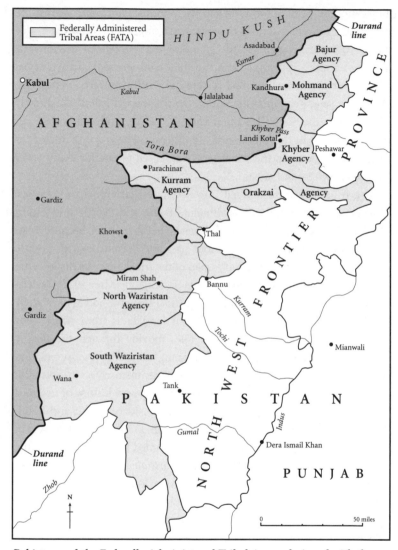

Pakistan and the Federally Administered Tribal Areas, designed with the help of the Army Press, Rawalpindi

Bajur and North and South Waziristan. Osama bin Laden was probably amongst them. Soon the Pakistani government was under US pressure to kill or capture the Al Qaeda members on its soil. The Western demands, however, put General Musharraf in an awkward position. Although he had offered the US full support after 9/11, intervening in the tribal areas would mean reversing over five decades of Pakistani policy. With the exception of a few limited operations to eradicate poppy production, the army had never been deployed in the tribal areas and the general knew full well that doing so would provoke a violent response.

That Waziristan had become a centre of Islamist activity, however, was undeniable, and Pakistan decided at least to give the impression of doing something. By the end of 2002 Musharraf had some 70,000 troops on the Pakistan–Afghan border. Patrolling, though, was one thing; fighting quite another. Musharraf wanted to avoid a full-blown conflict, preferring to resolve problems in the tribal areas in the traditional way: through talks. In 2003 the government began that process. It offered an amnesty to any foreigners such as Chechens and Uzbeks: if they surrendered to the government they would be allowed to stay in the tribal areas as long as they kept the peace.

Under heavy US pressure Musharraf did mount some operations against militants in South Waziristan in 2004. Unfortunately, though, he failed to coordinate the military and political processes. Tribal leaders no longer believed that the political administrators handling the negotiations were in control of events. Negotiators, too, complained that they made promises of ceasefires in good faith only to find that, within hours on some occasions, the military would launch an operation of which they had no knowledge. Decades before the British had found that if talks in the tribal areas were to succeed, the officials in charge of the negotiations needed to be able to call on military force if and when they deemed it necessary. The limited and controlled use of force to back up the political process had worked. Many believed it still could. But General Musharraf, and still more his American allies, were reluctant to hand over the management of one of the most important front lines in the US 'war on terror' to the relatively junior civilian officials responsible for maintaining relations with the tribal leaders.

Washington wanted direct control of the policy towards the tribal areas. A lot was at stake. Having initially been routed in Afghanistan after 9/11, bin Laden and his senior colleagues were now secure on Pakistani territory, planning attacks on the West. The Afghan Taliban, furthermore, were using the tribal areas as a springboard for attacks on US troops in Afghanistan. Musharraf, meanwhile, had other concerns. Although he had to do enough to satisfy Washington and keep the aid dollars flowing, he knew that if he did not attack the militants in the tribal areas they would not attack him and would instead concentrate on fighting the Americans in Afghanistan. It was a complicated mix of conflicting interests and differing perceptions. And on the ground it led to confusion.

Unable to resist US pressure, the Pakistan army's first major battle came in March 2004 when its troops fought for 12 days against an estimated 600 Islamic militants in South Waziristan. As many as 6,000 Pakistani soldiers were involved in the operation, and more than 130 people including 16 soldiers were killed. The army used light and heavy artillery, forcing thousands of people to flee their homes. When they returned many found their buildings in ruins, their livestock dead and the orchards destroyed.[56] Some in the military thought that the use of such overwhelming force was unwise. As one retired ISI chief, General Assad Durrani, put it:

> Military action was taken in haste. Regular channels of conflict resolution and dialogue should have taken precedence over the use of military force, which undermined the capacity of the administration and local tribesmen to neutralise, contain and de-weaponise the militants through non-military means.[57]

But having started, Musharraf persisted. Throughout 2004 the Pakistan army carried out operations to attack Taliban and Al Qaeda elements in South Waziristan. Increasingly, Musharraf and his men were seen by the tribesmen as American mercenaries. The harder the army fought, the more violent was the response and it became clear to many in the Pakistan army leadership, just as it had to the British colonialists, that they could never win a military victory in the tribal areas. Far from eliminating militancy, the use of force provoked more of it. Aerial bombing in particular pushed surviving civilians to support the radicals. But whereas the Pakistanis thought the use of force undermined their chances of long-term success, the US consistently insisted that Pakistan fight harder.

Searching for a different strategy, in May 2006 General Musharraf appointed a new governor of NWFP, Lieutenant General (retd) Ali Mohammed Jan Aurakzai, and gave him wide powers to negotiate. In September 2006 he struck a deal. The Pakistani state ordered the release of 221 prisoners, withdrew troops from checkpoints and returned captured weapons, vehicles and cash to the militants. It agreed to stop ground and air operations. In return the militants promised to cease cross-border infiltration, to stop harbouring Al Qaeda militants and to refrain from setting up a parallel administration. Foreigners, however, were allowed to stay in the tribal areas as long as they kept the peace. By resorting to talks under pressure the army had signalled its weakness and, by any standards, it was a very good deal for the militants. The Americans never liked it and did their best to undermine it. Just days after the agreements were signed the US bombed a madrasa in Bajur, killing 80 people. The militants reacted in the way some in the US had hoped they would: they rejected the ceasefire and started fighting once more.

But by this time Pakistani troops had been withdrawn. North and South Waziristan, in short, had been lost. Militants consolidated their position by killing anyone who opposed them, including an estimated 200 moderate tribal leaders.[58] They established parallel administrations which even raised taxes (a first in the tribal areas).[59] They imposed Taliban-style justice with public executions after rough and ready trials. In Bajur local militants managed to kill the head of the government's vaccination programme on the grounds that he was trying to sterilise Muslim children.[60] In Khyber the government from time to time even lost control of the main road leading to Afghanistan. The route was of critical strategic importance, carrying each year over 160,000 containers with fuel and other supplies for the Western forces in Afghanistan.

The militants next expanded their areas of influence outside the tribal areas and into NWFP itself. In towns that bordered the tribal areas such as Karak, Tank, Bannu, Kohat and Dera Ismail Khan girls' schools were closed, video shops bombed, barbers' shops destroyed and NGOs attacked.[61] The militant campaign also spread to Peshawar. In 2007 there was, on average, a suicide bombing, explosion or missile attack in the city once a week. By January 2008 the police in Peshawar were conceding that militants had effectively won control of strategic pockets on the outskirts of the city. They used these bases to launch attacks on army barracks and police stations.[62] The police were reduced to protecting themselves and government buildings.

Senior officials in Islamabad for the first time wondered in private whether eventually Peshawar might fall to the militants. Indeed, there was widespread despair at the deteriorating situation. Increasingly frustrated that its war on terror was being lost, the US upped the number of air strikes in the tribal areas resulting in a higher civilian death toll. There was an almost universal perception in Pakistan that innocent people were being killed because America was facing defeat in Afghanistan. During the campaign for the 2008 elections the politicians reflected the views of the voters, arguing that the emphasis should be on talks, not the use of force. So once again, just as it had in Swat, the policy switched and the government entered talks with the Pakistani Taliban leader, Baitullah Mehsud, who ordered a ceasefire promising that anyone who disobeyed would be 'strung upside down in public and punished'.[63] Clearly, he was involved in the dialogue process. The government, though, insisted that its strategy was to talk only to those, as the new prime minister Yousaf Gilani put it, 'who because of religious or ethnic considerations were misled into supporting extremists . . . to help drain the swamp in which terrorists fester and grow'. He insisted that it was not a repeat of the 2006 deal, because those agreements had been signed after militant groups 'bruised Pakistan's security forces in battle'. 'Now,' he said, 'we are negotiating from a position of strength.'[64]

The US, though, was committed to fighting, not dialogue. The US deputy secretary of state, John Negroponte, said that Pakistan should be arresting Baitullah Mehsud rather than talking to him.[65] Washington feared that the militants once again would use the talks process to regroup, reorganise and rearm. To demonstrate the depth of his frustration, in July 2008 President George W. Bush approved orders that allowed US ground forces to enter Pakistani territory without giving any advance warning to the Pakistani authorities.[66]

The fact that America was openly breaching Pakistani sovereignty worried the new army chief, General Ashfaq Kayani. Post-election talks between the government and the militants had got under way, and he had been making his own assessments about how to handle the insurgency. He could see that the American position was changing. The US had become convinced, Kayani thought, that anti-Americanism in Pakistan was so well established that there was not much point in US forces holding back for the sake of influencing hearts and minds that were already set against America. Kayani believed that the US also viewed stability in Afghanistan, in which they had troops, as more important than stability in Pakistan. And most pressingly of all Kayani could see that the Americans were no longer willing to tolerate the failure to dislodge Al Qaeda from the tribal areas, and that they could well mount more unilateral action. In 2007 the US National Intelligence Estimate had openly stated that Al Qaeda had an increasingly secure safe haven in the tribal areas and that it was becoming ever more capable of mounting attacks on US soil.[67] As he pondered these assessments Kayani concluded that the only way for Pakistan to prevent US incursions on Pakistani sovereignty was to fight harder itself. And he knew that the relationship with Washington was not irrevocably broken. For all its misgivings, in 2007 Washington announced an aid programme worth $750 million over five years. US officials said that the money would create 100,000 jobs in the tribal areas with a view to providing an alternative to militancy. The US planned 300–400 new schools, and some of the money was earmarked for equipping and training the Frontier Corps.

The US attitude to the Frontier Corps illustrated many of the dilemmas it faced in Pakistan. Historically, the corps had been seen as a way of keeping young tribesmen out of trouble by employing them and providing them with a small income. The chronically under-funded force had been given the bulk of the responsibility for the fighting in the tribal areas and Swat. But many of the corps did not believe in the war and did not want to fight. The US needed the

Frontier Corps to be more effective, but it feared it might be arming future enemies. There had been numerous reports of Frontier Corps units on the border helping the Taliban, but if the US and Pakistan could not win over the active support of men who had volunteered to join the corps then its cause in the tribal areas was surely lost.

Whilst Kayani pondered these problems he had to acknowledge that the 2008 election campaign had revealed unambiguously that most Pakistanis were opposed to military action. If he were to order his army to fight, Kayani concluded, he would need more political support. In July 2008 he met with the government leaders and laid out his case. The Americans were going to fight Al Qaeda with or without Pakistan, he said. He wanted to resist breaches to Pakistani sovereignty, but to do so he needed to show the Americans that he was making real military progress against the militants. The army was willing to fight but the politicians would have to offer vocal public support and to persuade the public that this was Pakistan's, not America's, war.

In August Kayani decided to move. The battle for Bajur, as it was known in the Pakistani press, became an intense conflict.[68] The military launched a ferocious offensive with 9,000 troops, heavy artillery, helicopter gunships and air strikes from fighter jets. A quarter of a million people fled the area seeking safety, many of them ending up in impromptu displacement camps. In September 2008 the army announced that it had killed as many as one thousand militants in Bajur in that month alone – 62 soldiers had also died. The officer in charge of the Frontier Corps force in Bajur, General Tariq Khan, saw the area as the key battleground between the state and the militants: 'If they lose here,' he said, 'they've lost almost everything.'[69] Yet whenever the estimated 5,000 surviving militants suffered further losses, they were reinforced by volunteers from other parts of the tribal areas and from Afghanistan. Financed by the huge profits from Afghanistan's poppy crop, the militants were also able to procure high-tech weaponry against which the Pakistan army found it difficult to compete. 'Even the sniper rifles they use are better than some of ours,' one official complained.[70]

In September 2008 General Kayani visited Bajur and appealed to the local tribal elders to support the armed forces. 'We will soon eliminate the militants and their supporters from the tribal areas and will establish the writ of the government,' he said.[71] As ever, the elders wanted to be on the winning side and, having seen how seriously the army was fighting, they responded to Kayani's appeal. The tribal support for the army came in the form of lashkars: private armies of tribal fighters who vowed to expel Taliban and Al Qaeda elements in their areas. There were a number of factors behind the lashkars. Tribal leaders who helped the government could expect financial rewards, but they were also reflecting public opinion in their areas. Although many people in NWFP respected the Taliban's fight against the US forces in Afghanistan, and many were attracted by the idea of a Taliban-style speedy justice system, they tended to change their minds once they had seen what sort of government the Taliban actually provided when it had control of an area. 'These Taliban call themselves Muslims, but they have been involved in all sorts of crimes,' said Malik Mohmand Habib, a tribal leader in Bajur with a 15,000-strong lashkar under his command: 'We want them out of our area.'[72] The lashkars worked closely with the army, often holding an area once the military had fought for it. In line with tribal tradition the elders repeatedly ordered that the houses of Taliban members be burnt down.[73] Once the lashkar movement got under way in Bajur it spread to other parts of NWFP, although in some areas the tribal elders said they were only prepared to confront the Taliban if the army agreed to stay out of their area. 'We will not allow the security forces to come into the district,' said one anti-Taliban tribal leader from Dir near the Afghan border. 'We have the capability and power to maintain peace here.'[74]

The militants were quick to see the threat the lashkars posed and in a series of targeted attacks tried to undermine them. When the ANP leader Asfandyar Wali Khan praised the lashkars, saying, 'it's going to be the people versus the Taliban,'[75] the militants responded with a suicide-bomb attack on his house (he survived). By October 2008 progovernment tribesmen were being beheaded,[76] and when hundreds of tribal elders in Orakzai met to discuss establishing a lashkar in their area, a suicide bomber drove into their jirga, detonated himself and killed more than 40 people.[77]

Asif Ali Zardari

For as long as Benazir Bhutto was alive her husband, Asif Ali Zardari, realised that she was the one who would have high office. It was she who could attract the massive crowds and whose support in Sindh was so great that she would always be a significant figure at the national level. To some degree this bothered him little: Zardari never had much interest in politics or religion and had no strong ideological views. He had on the other hand always been interested in power. When his wife was prime minister he secured himself ministerial portfolios and set up his own office inside the prime minister's house. After her murder in December 2007 he saw his chance to rule in his own right. For all his protestations of lack of interest, he wanted the presidency and worked hard to get it.

And once he had secured the job in September 2008, Ali Zardari was the most powerful civilian leader in the country's history. As president he could dismiss the parliament. He also controlled the government: the prime minister, Yousaf Gilani, had no independent power base. The victory of Zardari's party in the 2008 election, widely seen as amongst the freest and fairest in Pakistani history, gave him legitimacy. After nine years in power, the army was anxious to withdraw from front-line politics. That left the judiciary as the only possible source of authority that could challenge Zardari. But by a series of utterly unscrupulous manoeuvres, such as repeatedly promising to restore the chief justice Iftikhar Chaudhry who had been sacked by Musharraf, and then going back on the commitment, Zardari ensured that there was a sympathetic Supreme Court. Later popular protests fired Zardari to allow the chief justice to return to his job but, when he moved into President's House in September 2008, he was truly the master of all he surveyed.

He did have some problems, however. The 2008 elections had been held in the most favourable possible conditions for the Pakistan Peoples' Party. The PPP's iconic leader, Benazir Bhutto, had been assassinated and throughout Pakistan there was a wave of sympathy for her party. Before her death she had created a situation in which President Musharraf had remained implacably hostile to Nawaz Sharif whilst granting her and her husband amnesties. The official toleration of her return meant that the authorities let her run a more effective election campaign than Nawaz Sharif. Given the circumstances, the PPP should have won by a landslide. But to the dismay of many of its senior leaders, it secured only 97 seats in the National Assembly compared to 71 for Nawaz Sharif's Pakistan Muslim League (PML-N). Furthermore the pro-Musharraf party, the PML-Q, filled mainly with former Sharif supporters who could be expected to switch back to him at some time in the future, won 42 seats. Those electoral numbers, combined with the inevitable unpopularity faced by sitting governments in Pakistan, mean that the PPP faces the prospect of growing weakness in the future. It is a party in decline. Indeed, the party's support started to slip straight after the elections. By the time parliament and the Provincial Assemblies elevated Zardari to the presidency in September 2008, his national approval rating was down to 26 per cent.[78]

Zardari also had splits within his party. His management of the PPP in the months after Benazir Bhutto's death had been so adept that in virtually every internal party meeting nobody expressed any opposition to him. Indeed, in one session a member of the National Assembly went so far as to say he would commit suicide if Zardari did not stand for the presidency. The reluctance to challenge Zardari in public, however, concealed considerable private unease about him. For years PPP activists had tried to explain away the corruption allegations against Benazir Bhutto by arguing that it was her husband who had led her astray. Now the husband was in charge. Other party members had dynastic objections. Even though Benazir Bhutto had written a document naming Zardari, and their son Bilawal, as her political heirs, some party members, especially traditionalists in Sindh, objected to Zardari on the grounds that, whoever he might have been married to, there was not a drop of Bhutto blood in him.

There were also serious economic problems. Zardari came into power to find that inflation was at a 30-year high and the rupee at an all-time low against the dollar. In the 12 months before he became president, the Karachi stock exchange had fallen by a third. More seriously, over the same period the foreign exchange reserves, hit by rising global fuel and food prices, had fallen by 67 per cent to $4.7 billion.[79]

Pakistan seemed destined to return to the pre-Musharraf days of constant crisis management to stave off default. The deteriorating security situation contributed to the bleak outlook. Foreign direct investment, which had reached record levels under Musharraf, was replaced by capital flight. It was not surprising, then, that within a month of taking over, Zardari had made a somewhat desperate and utterly futile appeal for a $100 billion no-strings-attached international grant to shore up the Pakistani treasury.[80] After months of negotiations he secured an IMF deal of just $7.6 billion with lots of strings attached in the form of demands to cut back public sector spending.[81]

As Zardari looked ahead to his presidency, then, his political and economic problems were, by any standards, very tough. But they were dwarfed by the security situation. Initially Zardari hoped he could rely on his coalition partner, the ANP, to resolve the problems in NWFP. The ANP leader, Asfandyar Wali Khan, was well known for his opposition to the Taliban. His modernism had cost him votes. In the 2002 elections, the Afghan Taliban's resistance to the American-backed forces in Afghanistan had been widely admired throughout Pakistan and especially in NWFP. For the first time in its history the ANP won no seats in the National Assembly. By the 2008 election, however, the political situation had changed, albeit in complex and nuanced ways. The Afghan Taliban's struggle against Western forces remained highly popular. The emergence of a distinct Pakistani Taliban led by Baitullah Mehsud, though, had confused the situation. To some extent the Pakistani Taliban benefited from the reflected glory of the campaign in Afghanistan. But there were other aspects to Baitullah Mehsud's performance that attracted support. Many in the electorate welcomed the idea of Taliban-style speedy justice. Reflecting their Deobandi beliefs, many Pukhtoons had some sympathy for Pakistani Taliban's campaigns against lewd Indian films, uncovered women and other so-called manifestations of un-Islamic modernity. At the same time many people feared the Pakistani Taliban was too violent. They also worried that it could impoverish them. When they had governed Afghanistan, the Taliban leaders had been so unworldly that they had been utterly unconcerned by the dire poverty that surrounded them. Pukhtoons in NWFP had enjoyed sufficient improvements in their living standards in Pakistan to take a rather more materialistic view. There was one other important factor. The Taliban tended to be unpopular in places where it had governed in part because its presence generally attracted attacks by the US or Pakistani militaries, neither of which showed much ability to distinguish between their Taliban targets and the civilians around them. So although, in theory, the idea of Pakistani Taliban rule did not frighten many Pukhtoons, the practical reality of it was often less appealing.

It was against this background that the ANP achieved an electoral comeback in 2008, securing 13 seats. It was in large part a vote for an end to the conflicts in Swat, the tribal areas and other parts of NWFP. And after the elections the ANP leaders believed that they could talk to fellow Pukhtoons in the Pakistani Taliban, the TNSM and other organisations, and by appealing to Pukhtoon unity persuade them to stop fighting. President Zardari, then, had some good reasons for putting Asfandyar Wali in charge of the talks process: the ANP leader was a highly respected Pukhtoon for whom the Taliban would have some respect. That is how it seemed; but the reality was rather different. The Taliban was so extreme that even the JUI and JI, never mind the ANP, were looking like old-fashioned moderates out of touch with the most radical and politically dynamic elements of society. To his great dismay the ANP leader discovered that in the post-Red Mosque world the Taliban simply ignored him. If he wanted a united national movement, the Taliban argued, then the way to get it was by promoting radical Islam, not abandoning it.

So how big is the problem Zardari faces? Much depends on how one sees the Islamist movement. There are reasons for viewing it as a single, linked entity. Many of the militants who want to fight or to become suicide bombers move fairly freely between different organisations. Increasingly, there are young militants who want to attack a target and are not especially bothered which organisation provides them with the means to do so. There are also an increasing number of attacks organised spontaneously at a local level with apparently very little direction from the militant groups' hierarchies.[82] The various militant groups not only share an ideology, they also agree on some specific points including the view that President Zardari and even Asfandyar Wali are fighting Islam on behalf of America. Local security officials also believe that, even if it does not have direct control of groups such as the Pakistani Taliban, Al Qaeda has managed to pass on training in how to mount effective attacks.[83]

For all that, though, the various groups still have distinct leaderships, varying objectives and distinct constituencies. Al Qaeda predominates in North Waziristan, whereas the Pakistani Taliban is strongest in South Waziristan and Mohmand. The sectarian groups hold sway in Kurram, whilst in Khyber there is a violent struggle between two groups, Lashkar i-Islam and Ansar ul-Islam, which reflect religious divisions (between Deobandis and Barelvis) as well as a business dispute about carving up the local drugs trade.[84] In Swat, meanwhile, the TNSM tried to impose sharia law as their equivalents did, with some international jihadi support, in Bajur.

At the time he came into power the differences between these decentralised groups were one of Zardari's few opportunities for making progress against the Islamists. There was some potential for a policy of 'divide and rule'. Al Qaeda's central leadership was using the tribal areas as a sanctuary where it could make propaganda and plan global jihad in the form of more attacks on the West. It is the only Jihadi organization in Pakistan or Afganistan with global rather than regional ambitions. The Afghan Taliban under Mullah Omar, by contrast, seeks the withdrawal of foreign forces from Afghanistan. In January 2007 Omar made it clear that he did not have a formal relationship with Al Qaeda: 'We have never felt the need for a permanent relationship in the present circumstances. They [Al Qaeda] have set jihad as their goal while we have set the expulsion of American troops from Afghanistan as our target.'[85]

There were also differences between the Afghan and the Pakistani Taliban or Tehrik-e-Taliban, with Mullah Omar arguing that all Taliban fighters on both sides of the Durand line should make the fall of kabul their main goal. The Pakistani Taliban, formed to bring various militant groups together, preferred to focus on Pakistan itself. While each local Taliban group was free to undertake operations against the security forces as it saw fit, no single group was to enter negotiations with the authorities without the approval of the Tehrik-i-Taliban leadership as a whole.[86] Most of its initial demands were couched in defensive terms and involved resisting the presence of the Pakistan army in their areas.[87] The tribal areas are now also home to many former Kashmiri groups looking for a new role. Fighters from Harakat ul-Mujahideen, and Jaish-e-Mohammed (now Khudam ul-Islam), for example, have been active in battles against the Pakistan army near Peshawar and in Swat. Banned sectarian groups such as Lashkar e-Jhangvi have also made the move from Punjab to NWFP.

By the start of 2009, however, the possibility of weakening the Islamists by dividing them was diminishing. The ISI was maintaining its links with some elements of the Taliban such as the fighters led by Jalaluddin Naqqani and his son Sirajuddin but the jihadis were by that point running a full-blown and increasingly united insurgency. The frequent American air strikes within Pakistan may have destroyed some of the US's high-value targets but they also had the effect of unifying the various militant groups who vowed to come to each others' aid if need be. Increasingly, the demand for sharia law came to the fore as one on which all the different groups could agree. The failures of the Pakistani and Afghan judicial systems meant that it was also a relatively popular demand. There have been other indications of linkages between militant organisations. Baitullah Mehsud, for example, has claimed to have had contact with Abu Musab al-Zaqawi, the Al Qaeda leader in Iraq, before he was killed by the Americans. Mehsud has also used some Al Qaeda-type rhetoric about destroying New York, Washington and London.[88] The potential for creating divisions in the ranks of radical Islam, then, is increasingly limited.

The Pakistani author Ahmed Rashid has argued that any long-term solution in north-western Pakistan and southern Afghanistan must involve the area's economic and social development. He has urged the Pakistani government and its US backers to come up with a plan to introduce democracy, social reform and educational provision to the tribal areas.[89] 'Right now,' he has pointed out, 'only the extremists have a clear vision for the tribal areas.'[90] He is right. The struggle in north-western Pakistan is not just a military one. The failure of the Pakistani state to provide law and order has furnished the Islamists with an opportunity. Their battle for hearts and minds is enjoying some success, especially in Deobandi areas: while some Peshawarites worry that their city might actually fall to the militants, others fear that as attitudes there become ever more conservative and hostile to the US and its proxies in Islamabad, the city will just slip away from mainstream Pakistan as ever greater numbers sympathise with and even demand Taliban-style social restrictions.

Yet the social development of the tribal areas, however desirable, carries short-term risks. Modernisation will inevitably involve weakening the power of the tribal maliks. Yet the maliks represent the single biggest obstacle to the radical Islamists. The battle for Bajur revealed the maliks' potential as an anti-Jihadi force. The tribal structures have proved to be highly resilient. Even at the height of its power in NWFP the MMA religious-party alliance did not dare tackle some tribal traditions. Although MMA leaders, for example, said that in Islam widows could remarry, they did not support the practice because Pukhtoon tradition forbade it.[91] In the short term, the re-emergence of the tribal structures, however undesirable and regressive, represents a chance for the Pakistani government to defeat the radical Islamists. The choice for Western governments and Asif Ali Zardari may be between regressive theocrats with global ambitions and regressive tribal traditionalists who want to be left alone to govern themselves according to their own customs. The dilemmas facing Asif Ali Zardari could scarcely be more daunting.

Nationalism

My description of the partition as the greatest blunder in the history of
mankind is an objective assessment based on the bitter experience of the
masses. . . . Had the subcontinent not been divided, the 180 million
Muslims of Bangladesh, 150 million of Pakistan and about 200 million
in India would together have made 530 million people and, as such,
they would have been a very powerful force in undivided India.
— Muttahida Quami Movement (MQM) leader Altaf Hussain,
October 2000[1]

Introduction

'I have been a Baloch for several centuries. I have been a Muslim for
1,400 years. I have been a Pakistani for just over fifty.'[2] The tribal chief
Nawab Akbar Bugti Khan had no love for Pakistan. From his heavily
guarded, mud-walled fort deep in the Baloch desert, he ran a state
within a state. Pakistan may have been in existence for over half a
century, but he still considered any Pakistani troops in his vicinity as
part of an occupation army. And they saw him as a rebel. In 2007
General Musharraf ordered the death of Nawab Bugti. He went down
fighting. Firing from a cave, he killed 21 soldiers before he died. Many
people living in remote parts of Pakistan admired his stand. Islam was
meant to be the binding force – but, for many, ethnic ties have proved
to be stronger.

When Pakistan was created there were already over 70 million
Muslims living on the 'land of the pure' and they were by no means
united. As well as the Bengalis in East Pakistan, the new state had to
integrate five major groups: the Sindhis, the Baloch, the Pukhtoons, the
Punjabis and the incoming Mohajirs.[3]

Successive Pakistani leaders have shown little sympathy for Pakistan's various cultures. Mohammed Ali Jinnah himself insisted on loyalty and allegiance to Pakistan, and Pakistan alone. Speaking in Dhaka in March 1948, he said:

> What we want is not talk about Bengali, Punjabi, Sindhi, Baluchi, Pathan and so on. They are of course units. But I ask you: have you forgotten the lesson that was taught us thirteen hundred years ago? You belong to a nation now. You have carved out a territory, a vast territory. It is all yours: it does not belong to a Punjabi or a Sindhi or a Pathan or a Bengali. It is all yours. You have got your Central Government where several units are represented. Therefore, if you want to build yourself up into a nation, for God's sake give up this provincialism.[4]

Pakistani leaders since Jinnah have consistently echoed that line. In 1954 the first Pakistani commander-in-chief, Ayub Khan, wrote: 'The ultimate aim must be to become a sound, solid and cohesive nation . . .'[5] When he made his final address to the nation 11 years later, Ayub's view had not changed. Warning that some people wanted to destroy the country established by Jinnah, he said: 'I have always told you that Pakistan's salvation lay in a strong centre.'[6]

In 1971 Pakistan faced the most significant nationalist challenge of its short history when the Bengalis split away and formed Bangladesh. There are some in Pakistan today, such as some Pukhtoons or advocates of an independent Sindh called Sindudesh, for example, who would like to follow their example. One might think that the loss of East Pakistan in 1971 would have alerted Pakistani leaders to the dangers of ignoring local nationalist sentiment. It didn't. In 1974 Zulfikar Ali Bhutto was quite adamant on the matter. Speaking about Baloch demands for greater autonomy, he said the idea of confederation (rather than a more centralised federation) was 'a ridiculous one for a country that wants to count for something in the world. It will never work.'[7] General Zia saw it the same way. Asked in 1978 about the possibility of introducing a multi-national Pakistan in which the Baloch, Pukhtoons, Sindhis and Punjabis would be entitled to local self-rule, he replied: 'I simply cannot understand this type of thinking. We want to build a strong country, a unified country.

Why should we talk in these small-minded terms? We should talk in terms of Pakistan, one united Pakistan.' He went on to say that, ideally, he would like to break up the existing four provinces of West Pakistan and replace them with 53 small provinces, erasing ethnic identities altogether.[8]

On the face of it, General Musharraf took a different approach. He often spoke about devolution and repeatedly said he wanted to decentralise power. In reality he did no such thing. The main function of his devolution plan of 2000 was to answer those Western governments that, before 9/11, were pressing him to restore democracy. He used to tell them that he was doing just that by getting communities to elect mayors and councillors. The local leaders, however, had very little power and became a pliant tool of central government. As the International Crisis Group concluded, the devolution plan not only bypassed the provinces but also 'proved little more than a cover for further centralised control of the lower levels of the government'.[9]

Whatever their background, Pakistani leaders have consistently seen expressions of provincial feeling as a threat to the Pakistani state. Nationalist leaders in the provinces have tended to associate such centralist attitudes with Punjab. In reality, it has never been as simple as that. After all, Jinnah was a Karachiite, Ayub Khan was a Pukhtoon, Zulfikar Ali Bhutto came from Sindh and Musharraf was born in Delhi.

It is ironic that the nationalists in Pakistan's provinces have repeatedly cited, as a source of legitimacy, the very document that provided the basis for Pakistan itself: the Lahore Resolution. Although the resolution did not include the word 'federation', it did say that the new country it called for should have 'constituent units' which would be 'autonomous and sovereign'. The terms autonomous and sovereign are notoriously difficult to define. But national groups such as the Sindhis and the Baloch can certainly argue that, by any definition, sovereignty must include the power of a constituent unit to decide whether or not it remains in a larger entity.

This chapter will analyse some of the nationalist challenges to Pakistan. One of the most sustained campaigns has come from the least likely source: the refugees, or Mohajirs, who moved to Pakistan in 1947. Over the course of 60 years the attitude of those Mohajirs who ended up in Sindh has gone through an extraordinary transformation: Pakistan's

Provincial breakdown by population, 1951

Province	Percentage of WestPakistan	Percentage of East and West Pakistan
Punjab	62.1	27.7
Sindh	17.1	7.6
Balochistan	3.4	1.5
NWFP	17.4	7.8
Bengal	0.0	55.4
Total	100	100

Source: Keith Callard, *Pakistan: A Political Study*, George Allen & Unwin, Oxford, 1957, p. 156.

keenest advocates became the country's most bitter critics. The difficulty in explaining the turnaround in Mohajir attitudes, and the fact that the emergence of Mohajir nationalism was so closely intertwined with that of the Sindhis, means that most of this chapter must be devoted to developments in Sindh. It will also discuss the nationalists in Balochistan. Pukhtoon nationalism has been discussed in the previous chapter, and the breakaway of East Pakistan is the subject of chapter 4. There is no separate discussion of Punjab. As the dominant province in Pakistan, Punjab has never seen the need to press for greater autonomy.

When independence was attained, millions of people in northern India gave up their jobs, homes and communities, and began a terrifying journey to the 'land of the pure'. Most travelled on foot or by train and in doing so they risked their lives. An untold number never made it: they became victims of the frenzied violence triggered by partition. For those who crossed the rivers of blood that separated the two new nations, the feeling of relief was intense. Not only were they participating in the birth of a new Muslim nation; they had survived.

There are no reliable figures for the number of people who fled to Pakistan in the wake of partition. Ayub Khan estimated that there were 9 million.[10] Whatever the total, it is widely accepted that a majority of the incomers were Punjabis from the Indian side of the border who settled into Pakistan with relative ease. That is not to say there were no tensions. The East Punjabis tended to be better educated than the West Punjabis, and their need for suitable properties to live in did cause some resentment amongst the host population. To this day, the difference between

Punjab's traditional population and the post-partition incomers is reflected in voting patterns.[11] Nevertheless cultural, linguistic and, in some cases, family links meant that the assimilation process was relatively smooth. Compared to the refugees who headed for Sindh, the East Punjabis tended to have lower expectations of Pakistan. They suffered dreadfully during partition and many of those who survived the journey to Pakistan witnessed horrific acts of violence, including the murder of family members before their eyes. They did not arrive with a long list of demands: they were glad to be alive.

Most of the non-Punjabi migrants came from the United Provinces, Rajastan and other Hindu majority parts of northern India, and the majority headed for Sindh where they hoped they could find work in the new capital, Karachi. Despite the Mohajirs' repeated claims that they made huge sacrifices for Pakistan, the East Punjabis suffered more: the Mohajirs chose to move to build a new future, but the East Punjabis had to flee to save their lives. The Mohajirs had campaigned for Pakistan only to find that their own home areas in India did not become part of Pakistan. And the impact of the Urdu-speaking Mohajirs on Sindhi cities such as Karachi and Hyderabad was enormous. By 1951 the native Sindhi community in Karachi, for example, had been completely outnumbered; just 14 per cent of the city's population spoke Sindhi as opposed to 58 per cent who spoke Urdu. In other Sindhi cities the figures were even more striking. In Hyderabad over 66 per cent of the population was Mohajir.[12] It was quite possible for Mohajirs to live in these cities and seldom meet a Sindhi, never mind interact with one.

Many of the Mohajirs were well educated: in line with the imperial policy of divide and rule, the British had ensured that the Muslims who lived in Hindu-dominated provinces were well represented in the imperial bureaucracy and the professions. These were people with aspirations, if not to rule, then at least to govern. With some justification, the Mohajirs, especially those from the United Provinces, saw themselves as having been the driving force behind the creation of Pakistan. The Muslims living in the Hindu-dominated areas of British India had always had the most to fear from the end of the empire and they had always been the most enthusiastic promoters of Pakistan. This gets to the heart of the Mohajir issue. Their subsequent frustrations were a product of their earlier hopes and expectations.

Sindh: The Early Years

The Mohajirs presumed that their sacrifices for Pakistan would be rewarded and, at first, their expectations were largely met. Many fared relatively well in their new country. Since the Mohajirs did not fit into traditional power structures in Pakistan, they turned their attention to areas such as business and the bureaucracy in which success could be achieved on merit. The Pakistani government guaranteed that members of the British-run India civil service who moved to Pakistan would be given equivalent jobs in the new state. The local Sindhi population, with no middle class to speak of, were no match for the ideologically driven and highly motivated Mohajirs who took over businesses and homes abandoned by the many middle-class Hindus who had abruptly left Sindh for India.

In July 1948 the Mohajirs consolidated their pre-eminence by securing a significant symbolic gain: Karachi, despite the vehement opposition of the Sindhi chief minister Ayub Khuhro, became the Federal Capital Area under the control of the central government. Although there are many international precedents for a nation's capital being administered in this way, for the native Sindhis it was a big blow. Sindh's leading nationalist politician, G.M. Syed, later described the decision in the most vivid terms: 'Mr Jinnah dismembered Sindh by cutting off Karachi, its leading city, from it and handed it over to the central administration of Liaquat Ali Khan as its head, for colonisation of the city by Mohajirs.'[13] In 1948 the Sindhis were not sufficiently politically organised to block the move. But many still resented it. They began to wonder whether their national identity was under threat. Insensitive to such concerns, the Mohajirs pressed on with their demands, not least that Urdu should be Pakistan's national language. Urdu had become a symbol of Muslim identity and for the Mohajirs it was natural, even wonderful, that the language should acquire national status in Pakistan. It was unfortunate, then, that few Pakistanis spoke it.

The death of Jinnah in 1948 and the assassination of Liaquat Ali Khan in 1951 were setbacks for the Mohajirs. So too was the 1955 decision to declare West Pakistan as One Unit which amalgamated the provinces of Sindh, Balochistan, NWFP and Punjab into one administrative structure. The measure was meant to balance the power of East and West Pakistan and, superficially, it seemed to suit the Mohajirs well. It appeared that the provincial power bases, dominated by traditional leaders, would lose out to the new, Mohajir-dominated Pakistani elite. In the event, though, One Unit exposed just how unrealistic the Mohajirs' hopes of continuing to dominate Pakistani politics were. In 1951 Urdu speakers accounted for fewer than 5 per cent of West Pakistan's population. Inevitably, the Punjabis, who accounted for close to 40 per cent, started to assert themselves. One Unit helped them take jobs from the Mohajirs not only at the federal level but also in Sindh itself.[14] Furthermore, provincial objections to One Unit tended to strengthen rather than weaken the national movements in Balochistan, NWFP and, crucially for the Mohajirs, in Sindh.

The differences between the Mohajirs and the native Sindhis ran deep. From the Sindhi point of view, a wave of self-important, landgrabbing outsiders had turned up with colonial attitudes to match those of the departed British. The situation was hardly helped by the fact that many Mohajirs viewed the Sindhis as medieval vassals who needed to be dragged into the twentieth century. Some of the Mohajirs' policy initiatives were highly provocative. In 1957, for example, the University of Karachi forbade students from answering questions in Sindhi.[15] In the face of such discrimination it is hardly surprising that the Sindhis' sense of resentment was acute. They had been demanding greater provincial autonomy ever since 1917. For some, the decision to support the Pakistan project was based on a perception that a Muslim state would offer the best opportunity for pursuing Sindh's national interests.

In 1975 G.M. Syed tried to explain away the support he, and other Sindhi politicians, had given to the creation of Pakistan:

Some of us who all the time remained conscious of the national distinctness of the people of Sind and of their significant past history, participated in the movement for Pakistan solely for the purpose of ensuring thereby political independence, economic prosperity and cultural advancement of Sind. We remained convinced throughout of the validity of the teaching of our great political thinkers who considered the Sindhi people a separate nation.

The two-nation theory, he said, had been a 'trap' designed to establish 'Mohajir-Punjabi exploitative hegemony over the Muslim majority provinces'. The Sindhi nationalists had joined the Pakistan movement, he maintained, because they believed the Lahore Resolution would result in Sindhi independence and not 'the accident of history and freak of nature' that became Pakistan.[16]

G.M. Syed's role in first promoting Pakistan and later denouncing it has long been controversial. The record shows, however, that even before the transfer of power he was focusing on Sindhi as opposed to Muslim nationalism. In 1947 he wrote, 'The prospect of a unitary Pakistan looms ahead as a terrible nightmare in which the people of Sind will be trampled on as mere serfs by the more numerous and aggressive outsiders.'[17] In May 1948 the Sindhi nationalists joined forces with Bengalis, Pukhtoons and the Baloch to form the People's Organisation. Like its successor, the Pakistan Oppressed Nations Movement (PONM), the People's Organisation stopped short of explicitly demanding the break-up of Pakistan and was to make little impact. Nevertheless, the Sindhi nationalists did manage to send a message to the Mohajirs: many in Sindh did not welcome them.

In Pakistan's early years the Mohajirs were too confident to worry about the Sindhis. Even in 1958 when Ayub Khan, a Pukhtoon, took over, many Mohajirs remained optimistic. In line with Mohajir thinking, Ayub Khan wanted to create a strong central government, although he perhaps had a more secular vision than many Mohajirs would have been comfortable with at the time. Furthermore, the Mohajirs were well disposed towards the military, seeing it not only as a source of protection from India but also as a non-feudal meritocracy and the embodiment of Pakistani unity. But the Mohajirs' faith in the military was misplaced.

The Pakistan army was always, and remains, Punjabi-dominated: periods of military rule have generally seen a growth of Punjabi influence. Although there are no official figures, it is estimated that 65 per cent of officers and 70 per cent of the other ranks are Punjabis. That compares with the province's 56 per cent share of the population. Pukhtoons from NWFP, with 16 per cent of the population, constitute an estimated 22 per cent of officers and 25 per cent of other ranks. The Mohajirs have generally been over-represented in the officer corps and under-represented in the lower ranks. Despite some rather half-hearted efforts to correct these imbalances, the Sindhis and the Baloch have always been severely under-represented.[18]

Under Ayub Khan, Punjabis also took civilian jobs from the Mohajirs. Indeed, the situation was so acute that on a few occasions Mohajirs wanting to secure promotion tried to establish that they had Pukhtoon or Punjabi ancestry.[19] The Mohajirs' grip on the bureaucracy was further undermined when, in 1959, Ayub moved the capital from Karachi to Islamabad. It was a clear indication of the Mohajirs' diminishing influence and a significant blow in itself as it further limited their access to government jobs. The Mohajirs became increasingly disillusioned with Ayub Khan. It is no accident that in the 1965 presidential election the general's heaviest defeat in West Pakistan was in Karachi. Most Mohajirs voted for Fatima Jinnah, the sister of their beloved late leader, Mohammed Ali Jinnah.

Ayub Khan's successor, General Yahya Khan, did not suit the Mohajirs much better. True, he did reverse the policy of One Unit. The main beneficiaries of this, however, were not the Mohajirs but their provincial rivals who were able to reclaim power that had been taken over by Punjabis. The city of Karachi was returned to Sindh. This time it was the Mohajirs' turn to complain – some said they were surrendering a homeland for a second time. And by holding Pakistan's first ever national elections, Yahya heightened the Mohajirs' fears that their numerical inferiority would count against them. But Yahya's greatest contribution to the deterioration of ethnic harmony in urban Sindh was the failure of his policy over 1,000 miles away in East Pakistan.

The loss of Bangladesh in 1971 added significantly to the Mohajirs' sense of vulnerability. Ever since, their leaders have pointed to the loss of East Pakistan as evidence that the two-nation theory was dead and that the Pakistan project, for which they had made so many sacrifices, had failed. The Mohajirs' concerns went beyond the abstract: they were highly aware of the predicament of the Biharis. The Biharis were Indian Muslims who had moved to East Pakistan at the time of partition. Loyal to Pakistan, they were politically isolated in the new Bangladesh where the vast majority of the population was ethnically Bengali. Those who survived the 1971 war ended up in cramped 'refugee' camps where many families were to remain for decades. The Mohajirs have consistently argued the Biharis' case – but to no avail. And many Mohajirs saw the Biharis' plight as a warning: if the Bengalis could pull off independence then might not the Sindhis do the same? And might not the Mohajirs end up in the same situation as the Biharis?

But, if 1971 raised unwelcome questions for the Mohajirs, worse was to come. Under Zulfikar Ali Bhutto their disillusionment became complete. A Sindhi had, for the first time, achieved high office in Pakistan and Bhutto blatantly favoured his traditional constituency at the expense of the Mohajirs, not least by the use of the quota system. To the outrage of the Mohajirs it applied in Sindh but in no other province. Under the scheme, 40 per cent of government jobs and educational places were allocated to people living in urban areas, but 60 per cent went to rural areas where the native Sindhis tended to live. Much to the Mohajirs' discomfort, Sindhis started to take significant numbers of jobs in the lower and middle levels of the provincial bureaucracy. The MQM (Muttahida Quami Movement) leader, Altaf Hussain, later complained, 'if you were a Sindhi you got everything. If you weren't, you got nothing.'[20] The MQM's sense of having been treated unjustly was added to by the effect of Bhutto's nationalisation programme: it hit many Mohajir businessmen hard.

The Mohajirs' discontent found violent expression in 1972 when, on 7 July, Bhutto passed a Sindh Language Bill in the Sindh National Assembly. Again, the Mohajirs thought they were being singled out for discriminatory treatment: there were no similar bills in other provinces. Whilst making it clear that Urdu's status as a national language remained in place, the measure gave Sindhi the status of the sole provincial language and had a direct impact on the employability of Urdu speakers. Under the law, provincial government officials had to learn Sindhi, a language that many Mohajirs considered beneath them, if they were to keep their jobs.

Bhutto could be excused for thinking that he could push the Language Bill through without too much difficulty. Throughout Pakistan's early years Sindhi had been a compulsory language and many Mohajirs had learnt it. The requirement to learn Sindhi was dropped during the period of Ayub Khan's martial law because many officers stationed in Sindh said they did not see the point of studying the language when they would only be in Sindh for the duration of their posting. Bhutto, then, was restoring a practice that had existed before martial law. Nevertheless, the reaction to the Language Bill was swift and a warning of what was to come in later years. The day the bill was passed there were massive pro-Urdu demonstrations in Karachi. The police tear-gassed the protestors and announced a dusk to dawn curfew. The next morning's newspapers hardly helped calm the situation. The Urdu daily *Jang* bordered the whole of its front page with thick black lines. The banner headline ran: 'This is the funeral procession for Urdu: let it go out with a fanfare.' That day, 8 July, the Mohajirs returned to the streets. This time the police fired directly into the demonstrators killing 12 people, including a 10-year-old boy. The Mohajir movement had its first martyrs and the protestors responded with fury, burning down buildings throughout Karachi. Students from Karachi University targeted the Sindh department, setting all its records alight. On 9 July, with Bhutto insisting that the status of Urdu had not been undermined, ten more people were killed. Eventually calm was restored only when Bhutto passed an ordinance under which, for the next 12 years, no one could lose their job on the grounds that they did not speak Sindhi.[21]

By his overt support for his political heartland in rural Sindh, Bhutto had split the province in two. The importance of ethnicity was now plain for all to see. Increasingly, the Mohajirs began to identify themselves not as Pakistan's natural governors but rather as an embattled minority fighting for its rights. The Sindhis, by contrast, were emboldened. Bhutto's blatant bias in their favour gave hope and confidence to the Sindhi nationalists. At last the tide was turning in their favour. The idea that the Sindhis and the Mohajirs were compatriots, building a new state together was lost: the two communities were in enemy camps. G.M. Syed was talking in apocalyptic terms: 'You have already left India,' he warned the Mohajirs, 'the only other place of refuge for you may be the Arabian Sea.'[22]

Given Bhutto's record it is not surprising that many Mohajirs welcomed General Zia's coup. They found his family background encouraging: born in East Punjab, he had attended a school in Delhi and spoke Urdu. Already in the Indian army at the time of partition, he had opted for Pakistan. Better still, he had risen through the ranks on the basis of merit rather than family background – his father was no great landowner but a junior Raj official.[23] The Mohajirs also appreciated his Islamic outlook which was in line with their conception of why Pakistan had been created in the first place. And they were highly satisfied when he declared that the Mohajirs, having made special sacrifices for Pakistan, deserved special treatment. But Zia's cordial relations with the Mohajirs did not last. In the first place the Mohajirs wanted Bhutto's quota system reversed. Zia did not grant their wish. In rural Sindh many resented the execution in 1979 of their leader and champion, Zulfikar Ali Bhutto. Unwilling to further alienate the Sindhis, Zia extended the quota system in Sindh for a further ten years.[24]

If the Mohajirs were to become increasingly suspicious of Zia, many Sindhis were to develop outright opposition to his regime: they wanted to avenge the death of their hero, Bhutto. The tensions came to a head in 1983. As Zia's unpopularity grew throughout Pakistan, a broad range of politicians from all over the country formed the Movement for the Restoration of Democracy (MRD), which demanded free and fair elections. The Pakistan Peoples Party (PPP), now led by Zulfikar Ali Bhutto's daughter Benazir, dominated the MRD although ten other parties were also members. In 1981 it launched a campaign of agitation. Rather to the surprise of the salon politicians in Lahore and Islamabad, the MRD found its strongest support in rural Sindh. By August 1983 the PPP supporters and nationalists in Sindh (often the same people) rose up and mounted a sustained rebellion. Even if the uprising in Sindh was for the most part motivated by simmering resentment of General Zia's treatment of the Bhutto family, some in Zia's regime worried that it could develop into a full-blown nationalist struggle.

Zia's interior secretary, Roedad Khan, has recorded how the military regime was in fact able to turn this perception to its advantage:

Ironically, it was the intensity of the agitation in the interior of Sindh which aroused the suspicion of the people in the three other provinces, especially in Punjab. The MRD began to be viewed as a Sindhi movement for the redressal of Sindhi grievances and removal of their sense of deprivation and therefore lost its national appeal.[25]

The old British policy of divide and rule was alive and well and, for as long as the unrest remained localised, the military always felt confident they could crush it. Nevertheless, the Sindhi rebels put up a determined fight. For four months they participated in running battles with the security forces, and the army had to deploy thousands of men and even helicopter gun ships to quell the uprising. An estimated 400 people died in the violence.[26]

The MQM

The Mohajir Quami Movement (MQM), or Mohajir National Movement, has its roots in Karachi University. In 1978 Altaf Hussain and a group of like-minded students founded the All Pakistan Mohajir Student Organisation (APMSO). It was, in large part, a reaction to the existence of other student groups such as the Punjabi Student Organisation, the Pukhtoon Students Federation, the Baloch Students Organisation and the Sindhis' hardline Jiye Sindh Students Federation. Altaf Hussain, who was a student in the pharmacy department, argued that if these students' organisations would not accept the Mohajirs as members, then the Mohajirs should create an organisation of their own. Initially, the APMSO campaigned on minor issues, complaining with some justification that Mohajirs faced discrimination in university admissions and the allotment of rooms in the student hostels. But by 1981 the group was looking beyond the university campus.

Altaf Hussain could see that the Mohajirs had fears which he could exploit. Law and order in Karachi was deteriorating. In addition, new migrants were arriving in Karachi providing unwelcome competition for jobs. After the Soviet invasion of Afghanistan in 1979, Pukhtoons had fled to Pakistan in their millions. Many remained in the border area near Peshawar, but a significant number headed for Karachi where they started to work in their traditional fields: running transport networks, arms dealing and selling narcotics. Many Mohajirs now wanted an organisation that could represent and protect them.

Unlike many Pakistani politicians, Altaf Hussain has never enjoyed the benefits of a private income and a traditionally powerful family. He volunteered for military service but it was not a happy experience:

> The 1971 war started and I longed to go to East Pakistan and join in the fighting . . . I began to notice that some people received special treatment while others were discriminated against. . . . One night there was an argument with the Havildar [Sergeant] and he started abusing me. He said 'You Hindustorva [which roughly translates as "bloody Indian"], what sort of a war will you city dwellers fight? . . . After that I saw that the Havildar kept the Punjabis and Pathans in his own camp. I talked to the Mohajir boys there and pointed out how unfair all this was. The Pathans and Punjabis then turned against us, and there were fights, and we were punished again.'[27]

It was with those experiences in mind that Hussain founded the APMSO, and after a brief spell as a taxi driver in Chicago he set about the task of building a power base in earnest. He began by creating the MQM.[28] The young leader brooked no opposition. Whilst membership of the party was open, Altaf Hussain devised a system whereby taking an oath of loyalty to the organisation gave a member special status. And with urban Sindh's ethnic tensions steadily increasing there was no shortage of rebellious young Mohajirs, many of them second-generation unemployed graduates, willing to pledge themselves to the only organisation committed to advancing their interests.

In 1985 a minor incident – a traffic accident – demonstrated just how volatile Karachi had become. A student, Bushra Zaidi, was knocked down by a private transport wagon. Bushra Zaidi was a Mohajir. The reckless driver was a Pukhtoon. Karachi exploded. Throughout the city Mohajirs attacked Pukhtoon transport workers and their vehicles. The Pukhtoons retaliated in kind and by the end of the month over 53 people had died.

By the summer of 1986 Hussain was ready to flex his political muscles. On 8 August, despite heavy rain, tens of thousands of people gathered in Karachi's Nishter Park to hear him set out his political stall. To the rest of Pakistan the meeting was a revelation. Overnight, it seemed, a new political force had emerged. Crucially, Hussain called for the recognition of a Mohajir nationality. The size of the crowd – and the heavily armed bodyguards who surrounded the young leader – gave the Mohajirs confidence that they were now a force to be reckoned with. As the MQM's popularity grew, the biggest losers were the religious parties such as Jamaat-e-Islami and Jamiat Ulema-e-Pakistan which had traditionally attracted Mohajir support. The PPP was also hit hard. Although the bulk of the PPP's votes in Sindh came from rural areas, the party had also enjoyed substantial support in Karachi and Hyderabad and other Urdu pockets in interior Sindh. Altaf Hussain threatened to take those votes away. For an organisation that just a few years before had been arguing about room allocations in halls of residence, it was an impressive start.

Increasingly, ethnic rivalry drove the politics of Sindh. And as communal politics took hold, street violence in urban Sindh became so common that many parts of Karachi were under almost permanent curfew. The MQM proved to be an extremely well organised and effective outfit. This was partly because the central government could never summon up the political will to take it on. Given a free run, the MQM became ever more confident, fighting with all of urban Sindh's ethnic groups. Whilst its most formidable political opponent in Sindh was the PPP, various nationalist parties, such as Jiye Sindh, the Sindhi Baloch Pukhtoon Front and the Punjab Pukhtoon Ittehad (PPI) started to gain support. Punjabi settlers in Sindh, many of whom had arrived in the area before partition, and who were relatively non-political, started organising themselves. The trend was clear. Pakistan-wide parties, especially those rooted in Islam, were losing out to smaller nationalist parties that represented specific groups or communities.

Karachi had grown too rapidly. In 1947 there were 400,000 residents in the city: by the late 1980s that number had grown to 6 million. Many Mohajirs were living in the fetid slums and competing with the Pukhtoons, Punjabis and Sindhis in a desperate battle for Karachi's limited resources. No one collected the rubbish, the traffic lights did not work and the sewers overflowed. Few homes had water or sanitation facilities and most were subject to extortionate demands from corrupt landlords.

Karachi was ready to explode and on 14 December 1986 all hell broke loose. At 10 a.m. the loudspeaker of the Pirabad mosque on the outskirts of Karachi broadcast a pre-arranged signal. It was not a call to prayer but a call to arms. Minutes later, under the cover of heavy machine-gun fire, several hundred Pukhtoons swept down from the Pirabad hills. The Pukhtoons attacked Biharis and Mohajirs. Pukhtoon and non-Pukhtoon neighbours, who for years had lived in peace, began to slaughter each other without mercy. In some cases young Mohajirs tied the hands of Pukhtoons behind their backs and burnt them alive. The next morning the rioting spread.[29] Rival mobs were on the streets and the death toll climbed – at least 70 people died on the 15th. There was so much arson that a pall of thick black smoke covered Karachi. On the 16th exhaustion set in, but still 28 people were to die. The railway stations filled with people desperate to flee the city.

It is worth pausing at this point to consider the nature of the MQM's attitudes and demands by the late 1980s. The Mohajirs' dreams of forging a new Islamic nation were long gone. Many had even given up hope of achieving more mundane objectives such as a steady job in the bureaucracy. In 1959 the Mohajirs had 30 per cent of the top jobs in the civil service. By 1989 that figure was down to 7.1 per cent.[30] The idealists who had sacrificed their homes and security to reach Pakistan despaired of their future in a land they considered irreparably damaged by the events of 1971. Many Mohajirs felt that the traditional inhabitants of Pakistan were not just unsympathetic to their plight but even hostile to their presence in the country. When, in February 1987, Altaf Hussain asked a rally in Hyderabad whether they would rise to defend Pakistan in the event of an attack by India, they responded in the negative.[31] It was the answer he wanted: the Mohajirs were sending a message that their loyalty could not be relied upon unless the rest of Pakistan did more to reach out to them.

In terms of specific demands, the crucial question was whether the Mohajirs wanted a separate province. By Altaf Hussain's own admission, such a demand was fleetingly made when the MQM was formed in March 1984. 'When everyone else had a province, we said the Mohajirs should have one too.'[32] But it did not take the MQM leaders long to see that such a demand would set the new party on a collision course with every institution in Pakistan, not least the army. A different formulation was agreed – the Mohajirs should be recognised as the country's fifth nationality.

The MQM also wanted an end to the quota system and more government action to help the Biharis in Bangladesh. This was both a matter of principle and a pragmatic objective: the Biharis would increase the MQM's vote bank, a factor that made the MQM's political opponents reluctant to allow Biharis into Pakistan. In January 1993 an attempt to resettle some Biharis in southern Punjab ran into the vehement opposition of local Seraiki speakers who were themselves trying to transform their long-standing linguistic demands into a full-blown national movement.[33] Some Sindhis also opposed the Biharis' arrival and, to the disgust of the MQM, Prime Minister Nawaz Sharif bowed to the pressure and shelved the plan.

One of the most remarkable aspects of the MQM story is the total failure of successive central governments to address any of the Mohajirs' concerns. The Mohajirs believed that they should not have to ask any favours from Pakistan – they had earned their place in Pakistani society by virtue of their contribution to Jinnah's campaign. The failure of their indigenous compatriots to recognise the Mohajirs' sense of insecurity was, and remains, one of the country's most costly oversights.

The late 1980s and early 1990s marked the MQM's high point. The 1988 National Assembly elections provided solid proof that the party was a force to be reckoned with. It achieved a remarkable electoral breakthrough. Whilst the PPP remained dominant in interior Sindh, the MQM secured no fewer than 13 of Karachi's 15 seats. It had become the third largest political party in Pakistan. A party that could genuinely claim to have arisen from the people had swept the religious parties and feudal leaders in Sindh out of office. The result gave the Mohajirs new hope. Benazir Bhutto, who was trying to form the first post-Zia administration, now needed the MQM's support in the National Assembly. Consequently, on 2 December she signed a PPP–MQM pact called the Karachi Declaration. It covered no fewer than 59 points ranging from a promise to reform the quota to a pledge to construct road flyovers in

Karachi. The MQM's acceptance of the deal was enough to convince President Ghulam Ishaq that Benazir Bhutto could command a majority in the National Assembly.

The Karachi Declaration, however, was never implemented. Bhutto did not want to alienate her traditional power base in interior Sindh. Within a month of the declaration being signed, the PPP and MQM students at Karachi University were denouncing each other as terrorists. The killing rate, which had dipped immediately after the signing, picked up again. The MQM's frustrations on the national level were echoed in the Provincial Assembly. The party had one-third of the seats but that was not enough to push through its programme. Disillusioned MQM activists argued that the ballot box would never deliver any real gains. But the party's leaders were enjoying their new-found ability to wheel and deal with Pakistan's national political leaders. Frustrated with Benazir Bhutto, they entered secret talks with her opponents and by October 1989 reached a 17-point agreement with Nawaz Sharif's opposition coalition, the Islami Jamhoori Ittehad (IJI). In some respects, the MQM–IJI agreement went further than the Karachi Declaration. Rather than making a rather vague statement regarding the Biharis, for example, it included a specific commitment: 'all stranded Pakistanis in Bangladesh shall be issued Pakistani passports and in the meantime arrangements shall be made to repatriate them to Pakistan immediately'. There was also a clear condemnation of the quota system as 'unjust, biased and discriminatory'.[34]

But the MQM was about to discover for the second time that Pakistan-wide parties would promise the earth when they were trying to form an administration, only to renege on those commitments once in power. It was a process that encouraged the MQM's extremists to step up their campaign of violence. Furthermore, by throwing in their lot with a quintessentially Punjabi leader, Nawaz Sharif, they further alienated the Sindhis. The gulf between the Sindhis and the Mohajirs became wider and found ever more violent expression.

MQM politicians routinely deny any involvement in violence whatsoever. It is remarkable that journalists who have covered the MQM day in, day out, ever since its creation have never heard any of the party's leaders admit direct involvement in the violence. Despite the denials, there has been no shortage of people willing to accuse the MQM of sponsoring violence. Detained MQM activists have repeatedly admitted carrying out killings on party orders. For all the MQM claims that such confessions were obtained by force, most people in Karachi and Hyderabad believe they were genuine. Those accused include Altaf Hussain himself, who faces charges of murder, extortion, kidnapping and sedition. International human rights organisations have generally focused on the cases in which the MQM has been the victim of state power. Nevertheless in 1996 Amnesty International reported that: 'Most of the political groupings and parties in Karachi appear to maintain their own militia. ... Despite protestations by MQM leader Altaf Hussain that the MQM does not subscribe to violence, there is overwhelming evidence and a consensus among observers in Karachi that some MQM party members have used violent means to further their political ends.'[35]

It was a fair assessment. Each time Altaf Hussain called a strike, people in the city would die. Many of the city's businessmen were visited by MQM thugs demanding protection money. There was also the uncanny fact that whenever someone from the MQM was killed, a reprisal killing would follow in a matter of days. The MQM has never been just an electoral party. It is also a militant organisation. Its leaders know they cannot escape their party's bloodthirsty reputation. MQM senator Nasreen Jaleel neatly summarised the problem when she attended a diplomatic reception at the British High Commission in Islamabad in 1999. 'When I walk into a room like this,' she said, 'all these people see the word terrorist written all over my forehead.' Even if she has had no personal involvement in the campaign of violence, the reasons for such a perception are plain enough. It is no surprise that the MQM is one of the most disciplined parties in Pakistan. Contradicting the party line can result in death.

Despite these perceptions, Pakistan's central government took a long time to summon up the courage to tackle the MQM. The first serious attempt to break the organisation's street power came in 1992. Nawaz Sharif's IJI, like its PPP predecessor, had failed to honour its agreement with the MQM and his relations with the party soured. That alone, though, would not have led to a crackdown. The new factor in the equation was provided by the army, which was increasingly concerned that the MQM was undermining national development. In May 1992 the military declared its intention to bring peace to Karachi. The army operation began on 19 June, and for all the talk of even-handedness there was no doubting that the MQM militants were the primary targets.

The army's strategy included a plan to open up the MQM's internal divisions. These had been apparent ever since Altaf Hussain declared his intention in 1990 to broaden his party's electoral appeal, not least by changing the name of the Mohajir Quami Movement to the Muttahida Quami Movement, or United National Movement. His rhetoric now included passages about the problems faced not only by the Mohajirs but also by the underprivileged throughout Pakistan. He concentrated his political attacks not on other ethnic groups but rather on the landowners in the ruling classes. The strategy did not work: ethnic affiliations proved to be a stronger bond than class. The MQM continues to reign supreme in urban Sindh, but its message has never resonated elsewhere in Pakistan.

This was the least of Altaf Hussain's problems. Whilst he was looking beyond Sindh, the MQM's militant wing remained focused on the grievances of the Mohajirs and, as ever, expressed its point of view with violence. With this ideological split in the MQM becoming ever more apparent, the military saw its chance and backed a new, armed rival faction: MQM Haqiqi (the Real MQM). The Haqiqis set about their work with relish, ransacking and occupying MQM offices and creating a mini civil war in Karachi. For months, as the army crackdown continued, the city echoed with gunfire and the army, the MQM and MQM Haqiqi fought pitched battles in the streets. The military revealed the existence of MQM torture cells. The party's favoured method of extracting information from its opponents, it seemed, was to use an electric drill on the victims' knees and elbows. Altaf Hussain, meanwhile, afraid for his personal security, fled to London for 'medical treatment'.[36]

The torture chambers were a sign of just how far the MQM had gone in its campaign to be the sole representative of the Mohajirs. But in the midst of the struggle to survive, the MQM had lost its way. Rather than pressing for its basic demands, such as an end to the quota system, the leadership focused on more immediate issues such as the release of detained activists. Lacking clear direction, some MQM members became ever more extreme. Some argued that they needed to have an independent homeland, often referred to as Jinnahpur. The military claimed that in the midst of their clean-up operation they found maps of 'Jinnahpur' or 'Urdu desh' which showed how the Mohajirs wanted to carve Karachi, Hyderabad and some other areas out of Sindh.

The MQM insisted that the maps were not authentic. But by September 1994 it seemed that Altaf Hussain, still in London, had decided to make an explicit demand for the geographical division of Sindh. Certainly, he laid the groundwork by putting out a 'questionnaire' on the issue to all MQM members. He claimed to have received hundreds of thousands of letters in response. All but five or six, he said, had called for the establishment of a fifth, Mohajir, province.[37] But once again, he stopped short of making the demand an item of the party's official programme. The furthest he went was to talk of the *possibility* of 'changing geography' if the Mohajirs were not given their rights.

The violence, meanwhile, went on and on, and there was another crackdown; this time managed by Benazir Bhutto's second government. Her interior minister, General Nasrullah Baber, did not pull his punches. Unable to rely on the slow, intimidated and corrupt courts, which were always nervous to act, the security forces resorted to extra-judicial killings. Some 10 per cent of those who died in politics-related violence in 1995 were the victims of so-called 'police encounters'. In most cases the police would claim they had to open fire to prevent a detainee escaping. 'Peace has been restored in Karachi,' Baber said.[38] There was some truth in his boast. Whilst 1,586 people were murdered in Karachi in 1995, the figure slumped to 524 in 1996. It has never since exceeded 1,000 a year.[39]

The now familiar political cycle started to turn once more. The 1997 elections gave Nawaz Sharif's Muslim League just 14 of the 109 seats in the Sindh Provincial Assembly. Determined to keep out the better represented PPP, he once more needed MQM support. The 1992 crackdown, Sharif now assured Altaf Hussain, had been a mistake forced on him by the army. He would resign rather than oversee another attempt to quash the MQM by force. He promised prisoner releases, the opening up of Haqiqi-held 'no-go' areas and compensation for families who had suffered as a result of extra-judicial killings.

But once restored to power, Sharif again ran out of patience with the MQM. The trigger this time was the assassination on 17 October 1998 of the widely respected philanthropist and former governor of Sindh, Hakim Said. Apart from adding to the climate of fear in Karachi, the killing had no clear motive and it shocked the Pakistani nation. When Prime Minister Nawaz Sharif openly accused his MQM ally of organising the murder, it was inevitable that the MQM–Muslim League alliance would end. Sharif extended the quota system for a further twenty years, introduced Governor's Rule and established military courts which, he promised, would dispense 'speedy justice'. Remarkably, in all the years of politically inspired violence in Sindh, not one person had been given capital punishment. Nawaz Sharif promised that would change. Within weeks, though, the military courts ran into a series of constitutional challenges that were ultimately successful.

When he took over in 1999 it was General Musharraf's turn to promise he would address Mohajir grievances, but there was little sign that he would actually do so. Musharraf came from a family that had migrated to Pakistan from India. But once he settled into power he showed little sympathy for the MQM and did not open any dialogue with the organisation. Musharraf's initial coolness towards the MQM, however, gradually gave way to an inevitable political logic. With the PPP opposing his rule, Musharraf needed all the support he could get both in Sindh and in the National Assembly. The MQM was happy to oblige, joined his ruling coalition and took over the provincial administration. In March 2008 the depth of the MQM's relationship with Musharraf became plain for all to see. When the PPP, the Muslim League and the lawyers' movement had gathered their activists to hear a speech by the man Musharraf had sacked as chief justice, Iftikhar Chaudhry, the MQM went on the offensive. More than 40 people were killed in running street battles. Paramilitary forces and police stood by as armed MQM workers attacked the opposition. There was shock throughout Pakistan, but Musharraf defended the MQM: 'what happened in Karachi was mainly because of the chief justice, who went there ignoring the advice of the government'.[40]

The case of Sindhi nationalists is plain enough: they maintain that Sindh is theirs and that they should be governed by Sindhis. Mohajir nationalism is much more difficult to explain. When the Mohajirs came to Pakistan they were not a homogeneous ethnic group: they came from different parts of northern India. They did, though, share some attitudes. Many had been urbanised for two generations, they were relatively well educated and believed they had something to offer the new country. They looked forward to participating in, and providing leadership for, the construction of a new Islamic nation.

But the Mohajirs were always too small in number to govern Pakistan. Compared to Pakistan's longer-established inhabitants, they also lacked a political power base. They have never been strong enough to take on all of Pakistan's ethnic groups at once. At first they fought the Pukhtoons and then the Punjabis. Inevitably their early attempts to cultivate good relations with the Sindhis failed and by 1988, after the massacre on 30 September of over 200 Mohajirs in Hyderabad, the two communities were fighting each other. Finally, with the rise of MQM Haqiqi, the Mohajirs started targeting each other. Even though the Mohajirs were not an ethnic group, their peculiar situation in Pakistan forced them into becoming a homogeneous and politicised community. But once Mohajir unity broke down, it became inescapably clear that religion and Pakistani nationalism no longer provided the glue that bound them together. The Mohajirs became a confused community and, as a result, the MQM's *raison d'être* is utterly unclear. The party has no religious or territorial demands. Its members are Urdu speakers but the MQM is clearly more than a linguistic pressure group. On the one hand, the MQM has been a vehicle for demanding Mohajir rights. On the other, it has simply expressed the Mohajirs' frustration and bitterness about their experience in Pakistan. Most Pakistanis have no illusions about the nature of the MQM which is why they were both confused and sickened when, in 2001, the British government of Tony Blair made the extraordinary decision to grant Altaf Hussain a UK passport. By the turn of the century Hussain had no vision of the future whatsoever: his speeches and media interviews simply contained a long series of complaints about how partition had been a mistake. The scope of his ambition, it seemed, had been reduced: he looked far less like an energetic campaigner for Mohajir rights and far more like a would-be mafia boss determined to hang on to control of Karachi.

Balochistan

The politics of Sindh have presented successive Pakistani leaders with a highly complex problem that they have consistently failed to resolve. The recent history of Balochistan, by contrast, has been relatively uncomplicated. With varying degrees of assertiveness, some Baloch leaders have pressed for greater autonomy and, at times, for independence. The Pakistani state has, when necessary, employed all the force at its disposal to suppress such demands.

Many Baloch never wanted to join Pakistan in the first place. In the 1930s some Baloch leaders, foreseeing the eventual departure of the British, started to advance claims for independence. Such demands were most strongly advanced in Kalat, the largest, and by far the most powerful, of four princely states located in Balochistan. The other three, Makran, Kharan and Las Bela had, at various points of history, been part of the Kalat state. Indeed, in the second half of the eighteenth century the khan of Kalat, Naseer Khan, had managed more or less to unify the Baloch people.

By the time the British were preparing to leave South Asia, Kalat had lost much of its strength. Nevertheless, Naseer Khan's descendant, Mir Ahmed Yar Khan, argued that once the British had left, Kalat should be restored as a fully sovereign and independent nation. So as to advance his cause better in Delhi and Whitehall, he even appointed a Briton, Douglas Fell, as his foreign minister,[41] and in August 1947 the khan declared Kalat's independence.

Kalat may not have represented all the peoples in Balochistan, but there is no doubt that other Baloch leaders sympathised with the khan and wanted to see whether the new Pakistani government had the will and the strength to frustrate his bid for independence. Pakistani historians now portray Mir Ahmed Yar Khan as an isolated and recalcitrant individual who ungraciously failed to bow to the inevitable.[42] But for the new Pakistani government, incorporating Kalat into the country was far from easy: almost a year passed before this was achieved – and then only with the use of force. In April 1948 the Pakistan army marched on Kalat and, eventually, the khan signed an agreement of accession. After 225 days of independence, Kalat became part of Pakistan. The khan's brother,

Prince Abdul Karim, however, responded violently. Having based himself across the border in Afghanistan, he organised a guerrilla campaign which for some months harried the Pakistani forces. By June 1948, though, the army prevailed and both Kalat and the rest of Balochistan were secured as parts of Pakistan.

By no means can the fighting in 1948 be characterised as a Baloch-wide rebellion. But it is nonetheless of considerable significance that while other parts of Pakistan were fervently celebrating the creation of the new country, in Balochistan there was armed conflict. Ten years later, Baloch objections to One Unit, which they saw as a centralist measure that undermined their provincial rights, led to another violent confrontation. On 10 October 1958 the Pakistan army emerged victorious over a rebel force of around 1,000 men. Still the Baloch didn't give up. In the early 1960s Pakistani troops in Balochistan were subjected to a series of ambushes, raids and sniper attacks. There were large-scale confrontations involving hundreds of men on both sides in 1964 and 1965. The fighting continued sporadically until One Unit was abolished in 1970.

The first major Baloch challenge came in 1973. The trigger was Zulfikar Ali Bhutto's decision to dismiss Balochistan's provincial government in which the PPP had no representation. To help justify the move, Bhutto revealed a cache of 350 Soviet submachine guns and 100,000 rounds of ammunition in the house of the Iraqi political attaché in Islamabad. Bhutto claimed the weapons were destined for either Pakistani or Iranian Balochistan. Writing to President Richard Nixon, Zulfikar Ali Bhutto claimed that the discovery showed that 'powers inimical to us are not content with the severance of Pakistan's eastern part; their aim is the dismemberment of Pakistan itself'.[43]

Whether the arms were destined for Balochistan or not was never established, but there was no doubt that the Baloch were enraged by Bhutto's decision to remove their government. In response they mounted actions against the Pakistani army which, in turn, responded with force. With Bhutto describing the Baloch rebels as 'miscreants' (causing many to draw parallels with what had happened in Bangladesh), the army was given a free hand to restore Pakistani control. The fighting was to last for four years and the central government had to deploy no fewer than 80,000 troops to suppress an insurgency of 55,000 rebels.[44]

By 1974 the rebels had cut most of the main roads in the province. Their targeted attacks on survey teams forced Western oil companies to abandon their exploration projects in the area. In the largest single confrontation during the insurgency in September 1974, 15,000 Baloch tribesmen fought a pitched battle with the Pakistan army. The military had vastly superior equipment including Mirage fighter planes and Iranian-supplied (and piloted) helicopters. After three days of fighting, the Baloch ran out of ammunition and withdrew.[45]

The battle was the most intense moment of the conflict. Afterwards, the Baloch increasingly took to the hills and avoided pitched battles. As the pressure from the Pakistani troops increased, some Baloch rebels followed Prince Abdul Karim's example and set up camps in Afghanistan where they could regroup after bouts of fighting. As well as allowing the camps to exist, the Afghans provided the rebels with small amounts of financial support. Limited assistance also came in the form of a small number of leftist Punjabi intellectuals who went to the Baloch mountains to join the rebels.

What the rebels really wanted, though, was the support of the Soviet Union. They never got it. The Soviets had never backed the demands for an independent Balochistan but instead had called for greater Baloch autonomy within Pakistan. The Soviet Union's somewhat hesitant approach found echoes in Balochistan itself. From the very beginning of the uprising the Baloch were uncertain of their objective. Whilst some favoured a straightforward push for independence, others, notably in the Baloch People's Liberation Front, argued that secession was unrealistic and that the Baloch should settle for greater autonomy.

The army operation ended only after the 1977 coup when General Zia declared victory and ordered a withdrawal. Some have described the Baloch insurgency as a 'comparatively minor' affair.[46] This is an underestimation of what amounted to a serious and sustained challenge to Pakistan's very existence. Coming so soon after the loss of Bangladesh, this was a battle the Pakistan army had to win. And suppressing the rebellion was no easy matter – the conflict claimed an estimated 9,000 lives.[47]

The military's victory left a situation not unlike that in Sindh where nationalists continued to press the case for self-determination despite having little conviction that it could be achieved in the short term. The Baloch, though, have some specific grievances which, in 2000, under-pinned another phase of anti-Islamabad violence forcing the deploy-ment of tens of thousands of Pakistani army troops.

At the time of General Musharraf's coup in 1999 half of the members of the Provincial Assembly in Quetta were nationalists complaining about Punjabi 'colonisation' of their province. The elec-tion of so many nationalists had reflected growing discontent in Balochistan. Their primary complaint concerned energy. The Sui gas field in southern Balochistan provided over 35 per cent of Pakistan's total gas needs. Although the gas had been flowing since the early 1950s, it was not until 1976 that Quetta even got its first supply. And, as the Baloch rarely tired of pointing out, Quetta was only connected to the national grid when the army built a garrison there and needed some gas for itself. Sui was located in Nawab Bugti's tribal area and he had long demanded greater revenue from, if not total control of, the gas plant there. He had been bought off over the years with various bribes including a huge fleet of four-by-four Toyotas. Although he was happy enough to accept the cars, he never accepted the right of Pakistani occupiers, as he saw them, to take his gas.

The whole issue was a long-running sore in the relationship between Balochistan and the rest of Pakistan. It flared up in 2000 because, aware that Sui's gas supplies would run out by 2012,[48] Musharraf ordered increased oil and gas exploration activity. Unluckily for the Pakistani authorities, one of the most promising areas fell firmly within one of the most fiercely independent tribes of all, the Marris. When surveyors started explorations near the Marris' main town of Kohlu, fighting led to the deaths of ten people.[49] That sparked more militant activity. In August 2000, Marri tribesmen took direct action to stop coal mining on their land. They used rocket-propelled grenades and landmines to prevent coal-laden trucks leaving Balochistan. The federal government had to deploy over 1,000 or so security personnel to counter the rebel activity.

The tribal leaders had a second reason for taking on Islamabad: the construction of a deep-sea port at Gwadar on the southern Baloch coastline. Gwadar lies close to the Straits of Hormuz, and the govern-ment in Islamabad has big plans for what had always been a very remote and inaccessible area. The idea is to create a city for around a million people, complete with a port and warehouses and a free trade zone that will be used by no fewer than 20 countries including the Gulf States, the Central Asian 'stans', Iran, India and last, but by no means least, China. In fact, Beijing has provided much of the financial capital for the project and road links are being constructed to give China better access to Gwadar.[50]

The Baloch nationalists decided to confront Gwadar head on. They complained that it would attract Punjabis in such numbers that the Baloch could become a minority in their own province. The low levels of education in Balochistan mean that tribesmen were not able to take much advantage of the construction work: generally speaking, incomers have been doing the building. The campaign against Gwadar has been violent. In 2004, for example, 30 security personnel working there were killed, as were two Chinese engineers.[51]

The development of Gwadar, the Sui gas field and the exploration for more energy resources in Balochistan were three separate grievances most acutely felt by the three strongest Baloch tribes: the Mengals, Bugtis and Marris. And for once the Baloch propensity for disunity was overcome, as the three tribes joined forces in a common struggle. The significance of the alliance was not lost on Musharraf. He named the tribes' three leaders, Sardar Ataullah Mengal, Nawab Akbar Bugti and Nawab Khair Bakhsh Marri, as the only three out of 77 Baloch tribal chiefs who were 'anti-development and anti-democracy'. 'They do not want democracy,' Musharraf said, 'rather they want to exercise complete dictatorship and control in their areas.'[52] While Bugti became the pre-eminent leader of the insurgents fighting in Balochistan, Mengal looked after the propaganda battle. Having spent many years in exile in the UK where he had run an old people's home near the northern town of Warrington, he was delighted to be back in the thick of Baloch politics. He threw himself into the struggle, describing the rulers of Pakistan as 'temporary caretakers' of Balochistan. He said that half of the population of Balochistan was behind the insurgents, although he acknowledged that only a few hundred people in each area were actively fighting the Pakistani forces.[53] He urged the Baloch to 'arm themselves with sticks, axes, arms and enter the fight'.[54]

Throughout 2004 there were almost daily attacks against either government personnel or major plants such as garrisons and energy installations. Most were claimed by the Balochistan Liberation Army (BLA), an organisation that had been formed in the early 1980s at which time it was aligned with Moscow. Some of the fighting was extremely vicious. There were reported cases, for example, of Punjabis being pulled off buses travelling through Balochistan and murdered on the spot.[55] In January 2005 the conflict became more intense still after a female doctor working at the Sui gas field was raped – allegedly by two Pakistani soldiers. Had the army taken action against the relatively junior officers involved, the whole issue may have blown over. As usual, however, the army tried to avoid public admission of fault and a decision was taken to cover the incident up. Nawab Bugti now had an issue that he knew would motivate his tribesmen to fury. The traditional punishment for rape in the tribal areas is death. If a man suspected of committing rape does manage to flee the Bugti area, he cannot afford to return – ever. There have been cases in which a rape suspect has returned 40 years after the alleged crime and, within days, been killed by the victim's offspring.

After the rape, a pulse of extreme violence surged through Balochistan: there were an estimated 1,500 attacks on targets associated with the state, most of them in the Bugti area.[56] Musharraf warned that the state response would be ferocious. 'Don't push us . . . it is not the 1970s, and this time you won't even know what has hit you.'[57] But such bravado could not disguise the fact that the Baloch problems came at a bad time for the Pakistan army. There were many other demands on the troops who were also confronting Al Qaeda and the Taliban just north of Balochistan.

Deciding that a political settlement might be preferable, in April 2005 Musharraf dispatched two experienced politicians, Chaudry Shujjaat and Mushahid Hussain, to negotiate with Baloch tribal leaders. The Baloch took the process seriously. Between April and June 2005, when the talking was taking place, there was a complete cessation of Baloch attacks.[58] The parliamentarians suggested giving Balochistan more autonomy and a 10 to 15 per cent increase in the royalty on gas revenues paid to the province. It was a start, but it was never going to be enough to satisfy the Baloch leadership, which rejected the offer out of hand. The tribal chiefs complained that two of their demands had not even been addressed: that no more military garrisons be built in Balochistan and that the Gwadar development project be handed over to the Baloch. By May 2005 Baloch tribal leaders were describing the peace initiative as a total failure. 'They first said they would give the Baloch more than we can ever expect,' said Nawab Akbar Bugti. 'But they have gone back on everything.'[59]

The stage was now set for a major confrontation. In December 2005 insurgents fired six rockets at General Musharraf while he visited a paramilitary camp in the province. They missed, but he hit back. The army targeted Bugti in particular, launching a full-scale attack on his desert fort. Of the 25,000 people who lived in and around the fort, 85 per cent fled to the mountains including Nawab Bugti himself.[60] The insurgents blew up the two main gas pipelines to Punjab, cutting off the province's supplies. They also targeted gas production sites, railway lines and bridges.[61] In January 2006 there was an incident that revealed the depth of the mutual hatred between the state security forces and the tribesmen. After a landmine explosion seriously wounded three of their men, the Frontier Corps raided a nearby hamlet, burnt down some homes and arrested 12 local men. Later that day word came from the hospital that the three injured soldiers had succumbed to their wounds and died. Enraged, Frontier Corps personnel murdered the 12 men in their custody and sent a message that the bodies should be picked up. Some women arrived to do just that, but they were sent back and told that male family members should do the job. The next day two elderly tribesmen went to collect the bodies but they too were murdered.[62]

The conflict was fierce and unrelenting. But in August 2006 one particular army action made a difference. Nawab Akbar Bugti, still in hiding after the destruction of his fort, was located by the army and faced his final battle. The details of exactly what happened are contested but it seems that the army, using helicopter gunships and ground forces, tracked him down to a cave. The Nawab and relatives alongside him fought for hours before bombs from some helicopter gunships found their mark and collapsed the roof of the cave on top of the Baloch fighters.[63] Musharraf was strongly criticised for ordering

Bugti's death. But from the general's point of view the action worked: it demonstrated the power of the Pakistani state. Nawab Akbar Bugti, though, entered the pantheon of Baloch heroes. The manner of his death had guaranteed that he would go down in history just as he would have wanted, as a defiant Baloch leader fighting to the last.

Bugti's death also marked a moment of change in Baloch society. Ataullah Mengal, Khair Bakhsh Marri and Akbar Bugti represent the last generation of leaders with total personal authority over their tribes. The wider availability of the media, increased travel opportunities and slightly better provision of education have all chipped away at the traditional structures. Ataullah Mengal noticed the trend back in 2004: 'In Eastern Balochistan tribalism is coming to its dead end. It is more or less perishing and from the very ashes of the tribal system the Baloch nationalism will emerge.'[64] That is how he hoped it would work out. Like most Baloch tribal leaders Mengal was always far more nationalistic than religious. The mullahs, though, have different ideas. Their message to young Baloch tribesmen, frustrated by the stifling, old-fashioned ways of their elders, is that radical Islam offers a much more potent force for change than nationalism. The outcome of the competition between radical Islam and nationalism in Balochistan will define the province's future. As things stand the nationalists are holding sway. If the Baloch had been interested in fighting an anti-American jihad, there were no shortage of targets for them to attack. As part of its post 9/11 operations in Afghanistan the US had two significant military bases in Balochistan. So far they have, for the most part, been left alone. But with radical Islam such an obviously potent force, it cannot be too long before the Baloch start to wonder whether they should change their ideology and improve their chances of success.

Conclusion

In his book *Can Pakistan Survive? The Death of a State*, Tariq Ali wrote in 1983 that: 'The national question is the time bomb threatening the very structures of the post-1971 state. The hour of the explosion cannot be far away.' Twenty-six years later there has been an explosion of revolt against Islamabad, but the ideology of the insurgents has been more religious than nationalist.

The nationalists' complaints, however, have never gone away. It is now commonplace for the Baloch, Sindhis, Pukhtoons and Mohajirs to complain of Punjabi domination. Like the Bengalis before 1971, Pakistan's various national communities argue that they are economically deprived because the bureaucracy and the army are both Punjabi-controlled. The claim is difficult to refute. The armed forces and the civil service are the largest employers in Pakistan, and many Punjabi families clearly benefit from their province's dominance of these institutions. The national movements may be mainly political in character, but they are underpinned by genuine economic grievances.

For the most part though, the nationalists have held back from advancing demands for full independence and the key question is this: do the nationalists pose a threat to Pakistan's existence? The case of Bangladesh certainly provides a clear warning: a national movement has already led to territorial changes in Pakistan. The first half century of Pakistan's existence has proven that neither Islam nor Urdu has acted as an effective national cement. Although most Pakistanis now understand Urdu, fewer than 10 per cent speak it as a first language and most urban Pakistanis want to send their children to English-medium schools. After long careers in the army, many senior officers are keen Pakistani nationalists. But outside Punjab, few share their enthusiasm.

Before the growth of the Taliban in NWFP, the prospects for anti-Punjabi nationalists were not good. The Baloch, the Sindhis and the Mohajirs had all learnt that, if and when the need arose, the centre could find the determination and the strength to crush separatist forces. The various national movements were weak in part because they were divided. Their demands contradicted each other. If Altaf Hussain, for example, was to make a direct appeal for a separate province, he encountered the opposition not only of the Pakistan army but also the Sindhis. Organisations trying to unite the different national groups, such as the Pakistan Oppressed Nations Movement, failed to make significant headway.

The growing appeal of radical Islam, however, could make a significant difference. Pukhtoon nationalists have for decades been unable to get their case addressed by Islamabad. Now they have seen Pukhtoon tribesmen take on and, in some cases, defeat the Pakistan army. Many Pukhtoon nationalists may not like the idea of living under the Taliban, but an increasing number say they consider it preferable to living under a US-backed Pakistani government. Tariq Ali may have been nearly right. It's not exactly the national question that is the time bomb threatening Pakistan: it is the national and Islamic questions combined. They make a potent mix and whether the central state can withstand its force is still an open question.

3

Kashmir

Kashmir will fall into our lap like a ripe fruit.
—Mohammed Ali Jinnah, August 1947

In August 1947, Kashmir's autocratic ruler,[1] His Highness Maharaja Indar Mahindar Bahadur Sir Hari Singh, was faced with a momentous decision. The imperial government in London had always allowed some major landholders on the subcontinent a degree of autonomy and, technically, Kashmir had never been part of British India. The maharaja's ancestors had secured the right to govern some of their own affairs by recognising the paramountcy of the British Crown. The pact between the British and the maharaja's family was symbolised by the payment of a tribute: each year Hari Singh had to provide the British government with a horse, twelve goats and six of Kashmir's famous shawls, or pashminas.

When the British left, the maharaja had three options: Kashmir could try to become independent or join either India or Pakistan. The rulers of over 550 Princely States faced the same decision, but in the case of Kashmir the issue was especially sensitive. Its large population and proximity to both China and Russia gave the state considerable strategic importance. The matter was further complicated by religion: Kashmir was one of a handful of Princely States in which the ruler did not practise the same religion as most of his people. Whereas the maharaja was a Hindu, over three-quarters of his subjects were Muslims. The fact that Kashmir was not only predominantly Muslim but also contiguous with Pakistan convinced Muhammed Ali Jinnah that the maharaja's decision would go in his favour. 'Kashmir,' he said at the time of partition, 'will fall into our lap like a ripe fruit.'[2] It was a naive misjudgement of Himalayan proportions.

The maharaja had most of the foibles associated with India's decadent aristocracy. He was a hedonist and a reactionary whose main interests were food, hunting, sex and, above all else, horse racing. As his own son put it: 'Quite clearly, my father was much happier racing than administering the State . . .'[3] On one occasion in London's Savoy Hotel he had been tricked by a prostitute who proceeded to blackmail him.[4] He showed a similar lack of judgement in matters of state. In July 1947, with the transfer of power just weeks away, he took the view that 'the British are never really going to leave India.'[5]

The maharaja's ancestors had been blessed with greater political acumen. The State of Jammu and Kashmir had been established in the first half of the nineteenth century by a relatively minor Jammu chieftain, Gulab Singh. A combination of adept military conquests and astute financial deals enabled him to create one of the largest Princely States on the subcontinent. By 1850 he had moved on from Jammu (with its Hindu majority population) and added Ladakh (Buddhist majority), Baltistan (Muslim majority) and the Kashmir Valley (Muslim majority). In the latter half of the nineteenth century Gulab Singh's successors extended their control to another Muslim-majority area, Gilgit. They were Hindus ruling over a multi-ethnic state and their Muslim subjects were especially hard pressed.

In 1929 one of Maharaja Hari Singh's officials, Sir Albion Bannerji, resigned his post declaring that the Muslims were illiterate, poverty-stricken and 'governed like dumb driven cattle'.[6] Elsewhere in India, Mahatma Gandhi and his colleagues were campaigning against the British. In Kashmir the Muslims focused most of their discontent on the maharaja. He responded with force. The first significant crisis came in July 1931 during the trial of a radical Muslim activist, Abdul Qadeer, who advocated a violent uprising against Hari Singh's royal household. When protestors gathered outside the prison in which he was held, the police killed over 20 demonstrators.

By 1941 the Muslims' situation had not improved. A Hindu writer, Premnath Bazaz, reported that most Muslims in Kashmir were serfs working for absentee landlords: 'The poverty of the Muslim masses is appalling. Dressed in rags and barefoot, a Muslim peasant presents the appearance of a starving beggar.'[7] The maharaja himself hardly ever met his Muslim subjects. As his son later recalled: 'As for the Kashmiri Muslims, our contacts were mostly limited to the gardeners and the shooting and fishing guards.'[8]

As the British prepared to leave, it was clear that the maharaja wanted independence. He faced the opposition not only of Jinnah and Jawaharlal Nehru (who both hoped to incorporate Kashmir into their new countries) but also of the British. Mountbatten considered the future of the Princely States, which covered more than 40 per cent of the subcontinent's land mass, to be an important issue. In July 1947 many of the Princely State rulers gathered in their favoured forum, the Chamber of Princes, to hear Mountbatten speak. He urged them to opt for either Pakistan or India: 'You are about to face a revolution,' he said. 'In a very brief moment you'll lose for ever your sovereignty. It is inevitable.'[9] Mountbatten's success in persuading the vast majority of the Princely States to accept the new post-imperial dispensation and to abandon their hopes of retaining some autonomy was a remarkable achievement. But some of the more powerful rulers, including Maharaja Hari Singh, held out. This was despite the fact that Mountbatten had made special efforts in respect of Kashmir: despite his heavy workload in the run-up to the transfer of power, Mountbatten put aside six days for a visit to the maharaja's summer capital, Srinagar.

Mountbatten's talks in Srinagar have given rise to many controversies. Pakistani historians have argued that he improperly used his influence to steer the maharaja away from Karachi and towards Delhi. A typical Pakistani account can be found in the memoirs of the former Pakistani prime minister, Chaudri Muhammad Ali, who maintains that Mountbatten failed to give proper advice to Hari Singh. 'At no stage did he tell the maharaja, that, in view of the geographical and strategic factors and the overwhelmingly Muslim population of the State, it was his plain duty to accede to Pakistan.' In this, Ali maintains, Mountbatten was behaving inconsistently. When discussing similar issues with the Muslim leaders of Hindu majority Princely States, he urged immediate accession to India.[10] Although Pakistani authors complain about Mountbatten's conduct in Srinagar, their Indian counterparts take the diametrically opposed view, arguing that the viceroy behaved quite properly. Mountbatten, they insist, went to great lengths to advise the maharaja not only that the final decision was his alone but also that the Indian government would not consider it an unfriendly act if Kashmir did accede to Pakistan.[11]

Exactly what was said in Srinagar will never be known and, in any event, the issue is of limited significance. More serious charges are made about Mountbatten's part in creating the conditions for enduring conflict in Kashmir, not least his alleged role in trying to influence the findings of the Boundary Commission, which was responsible for implementing the partition of the subcontinent by demarcating the new international borders that would run through Punjab.[12] The terms of reference of the Commission stated that 'the Boundary Commission is instructed to demarcate the boundaries of the two parts of Punjab on the basis of ascertaining the contiguous majority areas of Muslims and non-Muslims. In doing so it will also take into account other factors.'[13] The man charged with drawing this highly important line was an austere and widely respected barrister, Sir Cyril Radcliffe. Since he had never even set foot on the subcontinent Sir Cyril could hardly be accused of prejudice. And to reinforce the Commission's image as an impartial body, Mountbatten said he wanted to isolate Sir Cyril from political pressures. He gave his staff explicit instructions to have no contact with him.

Two of Radcliffe's decisions have given rise to prolonged, angry debate. The first concerned a Muslim majority area called Ferozepur. Ferozepur was of strategic importance not only because it was home to an irrigation head-works, but also because it had the only arsenal that Pakistan could hope to have on its territory. There is now little doubt that Radcliffe intended to award Ferozepur to Pakistan and that Mountbatten persuaded him to change his mind. The most damning piece of evidence is a map that Radcliffe sent to the last governor of Punjab, Sir Evan Jenkins, on 8 August 1947. Jenkins received advance notice of all Radcliffe's awards so that he could get security personnel in place ahead of partition. The map showed that Ferozepur had been allocated to Pakistan. By the evening of 12 August, however, Jenkins had been instructed to change the map and to note that Ferozepur was now to be part of India. The matter came to light in 1948 when Pakistan managed to get hold of a copy of the original map that had been left in Jenkins's safe.

In 1989, Christopher Beaumont, the man who had worked in Delhi as Radcliffe's private secretary, published his account of what had happened. Having heard that Ferozepur was going to Pakistan, Mountbatten arranged a private lunch with Radcliffe. There is no record of exactly what was said, but by that evening Radcliffe had changed his mind. 'Mountbatten interfered,' Beaumont concluded, 'and Radcliffe allowed himself to be overborne: grave discredit to both.'[14]

Indian historians now accept that Mountbatten probably did influence the Ferozepur award.[15] Ferozepur, though, was of little importance in relation to Kashmir. Of far greater significance was another Muslim majority district, Gurdaspur, which provided the only practicable land link between India and Kashmir. If it were to be awarded to Pakistan then it would be difficult to see how the maharaja could realistically opt for India. Mountbatten was certainly aware of Gurdaspur's strategic importance. In June he publicly raised the possibility that, despite its Muslim majority, Gurdaspur could be awarded to India[16] and in early August he stated that if that happened then the maharaja's options regarding the future status of Kashmir would be kept open.[17]

Although Mountbatten's meddling in the Ferozepur award is now well established, there is less evidence concerning his role in the decision about Gurdaspur. While Pakistani historians claim that Mountbatten fixed the award, their Indian counterparts insist he did no such thing. The historians Larry Collins and Dominique Lapierre, for example, have argued that there was no foul play in the Gurdaspur award: 'Unintentionally, almost inadvertently,' they assert, 'Radcliffe's scalpel had offered India the hope of claiming Kashmir.'[18] It is interesting to note that although, Christopher Beaumont was convinced that the Ferozepur award was fixed, he did not believe the same was true of Gurdaspur. In his 1989 testimony he wrote: 'No change, as has been subsequently rumoured, was made in the northern [Gurdaspur] part of the line.'[19]

The motives behind the Gurdaspur award remain disputed. But even if Mountbatten's role in relation to the Boundary Commission was less neutral than he claimed, his many critics tend to overlook an important aspect of his views on Kashmir: he consistently supported a referendum to determine its future status. Since Kashmir was a Princely

State, Mountbatten could not insist on a referendum, but he did recommend one. When he met Hari Singh in June 1947 in Srinagar, he advised him to 'consult the will of the people and do what the majority thought best'.[20] Later, in October 1947, when India's first prime minister, Jawaharlal Nehru, was deploying Indian troops in Kashmir, Mountbatten insisted that any decision by the maharaja to accede to India would only be temporary prior to a referendum or, at the least, representative public meetings. When Mountbatten accepted the maharaja's decision to accede to India, he told him:

> . . . my Government have decided to accept the accession of Kashmir State to the Dominion of India. Consistently with their policy that, in the case of any State where the issue of accession has been the subject of dispute, the question of accession should be decided in accordance with the wishes of the people of the State, it is my Government's wish that as soon as law and order have been restored in Kashmir and its soil cleared of the invaders, the question of the State's accession should be settled by a reference to the people.[21]

Pakistani historians have never given Mountbatten credit for this: their feelings towards him have been best captured by Jinnah's biographer, Akbar S. Ahmed, who described the viceroy as the 'first Paki-basher'.[22] The acrimonious debate about Mountbatten's role has perhaps taken on an exaggerated importance, as the man who made the final decision about Kashmir was not Mountbatten but the maharaja. Too close a focus on Mountbatten's role also obscures the performance of another key player – Mohammed Ali Jinnah. Pakistan was to pay a heavy price for his complacent view that the 'ripe fruit' of Kashmir would fall into his lap. Throughout 1947 Jinnah's approach to Kashmir was inept, and at every stage his Indian counterparts outmanoeuvred him.

Jinnah's failure over Kashmir is all the more striking in view of the maharaja's dislike (or 'hate' as Mountbatten put it) of Nehru. Since his family originally came from the Kashmir Valley, Nehru had always taken a close interest in the state. As early as 1934 he identified the man who would become his main political ally there: the secular, nationalist intellectual, Sheikh Mohammed Abdullah. To the considerable irritation of

Hari Singh, Nehru and Abdullah became close friends. Abdullah was the son of a merchant in the Kashmir Valley and, although he did emerge as a strong political figure, he had opponents within the Muslim community. In 1939 some Kashmiris started to oppose Abdullah's alignment with Congress. The most significant was Ghulam Abbas who increasingly looked to Jinnah's Muslim League. In 1942, when Abbas came out in favour of Pakistan, the battle lines were drawn. Nehru backed Abdullah and Jinnah backed Ghulam Abbas. The maharaja was on his own. In May 1944, Jinnah visited Kashmir and declared his support for Abbas. It was the only time he ever went there. Even more remarkably, no other senior Muslim League leaders visited the state in the run-up to partition.

The Congress leadership had a completely different attitude towards Kashmir. Nehru visited it in July 1945 to address a massive National Conference rally. In July 1946, when Sheikh Abdullah was spending one of his many spells in prison, Nehru immediately headed for Kashmir to show his solidarity. He ended up being arrested at the border himself but eventually reached Srinagar and met the imprisoned Abdullah. By these visits – and a series of representations to the British on Abdullah's behalf – Nehru established his interest in Kashmir. It was to stand him in good stead. As the Pakistani historian Hasan Zaheer has written: 'The Muslim League leadership, overwhelmed by the issues arising from the creation of the new state, did not apply itself seriously to the Kashmir situation in the period preceding independence day, while India was systematically working at securing the accession of the state by any means.'[23] By the time the British transferred power, the maharaja still favoured independence. But the Congress leadership's lobbying effort meant that in the event of that option being ruled out, Hari Singh was at least giving serious consideration to the possibility of acceding to India rather than Pakistan. The Muslim League was paying the price for its passivity.

The maharaja's room for manoeuvre, however, was limited. Even before the transfer of power, the political situation in Kashmir had been deteriorating. Once the British left the subcontinent, the state started disintegrating. In Jammu, the maharaja's political heartland, the partition of Punjab sparked an outbreak of communal violence. Massacres forced hundreds of thousands of Kashmiri Muslims to flee their homes: many headed for the safety of Pakistan. From the maharaja's point of view, however, the situation was especially acute in Poonch where the violence was directly aimed at his rule. He had long considered the impoverished Muslims of Poonch to be amongst his least loyal and potentially most troublesome subjects, and he ordered all Muslims there to hand over their weapons. Feeling distinctly vulnerable, the Poonchis looked for another source of arms and found they were readily available from NWFP. The tensions reached a climax in the second week of September 1947, by which time an armed revolt had spread to the whole of Poonch. The uprising caused considerable interest in Pakistan where Jinnah and his colleagues hoped that it might force the maharaja to opt for Pakistan. On 12 September the country's prime minister, Liaquat Ali Khan himself, became involved in drawing up plans to help the rebels. He insisted, however, that Pakistan (unlike India which later showed no such inhibitions regarding troublesome Princely States) should not become associated with an invasion of Kashmir. Liaquat Ali Khan thereby formulated a policy that has continued for 60 years: that Pakistan fights for Kashmir by proxy.

Pakistan's effort to support the Poonchi rebels was small-scale and uncoordinated. The country's diplomatic campaign was equally unimpressive. In mid-October Liaquat Ali Khan sent a Foreign Office official, A.S.B. Shah, to Srinagar to urge accession to Pakistan.[24] It was too little, too late and Shah could not hope to reverse in a few days all the work that had been put in by Congress leaders over several months and years. Indeed, given the fact that the maharaja felt he was facing a Pakistani-backed rebellion in Poonch, he didn't even want to meet the envoy from Karachi. Whilst Pakistan was becoming the maharaja's enemy, the Indians continued their efforts to be seen as his friends.

In October a new factor came into the equation. Tribesmen from NWFP started making their way to Kashmir to fight alongside their Muslim brethren. Whilst it's not clear what role the central Pakistani government played in organising the invasion, there is no doubt that some officials in NWFP helped with logistics and supplies. Liaquat Ali Khan certainly knew about the operation, and British officials who had stayed in Pakistan after partition advised him to block the tribesmen's advance – advice that he rejected.[25] Some say Jinnah also knew about it and others insist he did not. Perhaps the most plausible account comes from the governor of NWFP, George Cunningham, who recorded that when Jinnah first heard about the tribesmen's move he said: 'Don't tell me anything about it. My conscience must be clear.'[26] The upright, constitutionally-minded Jinnah could easily have made such a remark. Kashmir, however, was never going to be secured by such ambivalent leadership.

Whatever the level of Jinnah's involvement, several thousand tribesmen crossed into Kashmir on the night of 21 October. At first they enjoyed considerable success defeating, or just as often, dodging the maharaja's forces. Muslim soldiers in the maharaja's army deserted their posts and joined the tribesmen, and by the end of October the Poonchi rebels and their Pukhtoon allies were within striking distance of Srinagar. Their most spectacular achievement was to sabotage Srinagar's power supply. As the city plunged into darkness the maharaja concluded that he was in serious trouble. His son has recalled what happened:

> On that fateful day I was left virtually alone in the palace while my father and members of the staff were attending the Darbar in the beautiful hall at the city palace on the Jhelum with its richly decorated papier mâché ceiling. Suddenly the lights went out – the invaders had captured and destroyed the only power house. . . . After a few minutes the eerie silence was broken by the sudden, blood-chilling howl of jackals. Weirdly the cacophony rose and fell, then rose again into a mad crescendo. Death and destruction were fast approaching Srinagar; our smug world had collapsed around us.[27]

At this crucial juncture, when Kashmir was ready for the taking, Pakistan paid the price of the haphazard nature of its operations. Rather than striking forward, the tribesmen became distracted by the opportunities for plunder. Their increasingly lawless conduct had a disastrous consequence. The local Muslim population, rather than seeing them as liberators, began to fear them and, far from providing help to the tribesmen, turned against them. These developments and the bad international press Pakistan was receiving as a result of the invasion dismayed the government in Karachi. Officials not only disowned the tribesmen but also obstructed them. Sherbaz Khan Mazari, a 17-year-old tribal leader from Baluchistan who tried to take some men to join in the fighting, later recounted that when he tried to enter Kashmir, 'I was stopped by Pakistani officials who told me in clear cut terms that I would not be allowed to cross into Kashmir. It became clear that they thought we were intent on partaking in the plunder that was taking place.'[28]

From the maharaja's point of view, however, the tribal invaders were still very much a threat. But he knew full well that any help from Delhi would come with a price: accession. Eventually he did sign an accession document. The precise timing of that act is one of the most keenly disputed aspects of the Kashmir issue. The basic question is whether he signed before or after Delhi despatched troops to Kashmir. No one disputes that the Indian troops were deployed at dawn on 27 October. The question is whether the maharaja signed the accession document on the 25th, 26th or the 27th. Pakistani commentators argue that if the act of accession took place after the Indian deployment, then India's move into Kashmir, and the subsequent occupation of parts of the state, was, and remains, illegal.

The historian Prem Shankar Jha has provided the most recent Indian version of these events. He relies on the evidence of Colonel (later Field Marshal) Sam Manekshaw who has said that he and one of the Congress party's most senior politicians, V.P. Menon, went to Srinagar on 25 October. According to Manekshaw, Menon told the maharaja that if he did not sign the Instrument of Accession there and then, Delhi would be unable to send Indian troops to help him. Faced with this ultimatum the maharaja signed the document on the evening of the 25th, and on the 26th Menon took it back to Delhi. Manekshaw did not claim to have actually seen the maharaja sign the document but he recalled that Menon came out of the maharaja's offices saying, 'Sam, we have got it!' According to Manekshaw, the Defence Committee of the Indian cabinet was handed the signed document on the 26th and sent troops to Kashmir that day.[29] There are, however, a number of problems with Manekshaw's account. To name just one, his claim that Indian troops were sent to Kashmir on 26 October is false. The airlift of Indian troops began on 27 October.

Prem Shankar Jha's reliance on Manekshaw's account in fact amounts to something of a tactical retreat in the Indian position on the signing of the Instrument of Accession. Previously, Indian historians had relied on V.P. Menon's memoirs. According to Menon, the maharaja signed the instrument not on the 25th but during the afternoon of the 26th, and the deployment of Indian troops followed on the 27th. There is also, however, a serious difficulty with Menon's account: he was not in Kashmir on the afternoon of the 26th. He was, in fact, at Delhi airport trying to get to Srinagar. Staff at the airport turned him back because, they said, it was too late to take off since the airport at Srinagar had no night-time landing facilities.[30]

The fact that Menon could not have secured the accession on 26 October, because he was not even in Kashmir, has led some to conclude that the Instrument was in fact signed on the 27th. By that time the maharaja had fled from Srinagar to Jammu. According to this version, V.P. Menon, having missed his flight from Delhi on the 26th, travelled to Jammu on the 27th and it was there and then – after the deployment of Indian troops – that the instrument was signed.[31] A recent, unbiased and comprehensive survey of all the available evidence adds weight to the view that this was what happened.[32]

The debate over when the instrument was signed has gone on for 60 years and a complete perusal of all the evidence could, in itself, fill a book. But, as even Jha has acknowledged, the conflicting Indian accounts 'could not fail to create the impression that the Indian government had something to hide'.[33] Remarkably, the Indian government denies historians access to the document the mahajara signed.[34] And, considered from Pakistan's perspective, the question of whether the maharaja did sign before the deployment of Indian troops remains, at the very least, unproven. Indeed, neutral historians tend towards the view that it was signed afterwards. But having said that, no one can dispute that the maharaja wanted Indian help and accepted that, to obtain it, he would have to accede. Whatever the precise timing, that is exactly what happened.

Far from plucking the ripe fruit of Kashmir, Jinnah watched it fall into Delhi's lap. Pakistani writers have tended to blame this outcome on Nehru, Mountbatten and the maharaja. But their own leader also played a significant role. The peculiar circumstances on the subcontinent before the transfer of power had played to Jinnah's strengths. He had managed to pull off a feat unprecedented in modern history: he created a new state entirely legally. He neither lifted a gun nor even ordered anyone else to do so. It's hard to think of anyone else who created a nation without spending even a single day in prison. In his whole life Jinnah was arrested just once – for disorderly behaviour at the 1893 Oxford–Cambridge boat race.[35] Jinnah's monumental achievement rested on a combination of talents that constantly frustrated the British: a refusal to compromise and a brilliant ability to grasp and articulate the most complex legal issues. But although these attributes helped Jinnah create Pakistan they became a handicap when it came to consolidating the new country. Jinnah's apologists argue that his failure to secure Kashmir should be forgiven. His administration was weak and over-whelmed by the arrival of refugees; he was sick and he was hampered by his British military commanders. These factors undoubtedly played a part. But they cannot conceal the extent of Jinnah's failure – especially in the period before partition. In terms of hard-nosed realpolitik the Indian leaders in Delhi were leagues ahead.

By the end of October there were thousands of Indian troops in the Kashmir Valley. The speed of the deployment bore testament to the extent of the planning Indian leaders had put into Kashmir. Pakistan, by contrast, was just beginning to realise that reliance on a few thousand tribesman to liberate the state was insufficient. On 27 October, Jinnah ordered Pakistani troops to go to Jammu and Kashmir and to seize Srinagar. The acting commander-in-chief of the Pakistan army, Lieutenant-General Sir Douglas Gracey, however, refused to obey the order. The Indian army, like that of Pakistan, still had a number of British officers in it and the general was not prepared to let them fight each other. Instead, Gracey called Delhi and told his supreme commander Field Marshal Claude Auchinleck. The next morning Auchinleck flew to Pakistan and persuaded Jinnah to back down. As Auchinleck recorded in a cable to the government in London: 'Jinnah withdrew orders but is very angry and disturbed by what he considers to be sharp practice by India in securing Kashmir's accession . . .'[36]

From Pakistan's point of view the situation was bleak. But it was not entirely lost. Some parts of Kashmir were under its control. The Poonch rebellion and the tribal invasion had secured significant amounts of territory. Furthermore, in Gilgit the Muslim-dominated Gilgit Scouts declared their desire to join Pakistan. The British commander of the Scouts, Major William Brown, wrote a telegram to the chief minister of NWFP, Khan Abdul Qayum Khan: 'Revolution night 31st to 1st Gilgit Province. Entire pro-Pakistan populace has overthrown [the maharaja's] Dogra regime. Owing imminent chaos and bloodshed Scouts and Muslim State Forces taken over law and order.'[37] Some areas under Indian control, such as Jammu, were of relatively little interest to Pakistan. The real problem for Jinnah and his new state lay in the most densely populated part of the state: the Kashmir Valley. Pakistan believed it should have it but the Indians were already there.

Once again, however, Jinnah failed to explore all the options open to him. One possibility was to make compromises over another Princely State, Hyderabad. The Muslim ruler, or nizam, of Hyderabad faced the same dilemma as Maharaja Hari Singh. He wanted independence but was far from sure he could achieve it. Jinnah realised that it was never realistic to expect the nizam to accede to Pakistan: Hyderabad was entirely surrounded by Indian territory. But he always hoped that the nizam could pull off independence. He considered Hyderabad to be the 'oldest Muslim dynasty in India',[38] and hoped that its continued existence as an independent state right in the heart of India would provide a sense of security for those Muslims who didn't move to Pakistan. Once again, however, Jinnah was thinking in terms of legally possible options rather than the political realities. In the long term the independence of Hyderabad, although constitutionally proper, was never going to happen. The new Indian leadership saw the issue clearly enough. When the nizam tried to strike a deal which would allow him to hang on to some degree of autonomy, Delhi flatly refused to consider the idea.

In retrospect most Pakistanis would agree that it would have been worth abandoning the aspiration for an independent Hyderabad if it meant securing Kashmir's accession to Pakistan. Furthermore, Jinnah had good reason to believe that such a deal could have been struck. In late November 1947 Nehru and Liaquat Ali Khan met to discuss the situation in Kashmir. To understand their conversation it is first necessary to consider briefly what had happened in yet another Princely State, Junagadh.

The Muslim nawab of Junagadh ruled over a million people, 80 per cent of them Hindus. Junagadh was located in western India and, even though it wasn't strictly contiguous with Pakistan, its coastline offered the possibility of sea links to the Muslim state that was just 200 miles away. The nawab of Junagadh, guided by his pro-Pakistani chief minister Sir Shah Nawaz Bhutto (the father of Zulfikar Ali Bhutto), decided to ignore the feelings of his Hindu population and acceded to Pakistan. It was the mirror image of the situation in Kashmir. The Indian government didn't accept the decision, blockaded Junagadh and then invaded it. Delhi then imposed a plebiscite and secured the result it desired: Junagadh became part of India.

When Liaquat Ali Khan met Nehru at the end of November he exposed the illogicality of India's position. If Junagadh, despite its Muslim ruler's accession to Pakistan, belonged to India because of its Hindu majority, then Kashmir surely belonged to Pakistan. When Liaquat Ali Kahn made this incontrovertible point his Indian interlocutor, Sardar Patel, could not contain himself and burst out: 'Why do you compare Junagadh with Kashmir. Talk of Hyderabad and Kashmir and we could reach agreement.'[39] Patel was not alone in this view. On 29 October 1947 officials at the American embassy in Delhi had told the US State Department: 'the obvious solution is for the government leaders in Pakistan and India to agree . . . [to the] accession of Kashmir to Pakistan and the accession of Hyderabad and Junagadh to India.' British officials in London concurred.[40]

Jinnah, however, never did the deal and the fighting in Kashmir carried on throughout 1948. The Pakistani leadership, fearing that they could lose control of those parts of Kashmir they already occupied, again asked the British commanders to deploy troops there. This time General Gracey had become more willing to fight for the Pakistani interest and, with India looking ever stronger in Kashmir, he advised the government in Karachi that:

if India is not to be allowed to sit on the doorsteps of Pakistan to the rear and on the flank at liberty to enter at its will and pleasure; if the civilian and military morale is not be effected to a dangerous extent; and if subversive political forces are not to be encouraged and let loose within Pakistan itself, it is imperative that the Indian army is not allowed to advance . . .[41]

Gracey was concerned that Pakistan's very existence was in jeopardy. Not only might India react to events in Kashmir by crossing the international boundary but, in addition, there was the risk that defeat in Kashmir could lead the Pukhtoon tribesmen to turn their anger on Pakistan itself, causing insurmountable law and order problems. The presence of the Pakistan army in Kashmir made a difference. By the end of the year Delhi controlled about two-thirds of Kashmir and Karachi one-third. Pakistan then planned a major counter-offensive in western Kashmir despite the clear risk that in doing so it might tempt India to invade Pakistan itself and strike for Lahore. The fear of an all-out war between the two countries was real and persuaded the British, who still had officers commanding both armies, that the fighting had to stop. The Indian and Pakistani governments agreed, and one minute before midnight on 1 January 1949 a ceasefire came into effect.

1949–1965

As the ceasefire took hold, the politicians on both sides considered their options. Liaquat Ali Khan decided that two areas under Pakistani control, Gilgit and Baltistan (which became known as the Northern Areas), should not be fully incorporated into Pakistan's democratic structures. Instead, the area was kept constitutionally separate from the rest of Pakistan and ruled directly by the Ministry of Kashmir Affairs in Karachi. Liaquat calculated that if a Kashmiri referendum were ever held, Pakistan might need the votes of the Muslims there. (To this day Pakistan's Foreign Office advises governments that any move to incorporate the Northern Areas into Pakistan would undermine Islamabad's case that the whole issue of Kashmir should be resolved on the basis of UN resolutions.) Pakistan also let things remain largely as they were in

Azad (or Free) Kashmir. This was an area in which the local Muslim populace had declared independence and started establishing rudimentary governmental structures.

India had to pursue a much more proactive policy. Its overall objective was to consolidate the maharaja's accession. To do this the leadership in Delhi looked to their old ally Sheikh Abdullah. In March 1948 the maharaja had reluctantly recognised the popularity of the 'Lion of Kashmir', as Abdullah was universally known, and made him prime minister. Predictably enough, the two men disagreed about almost everything, not least Abdullah's plans to take land from the (predominantly Hindu) elite and give it to the (predominantly Muslim) peasantry. The two men's relationship was unsustainable. Delhi sealed the maharaja's fate in June 1949. Having persuaded him to take a holiday outside of Kashmir, the Indian government advised him to stay out of the state indefinitely and his son Karan was appointed as regent. Hari Singh never returned to Kashmir: he died 13 years later in Bombay.

There was now no one in Kashmir to rival the popularity and authority of Sheikh Abdullah. But to Delhi's dismay, when it came to the big questions of Kashmir's constitutional status, he pursued a remarkably similar line to his old royal adversary. In public Abdullah stated his commitment to a secular India; in private he made no secret of his desire for independence or at least a considerable degree of autonomy. In September 1950, for example, he told the US ambassador to India, Loy Henderson, that he favoured Kashmiri independence.[12] But as Abdullah was to discover, Kashmir was already locked in a vice. From the moment the maharaja signed the document of accession the voice of the Kashmiris was drowned out by those of the politicians in Pakistan and India.

Abdullah was not working in isolation. The United Nations was also involved in seeking a solution that would bring stability to the mountain state. From the moment the issue was referred to it by India in January 1948, the UN made great efforts to broker a solution. In general terms the various UN proposals can be summarised thus: there should be some form of plebiscite in Kashmir. Initially both India and Pakistan said they agreed with this. Nehru repeatedly pledged that he would consult the wishes of the Kashmiri people. In October 1947 he had written to Liaquat Ali Khan saying:

Our assurance that we shall withdraw our troops from Kashmir as soon as peace and order are restored and leave the decision regarding the future of this state to the people of the state is not merely a pledge to your government but also to the people of Kashmir and to the world.[43]

The devil, though, was in the detail: India insisted that the first priority was to withdraw the tribesmen and any Pakistani forces in Kashmir. Pakistan meanwhile argued that no referendum would be fair if the Indian troops remained in place. With both sides afraid of losing whatever territory they held, the issue ran into interminable deadlock. The Kashmir dispute was one of the first to expose the UN's weakness: it could, and did, launch a whole series of initiatives. But the parties to the dispute resisted a compromise and the UN was powerless to impose one. The situation was complicated by the influence of the cold war. Whilst Pakistan increasingly looked to the United States for big-power support, India sought to improve its relations with the Soviet Union which, in return, liberally used its veto power on the Security Council in Delhi's favour.

China also got involved. In 1957 a Chinese magazine published a map showing the location of a road that Beijing had constructed in Aksai Chin, a desolate and largely uninhabited area in eastern Kashmir. Ever since the 1920s the Chinese and the British had wrangled over border demarcation issues: one of them concerned Aksai Chin. Following the transfer of power, the Chinese had occupied Aksai Chin and built a road across it without India even noticing. The publication of the Chinese map rang alarm bells in Delhi, and the relationship between Delhi and Beijing rapidly deteriorated. By 1962 the two countries were fighting. China's overwhelming defeat of the Indians sent shock waves through the Western world. The significance of the conflict lay not in Aksai Chin itself but in its impact on the regional strategic balance. Concerned about Chinese expansionism, the US and some Western European powers offered significant supplies of weapons to Delhi.

Pakistan, which had long hoped that US pressure might force a settlement in Kashmir, was left as a frustrated bystander. The only initiative that it could make was to recognise the Chinese claim to

Aksai Chin. The Pakistani recognition was qualified. Pakistan said that if the Chinese-occupied area should ever be granted to Pakistan then it would not challenge the Chinese presence in the area. Predictably enough, India complained bitterly that Pakistan had given up territory to which it had no right and which it did not even control.

Despite the reverse in Aksai Chin, India felt it was making progress elsewhere in Kashmir. Throughout the 1950s it consolidated its rule over the state. In 1953 the Congress leadership decided that Abdullah had become too much of a loose cannon and engineered his dismissal. The decision was welcomed by both the Hindus in Jammu and the Buddhists in Ladakh who feared that Abdullah was creating a Muslim one-party state in which they had little stake. Abdullah was succeeded by one of his closest advisers, Bakshi Ghulam Mohammed, who proceeded to order the arrest of his long-time friend and master. For Abdullah it was the start of a long stretch in prison; he was to remain in detention for most of the next 15 years. Bakshi, who fully appreciated that he owed his position to Delhi, acted accordingly. His ten-year administration was marked by one policy above all others: increasing India's influence and authority in Kashmir. As far as Delhi was concerned, Kashmir had become an integral part of its territory and there would be no more talk of a plebiscite. The demand for a referendum, however, did not go away. In one of his brief periods out of prison, Abdullah, who by this stage was perceived as a hero in Pakistan, insisted that the Kashmiri people themselves must decide on their future. Within a matter of days he was back behind bars.

The Indians believed that the internal political situation in Kashmir was stabilising, but in 1963 Delhi received a brutal reminder that, in fact, the state remained highly volatile. In December of that year a devastating rumour, later confirmed as true, spread through the Kashmir Valley. A religious relic, a hair from the Prophet's beard, had been stolen from a shrine near Srinagar. The hair was eventually returned but the incident produced an intense outburst of Muslim feeling and provoked a wave of social unrest in Kashmir. The incident made Pakistanis wonder whether the time was ripe to push the Indians a little harder.

The 1965 War

The 1965 war between Pakistan and India was a particularly futile conflict. At the end of it the two sides agreed a ceasefire line identical to the one with which they had started. So, why did the two countries join battle in the first place?

The conflict of 1965 was just waiting to happen. Both India and Pakistan had a sense of insecurity. Ever since partition, Pakistan had distrusted Indian intentions. Senior politicians and military officers feared that their counterparts in Delhi secretly hoped and, in many cases, believed that the whole Pakistan project would fail and that the subcontinent would be reunited. India also had genuine concerns: after its defeat at the hands of China in 1962, the country faced a major crisis of confidence. One contemporary American observer who tried to catch the mood of the two young nations described the volatile mix of distrust and disdain that marked public opinion on both sides of the border:

> Again and again I have heard Pakistanis say that India does not accept Pakistan and is determined to destroy it; that Indians can't fight and won't fight . . . again and again I have heard Indians say that Pakistan is a ruthless dictatorship and theocracy; that Pakistan is bent on destroying India and determined to destroy the large Hindu minority in Pakistan.[44]

Regional politics also played a part. Pakistan's improving relationship with China affected its perceptions of its strength vis-à-vis India. Ayub Khan visited China in March 1965. He was given a rapturous reception and secured China's firm support for a plebiscite in Kashmir. In addition, Ayub also visited Moscow. Even though the results of the Soviet trip were less striking, the fact that a Pakistani leader was cordially received in Moscow inevitably caused concern in Delhi. Moscow, an important Indian ally, seemed to be wavering.

Ayub Khan and his young foreign minister Zulfikar Ali Bhutto were further encouraged by their perception of the state of opinion in Kashmir itself. The riots that followed the disappearance of the hair of the Prophet's beard led them to believe that the people of Kashmir were ready for a fight. Speaking immediately after the incident, Bhutto said the people of Kashmir were 'in revolt. Unmistakably in revolt.'[45] Pakistani intelligence reports seemed to confirm that the levels of discontent in Kashmir had reached new heights. If Pakistan could show the Kashmiris that removing the Indians was a real possibility, Bhutto believed, they would readily join an anti-Indian uprising. There were also signs that Sheikh Abdullah was pursuing an increasingly independent line and that he could even side with Pakistan. In March 1965, much to India's annoyance, Abdullah met the Chinese prime minister, Chou En-Lai. A few days before the encounter Abdullah had said that 'we did not make those sacrifices all these years for our rights in vain, and we will not leave it now because of fear of India's might. It is wrong to say that Pakistan is instigating us.'[46]

Ayub was also increasingly confident about Pakistan's military capability. Immediately after independence, Pakistan's armed forces had been hopelessly weak and had proved incapable of playing a decisive role in the war of 1947–8. Ayub had subsequently given high priority to creating an effective military machine, and by the early 1960s it was widely believed that he had succeeded. Pakistan may have had less manpower than India, but the close Pakistani–US relationship ensured that its personnel were better trained and better equipped. Pakistan was increasingly prepared to test its strength and Bhutto in particular itched for an opportunity to do so. Ever since he became Ayub's foreign minister in 1963, Bhutto had focused on the Kashmir dispute. He had also taken care to foster good relations with senior military officers, and was well aware that the generals in Rawalpindi were also devoting considerable time to the issue. By late 1964 they had developed a strategy that would become known to the world as Operations GIBRALTAR and GRANDSLAM. In Operation GIBRALTAR armed militants would cross into Indian-controlled Kashmir and instigate a general revolt. They could be backed up, if necessary, by Operation GRANDSLAM in which Pakistani troops would be deployed with the same objective. The idea was to restrict any fighting to Kashmir itself and avoid an escalation into full-scale war.

Excited by the prospect of decisive action in Kashmir, Bhutto advised Ayub that the time had come to fight. Both UN resolutions and bilateral talks, he argued, had failed. He spoke of the possibility that

China would intervene on Pakistan's side. India, he said, was too weak to engage in a major war and would never dare invade over the Punjab border. Furthermore, he told Ayub, the opportunity might slip away. Ever since Delhi's defeat in 1962, the Western powers had been pouring arms into India so as to contain Chinese expansionism and, in the long run, the military balance was bound to tilt in Delhi's favour. Ayub, he argued, had already missed one opportunity by failing to move troops into Kashmir in 1962 when the Indians were in disarray. He must not, he urged, make the same mistake twice.

As he considered his options, Ayub took heart from the outcome of a recent military clash between India and Pakistan on a tract of marshland off southern Sindh, the Rann of Kutch. The Rann had been disputed territory ever since 1947. As an imperial power, the British had stated that the Rann of Kutch, as its name implies, was part of Kutch State. Since Kutch went to India, so too did the Rann. Pakistan, however, argued that since the Rann was flooded each monsoon it was really a sea. Consequently, Pakistan maintained, the boundary line should be drawn halfway through the Rann between, as it were, the two shores. The dispute had far more symbolic than strategic importance: the Rann had no economic significance whatsoever. As one Pakistani military historian put it: 'A minor border dispute was escalated to a point where restraint by either side would be contrived by the other as chickening out.'[47] Fighting in the Rann began in early 1965 with a series of small-scale exchanges in which the two sides attacked each other's posts.

As the monsoon approached, both India and Pakistan recognised the inevitable: the forces deployed in the Rann would have to stop fighting because the area would become flooded. They agreed to a British-sponsored ceasefire that also allowed for a UN tribunal of three members to resolve the basic dispute in the Rann. The international diplomacy eventually took both sides to Geneva where a three-man panel (with representatives from Yugoslavia, Iran and Sweden) considered the issue and searched for a settlement. India had apparently conceded the principle that it would, after all, accept international mediation to resolve a bilateral dispute with its Muslim neighbour. But, far from contributing to stability on the subcontinent, the international mediation created new resentments in India and fresh hopes in Pakistan.

In July 1965, Ayub finally made up his mind: he would take Bhutto's advice. The infiltration of Kashmir outlined in Operation GIBRALTAR began and, on 10 August, a body no Kashmiri had previously heard of, the Revolutionary Council, called on the people to rise up against their Indian occupiers. The Council declared that, having formed a National Government of Jammu and Kashmir, it would henceforth be 'the sole lawful authority in our land.'[48] The anticipated Kashmiri revolt, however, never occurred. Pakistan had not put the necessary preparations in place. Kashmiri leaders had not been consulted about Operation GIBRALTAR. Some even suspected that the infiltrators were Indian provocateurs. When the militants contacted supposedly sympathetic mullahs, they found that most were reluctant to help.[49]

From Pakistan's point of view the results of Operation GIBRALTAR were disappointing. For India, though, the situation was alarming. Bruised by accusations of weakness over the Rann of Kutch affair, the Indian prime minister, Lal Bahadur Shastri, opted for an all-out military campaign. In mid-August the Indians launched a major offensive. In doing so they crossed the 1947 ceasefire line so as to prevent further infiltration. The Indians were soon able to cut off the militants' supply lines, leaving the infiltrators short of material and completely isolated.

Some Pakistani generals could see the writing on the wall. But Bhutto urged Ayub to carry on. He said he would not 'even consider allowing this movement to die out . . . such a course would amount to a debacle which could threaten the existence of Pakistan.'[50] On 29 August, Ayub once again accepted his minister's advice and opted for war. He sent a top-secret order to his army chief, General Mohammed Musa:

1. . . . to take such action that will defreeze Kashmir problem [sic], weaken India's resolve and bring her to the conference table without provoking a general war. However, the element of escalation is always present in such struggles. So, whilst confining our actions to the Kashmir area we must not be unmindful that India may in desperation involve us in a general war or violate Pakistani territory where we are weak. We must therefore be prepared for such contingency.

2. To expect quick results in this struggle, when India has much larger forces than us, would be unrealistic. Therefore our action should be such that can be sustained over a long period.

3. As a general rule Hindu morale would not stand for more than a couple of hard blows delivered at the right time and the right place. Such opportunities should therefore be sought and exploited.[51]

Two days later Pakistan's armed forces launched Operation GRANDSLAM with a major offensive in western Kashmir. Initially the Pakistanis enjoyed considerable success. Within five days they were threatening India's only all-weather land route to Kashmir. But the Pakistani plans contained a fatal flaw. The military leadership in Rawalpindi was relying on its extraordinarily complacent assumption that India would not extend the fighting beyond Kashmir. India saw no reason to show such restraint. On 6 September, Delhi opened up a 50-mile-wide front near Lahore, launched an offensive in Sindh and made a drive for the Pakistani city of Sialkot. Despite the predictability of the Indian action, the Pakistani planners were taken by surprise.

In a matter of hours Pakistan's strategy was turned on its head. All thoughts of offence were abandoned. The priority now was to save Lahore. Ayub Khan himself conceded privately that the situation was dire. 'It is catastrophic,' he told the American ambassador on 7 September. 'We are getting ready for a desperate fight.'[52] He knew that Lahore was extremely vulnerable. The commander in charge of the city's defence, Major General Sarfraz Khan, had been specifically ordered to put no defensive measures in place. When a junior officer implored him to deploy troops in defensive positions he had replied: 'Sorry, GHQ has ordered no move, no provocative actions.'[53]

Despite being unprepared, the Pakistanis did manage to halt the Indian advances on Lahore and Sialkot. Ayub Khan realised that if he was to achieve his original war objectives in relation to Kashmir he would need outside help, and he looked to China. There were some indications that Beijing might play a decisive role. Whilst the fighting in Kashmir was underway, China had resuscitated a long-standing territorial dispute concerning some Indian military installations that, Beijing maintained, were on Chinese territory. After some opening diplomatic exchanges, China declared on 16 September that India would face 'grave consequences'[54] if it did not dismantle its military installations within three days. For good measure, Beijing also demanded the return of 800 sheep and 59 yaks which it claimed India had kidnapped.

Ayub and Bhutto visited Beijing on 20 September to see whether China was prepared to back up these statements by launching an offensive on India. Their hosts offered plenty of moral support but not much more. Beijing realised that attacking India could provoke a devastating Western response and suggested instead that Ayub could abandon some major Pakistani cities near the border and conduct a 'people's war' against India. It was not the kind of advice he was looking for. On 21 September, China de-escalated the crisis in its relations with Delhi by announcing that India had dismantled its military installations. The sheep and yaks were forgotten. Ayub's last card had been played. By the time he returned to Pakistan he was determined to agree a ceasefire. India, which had achieved its objective of preventing the loss of Kashmir, was like-minded. With both parties to the conflict in search of a settlement, the UN's peace brokers were, for once, able to achieve something. The fighting stopped on 23 September 1965.

As the situation in Kashmir stabilised, India and Pakistan came under increasing pressure to talk. In January 1966 they did so in Tashkent and the two sides agreed to go back to their pre-war positions. For the Pakistani public it was a shocking and disappointing outcome. Even after the ceasefire the official media in Pakistan had given the impression that India had suffered a humiliating defeat: it was now perfectly clear to everyone that the true result was closer to a draw. The joint statement made at Tashkent merely noted the existence of the Kashmir dispute. This amounted to a significant climb-down by Ayub Khan. When Pakistan had agreed to a ceasefire in 1949, it had not only secured control of the one-third of Kashmir that was under Pakistani control but also won an Indian pledge to hold a referendum. The exaggerated hopes that Ayub's regime had encouraged and the subsequent let-down at Tashkent began the process that eventually forced the field marshal to relinquish power.

The greatest beneficiary of the Tashkent talks was Zulfikar Ali Bhutto. Despite the leading role he had played in instigating the 1965 war, he successfully disassociated himself from the Ayub regime and relentlessly pursued his drive for power. He achieved it six years later, after Pakistan had fought and lost another battle against India. In 1971, with Indian military help, the eastern wing of Pakistan broke away to become Bangladesh and it fell to Bhutto to re-establish a modus vivendi with India. In June and July 1972 Bhutto met his Indian counterpart Indira Gandhi at Simla. The talks concentrated on issues such as the return of the Pakistani prisoners of war captured in 1971, but Simla is best remembered for its impact on the Kashmir dispute. In the first place Bhutto agreed to the use of the term 'line of control' rather than 'ceasefire line'. It may have seemed like a semantically insignificant point but, after Simla, Bhutto was repeatedly accused of having sold out Pakistan's interests. His critics maintained that the change in terminology signalled Bhutto's willingness, at some stage in the future, to transform the ceasefire line into an international border. Some Indian participants at Simla have said that this was indeed their impression of Bhutto's intentions.[55] Bhutto himself always rejected this interpretation of Simla and insisted that he gave no secret undertakings. The second important development at Simla was the agreement that the two sides would 'settle their differences by peaceful means through bilateral negotiations or by any other peaceful means mutually agreed between them'.[56] Ever since, successive Indian governments have relied on Simla to reject Pakistani demands that the Kashmir dispute should be the subject of international mediation.

For the Muslims of Indian-controlled Kashmir the 1965 war was a disaster. It was not a conflict of their own making and yet they paid the price. After 1965 India tightened its grip. A plebiscite was out of the question, but Indira Gandhi could see that a political rather than military solution gave India the best prospect of long-term success in Kashmir. By 1974, like Nehru before her, she had come to the view that Sheikh Abdullah held the key. Persuading Abdullah to work with the Indian government was not easy. Not only had he spent a good proportion of his life in Indian jails, but he also refused to give up on the idea that the Kashmir people, and not the politicians in India (or, for that matter, Pakistan), should determine the future of the state. Despite these apparently significant obstacles the Indian government and

Abdullah did reach an agreement. Under the Kashmir Accord of February 1975, Abdullah accepted that Kashmir was 'a constituent unit of the Union of India' albeit with special status.[57] In return he became chief minister.

Abdullah's Kashmiri opponents and the Pakistani government denounced the Accord as a sell-out, and there was no escaping the fact that it represented a great achievement for Indira Gandhi. In October 1975 she celebrated her political breakthrough by paying a state visit to Srinagar. Sheikh Abdullah laid on a traditional boat procession. When 32 turbaned oarsmen carried the Indian leader across the Dal Lake, the banks were lined by thousands of people. Given what has happened in Kashmir since 1975, it is remarkable that they cheered her on her way.

If the Indian government was making some limited moves to find an accommodation with the Kashmiri people, it remained determined to ensure that Pakistan be kept at bay. The latent hostility between Islamabad and Delhi found violent expression in 1984 when the country's two armies clashed once again, this time fighting on the Siachin Glacier in the east of Kashmir. Despite all the attention paid to ceasefire lines in 1948, at Tashkent and at Simla, no one had seen any point in demarcating the icy wasteland that lay at the eastern end of the line of control. In any event, the glacial territory was so hostile that independent survey teams were unable to access it. Consequently, the line of control stopped short of the glacier and there was no internationally recognised line that clarified which parts of it belonged to which side. The crisis over the Siachin Glacier had been developing for some years. In the late 1970s, India was concerned to note that some mountain-climbing expeditions were seeking Pakistani, rather than Indian, permission to climb on the glacier. In 1984 Delhi became even more worried: some recently published Pakistani maps showed the glacier as part of Pakistani-controlled Kashmir. Delhi responded to this 'cartographic aggression' by deploying troops on the glacier, capturing the high ground that they have never subsequently relinquished. The two sides have fought for the glacier ever since, although the severity of the climate means that more people die as a result of the cold than through military actions.

The Insurgency

As she glided across the Dal Lake in 1975, Mrs Gandhi may have thought she was well on the way to solving India's Kashmir problem. But even as she was feted, new forces were developing in the state. For as long as he lived, Sheikh Abdullah, with his immense popularity and increasingly authoritarian habits, was able to keep a lid on the pressure that was building up; but after he died in 1982 a new generation of activists, many of them Pakistanis inspired by Islamism as much as Kashmiri nationalism, found their voice. True to South Asian tradition, Abdullah's son Farooq took over the reins of power, but he was never as strong as his father. For all his political manoeuvring, Sheikh Abdullah's long years in prison had made him the symbol of Kashmiri defiance in the face of Indian authority. Farooq, by contrast, was seen as a lightweight political dilettante and he could not walk the impossibly fine line of keeping both Delhi and the Kashmiri people content.

During the 1980s anti-Indian opinion steadily hardened and Kashmir's Jamaat-e-Islami, an offshoot of the Pakistani party of the same name, emerged as a force to be reckoned with. Although Jamaat favoured union with Pakistan, another group, the Jammu and Kashmir Liberation Front (JKLF), advocated independence. The organisation first came to prominence in 1984 for its alleged role in the kidnapping and subsequent murder of an Indian diplomat in the British city of Birmingham. By the late 1980s the JKLF was becoming active in Kashmir itself and it found that many people in the state were ready to respond.

On 31 July 1988, Srinagar rocked to a series of explosions. They were claimed by the JKLF although in reality their provenance was rather more complicated. The JKLF, it is true, had laid the bombs. But the materials had been provided by the Pakistani state, and, more precisely, the ISI. In 1987 the ISI and the JKLF had, with General Zia's approval, struck a deal. The JKLF agreed to recruit would-be militants in Indian-held Kashmir, bring them across the line of control and deliver them to ISI trainers. The ISI in turn agreed to provide the JKLF fighters with weapons and military instruction. The young men were then sent back across the line so that they could mount attacks.[58]

The 31 July explosions marked the start of the 'insurgency', Kashmir's version of the Palestinian intifada. The levels of violence were extraordinary. The Kashmiri political parties estimate the dead since 1988 at between 80,000 and 100,000. Neutral observers tend to estimate 60,000, whereas India claims the figure is closer to 30,000.[59] By all accounts far more people have died as a result of the insurgency than in the wars of 1947 and 1965 put together.

When the insurgency began the JKLF, with its ISI backers, was clearly the dominant force. But there was a problem: the ISI became increasingly concerned about the JKLF's pro-independence position. It was perhaps inevitable that the ISI would look for more politically amenable clients in Kashmir, and it turned to Jamaat-e-Islami's armed wing, Hizb ul-Mujahideen. The organisation, which supported the union of Kashmir and Pakistan, duly received considerable logistical and financial support from Islamabad and the JKLF found itself eclipsed. The new awkwardness in the relationship between the Pakistani government and the JKLF was fully exposed in 1992 when the JKLF leader, Amanullah Khan, tried to demonstrate his opposition to the division of Kashmir by leading a peaceful march across the line of control. The Pakistani authorities stopped the march by force, killing seven JKLF activists in the process. Pakistan's hostility to the JKLF was soon reflected on the ground in Kashmir itself where JKLF and Hizb ul-Mujahideen militants started targeting each other.

Even if they were in conflict the JKLF and Hizb ul-Mujahideen did have one thing in common: most of their fighters were Kashmiris. Many other groups that emerged in Kashmir in the 1990s relied more on Pakistani recruits. Lashkar-e-Toiba (now renamed Jamaat al Dawat) and Jaish-e-Mohammed (now Khudam ul-Islam) both demonstrated the capacity to mount devastating suicide attacks. The two organisations clearly benefited from the support of Pakistan's state institutions, especially the ISI. Other Pakistani-backed outfits included Al Badr, which has a history dating back to the war of 1971 in East Pakistan. It subsequently fought in Afghanistan before switching its focus to Kashmir. Tehrik-e-Jihad had especially close links to the Pakistan army; many of its members were Kashmiris who used to serve in the Pakistan military. While Tehrik-e-Jihad was almost exclusively focused on Kashmir (the organisation accused in 2007 of involvement in the attempted assassination of Benazir Bhutto in Karachi), Harakat-e-Jihad-e-Islami, conducted operations not only in Kashmir but also Burma, Uzbekistan, Tajikistan and Chechnya. In November 2001, 85 of its fighters who were supporting the Taliban's attempts to defend the northern Afghan city of Mazar i-Sharif were killed by US bombing.[60] Harakat e-Jihad e-Islami was closely related to Harakat ul-Mujahideen. Both organisations were factions within Harakat ul-Ansar before it disbanded and recreated itself when the US put it on its list of banned organisations. The list of militant groups goes on and on. Shias who wanted to fight in Kashmir, for example, could join Hizb ul-Momineen, whilst Kashmiris with a pro-Pakistani political position felt at home with Jamiat-ul-Mujahideen.

The militants' struggle has provoked a terrible response. India's atrocious human rights record in Kashmir is an established fact. Amnesty International, Human Rights Watch and India's own National Human Rights Commission have all produced copious reports documenting the repressive conduct of the Indian security forces. Year after year the US State Department's human rights reports have spoken of extrajudicial killings on an almost daily basis, the systematic use of rape as a weapon of terror and the routine recourse to torture to extract information from suspected militants. Methods used by the Indian army, the border security force and the police have included beating, sexual abuse, burning with cigarettes and hot rods, suspension by the feet, the crushing of limbs by heavy rollers, and electric shocks. Security force personnel have carried out those activities with virtual impunity and only a tiny proportion has faced prosecution.[61]

Throughout the 1990s this brutal display of state power failed to defeat the insurgency. But the militants, too, have been responsible for gross human rights violations. In addition to targeted killings of security force personnel and anyone who dared speak out against their campaign of violence, the militants have carried out several mass murders of civilians. In 1998, for example, there was a series of six attacks on Hindu villages in which nearly a hundred men, women and children were killed. The militants have also carried out hundreds of kidnappings. In November 1997 the Indian government claimed that since 1989 there had been 1,900 kidnappings and that in 700 of those cases the captives were killed.[62]

The relationship between Pakistan and the Kashmiri people is an awkward one. As Pakistan's support for the insurgency grew in scale, many Kashmiris came to resent the way in which their conflict with the Indian security forces was being overshadowed by the dispute between the Indian and Pakistani governments. And many in Kashmir were also disturbed by the way in which the insurgency was becoming coloured by communal considerations. Kashmir had always been home to a mix of different religious and ethnic communities, and at a local level there had always been high levels of tolerance. Under the pressure of the insurgency some of those long-established relationships started breaking down.

The single most important event in this process was the exodus of a large proportion of the Hindu population from the Kashmir Valley in 1990. The Hindus there claimed that the Islamic groups were singling them out for targeted assassinations. The scale of their migration has been disputed. Officially-inspired Indian versions claim that as many as a quarter of a million Hindus left the valley. More considered Indian accounts put the figure at around 100,000.[63] Most moved to refugee camps in Jammu and Delhi. Their departure was used by propagandists in Delhi to assert that Hindus, too, were the subject of human rights abuses in the Kashmir Valley.

The number of groups operating in Kashmir weakened the insurgency and at times there were fierce and deadly clashes between different organisations. The anti-India politicians in Kashmir have made some efforts to present a united front. In 1993 they founded the All Parties Hurriyat Conference (APHC), an umbrella group for Kashmiri political parties, including Jamaat-e-Islami, of Indian-controlled Kashmir and the Muslim Conference. The APHC claims to represent Kashmiri opinion and was founded to press for an end to Indian rule through peaceful means. Having said that, some of its leading members have tried to increase their political strength by creating allied militant groups. The APHC, however, has faced many challenges, not least from hardline groups that have disagreed with its strategy of holding occasional rounds of talks with the Indian authorities. Inevitably, the splits between the militant groups have worked to the advantage of the Indian security forces. The rifts also undermined the standing of the liberation struggle in Kashmiri popular opinion. Although the militants still enjoyed a wide platform of support, a significant number of Kashmiris began to have their doubts. Far from seeing the fighters as liberators, some perceived them as a disruptive element waging a communal, internecine and possibly futile struggle. The militants' practice of turning up unannounced at people's houses and demanding sanctuary left many householders scared and resentful. Families also objected to the pressure to provide not only funds but also their young men for the struggle, and many did not appreciate the efforts of some militants to force the Kashmiris to adopt a more Islamic lifestyle.

The insurgency, or Tahrik, in Kashmir has passed through a number of phases.[64] The militancy of the first years gradually gave way to a parallel political effort managed by the APHC. Neither tactic made any progress, leading to a period in the 1990s of even more intense conflict.

The figures given below should not be taken at face value: many in Pakistan and Kashmir believe them to be an underestimate. They do, nonetheless, demonstrate trends. In the late 1990s the militant

Kashmir killings, 1995–September 2008

	Civilians	Security forces personnel	Militants
1995	1050	202	1308
1996	1214	94	1271
1997	918	189	1114
1998	867	232	999
1999	821	356	1082
2000	762	397	1520
2001	971	706	2119
2002	966	521	1747
2003	795	314	1494
2004	707	281	976
2005	557	189	917
2006	389	151	591
2007[1]	349	168	599
2008[2]	68	71	268

Source: US Department of State, Human Rights Reports 1995 to 2000. The figures for 1995 and 1996 are based on Indian press reports. The figures for 1997–2000 are official Indian government figures. See www.state.gov/www/global/human_rights/hrp_reports_ mainhp.html

[1] http://satp.org/satporgtp/countries/india/states/jandk/index.html

[2] http://satp.org/satporgtp/countries/india/states/jandk/timeline/index.htm

campaign, and the Indian response to it, became ever more intense. The steady fall in the number of civilians, as opposed to militants, killed in the insurgency is partly explained by the fact that after a decade of experience, the Indian security forces became more adept at ensuring that civilians were not caught in the crossfire. A growing belief in Kashmir that fighting India was futile, coupled with General Musharraf's 2002 decision (see below) to stop infiltrations across the line of control, clearly made a significant difference. The number of deaths from that time came down more slowly than might have been expected, in part because many militant groups had enough personnel and munitions to sustain the fight for some years – albeit with a reduced capability.

Kargil

Karnal Sher Khan was always destined for a military career. The name Karnal, selected by his grandfather, was a corruption of 'colonel' and it revealed his family's ambitions. By the summer of 1999 Karnal had made it to the rank of captain in Pakistan's Northern Light Infantry. He never did become a colonel. He died in the Kargil campaign. In one way, though, the captain exceeded his family's expectations. He fought with such courage that he was posthumously awarded Pakistan's highest military honour, the Nishan-e-Haider, and became a national hero. His picture, repeatedly published in the Pakistani press, became a symbol of Pakistani pride. He was recommended for the award by an Indian officer, who had seen Captain Karnal Sher Khan's valour at first hand and who insisted that his memory should be treated with due respect. 'We are a professional army,' the Indian officer said, 'and respect another professional soldier, even when he is from the enemy side. And we would feel happy if a soldier like Karnal Sher gets recognition for his bravery.'

Captain Karnal Sher Khan's last moments were spent in a hopeless attempt to hold on to a post high in the Himalayas in Kashmir. Having been shelled and strafed for three days and nights, he and the men under his command were surrounded by Indian troops. After repelling two Indian attacks they were exhausted, outnumbered and outgunned: surrender was their only realistic option. But the captain would not

Kashmir, 2001

give up. Instead he ordered a counter-attack. His final battle lasted just a few minutes. By the end of it Karnal Sher Khan was out of ammunition and surrounded by Indian soldiers. Undaunted, he tried to carry on fighting with his rifle butt. The Indians shot him dead. 'It was suicidal for Sher to launch the attack in broad daylight because we could see his movements,' the Indian officer recalled, 'yet in the highest military traditions he launched the attack.'[65]

That much both India and Pakistan could agree on. But virtually every other aspect of Captain Sher Khan's last hours was controversial. At the time the Pakistanis claimed the captain had died at a post on the line of control. The Indians, by contrast, insisted he, and hundreds more Pakistani troops, were well inside Indian-controlled territory. The difficulty for Pakistani officials was that the captain's body was in Indian hands – indeed it had been flown to Delhi. Pressed to explain how the Indians had managed to get the body from the Pakistani side of the line of control, Pakistani spokesmen suggested that the Indians had dragged the corpse across the line so as to mount a propaganda offensive.

The fate of Karnal Sher Khan's remains became an international issue. The Indian authorities, who released television pictures of the body, said they would not hand it over unless Pakistan admitted that the captain had been a member of the army who had been deployed on the Indian side of the line of control. Delhi suggested that Pakistan could send some officials and relatives of the captain to identify the corpse. Pakistan demanded that the remains should be sent to Islamabad for verification.[66] Eventually the two sides reached a compromise: Pakistan did not send anyone to Delhi, but did accept that the captain was a member of its army. Two weeks after Sher Khan died, the Indian government handed over the body to the International Committee of the Red Cross and his coffin, draped in a Pakistani flag, was flown to Karachi.

Three months later, General Musharraf implicitly conceded that Captain Sher Khan had indeed been on the Indian side of the line of control. At a ceremony to pay tribute to the Pakistani soldiers who had died in Kargil, he said that Captain Karnal Sher Khan had killed 15 enemy personnel while carrying out 'offensive defence'.[67] Despite Musharraf's use of the phrase 'offensive defence' and, on another occasion, 'aggressive patrolling', Pakistani officials still insisted, at least in public, that none of their troops were involved in the Kargil campaign. The whole operation, they maintained, was carried out by Kashmiri militants who, on their own initiative, decided to step up their campaign against the Indian forces in Kashmir.

Throughout his time in power, General Musharraf refused to admit that one of his first acts as army chief had been to order his men into Indian-controlled territory in Kashmir and thereby launch the Kargil campaign. His denials were partly explained by his need to be consistent. From the outset he maintained that Kargil was the work not of his soldiers but of militants intent on liberating their homeland. He had his story and he stuck to it. The international community has helped to sustain the myth. In private, foreign governments made it clear to Islamabad from the outset that they simply did not believe the claim that no Pakistani regular troops were involved in the offensive. To mount such a large-scale operation in such harsh terrain, they pointed out, was clearly beyond the capability of the militant groups. But throughout the Kargil campaign politicians in Washington and Europe assiduously avoided making any public accusation about Pakistan's official involvement in Kargil. The furthest they went was to talk about 'Pakistani-backed forces'. The Western diplomats were reticent for a simple reason: they wanted to make it easier for Pakistan to de-escalate the crisis by withdrawing. After all, if Pakistani troops had never crossed the line of control then it was far easier for the Pakistani prime minister, Nawaz Sharif, to withdraw them without losing face.

When they speak 'off the record', Pakistani politicians and army officers freely concede that the denials about Kargil were nothing more than barefaced lies. The Northern Light Infantry, they admit, did cross the line of control. The truth is that, just as in 1947 and 1965, Pakistan tried to fudge its offensive by saying it was carried out by volunteers and not regular troops. In reality the Islamic militants probably accounted for no more than 10 per cent of the total force and were given only portering duties.

For the Pakistani generals who organised the Kargil campaign, it all seemed to start so well. In the spring of 1999 their troops occupied well over 100 square kilometres of Indian-controlled territory without firing a single shot. The operation relied on stealth. Between 1,000 and 2,000 men crossed the line of control (supposedly one of the most heavily guarded frontlines on earth) and moved 10 kilometres into Indian territory before they were even identified. To the considerable embarrassment of India's massive intelligence apparatus, the Pakistani intruders were first spotted by a couple of shepherds. When the Kargil conflict was over, the failure to notice, let alone predict, the incursion was closely examined by an official committee of enquiry in India. The committee's report suggested that the intelligence agencies could perhaps be forgiven: no one could have thought that Pakistan would deploy troops in an area which was so high and so cold that surviving, not to mention fighting, was a major challenge. The report pointed out that over the years the Indian military had undertaken various war-gaming exercises in which the possibility of a Pakistani offensive around Kargil had been considered. Each time it had been ruled out as totally impractical. 'Pakistan's action at Kargil,' the report concluded, 'was not rational.'[68]

India's tactics for controlling the territory around Kargil were largely determined by the area's hostile climate. In view of the fact that the winter temperatures regularly drop to as low as minus 20 degrees Celsius, the Indian army had developed the practice of vacating some of its posts around Kargil each October and then reoccupying them the next March. Pakistan's military planners calculated that if they took advantage of the spring weather a few weeks before the Indians, they could move into Indian territory unopposed – which is exactly what they did.

It is not clear precisely when the operation began, but some Pakistanis, presumably on reconnaissance missions, crossed the line of control as early as October 1998. On 13 October the body of a Northern Light Infantry soldier, Haider Khan, was returned to his village in Pakistan's Northern Areas by four of his NLI comrades. The four men were ordered not to divulge how or where he had died, and Haider Khan's family were given no information. Later it emerged that he was probably the first victim of the Kargil campaign. In June 2000, when the Pakistani government decided to honour the NLI for its role in the Kargil campaign, Haider Khan's name was included in the list of those who had died.[69]

Many more Pakistanis crossed the line of control in the first six weeks of 1999 and established a series of logistics bases on the Indian side. In March their work was held up by heavy snow: an avalanche claimed the lives of some Pakistani troops and the operation had to wait for the weather to clear. By April the conditions had improved and a far larger group of men crossed the line. Not all of them were from the NLI: some were commandos from the Special Services Group and others were civilians recruited from Islamic militant groups. As they went forward, the Pakistani troops and their civilian counterparts moved surreptitiously. The Indians did have regular helicopter flights patrolling the area, but every time the intruders heard a helicopter coming they simply ducked for cover. By the end of April they were both delighted and somewhat amazed that they were still undetected.

The high command in Rawalpindi could not have asked for more. The operation to infiltrate and then dig into Indian-controlled territory had exceeded their expectations. But, as so often with Pakistani military operations, the objectives were somewhat unclear. At a tactical level the plan was simple enough. The planning for Kargil had begun in 1994 when the Indians managed to cut the Neelum Valley road that lay just inside Pakistani-controlled Kashmir. The Indian action was highly disruptive: the Pakistan army was forced to move supplies to the local population by mules until it was able to construct a bypass protected from Indian artillery positions.

As it took stock of what had happened in the Neelum Valley, the Pakistan army considered various possible responses. By 1996 it had drawn up a detailed plan that concentrated on a road from Srinagar to Leh in Indian-controlled Kashmir. It was the only land route available for supplying the Indian troops at the Siachin Glacier. The road had long frustrated Pakistan's military planners. For several years artillery emplacements on the Pakistani side of the line had tried to target the road, but since they were unsighted, hitting it was more a matter of luck than judgement. The planners concluded that if they could hold the high ground above Kargil, they would not only be able to direct artillery fire towards the Srinagar-Leh road with greater accuracy, but also be close enough to use small arms against Indian targets. And if the road was cut, then the Indians would have to move in all their supplies to Siachin by air – a hugely expensive proposition.

Attacking the road, then, was the immediate objective. But the Pakistani strategists had other goals in mind as well. Many senior officers feared that the anti-Indian insurgency was on the wane. They worried that many Kashmiris, tiring of the violence, might settle for a compromise favourable to Delhi. The army hoped that a major operation in Kargil would provide the insurgency with a shot in the arm and thereby keep up the pressure on India. There were also broader objectives. The army hoped that the Kargil incursion would increase the level of international diplomatic involvement in Kashmir. Once the Pakistani move became known, the thinking went, the international community would become concerned about a possible nuclear exchange and exert strong pressure for a ceasefire. Pakistan would not only have increased the amount of territory under its control but would also have drawn international attention to the Kashmir dispute.

The Pakistanis had considered India's likely response to the Kargil incursion. The crucial question was whether India's high command would order a repeat of 1965 and extend the conflict beyond Kashmir by launching an attack on Pakistan itself. General Zia had rejected an earlier version of the Kargil operation precisely on the grounds that it could lead to all-out war with India.[70] The various war-gaming scenarios played out by the Pakistani planners indicated that this was no longer a problem. The Indian army, they figured, still enjoyed a considerable numerical superiority over Pakistan, but the extent of that superiority had steadily diminished throughout the 1990s. The Pakistanis predicted that Delhi would move some divisions from the border with China to Kashmir and would then find that it did not have enough strength to guarantee a victory over Pakistan itself. It was also thought that the nuclear dimension would act as a constraint on Delhi.

India, in short, would find itself in a very awkward position. The Pakistani troops, the plan went, would be occupying posts so high that they were impregnable. According to a late addition to the Pakistani plan, Pakistani-backed militants would then up the ante by launching attacks on military installations throughout Indian-controlled Kashmir. This would serve a number of objectives: the insurgents would be encouraged; the pressure on the Pakistani troops occupying the heights would be relieved; and, because more Indian troops would have to be deployed throughout Kashmir, the risk of an attack on Pakistan would be further reduced. The Pakistan army also calculated that if the plan went wrong for any reason, they could deny involvement and say that militants over whom they had no control had carried out the whole operation. As exit strategies go, this was woefully inadequate. One Pakistani cabinet minister later put it that 'the army had climbed up a pole without considering how it would get down'.[71]

The incursion was eventually discovered in the first week of May. Having been tipped off by the shepherds, Indian army patrols confirmed that a significant number of infiltrators had crossed the line. Delhi, however, still did not appreciate the scale of the Pakistani operation and the Indian prime minister, Atal Behari Vajpayee, was not informed until 9 May.[72] As late as 16 May the defence minister, George Fernandes, was predicting that the 'intruders will be evicted in 48 hours'.[73] It was a hopelessly optimistic assessment. The Pakistanis had dug in on high, very defensible positions. On 21 May the Indian air force conducted an air survey of the Kargil sector. It was only then that Delhi realised what they were up against: the photographs revealed that as many as eight helipads were in place on the Indian side of the line of control.

Atal Behari Vajpayee had a lot to worry about. He was faced with a major political and military challenge. To complicate matters still further, his coalition government led by the Bharatiya Janata Party (BJP) had in March suffered a parliamentary defeat and consequently was in the midst of an election campaign. The opinion polls indicated that Vajpayee was in a precarious position: the outcome of the election was far from certain and anything that could be interpreted as defeat in Kashmir would clearly reduce his chances of winning another term. Vajpayee also felt betrayed. Just three months before, in February 1999, he had gone to Lahore to talk peace with his Pakistani counterpart, Nawaz Sharif. Although the formal text that came out of the summit, the Lahore Declaration, contained only one reference to Kashmir, the two leaders had discussed the issue in some depth. Sharif and Vajpayee had a one-hour session at which no one else was present and during which they reached a private understanding. They agreed that they should try to find a solution to the Kashmir problem by the next millennium or, in other words, by the end of the year. The two prime ministers decided to set up a diplomatic back channel. Each leader would appoint an expert who would be charged with conducting the secret talks. Since the back channel would be entirely deniable, it was hoped that the two sides could discuss fresh approaches to the Kashmir dispute. Vajpayee appointed the prominent Bombay newspaper publisher, R.K. Mishra, and Sharif opted for a retired diplomat, Niaz Naik.

And so began a series of extraordinary meetings. On 27 May, Naik and Mishra met in a luxury suite in Delhi's Imperial Hotel. Having unobtrusively slipped into India on a PIA flight, Naik was determined to keep a very low profile and barely left his room. For several days, between endless rounds of room service, he and Mishra discussed possible solutions to Kashmir. Both agreed that they would have to go beyond their governments' public positions on the issue. Delhi would have to stop talking about Kashmir being an integral part of India and Islamabad would have to stop asking for the implementation of UN resolutions and, in particular, give up the demand for a plebiscite. The two men also agreed that any solution had to be balanced: it must take into account the requirements of Pakistan, India and the Kashmiri people. Having established these initial rules of the game, the two men informed Vajpayee about their discussions. The Indian prime minister added one new element: any solution, he said, must be final and not partial.

Naik and Mishra then started discussing possible solutions. This was in itself a remarkable fact. Two men, directly appointed by the Indian and Pakistani prime ministers, were seriously discussing how to solve the Kashmir dispute. As they did so, the scale of their task became ever clearer. Many proposals were immediately rejected as being unacceptable to one side or the other. Naik ruled out the idea of converting the line of control into a border: 'It's the status quo,' he said. 'If we accept that, then why did we fight two wars?' Mishra was equally dismissive of the idea of Kashmiri independence. India, he argued, could not allow such a precedent for fear that other Indian states would also try to break away. They also rejected other possibilities such as greater autonomy, and a division of Kashmir on the basis of the religious affiliation with Muslim majority areas going to Pakistan and Hindu majority areas to India. Mishra thought the result would be the same as it had been 50 years before, during partition: 'It will result in a blood bath,' he said.[74]

Naik and Mishra in fact knocked down every possibility they could think of. They considered regional plebiscites and models for joint sovereignty. They discussed how the city of Trieste was governed after the Second World War, and they considered the model of the British and Irish governments' arrangements for Northern Ireland. As the discussions continued, the two men gradually came to the point where they shared some ground. If a solution were to endure, it would have to be based on a new, verifiable, clearly defined international border. Kashmir would have to be carved up between Delhi and Islamabad. But where would that border be?

Naik suggested that India should keep everything south and east of the Chenab river. Since Mishra did not know exactly where the river was, Naik went to the hotel bookshop to buy a tourist map. As he looked at the map, Mishra wondered whether maybe it could work. He neither accepted nor rejected the idea. It was progress, and on 1 April Naik and Mishra decided they needed to pause and report back to their prime ministers before meeting again. But it was never to be. The peace initiative was shattered by the Kargil offensive. As soon as the Indians became aware of the Pakistani infiltration, the back channel was diverted from long-term thinking into immediate crisis management. It is difficult to believe that the Chenab river proposal would have been acceptable to the Indian government. Nevertheless, a great opportunity for genuine dialogue had been missed.

Instead of seeking a solution to the Kashmir dispute, Vajpayee was now focused on the immediate task of expelling the Pakistani intruders. On 25 May he approved the use of air power. The next morning the airfield at Srinagar was used to launch over 40 sorties of MiG-21, MiG-23 and MiG-27 fighter aircraft. Mi-17 helicopters were also used for air strikes. The aircraft, however, made little impact. Since many of the targets were located at between 13,000 and 17,000 feet, the planes had to fly in at over 25,000 feet to avoid the Pakistanis' anti-aircraft fire. The Indian pilots descended to around 20,000 feet at the last moment before firing and making good their escape. At these heights the planes and their missiles were pushed beyond their technical limits. The thin mountain air affected the bombs' performance and the Indians found themselves having to recalculate predicted trajectories. And even if they could work out which direction the bombs would take, locating the tiny Pakistani positions in the mountainous terrain was virtually impossible. This was, in part, because the air force could not use its laser-guided bomb systems. Indian officials have claimed that this was because of cost considerations.[75] The real reason was that the Indian forces did not have a direct line of sight to most of the Pakistani positions: it was impossible for Indian ground troops to fix laser beams on any targets.

The Indian aircraft faced another problem. Many of the targets were very close to the line of control and the pilots found it difficult to remain inside Indian-controlled air space. On 27 May the Pakistanis shot down a MiG-27 and a MiG-21, claiming that both had strayed across the line of control. The next day Pakistani troops on the Indian side of the line shot down a Mi-17 helicopter. Concerned by the extent of the losses after just four days of the air campaign, the Indian air force decided to deploy some French-built Mirage 2000 fighter-bombers. The new planes not only had better defensive equipment but also gave the Indians the possibility of flying at night. Indian officials subsequently claimed that the

Mirage planes were far more accurate and enjoyed a far higher success rate than the MiGs.[76] If the Mirages did perform better, that was partly because the air force switched its emphasis from searching for the Pakistani positions on the peaks and instead concentrated on rearward camps and logistics bases. It was a longer-term strategy but it worked: the Pakistani supply lines were successfully disrupted.

The Indian air force may have been improving its performance, but the Indian ground troops still faced a daunting task. The Pakistanis had occupied over 130 separate positions. To reach them the Indian soldiers had to climb thousands of feet. As they approached the summits, they entered a killing zone. The Pakistanis could fire at will, picking off the Indians one by one. Furthermore, the craggy nature of the terrain meant that, on most of the peaks, the Indians could deploy no more than 10 to 20 men in any single attack. If there were more men than that, they would end up forming queues vulnerable to Pakistani attack.

As the Indian army considered its options, it concluded that two Pakistani positions – at Tololung and Tiger Hill – were the most vulnerable. Both had a direct line of sight to the Srinagar-Leh road and to the Indian military cantonment at Dras. From the Pakistani point of view that made the positions invaluable – they could direct accurate fire at the Indians. But the direct line of sight also offered India an opportunity to aim artillery fire back at the Pakistani soldiers. And once a battery of Bofors guns was moved into position that is exactly what happened. The artillery onslaught was unrelenting and forced the Pakistanis to shelter behind the crest of the peaks. That in turn enabled Indian troops to climb up towards the peaks unopposed.

Tololung fell first, but taking the second, Tiger Hill, was still a monumental task. An Indian journalist's account of the battle for Tiger Hill gives an impression of the difficulties the Indians faced:

> Soldiers of three crack infantry units have been at it since mid-May in a vain attempt to dislodge Pakistani troops at the crucial peak. The scenario is near hopeless: hauling yourselves up on ropes at 15,000 odd feet, over a killing 80 degree gradient mountain face, weighed down by 40 kg backpacks, braving icy winds and sub-zero temperatures. Forget enemy guns, even boulders flung from the top take lives.[77]

The decisive battle for Tiger Hill took place on the night of 3 July and lasted 11 hours. The Indian infantry made its move on the evening of that day, planning to reach the 16,000-foot peak around midnight. They attacked from three sides. By that time over 30,000 rounds had been fired into the mountain. As the Indian troops neared the summit the artillery stopped. For the Pakistanis on the summit it might have seemed like a blessed relief, but this didn't last long. The first Indian soldiers to reach the peak ascended an almost vertical cliff. One of them, 19-year-old Yogendra Singh Yadav, later described what happened. 'It was a near-90 degree incline and we had to climb with the help of ropes,' he recalled. Yadav was one of the first to reach the summit and when he got there he could see that the Pakistanis were taken by surprise: they had not expected anyone to make it up the cliff face and consequently had left it undefended. Yadav then saw a bunker in which some Pakistanis were sheltering. 'There were four men inside. I hurled my grenade inside and saw two of them die.' By the time Yadav was joined by the other two assault teams many of the 50 or so Pakistani defenders had decided to slip away and in the end, the Indians said, they found only seven Pakistani bodies on the top.[78]

The recapture of Tololung and Tiger Hill were significant victories for the Indian forces. The Indian defence minister, George Fernandes, caught the mood: 'We will now be able to dictate terms to the intruders. Our army is in a position to do anything,' he said.[79] The truth was very different. The peaks above Dras had only fallen because the Indians had a clear line of sight that enabled them to use artillery fire. Most of the Pakistani positions were not visible to the Indians and it was much more difficult to ensure that artillery shells found their mark. Despite this crucial distinction, the battles above Dras did have a decisive impact. While Indian morale soared, the Pakistani politicians and even some in the military began to wonder whether they had overextended themselves.

When Tiger Hill fell, Nawaz Sharif concluded that the military position was becoming untenable. His military commanders had assured him that all of the positions they had occupied were impregnable. Sharif now believed they had been overconfident. Two important posts, after all, had just been overrun. The military top brass insisted – with considerable justification – that they could still hold on to large tracts of Indian territory, but Sharif no longer trusted their judgement. With the supply lines cut and no chance of sending in reinforcements, he believed it was only a question of time before the Indians secured a complete victory.

Sharif wanted a way out but it was far from clear how he could extricate himself from Kargil. He knew that any order to withdraw would be deeply unpopular and seen by many Pakistani voters as a cowardly abandonment of the Kashmiri cause. But withdrawal, he believed, it had to be. A senior American official involved in the issue described the Pakistani prime minister as 'increasingly desperate as he realised how isolated Pakistan was'.[80] Eventually he decided to go to the United States in search of some political cover. In one of his meetings with President Bill Clinton, Sharif was told, apparently to his surprise, that the Pakistani army was preparing its nuclear arsenal for use.[81] To an extent Clinton provided the cover Sharif was seeking. In return for Sharif's commitment to 'take concrete and immediate steps for the restoration of the line of control' – in other words to withdraw – Clinton agreed to two things. First, he would make no statement about the fact that Pakistani regular troops had been involved in the conflict and, second, he would make a public statement about his personal commitment to finding a solution to the Kashmir dispute. It wasn't much, but it was all Sharif could get.

Indian sources have claimed that by the time Sharif met President Clinton over 80 per cent of the Pakistani intruders had been dislodged from their positions.[82] Neutral observers, probably relying on Pakistani sources, have suggested that the Pakistani troops had been dislodged from only 12 of 134 defended positions.[83] Another estimate suggests that India had overrun only 4 out of 132 positions.[84] Whatever the precise figure, the important point is that Pakistan remained in control of a large area and would in all likelihood have been able to hang onto it for the remaining weeks of the summer. Its troops could then have dug in, maintained a light presence and waited to see whether there would be any diplomatic movement before fighting could resume the next spring. The planned militant attacks on Indian installations in the rest of Kashmir would add to Delhi's discomfort.

The Pakistanis' strength on the ground helps explain why so many in the military establishment resented the order to pull back. The former director general of the ISI, General (retd) Hamid Gul, for example, claimed after the conflict that Sharif 'lost a war in Washington that had already been won in Kargil'. Hamid Gul is known for the extremity of his views, but on this occasion a significant number in the Pakistan military agreed with him. In the days immediately before Sharif went to Washington the army had no plans for a rapid pull-out. On the contrary, some senior officers were still drawing up plans to establish permanent posts on those positions that remained under Pakistani control. The views of the army chief, General Musharraf, remain unclear. Most insiders, though, say that he was in full agreement with Sharif's decision to go to Washington.

Even if Musharraf and Sharif were able to present a united front over Washington, the Kargil campaign did create a deep and lasting rift between the military and civilian leaderships that eventually manifested itself in the October 1999 coup. During his trial, after Musharraf's takeover, Sharif made a remarkable claim that exposed the extent of that divide. He said he had had no advance knowledge of what the army was planning to do in Kargil: 'This ill-planned and ill-conceived opera-tion was kept so secret,' Sharif complained, 'that the Prime Minister, some Corps Commanders and the Chief of Navy and the Air Force were kept in the dark.'[85]

Sharif's comments echoed claims made during the Kargil campaign. On 11 June the Indian government had released two tapes of conversa-tions between General Musharraf and his chief of general staff, Lieutenant General Mohammed Aziz. At the time of the second conversation on 26 May, General Musharraf was on a trip to China and, although it was never clear which intelligence agency had recorded the tapes, no one seriously doubted their authenticity. One remark made by Aziz suggested that the prime minister may indeed have been uninformed about Kargil. Aziz had had a meeting with Nawaz Sharif and he described what had happened to General Musharraf: 'We told him [Sharif] there is no reason for alarm and panic. Then he [Sharif] said that: "I came to know seven days back, when the Corps Commanders were told".' Aziz then told Musharraf how he had told Sharif that 'the entire reason for the success of the operation was total secrecy. Our earlier efforts failed because of lack of secrecy. So the top priority is to accord confidentiality to ensure our success.'[86]

When Indian ministers heard this tape some concluded that Nawaz Sharif had not been told about Kargil in advance. The suggestion fitted in with a remark made by Sharif on 10 May. When Vajpayee had called him that day to complain about the incursion at Kargil, Sharif had claimed he knew nothing about it.[87] The Pakistan army has consistently denied this claim. During the Kargil campaign Musharraf pointedly told a television interviewer that 'everyone was on board' the Kargil operation. Sharif's and Musharraf's versions contradict each other. But there is considerable evidence that the military did hold back significant amounts of crucial information from the prime minister.

Army officers claim that the Kargil operation was first mentioned to Sharif in a meeting that took place in the ISI office, Lahore, in February 1999. The meeting was routine and took the form of a regular quarterly briefing in which the ISI briefed the civilian leadership about latest developments in Kashmir. As usual, the ISI invited the prime minister, the chief of army staff and some of their senior colleagues. According to the military version, Sharif was told about Kargil at this meeting. Army officers say the prime minister had a famously short attention span and he may not have fully understood everything that he was told. They claim that Sharif seemed bored by the briefing he was being given and asked for it to be shortened.

Sharif and two other participants at the meeting[88] have a different version. They say that although there was talk about the need to bolster the insurgency, no one ever mentioned the possibility of the Northern Light Infantry being deployed in Kashmir. Indeed, it would have been unusual for such an issue to be raised at the ISI briefing. For many years the military operations in Kashmir had been the preserve of the army, while the ISI had responsibility for supporting the insurgency. If the army was planning an initiative in Kashmir, it would have been more normal for it to organise a separate briefing for the prime minister either in his office or in army headquarters in Rawalpindi.

The February meeting is of interest because it took place before the Lahore summit and raises the possibility that Nawaz Sharif knew about the plan to deploy troops in Indian-controlled Kashmir when he invited Atal Behari Vajpayee for talks. But no one suggests that any final decisions were taken in February. As far as the army is concerned, the prime minister granted his formal approval of the Kargil plan in the second week of March at a meeting held at ISI headquarters in Islamabad. The meeting was attended by the ISI chief General Ziauddin, the chief of army staff General Musharraf and his two most powerful colleagues, Generals Mehmood and Mohammed Aziz. The air force and navy chiefs and other corps commanders were excluded. On the political side Sharif was joined by his religious affairs minister Raja Zafar ul-Haq, his foreign minister Sartaj Aziz and the minister for Kashmir affairs, Lieutenant General (retd) Majid Malik.

Two eyewitnesses at this meeting have claimed that even this stage (when the military intervention was already well under way) there was no mention of troops crossing the line of control. According to their version, although there was talk of increasing the level of militant activity in Kashmir, the discussion was framed entirely in terms of the insurgency. The army stated its fear that the resistance movement could die out. It argued that if the Lahore process was to bear fruit then the Indians must be made to believe that the pressure in Kashmir would not go away. The army failed to disclose the role of the Northern Light Infantry and did not identify Kargil as a military objective.[89] It's widely agreed, however, that at this meeting the army secured Sharif's agreement to 'increase the heat' in Kashmir. The intriguing question is whether the army wilfully misinterpreted an endorsement of increased militant activity as an order to go ahead with the full-blown Kargil campaign. According to the Sharif version of events, that is exactly what happened and he was not told about the role of the NLI until after the Indians had discovered the intrusion in early May. In a meeting in the second week of that month, one participant recalled, 'Sharif heard it for the first time.' It is an incredible claim that, if accurate, would lend weight to the Indian allegation that Pakistan has a rogue army.

It is difficult to draw firm conclusions about what happened in the run-up to Kargil. The two versions are utterly contradictory. The most likely explanation is that the army did tell Sharif what was happening, but for a number of reasons a full discussion did not develop. First, the army did not believe that Kargil would become such a big issue. The planners thought they were mounting a relatively limited operation. Had the Pakistani intrusion been discovered and stopped earlier, this is exactly what would have happened. Secondly, Sharif never took much interest in detailed military matters. If the army wanted to scrap for a few posts near the line of control he was not the man stop them. Thirdly, the army would not have wanted Sharif to get too closely involved in the decision-making process. Senior officers not only resented civilian involvement in such issues, but also wanted to keep the whole matter secret. It's widely accepted that those corps commanders who were not directly involved in Kargil were not told about it until after it had happened.

Yet even if one takes the army's version at face value, it indicates a hopelessly inadequate approach to decision-making. The army's claim that Sharif was told about Kargil in advance but failed to take in what he was told suggests that nothing was put down on paper. It indicates that, at the very least, there was no thoroughgoing debate about the implications of the Kargil operation. The foreign office was not asked for its opinion and little thought was given to what would happen if India responded with a major counter-attack. Just as in 1965, no one seemed to scrutinise the prediction (this time accurate) that India would not extend the war beyond Kashmir and launch an attack across the international boundary. It was a remarkably casual way for a nuclear power to run a war.

Kargil was a disaster for Pakistan. Afterwards the international community insisted with even greater vehemence than hitherto that the line of control was inviolable and that Pakistan should respect its sanctity. For all its efforts to concentrate world opinion on India's human rights abuses in Kashmir, Pakistan had instead managed to enhance its image as an aggressive and unpredictable state.

Musharraf after Kargil

When General Musharraf grabbed power in Islamabad in October 1999, he espoused the traditional Pakistani position on Kashmir. He believed the former Princely State was an integral part of Pakistan and that, in accordance with UN resolutions, there should be a plebiscite of the Kashmiri people so that they could achieve self-determination. He supported the Pakistan-backed Kashmiri insurgency as the only way to put pressure on Delhi. He insisted that improved relations between India and Pakistan were contingent on a resolution of the Kashmir dispute. Kashmir trumped all other bilateral issues. 'There is no other dispute,' he said.[90]

In theory, previous Pakistani governments had taken much the same line. But in practice they had repeatedly veered away from it. When Benazir Bhutto became prime minister in 1988, for example, she reached out to her Indian counterpart, Rajiv Gandhi, despite his having given no ground on Kashmir. The two leaders set up a hotline between Islamabad and Delhi and signed an agreement on nuclear safety: 'The Prohibition of Attack Against Nuclear Installations and Facilities'. A decade later Benazir's great political rival, Nawaz Sharif, invited the Indian prime minister, Atal Behari Vajpayee, to Lahore. In the Lahore Declaration of February 1999, Pakistan agreed in principle to some confidence-building measures despite, again, India making no movement on Kashmir. On the contrary, if anything, Vajpayee secured a Pakistani concession in the form of a reiteration by Sharif that the dispute should be resolved bilaterally. Although this had always been the formal position, as stated in the Simla Accord, Pakistan had repeatedly called for third-party mediation. The Lahore Declaration reaffirmed that it was a bilateral matter.

On both these occasions the Pakistani military was suspicious that the civilians were making too many concessions. And on both occasions it undermined the peace initiatives. Bhutto's attempt to forge a relationship with Rajiv Gandhi was overwhelmed by the ISI's increasing support for the Kashmiri insurgency. And nearly a decade later, even as Nawaz Sharif was signing the Lahore Declaration, his army was launching the Kargil operation in Indian-controlled Kashmir. But although the military seemed unwilling to accept civilian leaders making overtures to Delhi, the army had in fact made very similar moves when it was in power. In 1987, for example, General Zia ul-Haq famously engaged in 'cricket diplomacy' by attending a test match between India and Pakistan in Jaipur and then reaching a series of understandings that helped reduce a build-up of armed forces on both sides of the Rajasthan Desert – all this despite securing no concessions on Kashmir.

Over the years, then, Pakistan had given some mixed messages on Kashmir. Although it demanded a resolution of the issue on its terms, it had failed to implement a consistent diplomatic policy to achieve that goal. That was one reason why Kashmiri activists were so encouraged by General Musharraf's coup. As the architect of the Kargil campaign, Musharraf's credibility on the Kashmir issue was insurmountable and Kashmiri activists believed he would take a hard line. They were wrong.

Although General Musharraf had in the past given some very general thought to what a solution to Kashmir might look like,[91] the first indication that he might be willing to show real flexibility came in July 2001. In a move that caught the imagination of the South Asian media, the Indian prime minister Atal Behari Vajpayee invited Musharraf to talk peace in the city of Agra. The general seized the initiative by telling a group of Indian journalists that he was willing to 'move on all issues in tandem'.[92] In other words, a solution to Kashmir did not have to precede discussion of any other issues. At the same time, he argued, India had to recognise the centrality of the Kashmir dispute.

The most remarkable aspect of Agra was that the two leaders had not asked officials to negotiate a draft agreement in advance of their encounter. After Agra collapsed, Musharraf and Vajpayee were scoffed at by professional diplomats who argued that the two leaders had been naive in thinking they could reach agreement themselves. In fact, they had good reasons for using such an unconventional negotiating technique. In the past various initiatives had failed because civil servants in Delhi and Islamabad were so afraid of being accused of a sell-out that they stuck rigidly to their most hardline national positions, guaranteeing that no progress could be made.

The approach of the two leaders may have been brave and innovative, but it did not work: the Agra summit collapsed amidst great acrimony. According to General Musharraf's version the two leaders, in a one-on-one session, actually wrote a joint declaration. As Musharraf was getting ready for the signing ceremony, his officials told him that the Indians had backed out. As a military ruler Musharraf had little sympathy for the constraints under which Vajpayee was working. 'There is the man and the moment,' he later wrote. 'When man and moment meet history is made. Vajpayee failed to grasp the moment and lost his moment in history.'[93]

As well as criticising what he saw as Vajpayee's weakness, General Musharraf was quite clear in pinning blame for the collapse of the summit on the hardline Indian nationalist and deputy prime minister, Lal Krishna Advani. 'The Agra summit saw a great breakthrough,' Musharraf later wrote on his presidential blog, 'but ended up in a disappointing failure under the negative influence of some radical Indian Government functionaries in particular Mr. Advani.'[94] It's a reasonable conclusion. Despite having the support of his foreign minister, Jaswant Singh, Vajpayee could not get the declaration past Advani, who wanted a clear statement that the violence in Kashmir was terrorism, not freedom-fighting. In explaining the failure of Agra, Advani later said that in 'all the drafts prepared they were not willing to concede that there is any such thing like terrorism.'[95] Vajpayee has subsequently confirmed that this was indeed the problem: 'During the talks, he [General Musharraf] took a stand that the violence that was taking place in Jammu and Kashmir could not be described as terrorism. He continued to claim that the bloodshed in the State was nothing but the people's battle for freedom.'[96]

As the dust was settling on the Agra summit, General Musharraf faced a crisis that reinforced the idea that the time had come for a rethink of Pakistan's Kashmir policy. The 9/11 attacks raised an obvious difficulty. There was a very real possibility that the US would now perceive the Pakistan-backed insurgents as jihadis not unlike those who attacked America. When the insurgency had begun in 1988 most of the fighters had been Kashmiri nationalists. Over the years these relatively secular fighters had been joined by better-financed, Pakistan-based, jihadi outfits, some of which had training camps in Afghanistan. The connection between what had been happening in Afghanistan and what was still going on in Kashmir was plain for all to see. Nevertheless, immediately after 9/11 General Musharraf did his best to obscure the link and American officials agreed not to push the point. Apart from wondering whether Kashmir could become a safe haven for the Taliban and Al Qaeda, they could not see any reason to open up another front line: 'We did not treat it as part of the war on terror,' recalled Ashley J. Tellis, who was based at the US embassy in Delhi at the time.[97] That stance, however, proved to be unsustainable.

On 13 December 2001, five men armed with AK-47s, plastic explosives and grenades drove towards the Indian Parliament. Their car, an Ambassador, was of the kind used by many Indian ministers. Since it was painted with official markings and had a red light on its roof, the guards assumed that it was on legitimate business. As the car drew up to the Parliament building, the occupants were eventually challenged. The five men then seemed to panic. They jumped out of the vehicle and started firing. During a 30-minute gun battle the attackers killed six Indian security personnel and a gardener before they, too, were shot down.[98] Nobody claimed responsibility for the attack, but Indian leaders immediately blamed the ISI and two Pakistan-backed militant organisations, Lashkar-e-Toiba and Jaish-e-Mohammed. On 26 December the Americans implicitly accepted the Indian claim by putting both groups on the State Department's list of designated terrorist organisations.

India responded to the attack with predictable fury. 'Our fight is now entering the last stage,' Atal Behari Vajpayee told the Indian people in a televised address. 'A decisive battle [will] have to take place.'[99] In time-honoured fashion the Indian government withdrew its high commissioner from Islamabad and cut rail and other transport links. But it also went much further. Hundreds of thousands of Indian troops were deployed on the Pakistani border.

With the international community fearing war, Musharraf was now under growing pressure to reverse Pakistan's long-standing policy of backing the Kashmiri insurgency. His response broke new ground. On 12 January 2002 he delivered a major speech in which he declared that 'violence and terrorism have been going on for years and we are weary and sick of this Kalashnikov culture'.[100] He went on to announce bans on both Jaish-e-Mohammed and Lashkar-e-Toiba. Jaish had not existed for long. It had been founded by Mullah Masood Azhar, a former Harakat ul-Ansar member, after he was released from an Indian prison in December 1999 in exchange for 155 hostages who were on board a hijacked Indian Airlines plane forced to land in Afghanistan. Within weeks Mullah Masood was recruiting new members for his organisation at a series of public rallies in Pakistan. Musharraf's decision to ban Jaish was partly motivated by the fact that on 1 October 2001 a Jaish suicide bomber had killed himself and 38 others by driving a truck full of explosives into the legislative assembly building in Srinagar. Coming so soon after 9/11 it was perhaps inevitable that the operation was perceived as a terrorist attack rather than as a legitimate action in a freedom struggle.

The second group to be banned, Lashkar-e-Toiba, was based on a 190-acre site in the town of Muridke just outside Lahore. Lashkar-e-Toiba had always put Islam at the heart of its ideology. It wasn't just fighting for the liberation of Kashmir but also for its Islamisation. In fact, Lashkar's extreme Islamic radicalism – manifested, for example, by throwing acid in the faces of Kashmiri women who did not wear a burqa – managed to alienate the organisation from many of the people it was supposed to be liberating.[101] Lashkar had also demonstrated the extent of its extremism by mounting operations not only in Indian-controlled Kashmir but also in India itself. In December 2000 it had claimed responsibility for a suicide attack on an Indian army installation inside the Red Fort in Delhi. And while, a year later, Lashkar denied involvement in the attack on the Indian Parliament, few doubted that Lashkar was perfectly capable of mounting such an operation.

Although he banned Lashkar and Jaish, Musharraf did not abandon the insurgency altogether. He made no move against the most prominent of all the militant groups active in Kashmir, Hizb ul-Mujahideen. Like Jaish and Lashkar, Hizb ul-Mujahideen had many close links with Pakistan. Besides its relationship with Jamaat-e-Islami, its leader, Syed Salahuddin, was based in Pakistani-controlled Kashmir. Despite that, Hizb ul-Mujahideen had managed to sustain its image as a predominantly indigenous group, not least because some 80 per cent of its militants were of Kashmiri origin. Unlike Lashkar and Jaish, Hizb ul-Mujahideen had never required its recruits to be strongly religious.[102] Musharraf was also able to argue that Hizb ul-Mujahideen had few links with Afghanistan. Although it had had some camps there in the past, the Taliban, which was hostile to Jamaat-e-Islami, had closed them down.

Musharaff's 12 January speech made a huge impact in Pakistan. For the first time in decades a Pakistani leader seemed to be charting a genuinely new course: 'No organisation will be able to carry out terrorism on the pretext of Kashmir,' he declared.[103] But there were still doubts about the apparent U-turn. Certainly India was unconvinced and maintained its heavy troop deployments on the border. The risk of war, possibly nuclear war, did not go away. Western capitals took the threat seriously, with the US embassy in Delhi even considering the construction of a hardened bunker to give its diplomats some chance of surviving a nuclear exchange.[104] In the end the US and British governments settled on a travel warning and partial evacuation of their embassies in Delhi. It was an astute move. India's politicians were forced to realise that their sabre-rattling with Pakistan jeopardised inward foreign investment and the economic growth that came with it.

But even if Delhi was beginning to see that its threats were empty, Vajpayee needed more Pakistani concessions before he could persuade the Indian electorate that the troops should be demobilised. In June 2002 the US deputy secretary of state, Richard Armitage, paid a visit to General Musharraf to see what might be on offer. A veteran diplomat with a famously blunt manner, Armitage spent the next two hours probing Musharraf, asking, 'What can I tell the Indians?' Musharraf had already pledged to halt terrorist infiltrations in the Indian-controlled part of Kashmir. Armitage wanted to go a step further: Would Musharraf now promise a 'permanent end' to the terrorist activity long encouraged by Pakistan? 'Yes,' Musharraf replied.[105] It was a major development reversing over a decade of policy.

After Musharraf made the commitment to Armitage, the level of infiltration across the line of control declined rapidly. Militant leaders complained that for the first time in 13 years, Pakistani soldiers were not only failing to help fighters cross the line of control but also actually blocking them. 'Now we have two armies against us,' one said, 'the Indian and Pakistani. Our problems have doubled.'[106] But General Musharraf wasn't yet ready to abandon the Kashmir cause entirely. To keep the militants on side he increased the payments made to them by the military and in the autumn of 2002 he allowed them to resume their campaign, albeit on a reduced scale. He was hoping to disrupt the October 2002 Kashmir elections, and prevent India claiming that there had been a free and fair vote and a significant step towards the normal-isation of the political process there. As polling day drew closer,

Pakistani-based militant groups confirmed that Islamabad had given them the green light to resume small-scale infiltrations.[107] The Pakistan army's strategy was to encourage 'smaller but better' forces to carry on the insurgency.

Inevitably, Delhi and Washington noticed the resumption of infiltrations across the line of control and wondered whether Musharraf's stated policy on Kashmir amounted to a tactical feint rather than a genuinely new approach. Not for the first time (nor the last) Musharraf found himself caught between two competing camps: domestic hardliners and international opinion. Whilst he reassured some at home that the struggle for Kashmir would continue, he simultaneously had to convince the West that he was serious about changing the policy. Inevitably, the process involved some ducking and weaving as he appeased one group and then the next. His attempts to satisfy both camps made it difficult to establish where he stood. So what was he thinking?

Ever since he had come to power General Musharraf had faced increasing evidence that the Kashmiri people themselves were becoming exhausted by the struggle. While many Kashmiris continued to view the Indian forces as repressive occupiers, they were at the same time becoming disillusioned by an insurgency that seemed unlikely to deliver results. Pakistan-based militants were making up an ever-greater proportion of the insurgents. An increasingly clear split emerged between indigenous and Pakistan-based militant organisations. While some of the indigenous groups maintained their traditional pro-Pakistan position, most were now fighting a traditional, pro-independence struggle to expel what they saw as the occupying Indian army. Aware of the evolving views of the Kashmiri people, the relatively indigenous, nationalist groups showed greater flexibility than their more religious counterparts. Hizb ul-Mujahideen, for example, announced a ceasefire in July 2000. Although it did not hold, many Kashmiris were delighted by this development: they may have admired the militants' bravery, and shared their anti-Indian sentiment, but they were also increasingly sceptical that the jihadis really represented Kashmiri opinion.

Assessing public opinion in Kashmir is difficult. Elections in Indian-controlled Kashmir have been so routinely rigged that they are no guide. Furthermore, the security situation and highly charged political atmosphere mean people are reluctant to give honest opinions to strangers. In 2002, however, there were two serious attempts to discover what Kashmiris were thinking.

In March 2002 a British company, MORI, polled 850 people in Jammu and Kashmir. Inevitably the exercise had some flaws. MORI asked its Indian affiliate to carry out the survey and many Kashmiris feared it was a thinly disguised attempt by the authorities in Delhi to identify militant sympathisers. Some of the responses did not ring true. For example, an implausibly high number of respondents – 54 per cent – expressed the opinion that human rights violations by the Indian security forces in Jammu and Kashmir were non-existent. Nonetheless, some of the findings were in line with the anecdotal evidence that had been reaching the army leadership in Rawalpindi for the previous two or three years. No fewer than 88 per cent of the people said they wanted militant infiltration across the line of control to stop. Those surveyed wanted the Kashmiri people (as opposed to Delhi and Islamabad) to be at the forefront of the search for a settlement: 86 per cent said the first step should be the election of genuine Kashmiri representatives through free and fair elections. In a sign of how much ground Pakistan had lost, 61 per cent said they would be politically and economically better off as Indian citizens compared to 6 per cent who thought they would benefit materially from Pakistani citizenship. Strangely, the MORI pollsters did not ask the respondents about independence.[108]

The second survey was conducted by the International Crisis Group (ICG) and involved interviews with a smaller sample of 80 people in Srinagar and the Kashmir Valley.[109] The ICG found that although many believed the Kashmiri militants were justified in fighting what they viewed as oppressive Indian rule, they were also exhausted by the conflict and sceptical of Pakistan's motives in Kashmir. Of the poll respondents, 70 per cent favoured the borders between Pakistan and Indian Kashmir being opened for more trade and cultural exchange.

The Pakistan-based militant groups knew full well that their support in Kashmir was gradually eroding and they took out their frustration on General Musharraf. On 14 December 2003, as Musharraf was being driven to Army House in Rawalpindi, his car was blown off the ground. Explosives had been packed into the base of a bridge on which his convoy regularly travelled. The attackers had tried to detonate their huge bomb with a remote-control device that failed because of a radar-jamming system fitted to the general's car. The radio signal to the bomb got through a few seconds too late, once the general's car had passed. Makeshift repairs were still being made to the bridge when there was a second attempt on his life. On 25 December the general was crossing the bridge again and this time the attackers used a different tactic. Just after the bridge they had lined up three suicide bombers in Suzuki vans packed with explosives. All three failed to hit their target. The first drove into a policeman and detonated too early. The second was rammed by a police van and again missed its mark. The third never materialised: the bomber either reckoned the deed had been done or simply took fright and drove away.

Mobile-phone records enabled the Pakistani authorities to arrest virtually all of those involved in the two plots. Musharraf was appalled to discover that some of those responsible belonged to Pakistan-based Kashmiri militant organisations that for years had been trained and supported by the Pakistan army. General Headquarters in Rawalpindi perceived the assassination attempts as a gross act of betrayal by former clients. The attacks made a difference. General Musharraf could see in starkest possible terms that there was some truth in the repeated warnings of Pakistani liberals who had long argued that supporting jihadis in Kashmir risked blow-back in Pakistan. In international terms the assassination attempts helped Musharraf convince sceptical Westerners that he was indeed serious about tackling the militants. It was difficult, after all, to counter the argument that he wanted to confront those who were trying to kill him.

Musharraf's thinking on Kashmir was also affected by economic and regional factors. He believed that Pakistan's economic prospects would be greatly improved if Pakistan and India could trade. Traditionally Pakistani generals, like their Indian counterparts, had tended to measure each other's power in strictly military terms. But in the 1990s India's economic deregulation had led to sustained, substantial economic growth. Increasingly, the Pakistan army could see that economics played a part in the military balance. India, with its vast population and growing inward investment, would be able to out-gun Pakistan. To compete, Pakistan needed growth of its own – and the most obvious way to secure it was to end the decades-long ban on trade with India itself. Furthermore, the military's hold on power in Pakistan was always going to be tighter if it could deliver a rising standard of living to the Pakistani people.

There were other regional considerations – not least the lessons General Musharraf had been forced to learn from the Kargil stand-off. Although he adeptly managed to shunt the blame for his own adventurism onto Nawaz Sharif, he could not avoid the conclusion that during the Kargil crisis the Pakistani army's tactical military success counted for nothing: the threat of international isolation had forced it to retreat. Musharraf had come to understand that victory in Kashmir could not be achieved by military means alone. The experience of Kargil also changed opinions within Kashmir. The idea that Pakistan was making sacrifices for the eventual well-being of the Kashmiri people had been replaced by a more sceptical belief that Pakistan was serving its own national interests. The Pakistani withdrawal had made many Kashmiris think that, when it came to the crunch, Pakistan would put its own relationship with the international community ahead of the hopes and aspirations of the Kashmiri people.

As well as considering these developments within Kashmir and Pakistan, Musharraf had to be mindful of changing US perceptions. From the start of his presidency, Bill Clinton had considered the idea of forging a new relationship with India. Ironically, the Indian nuclear test of 1998 made that easier. Washington became actively engaged in managing India's de facto nuclear status. Clinton's deputy secretary of state, Strobe Talbott, and the Indian foreign minister, Jaswant Singh, held no fewer than 14 face-to-face sessions over two and a half years. Traditionally, Washington would have taken care to balance such encounters with a similar number of meetings with Pakistani officials. But the US perceptions had changed. India's democratic record, coupled with its expanding economic might, meant that the US no longer saw the need to treat India and Pakistan as diplomatic equals. For Pakistani politicians and diplomats Talbott's memoir makes grim reading. They are portrayed as insecure, unreliable, aggressive, unsophisticated fantasists. India, on the other hand, is described as an emerging great power with which the US needs a better relationship. Furthermore, although most of the Talbott–Singh dialogue centred on nuclear issues, it had significant ramifications for Kashmir. The US administration no longer perceived Kashmir as a legitimate dispute. Echoing language used by the Indian foreign minister, Talbott had come to see the Pakistani dream of recovering Kashmir as a 'fantasy'.[110]

Composite Dialogue

For a number of reasons, then, Musharraf's Kashmir policy was changing and he did communicate his developing ideas to the Indians. After the failure at Agra, Atal Behari Vajpayee had again suggested a private back channel of communication. Musharraf was represented by Tariq Aziz, his trusted friend and secretary of Pakistan's National Security Council. The Indian interlocutor was Satinder K. Lambah, a former high commissioner to Islamabad. Although the details of their talks remained secret, the public manifestations of their private diplomacy soon became evident.

In November 2003, Musharraf announced a unilateral ceasefire along the line of control. There had been so many ceasefires in the past that the statement made little impact, and many remained sceptical that this one would last. But it did. India reciprocated and the artillery exchanges came to a halt. Within weeks the two sides had also agreed some confidence-building measures including the restoration of transportation links. The next month Musharraf gave a television interview in which he remarked that there were 10 to 12 possible solutions to the Kashmir dispute, although he didn't give any details of what he had in mind.[111] A couple of weeks later he made a much more significant statement in which he confirmed a major concession that he had earlier hinted at: the long-standing Pakistani demand for a plebiscite in Kashmir could be dropped. 'We are for United Nations Security Council resolutions,' he said. 'However, now we have left that aside. If we want to resolve this issue, both sides need to talk to each other with flexibility, coming beyond stated positions, meeting halfway somewhere. We are prepared to rise to the occasion, India has to be flexible also.'[112]

A few weeks later, Atal Behari Vajpayee was in Islamabad for a summit of the South Asia Association for Regional Cooperation, where he signed up to a statement very like the one that he had agreed with Nawaz Sharif back in Lahore five years previously. But this time there were two important differences. First, the back-channel diplomacy had allowed a degree of trust to be built up between the two sides. Second, Vajpayee was no longer dealing with a civilian prime minister who could be undermined by the army: he had secured agreement from the Pakistan army itself. Even though the Islamabad Declaration was a significant achievement for Vajpayee, he was not to get the chance to see it through.

Within four months Vajpayee had been voted out of office and it fell to Manmohan Singh to keep up the 'composite dialogue' with Pakistan. He did just that. More confidence-building measures were agreed including a bus service across the line of control, meaning that families which had been separated for decades could at last be reunited. Interestingly, the militants opposed the bus service, fearing it would help persuade the Kashmiri people that there could be significant benefits in settling for something less than a complete end to Indian occupation. There was also significant progress on bilateral trade which by 2006 was worth $1 billion a year.[113]

The Indians were becoming increasingly convinced that Musharraf was serious about implementing his commitment permanently to stop infiltration across the line of control. In December 2004 India's chief of army staff, General N.C. Vij, reported that the level of infiltration across the line was 90 per cent lower in October and November compared to the same period a year before.[114] Mosques in Pakistan were told to stop taking financial collections for militants fighting in Kashmir.[115] A further sign of the Pakistani's serious intent came in the form of three resettlement camps, within Pakistan itself, for Kashmiri militants who gave up the fight. In a complete reversal of past practice, militant leaders now received payoffs for not fighting: they got $800 for stopping their fight and another $800 for settling into civilian life by getting married.[116]

There were, however, limits as to how far Musharraf would go. He made it clear from the outset that he could not accept India's preferred option of making the line of control into an international border. For its part Delhi insisted there could be no change to its international borders and no division of Kashmir along religious lines. With those conditions in mind General Musharraf narrowed his 10 or 12 solutions on Kashmir to a four-point plan. He proposed that Kashmir be geographically defined, gradually demilitarised, given powers of self-governance; and that some parts of Kashmir be subject to joint Indian, Pakistani and Kashmiri supervision. As part of the plan, the line of control would be opened up and made irrelevant. In the event of a solution along these lines, Pakistan would be willing to give up its claim to Kashmir.[117]

These were genuinely ground breaking proposals and, according to some Pakistanis involved in the process, they nearly produced an agreement. President Musharraf's foreign minister Khurshid Kasuri has said that the two sides had 'worked out everything' for an agreement on Sir Creek.[118] They had also drawn up 'certain schedules of disengagement' for Siachin, although Kasuri added that while some elements of the Indian government wanted to compromise on Siachin, others did not. On Kashmir, Kasuri said, the two sides had made progress in the four areas identified by Musharraf. On demilitarisation, he said, the principle but not the detail had been agreed: there was also common understanding on regionalisation which meant allowing people to cross the line of control more easily, greater self-rule for Kashmiris on both sides of the line, and finally, the overarching joint mechanism.

The problem according to Khurshid Kasuri was 'sheer bad luck': just as the Sir Creek deal was due to be signed in early 2007, President Musharraf sacked the chief justice, Iftikhar Chaudhry, thereby starting a process in which the president's authority steadily drained away. Musharraf was no longer strong enough to sell an agreement to the Pakistani people. The Indians, meanwhile, were going through five state elections, so from their side too it was a difficult time to be making concessions. Fearing that public rejection of the agreement on either side of the border would waste all their hard-won diplomatic ground, both sides agreed to delay.

That is Kasuri's version. Others believe India got cold feet. In his autobiography General Musharraf complained that on the issue of Kashmir: 'the initial signs of sincerity and flexibility that I sensed in Manmohan Singh seem to be withering away. I think the Indian establishment – the bureaucrats, diplomats and intelligence agencies and perhaps even the military – has gotten the better of him.'[119] After Kasuri went public with his view that a deal had nearly been reached, Indian officials downplayed his remarks as just 'Kasuri's perception.'[120] The chief minister of Kashmir certainly thought India had missed a great opportunity and had 'funked it' by failing to reach a deal with Musharraf whilst he was in power.[121] Officials in Delhi said their reluctance was in part due to concern that any deal made by Musharraf would not stick once he was out of power. These sceptics felt their doubts were vindicated when, following his fall from power, Lashkar-e-Toiba, which they presumed was acting on the instructions of the ISI, once again started mounting attacks in Kashmir and in 2009 in Mumbai.[122]

With so much international attention on Iraq and Afghanistan, Pakistan received very little international recognition for its concessions over Kashmir. It had, after all, stopped support for the insurgency and given up the demand for a plebiscite. Before Musharraf such policies seemed unimaginable. Islamabad has difficulty claiming credit for its moves, in part because it can hardly boast about changing a policy – support for the insurgency – the existence of which it had always denied. Musharraf was also fearful that if he made too many public statements about his new Kashmir policy he would provoke a domestic political backlash. US pressure on India could have made a difference, but that was never likely to happen. Like President Clinton before him, President Bush apparently decided before he took office that improved relations with India could be one of his memorable legacies.[123] America's tilt towards India under Clinton became a lurch under Bush and culminated in a deal that implicitly recognised India's right to possess nuclear weapons.

India has won diplomatic victories in Europe too. When it comes to defining Kashmiri militants as terrorists, the European Union has gone even further than the US. Recognising the largely indigenous and relatively nationalist nature of Hizb ul-Mujahideen, Washington has never designated it as a terrorist organisation, instead listing it as a 'group of concern'. In November 2005, however, the EU did name Hizb ul-Mujahideen as a terrorist organisation. And the EU's sympathy for the Indian position reached a new level in 2006 when the Liberal Democrat MEP, Emma Nicholson, presented a report on Kashmir to the EU Foreign Affairs Committee. In a very pro-Indian document she casually dismissed the Kashmiri case for self-determination. She criticised General Musharraf's attempts to stop the movement of militants across the line of control as insufficient, and described the demand for a plebiscite as 'meaningless' and 'wholly out of step with the needs of the local people and thus damaging to their interests'.[124]

Partly because it was so encouraged by these various developments, India missed the opportunity Musharraf presented to resolve the Kashmir dispute. As soon as he fell from power in August 2008, Pakistan reverted to a more hawkish stance. On the election campaign trail in 2008, civilian politicians made bellicose, populist statements about Kashmir. In Kashmir itself in the summer of 2008 there was an outburst of frustration and anger resulting in some of the biggest ever protests in Kashmir as hundreds of thousands of Muslim demonstrators took to the streets, showing once again that even if their movement was coloured by outside intervention, at its heart lay an indigenous demand for, as the protestors put it, 'freedom'. The authorities imposed an indefinite curfew in all parts of the Kashmir Valley for the first time in 13 years. The spark had been a decision by the Kashmiri authorities to grant some land to a Hindu shrine in a cave that housed a large ice stalagmite. But few doubted that the underlying cause for the unrest was the continued resentment at oppressive Indian rule and the failure to achieve anything remotely resembling a permanent solution in Kashmir. While most of the protestors spoke of their desire for independence, rather than union with Pakistan, the unrest reflected a realisation by many Kashmiris that the hope of any genuine movement, which Musharraf had represented, had been thwarted by Indian intransigence.

Despite the fact that the Indian forces repeatedly fired on protestors, the demonstrations for the most part remained peaceful. But there were some violent incidents. In July 2008, Hizb ul-Mujahideen claimed responsibility for a bomb attack which killed nine soldiers travelling in a bus near Srinagar.[125] There was also a reversion to previous patterns of conduct on the line of control. In July 2008 the Indians complained that small-arms fire across the line had resulted in the death of an Indian soldier and amounted to 'the biggest violation of the ceasefire in the last five years'.[126]

By the time Musharraf left office, then, the situation in Kashmir was looking grim, with the Kashmiri people once again on the streets expressing their view that the status quo was unacceptable. In Islamabad meanwhile, the new president, Asif Ali Zardari, infuriated many Pakistanis by describing the militants in Kashmir as terrorists. He insisted that India was not a threat to Pakistan and, a businessman to the core, repeatedly stated that Pakistan's economic salvation lay in increased trade with India.[127] His desire to pick up where Musharraf left off may well have been genuine. But it was likely to be frustrated. As a civilian leader it would be far harder for President Zardari to get military agreement for significant compromises over Kashmir than it would have been for Musharraf. Furthermore, with the insurgency on the Afghan border gaining ever greater strength, the option of relieving the pressure in the northwest of Pakistan by diverting the militants back to Kashmir looked increasingly attractive.

The fight for Kashmir has been hugely costly, and not only in terms of human life. The sustained conflict between the two biggest powers in South Asia has held back the region's economic development. For Pakistan the conflict has carried an especially high price. Not only has the Kashmir issue diverted attention from more important national objectives, such as reducing poverty, it has also contributed to a destabilising radicalisation of opinion among youths in Pakistan. India, too, has suffered because of Kashmir: the dream of Gandhian principles governing the world's largest democracy has been shattered by the Indian security forces' brutal suppression of Kashmiri opinion. Ever since 1947 the views of the Kashmiris themselves have been obscured by the dispute between India and Pakistan. Most Kashmiris are sick of conflict and desperate for a peaceful settlement. But for both India and Pakistan the symbolic importance of the Kashmir dispute means that they will inevitably follow their own perceived national interests rather than those of the Kashmiri people. If the Kashmiris had been conducting a straightforward fight for independence in the same way as the Chechens or East Timorese, they would have had a greater chance of success. The tragedy of Kashmir is that the voices of its own people have been drowned out by the Islamists, nationalists and ideologues in both Islamabad and Delhi.

4

Bangladesh

This was a war in which everything went wrong for the Pakistan armed forces. They were not only out-manned but also out-gunned and out-Generaled. Our planning was unrealistic, strategy unsuited, decisions untimely and execution faulty.

—Hamoodur Rehman Commission Report[1]

The order went out at 11.30 p.m. on 25 March 1971. Operation SEARCHLIGHT was under way and all over the East Pakistani capital, Dhaka, Pakistani troops fanned out to secure key objectives. After months of talks, the junta in Pakistan had decided on military action to bring the East Pakistani leadership into line. Pakistan's military planners realised from the outset that Operation SEARCHLIGHT could alienate Bengali personnel inside the police and armed forces, and that many Bengalis would disobey orders to suppress their fellow people. Worse still, they could take their weapons and use them in a fight for an independent Bangladesh. Consequently, one of Operation SEARCHLIGHT's first objectives was to disarm any Bengali soldiers or police officers. In many places the plans went awry.

In Chittagong, home to the Eighth East Bengal Regiment, most of the soldiers were East Pakistani Bengalis but some of the officers came from West Pakistan. As soon as the disarming operation began the Bengalis resisted. Hundreds of Bengalis in the Chittagong cantonment were killed before Major Zia ur Rehman (who later became president of Bangladesh) took the initiative. When he found out what was happening he did not hesitate. 'We mutiny!' he said. At midnight he went with a group of Bengali soldiers to the house of his commanding officer, Lieutenant Colonel A.R. Janjua, and called him to the door. 'I am taking over and you are under arrest,' he said. Within minutes Janjua and six other officers from West Pakistan were locked in an office. The Bengali soldiers wanted revenge. At half past midnight the arrested officers, all from Punjab, were shot dead in the office. Addressing Bengali soldiers shortly afterwards, Major Zia proclaimed, 'We have mutinied. From this moment on we are in independent Bangladesh. Pakistan is no more.'[2]

In another incident in Jessore on 29 March the most senior Bengali officer in the First East Bengal regiment, Lieutenant Colonel R. Jalil, was woken at midnight. He was told that he, and all the other Bengalis in his battalion, were going to be disarmed. 'This is an insult,' he retorted, 'it means we are not being trusted.' Eventually, though, he yielded and agreed that he and his Bengali men would gather their weapons and hand them over the next morning. But when the moment came and the hand-over was about to take place, the Bengali battalion commander took off his Pakistani badges of rank and threw them on the ground. 'This means we don't belong to this army,' he said. It was a pre-arranged signal: the Bengali soldiers opened fire on Pakistani officers and men who, 12 hours before, had been their comrades-in-arms. The action was a suicidal gesture. The Bengalis were outnumbered and by the end of the day 69 of them had been killed.[3]

In the year 1971 the future of East Pakistan depended on a struggle between three men: a habitual drunk, General Yahya Khan; a professional agitator, Sheikh Mujibur Rahman; and a political operator par excellence, Zulfikar Ali Bhutto. Relying respectively on military force, street power and pure guile, this volatile trio pursued their incompatible objectives. Yahya, Pakistan's military ruler, repeatedly claimed that he had one, and only one, objective: to keep the east and west wings of Pakistan united. If unity was assured then he was prepared to offer East Pakistan substantial autonomy. In fact, Yahya did go further than any other Pakistani leader in trying to make the necessary compromises to find a solution for East Pakistan. A durable settlement, though, eluded him. Ever since the defeat by India in 1971, many Pakistanis had complained about Yahya's drinking and his womanising. But those were the least of his problems. Yahya was simply outclassed. Politically, intellectually and in terms of sheer drive, he was never in the same league as either Zulfikar Ali Bhutto or Mujibur Rahman.

Yahya viewed politicians with disdain and Mujibur Rahman was a politician to the core. He started out as an angry activist addressing groups of 10 to 20 students. He ended up as the founder of Bangladesh, speaking to the hearts of many millions. His creed never altered: he believed in Bengali nationalism. When Mohammed Ali Jinnah struggled for Pakistan he relied on legal arguments. Mujibur Rahman had to engage in a far rougher, dirtier fight for Bangladesh and, unlike Jinnah, he spent long periods in jail. From the moment he became interested in politics at Dhaka University, he was never afraid of defying the authorities; on the contrary, he relished it. No one doubts that Mujibur Rahman deserves the title 'founder of the nation', but there are sharp differences of opinion as to exactly when Mujib became irrevocably committed to Bengali independence. Many believe this was his goal from the outset. Speaking after independence, Mujib himself claimed that he had been planning to divide Pakistan ever since 1947. As we shall see, however, there is good evidence that even as late as December 1970 or even February or March 1971 he was still thinking in terms of a united Pakistan and did not foresee a complete division.

The third contestant in the struggle for East Pakistan had no particular interest in the place. Zulfikar Ali Bhutto may have preferred to keep Pakistan united, but he shed few tears when Bangladesh broke away. Bhutto's role in the 1971 crisis has been fiercely debated. He has argued that he did his best to save the country from being split up, but many believe he played a sophisticated, cynical game to fulfil his personal ambitions even if the Pakistani nation was broken in the process. Bhutto was a man in a hurry. After the 1970 elections one senior minister told Yahya that if Bhutto did not become prime minister within a year he would literally go mad.[4] Bhutto himself made little secret of his lust for power and, at the start of 1971, General Yahya and Mujibur Rahman were standing in the way of his becoming prime minister. By the end of 1971, having lost a war with India, Yahya was in disgrace and Mujibur Rahman was ruling Bangladesh. The path was clear for Bhutto to take over in the west.

The complicated interplay between Yahya, Mujib and Bhutto had a decisive role in the break-up of Pakistan and the creation of Bangladesh. But Bengali nationalism was alive and well before any of them were even born. The British had always considered Bengal to be a troublesome province: the Muslims there had been the most vociferous champions of Muslim rights and a Muslim homeland on the subcontinent. In 1906 the All India Muslim League was inaugurated in Dhaka, and 34 years later it fell to a veteran Bengali politician to propose what is now seen as one of the fundamental texts of Pakistan, the Lahore Resolution. The resolution declared: 'the areas in which the Muslims are numerically in the majority, as in the north-western and eastern zones of India should be grouped to constitute "Independent States" in which the constituent units shall be autonomous and sovereign'. The resolution plainly indicated a desire for 'Independent States' and not one independent state. Some leading Bengali Muslims were highly conscious of the distinction. Speaking in Lahore, for example, the Bengali nationalist and future Pakistani prime minister, Husain Shaheed Suhrawardy, made it quite clear that: 'Each of the provinces in the Muslim majority areas should be accepted as a sovereign state and each province should be given the right to choose its future Constitution or enter into a commonwealth with a neighbouring province or provinces.'[5]

Those Bengali leaders who wanted two separate states had a problem. They could never control the Muslim League. Muslim activists from minority provinces in northern India, notably the United Provinces, had far more weight in the organisation. Their predominance, and the Bengalis' relative weakness, had important consequences. At what turned out to be a crucial meeting of the India-wide Muslim League Legislators' Convention, held in Delhi in April 1946, it was decided that the north-western and eastern zones referred to in the Lahore Resolution should form one country: a united Pakistan. In geographical terms the proposition seemed absurd, but politically it made sense. A united Pakistan was not only in line with the-two nation theory, it also countered British concerns about creating too many independent countries on the subcontinent. But some Bengali leaders were unhappy with the change. A senior Bengali Muslim League official, Abul Hashim, objected that the demand for a united Pakistan amounted to an amendment of the Lahore Resolution. He was ruled out of order. Even though it was not clear that the Delhi Convention had the right to amend the Lahore Resolution,[6] the demand for a unified Pakistani state had been approved.

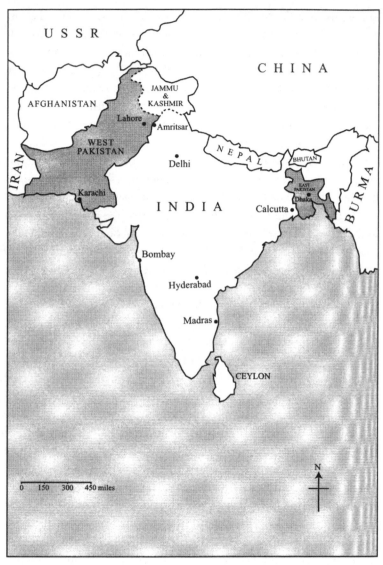

Pakistan, 1947

When Abul Hashim made his complaint, Jinnah, the lawyer, could see the problem clearly enough but his first attempt to get around it was feeble in the extreme. He suggested that the letter 's' after the word 'State' in the Lahore Resolution was a typographical error. When Liaquat Ali Khan produced the original minutes of the meeting, Jinnah had to concede that he was wrong and that the word 'States' was indeed in the original text.[7] He then fobbed off Abul Hashim by assuring the convention that the Lahore Resolution had not been amended. The resolution, he said, would be the document laid before the future Pakistani Constituent Assembly that, as a sovereign body, would take all final decisions.[8]

After the Delhi meeting Jinnah took care to align himself with more amenable Bengali leaders such as the Dhaka-based, Urdu-speaking notable Khwaja Nazimuddin. Like many of his fellow Bengalis, Nazimuddin had voiced support for two separate Muslim countries. As late as April 1947 he said that 'it is my considered opinion that an independent sovereign Bengal is in the best interest of its people'.[9] But Jinnah knew that, above all else, Nazimuddin was loyal and would follow his leadership. And having made the decision to support a united Pakistan, Nazimuddin never wavered. After Jinnah's death he held the two top jobs in Pakistani politics: first he became governor general and, later, the federal prime minister. In both posts he promoted the interests of the central government in Karachi rather than those of the provincial politicians in Dhaka.

Pakistan's founders had set themselves an enormous task. They had to govern two chunks of territory 1,000 miles apart. The eastern wing, or East Pakistan,[10] was the more populous. When the first census was carried out in 1951, there were 42 million people living in the east and 34 million living in the west. Compared to West Pakistan, the east was linguistically homogeneous: both Hindus and Muslims in Bengal spoke Bangla and, according to the census, only 1 per cent spoke Urdu. West Pakistan, by contrast, was an ethnic cocktail and brought together Punjabis, Sindhis, Pukhtoons and the Baloch, as well as the newly arrived Urdu speakers.

In the euphoria that accompanied the creation of Pakistan the question of East Pakistan's place in the new state was put on hold, but not for long. The initial problem was this: Pakistan's new rulers, many of whom had

Languages spoken, 1951, East and West Pakistan

Language	Percentage
Bangla	54.6
Punjabi	28.4
Urdu	7.2
Pukhto	7.1
Sindhi	5.8
English	1.8

Source: Keith Callard, *Pakistan: a Political Study*, Allen & Unwin, Oxford, 1957, p. 181. The total adds up to more than 100 per cent as some people declared more than one language.

moved to Pakistan from the United Provinces, believed that if Pakistan were ever to get its economy and armed forces in order there would have to be a strong central government and just one national language: Urdu. The leadership's concerns were not limited to East Pakistan. They were also anxious about provincialism in Sindh, Balochistan and NWFP. East Pakistan, though, plainly had the most fissiparous potential. Not only was it a long way away, but it was also considered an especially suspect element in the new Muslim state because so many Hindus stayed there after 1947.

In February 1948 Bengalis started articulating their concerns about the language issue. A Hindu Bengali in the Constituent Assembly, Dhirendra Nath Dutta, formally proposed that, alongside Urdu, Bangla should be used in Assembly sessions. Prime Minister Liaquat Ali Khan rejected the idea out of hand declaring: 'It is necessary for a nation to have one language and that language can only be Urdu and no other language.'[11] To many East Pakistanis the statement, which was widely publicised by the Dhaka newspapers, seemed uncompromising, arrogant and unreasonable. A man who had never previously lived in the territory of Pakistan was insisting that his language, the language of just 7 per cent of the people, should become the national language.

By March the debate turned violent: a student demonstration in Dhaka was baton-charged and some language activists were arrested. The chief minister of East Pakistan, Nazimuddin, realised that the problem was getting out of hand and asked Jinnah to revive some enthusiasm for the Pakistan project by visiting Dhaka. In spite of the fact that Jinnah himself spoke poor Urdu, he had long believed in the language's potential nation-building role. At a mass meeting in Dhaka he insisted that 'the state language of Pakistan was going to be Urdu and no other language. Anyone who tries to mislead you is really an enemy of Pakistan.' Amazingly, the Quaid-e-Azam was shouted down. A group of students (rumour has it that Mujibur Rahman was one of them) shouted 'No! No!' as the founder of Pakistan spoke. At the time Jinnah was treated as a living saint: such barracking was unheard of and should have alerted him to the depth of the problem. It did not. A session with the students after the meeting soon became a slanging match, but Jinnah held firm and reasserted that Bangla had no place at the national level.[12]

Jinnah was not alone in failing to understand the depth of the discontent in East Pakistan. In January 1952, Nazimuddin told a public meeting in Dhaka that Jinnah had been right: for the sake of Pakistani unity, Urdu must be the official language of Pakistan, East and West. The fact that Nazimuddin could himself barely speak Bangla hardly helped him win popular support for this stance. It was a disastrous speech that provoked a general strike and, on 21 February 1952, riots, in response to which the police opened fire killing three students.[13] The Bangla language movement had its first martyrs. Eventually, in May 1954, Nazimuddin's successor as prime minister, Muhammad Ali Bogra, announced that Bangla would be accepted as an official state language alongside Urdu. The demand had been granted – but too late.

The failure of both Jinnah and Nazimuddin to read the feelings of the Bengali people reflected a more general problem. The central government and the federal bureaucracy were located in West Pakistan. So too were all the military's main establishments. The fact that East Pakistan was so remote helps explain why West Pakistani leaders never appreciated the intensity of feeling there. For the next 20 years senior figures in the federal government and the Pakistan army consistently viewed disturbances in East Pakistan as issues of law and order rather than politics. Bengali activists were dismissed as anti-Pakistan conspirators infiltrated by Hindus. At no point were they perceived as citizens with legitimate grievances.

When Nazimuddin made his disastrous speech he was both prime minister and leader of the Muslim League. In March 1954 the East

Pakistani electorate punished him. A provincial election campaign was turned into a civil disobedience movement on the language issue and, just seven years after leading Pakistan to independence, the Muslim League was wiped out; it won just 10 of the 309 seats contested. Karachi no longer had a political base in East Pakistan. During the campaign the Muslim League leaders had repeatedly warned the electorate in East Pakistan that the future of the country was at stake. Apparently the voters didn't care. As a result of the election a new provincial administration, led by Fazlul Huq, the man who 14 years earlier had proposed the Lahore Resolution, was sworn in. But his government would not last. In May 1954 he caused havoc in Karachi by telling two foreign correspondents that he favoured the independence of East Pakistan.[14] At the time, the federal prime minister in Karachi was Chaudri Mohammed Ali (he held the job for just 13 months), whose background as a Punjabi-speaking Mohajir and senior civil servant made him particularly unsympathetic to such unpatriotic sentiments. He launched a vituperative attack on Fazlul Huq, describing him as 'a self confessed traitor to Pakistan' and putting him under house arrest.[15] Fazlul Huq's provincial government was dismissed and replaced by direct rule from Karachi.

As Fazlul Huq had made clear, the concerns of East Pakistan's political activists were not limited to the language issue. From the very outset Bengalis complained that British colonialists had been replaced by West Pakistani colonialists. There was also a series of rows over constitutional issues. The task of writing a constitution threw up some genuinely difficult questions. The Objectives Resolution of March 1949, which laid down the framework of the new constitution, had opened with the observation that 'sovereignty over the entire Universe belongs to Allah Almighty alone and the authority which He has delegated to the State of Pakistan through its people for being exercised within the limits prescribed by Him is a sacred trust.'[16] It may have been in line with the two-nation theory but, at a stroke, the formulation destroyed any faint hopes of co-opting East Pakistan's substantial Hindu community into the Pakistan project.

There was also the question of how the central and provincial government would divide power. The Constituent Assembly's first Interim Report of September 1950 gave the central legislature authority over a long list of subjects. The Awami League hit back with proposals that the central, federal government should have limited tax-raising powers and competence in just two policy areas: defence and foreign affairs. The provinces, it argued, should control everything else.

The most awkward constitutional question of all concerned East Pakistan's numerical representation in the proposed parliament. The Constituent Assembly at first ducked the issue altogether by failing to state clearly how many representatives each province would have. The Bengalis, who made up 55.4 per cent of Pakistan's population, took that to be an effective denial of their natural, democratic majority. With the Assembly unable to resolve the matter, further discussion was postponed. When the Assembly revisited the issue in 1954, it considered suggestions that the two houses of parliament should have parity. But now the Punjabis started to assert themselves, resisting any proposal that would have allowed East Pakistan's representatives to form alliances with the smaller provinces and thereby outvote Punjab. Again, the Constituent Assembly was deadlocked.

The matter was eventually resolved, at least temporarily, with the adoption of the 1956 Constitution. East and West Pakistan would be given an equal number of representatives (150 each) in a unicameral parliament. The Punjabis had been bought off by the imposition in 1955 of One Unit under which the four provinces of West Pakistan were amalgamated into one administrative structure that the Punjabis were confident they could dominate. By exploiting splits among the Bengali leadership, Chaudri Mohammed Ali was able to force the constitution through. But many Bengalis (notably supporters of the Awami League) saw it for what it was: a denial of their democratic majority.

By the time General Ayub Khan took over in 1958, Bengali opinion was more hostile to the notion of Pakistan than it had been in 1947. The existence of a military government made matters worse. Previously, advocates of Bengali rights had at least been able to air their opinions quite freely. With the military in charge, that was no longer possible: political parties were banned. The army was even more prone than the bureaucrats to seeing Bengali activists as unpatriotic troublemakers. Indeed, the decision to mount a coup was in part motivated by concerns about East Pakistan. It was clear that any elections held under the 1956

Constitution would result in a clear victory in East Pakistan for the increasingly nationalist Awami League. With student activists in Dhaka still organising street protests, the military responded with arrests and detentions. Leading political players were interned. In January 1962 even former Prime Minister Suhrawardy, who had just been on a tour of East Pakistan, was arrested for anti-state activities. The Bengali students responded to his detention with riots that in turn led to army intervention and the arrest of Awami League leaders. Ayub's 1962 Constitution confirmed the trend, putting all key powers in the hands of the president. This was light years away from the kind of solutions that had been discussed in the Constituent Assembly. It should have been no surprise when, in the presidential election of 1965, Ayub's worst results were in East Pakistan where 47 per cent of the electorate voted against him. Had the vote been held on the basis of universal suffrage, Ayub would almost certainly have suffered an even worse result.

The East Pakistanis' disillusionment with Ayub in part reflected the fact that they were poorly represented in the military and consequently had little say in his regime. At the time of independence they accounted for only 1 per cent of the members of Pakistan's three armed services, and there were only 155 Bengali soldiers in the army.[17] The British military had always favoured recruiting Punjabis and Pathans whom they considered more warlike, and the imbalance that Pakistan inherited was not easy to correct. Ayub Khan did make efforts to recruit more East Pakistanis, but he came nowhere near achieving a representative army. By 1963 Bengalis accounted for just 5 per cent of officers and 7 per cent of other ranks.[18]

It wasn't just a question of numbers. Ayub believed that the impossibility of defending East Pakistan's long borders meant that, in the words of his famous dictum, 'the defence of the East lay in the West'. Militarily he may have had a point; politically, the strategy was a disaster. It convinced the East Pakistanis that they were being kept dependent on West Pakistan. Similarly, the west's refusal to place major military bases in the east (it was proposed, for example, that the naval base should be moved from Karachi to Chittagong) may have been justifiable in terms of logistics and expense, but it further alienated the Bengalis.

At a time of military rule the composition of the army was especially important. But the national origins of the senior civil servants told much the same story. In 1966 East Pakistani civil servants accounted for less than a quarter of the senior staff in the following ministries and departments: Finance, Defence (in which they held just 8.4 per cent of the jobs), Foreign Affairs, Health and Social Welfare, Agriculture, Home and Kashmir Affairs and Natural Resources.[19] The Bengali grievances, then, were numerous and in 1963 the Awami League elected a leader who could articulate them: Sheikh Mujibur Rahman. In 1966 he crystallised the Bengalis' demands into Six Points, which together were to become the central issue in Pakistani politics for the next five years:

1. There should be a Federation of Pakistan on the basis of the Lahore Resolution.
2. The federal government should be limited to Defence and Foreign Affairs.
3. There should be two separate currencies for the two wings, or measures to stop capital flight from East to West.
4. The centre should have no tax-raising powers.
5. Foreign-exchange earnings of each wing should remain with each wing.
6. A militia or paramilitary force for East Pakistan should be set up.[20]

All these demands had been made before, but the Six Points came to acquire symbolic status and won almost universal support in East Pakistan. And they were widely denounced by the west as a thinly veiled demand for secession.

That the Bengalis felt economically deprived was clear from the fact that three of the Six Points directly addressed economic issues. The Bengalis complained that Karachi, as the new capital, had better chances of directing foreign investment and generating some economic activity. Worse still, the Pakistani exchequer came to rely on the hard currency generated by East Pakistan's jute exports. Meanwhile, West Pakistani business concerns moved into the east, taking the place of Hindu entrepreneurs who had left at the time of independence. By 1970 six non-Bengali industrialists controlled over 40 per cent of all East Pakistan's manufacturing assets.[21]

The wealth gap between East and West Pakistan grew throughout the 1950s. The government in Karachi was so short of resources that it was hardly in a position to begin a programme of subsidised development in the east. Nor was Ayub Khan indifferent to the economic situation in East Pakistan. Indeed, his 1962 Constitution required the removal of the disparity between the east and west, but that objective was never given sufficient priority and Ayub failed to honour his pledge. In 1960 the per capita income in West Pakistan was 32 per cent higher than in the east. Although growth rates in the east did improve in the 1960s (the average for the decade was 4.2 per cent), there was a still faster growth rate of 6.2 per cent in the west. By the end of Ayub's period in office the gap between east and west had widened: per capita income in the west was 61 per cent higher than in the east.[22]

Relations between East and West Pakistan deteriorated still further with the unmasking of the Agartala Conspiracy in December 1967. The plot was named after the Indian border town of Agartala where some Bengali nationalists were said to have made contact with Indian army officers. The conspiracy was uncovered when a plain-clothes security official overheard some men in the Chittagong Club discussing their plans to assassinate Ayub Khan on a PIA flight from Dhaka to Chittagong. Having killed Ayub, they intended to establish an independent state in East Pakistan. Over 50 Bengali civil servants, military personnel and politicians were accused of complicity and many of them put on trial. Ayub Khan then upped the ante by trying to implicate Mujibur Rahman in the conspiracy. In a move that rapidly backfired, he was put on public trial. The more the Bengali public learnt about the conspirators, the more they admired them. Before the trial few in East Pakistan dared to discuss secession in public. But as the papers printed more and more details of the proceedings, debate about breaking away became a normal part of public discourse. Mujibur Rahman, meanwhile, secured his place as a political martyr and his support base became ever more solid. As backing for Ayub Khan, in both East and West Pakistan, slipped away, the atmosphere in Dhaka darkened. The army was frequently called out to restore law and order, and the pro-Mujib protests became so intense that Ayub was forced to withdraw the Agartala Conspiracy case and release Mujib from prison. By the time Yahya Khan took over power from Ayub, in March 1969, there were almost continual protests in Dhaka.

At the end of the Ayub period there was an immense gulf between East and West Pakistan. As we have seen, this happened first, and perhaps foremost, because Pakistan had set itself the very difficult task of maintaining national unity despite a lack of geographic contiguity. Shortly after partition, Mountbatten predicted that East Pakistan would break away within a quarter of a century. He was right, with one year to spare.[23] The Bengalis may have been Muslims, but they had a distinct identity that West Pakistanis neither valued nor even recognised. Economic factors were also important. One West Pakistani who travelled to East Pakistan in 1970 recorded his impressions of the Dhaka suburbs:

> the women had hardly a patch of linen to preserve their modesty. The men were short and starved. Their ribs, under a thin layer of dark skin, could be counted from a moving car. The children were worse. Their bones and bellies were protruding. Whenever I stopped beggars swarmed around me like flies. I concluded that the poor of Bengal are poorer than the poorest of West Pakistan.[24]

Some contemporary observers thought a profound crisis was inevitable. The UK deputy high commissioner in Dhaka, for example, took the view in June 1969 that East Pakistan was bound to break away. The martial law administration, he thought, would be forced by public disorder to hold elections in which Mujibur Rahman would emerge the clear winner. His government would demand a large degree of provincial autonomy that would lead to the imposition of martial law. This would be followed, the deputy high commissioner predicted, by a general uprising that the Pakistan army would not be able to control.[25] As we shall see, he wasn't far wrong.

Yahya inherited a difficult situation and he realised that to achieve a lasting constitutional settlement he would have to address the relationship between East and West Pakistan. At heart, Yahya believed that politicians could only be relied upon to break their word, but he nevertheless accepted that he would have to negotiate with them. He also realised that it would be futile to try to create a pliant Bengali leadership with whom he could do business. Yahya understood that the most popular man in East Pakistan was Mujibur Rahman and, if any settlement were to work, Mujib would have to be on board. The crucial question for Yahya was whether Mujib could ever compromise on his Six Points. Like many of his military colleagues, Yahya believed that the Six Points would leave the centre with so little authority that a united Pakistan could not survive. Throughout 1970, Yahya organised a number of meetings with Mujib and other politicians. Some of these encounters were face to face; others were conducted through intermediaries. Mujib did not hesitate to put forward his demands. He said he wanted elections to be held on a one-man one-vote basis that would reflect East Pakistan's numerical majority. He also wanted a clear statement on the division of powers between the centre and the provinces. If these demands were granted, he said, then his Six Points were not 'the Quran or the Bible.' And he insisted that his objective was autonomy and not secession.

Yahya reassured the Bengali leader that the army would accept any arrangements, including elections, that left Pakistan intact. In March 1970 he announced a Legal Framework Order (LFO). Despite the misgivings of some members of the junta, the LFO stated that there would be elections to a unicameral National Assembly that would reflect East Pakistan's numerical superiority. As before, the Assembly would have 300 seats. Under the 1956 Constitution, however, both provinces had been given 150 seats each. Now, East Pakistan would have 162 seats whereas West Pakistan got just 138. The Assembly would be charged with drafting a new constitution within 120 days. The LFO made no stipulation about the size of the majority needed to pass the new constitution but stated that 'the National Assembly shall decide how a decision relating to the Constitution Bill is to be taken'.[26] For all intents and purposes that meant the constitution could be passed by a simple majority, which was exactly what Mujibur Rahman had been demanding. The constitution would set out the degree of regional autonomy for Pakistan's two wings. Even if these arrange-ments left many fundamental questions unanswered, the LFO amounted to a major, and long overdue, concession by West Pakistan.

But while Yahya was trying to negotiate with Mujib in good faith, Pakistan's intelligence agencies remained suspicious. In late 1970 they hit gold. Having successfully bugged a meeting between Mujibur Rahman and his senior colleagues, they were able to play Yahya a devastating tape. On it Mujib was clearly heard to say: 'My aim is to establish Bangladesh: I will tear the LFO into pieces as soon as the elections are over. Who could challenge me once the elections are over?' One of Yahya's senior political advisers, G.W. Choudhury, was present when Yahya heard the tape:

> When Yahya listened to this 'political music' played by his intelligence services, he was bewildered. He could easily recognise Mujib's voice and the substance of his recorded talk. The next morning when I saw him he was still in a bewildered state; but he was never a serious administrator, so he soon recovered from his shock and told me: 'I shall fix Mujib if he betrays me.'[27]

It is difficult to assess Mujib's intentions at this time. He told some that he wanted to keep Pakistan united and others that he did not. It has been argued that Mujib was unable to resist the pressure of hardliners within the Awami League. That was certainly the view of the Hamoodur Rehman Commission which, somewhat surprisingly, concluded that Mujibur Rahman was genuine when he said that he did not want to break up Pakistan. In its report on the events of 1971 the Commission argued that:

> We must give full weight to the fact that before the elections he [Mujib] offered the Council Muslim League and the Jamaat-e-Islami a number of seats in East Pakistan which would have still permitted him to obtain the majority of the East Pakistan seats but not to have a clear majority in the whole house. Quite clearly his purpose was to be able to play the role of the leader of the largest single party without being under pressure for [sic] members of his own party to go through with the Six Point programme on the basis of an overall majority in the house. This fact clearly established that Sheikh Mujibur Rahman, at that time at least, had not decided on secession.[28]

When the election results were released, however, it became clear that such attempts to manage the outcome were futile. Pakistan's first ever national elections laid bare the yawning divide between east and west. Mujib campaigned on the Six Points and won almost total victory. In the east his Awami League secured 160 out of the 162 directly elected constituencies – enough for an absolute majority in the National Assembly. It won no seats in the west. Zulfikar Ali Bhutto's Pakistan People's Party (PPP), meanwhile, gained 81 out of 138 seats in the west, with a strong showing in Punjab and Sindh. It won no seats in East Pakistan. The clearest losers were the military, which had always hoped that no single party would secure an absolute majority, thus allowing the generals to play a mediating role. The fact that the scale of the Awami League victory came as a shock to Yahya once more demonstrated the inability of West Pakistani leaders and officials to read Bengali opinion. Intelligence reports produced for the military had repeatedly predicted that the Awami League would win no more than 60 per cent of the votes in East Pakistan.[29]

Mujib was jubilant. Secure with his massive mandate, he declared that no one could stop him from framing a constitution on the basis of the Six Points. He could hardly say anything else. During the campaign he had repeatedly described the election as a referendum on the Six Points – and the result was unambiguous. In January 1971 the Awami League's successful election candidates made a pledge:

In the name of Allah the Merciful the Almighty; in the name of the brave martyrs and fighters who heralded our initial victory by laying down their lives and undergoing the utmost hardship and repression; in the name of those peasants, workers, students, toiling masses and the people of this country; we, the newly elected members of the National and Provincial Assemblies, do hereby take oath that we shall remain whole-heartedly faithful to the people's mandate on the Six Points . . .[30]

Mujib's growing intransigence left Yahya dismayed. In January 1971 he went to Dhaka for talks with the Awami League leader. On the eve of his meeting with Mujib, Yahya once again revealed his remarkably casual attitude to high office. He asked the Awami League to provide him with a copy of the Six Points. The East Pakistanis were understandably bewildered that Yahya seemed to be ignorant of the Six Points which had, after all, been at the centre of political discourse throughout his period in power. When the two men did meet, Mujib repeated his demand for the Six Points to be respected. Yahya implored Mujib to reach out to West Pakistan's politicians. He even went as far as saying that he had 'nothing against the Six Points programme but you will have to carry the West Pakistan leaders with you'.[31] Despite that statement, there is little doubt that Yahya did think the Six Points would have to be amended if only to secure the support of his military colleagues for any future constitutional settlement. In the run-up to the elections he had repeatedly told Mujibur Rahman that the Six Points would have to be modified. In response Mujib had repeatedly promised that he could compromise on them. Many of Yahya's colleagues had distrusted those assurances and now Yahya believed he should have listened to their advice: 'Mujib has let me down,' he said. 'Those who warned me against him were right. I was wrong in trusting this person.'[32] Publicly, though, he told reporters: 'Sheikh Mujibur Rahman is going to be the future prime minister of the country.' Yahya, perhaps, hoped that the prospect of actually taking office might make Mujib realise that it would be worth his while showing greater flexibility.

Having made little progress in Dhaka, Yahya moved on to Larkana for talks (and a duck shoot) with Zulfikar Ali Bhutto. Throughout the period when the LFO was being negotiated, Yahya had repeatedly asked for Bhutto's opinions on issues such as the Six Points, one-man one-vote and the abolition of One Unit, but Bhutto had not wanted to commit himself and refused to declare his hand. After the elections, though, Bhutto could see things more clearly. Mujibur Rahman had won an overall majority and was in a position to prevent Bhutto from becoming prime minister. Even though Bhutto had exceeded all expectations in the elections, there was no getting around the fact that his PPP still had far fewer seats than the Awami League. With Yahya Khan still the military leader and Mujib ur-Rahman the prime minister in waiting, Bhutto had a problem.

The election results were a major blow for Bhutto but he refused to recognise the setback. 'No constitution,' he proclaimed, 'could be framed, nor could any government at the centre be run without my party's co-operation.' Plainly, this was not true. The new parliament could take decisions by a simple majority and the PPP did not have enough seats to veto anything. Despite those hard facts Bhutto insisted that the PPP was 'not prepared to occupy the opposition benches in the National Assembly'.[33]

As he prepared to welcome Yahya to Larkana, Bhutto was determined to turn the election result in his favour. The two men's talks have long been very controversial. Some believe that Yahya and Bhutto reached a secret deal to work against Mujibur Rahman. This view has been most forcefully expressed by the man who went on to run West Pakistan's unsuccessful military campaign in East Pakistan, Lieutenant General A.A.K. Niazi:

> Bhutto was not prepared to accept the role of opposition leader in a united Pakistan: his endeavours were therefore directed at compromising Mujib's right to form the government, which would only be possible if East Pakistan gained independence. The final plan for the dismemberment of Pakistan was hatched between General Yahya and Bhutto at Larkana.[34]

Various conspiracy theorists have tried to prove much the same point, but there is little hard evidence to back up their claims. Certainly the accusation seems unfair in respect of Yahya. Although he had arrived in Larkana deeply frustrated by Mujib's attitude, there is no reason to suggest that he was not still committed to a united Pakistan. Indeed, his subsequent use of military force to keep Pakistan united demonstrated Yahya's determination to keep the country together. For Bhutto, though, it was a different story. He was already thinking that Mujib was an obstacle to his ambitions. Shortly after the Larkana meeting Bhutto went to Dhaka to meet Mujib. Yahya had asked Bhutto to prevail upon the Bengali leader to be flexible about the Six Points, but Bhutto had a different agenda. As one of the Awami League negotiators put it: 'He showed no interest in the basic constitutional issues. He spent all his time discussing his share of power and the allocation of portfolios.'[35] Bhutto's attitude infuriated Mujib who felt that, once again, arrogant

West Pakistani politicians were failing to take East Pakistan seriously. He had, after all, won the elections, yet Bhutto was insisting that the PPP had a right to be in the government.

Although determined to prevent it happening, Yahya knew that the break-up of Pakistan was now a distinct possibility.[36] He was also aware that some elements of the military leadership could never accept the Six Points.[37] Nevertheless, he had started a process and had little option but to see it through. He could only hope that Bhutto and Mujib could come up with a political compromise, and later a constitution, that would ensure the country's survival. Privately he made no secret of his frustration with Mujib and told fellow officers that he wanted 'to sort this bastard out'.[38] Whilst Yahya, Mujib and Bhutto acrimoniously negotiated in ever-diminishing circles, one issue came to the fore: the date the National Assembly would be convened. Mujib wanted it to begin as soon as possible, suggesting mid-February. Bhutto, still uncertain that he could get into government, wanted it delayed until the end of March. Yahya split the difference and announced it would take place on 3 March.

It is at this point that Zulfikar Ali Bhutto made his most significant contribution to the dismemberment of Pakistan. Frustrated that the Awami League was offering him no guarantees about his future role, he told a mass rally in Lahore that the PPP would not attend the National Assembly's opening session. More than that, he declared that no other party from West Pakistan would attend it either. If any members of the Assembly did attend, Bhutto said, he would see to it that their 'legs will be broken'.

Bhutto had ended any possibility of resolving his differences with Mujib through constitutional means. He did attend more talks with both Yahya and Mujib but never made any significant concessions. Bhutto knew that he had support from some of Yahya's senior military colleagues who increasingly favoured a military solution. They felt that they had given Yahya a relatively free hand to come up with a workable constitution and that he had botched the job. Bhutto could now see the way ahead. If Mujib stuck to the Six Points then the military would be left with only one democratically elected leader whom they could consider acceptable: Bhutto himself. Yahya's tragedy was that neither Bhutto nor Mujib had an interest in helping him find a compromise.

Yahya is often written off as a weak, lightweight drunk lacking the intellect and foresight to manage the national crisis he faced. It is only fair to point out, though, that up to this point he had pursued a highly controversial but nonetheless fairly consistent course. With more realism than most of his military colleagues, he had understood that if East Pakistan was to remain part of a united country, it must be given major concessions. Elections had been held and East Pakistan's numerical majority was to be reflected in the new National Assembly. Yahya's mistake was that he played his most important cards – an East Pakistani majority in an Assembly with constitution-making powers – early. Worse, he got nothing in return. He believed that he had to make this concession if the elections were to have any credibility. He had a point. But after his overwhelming election victory Mujib was never going to make any concessions on the Six Points. The only hope would have been to blur the Six Points before setting out the terms of the Legal Framework Order and, in particular, the composition of the National Assembly. However, it must be said, it's far from clear how Yahya could have persuaded Mujib to give any public declaration to this effect.

As Yahya's talks with Mujib and Bhutto ground on, it became clear that the attitudes of the two politicians were hardening. Mujib now wanted an immediate end to martial law. Yahya and his negotiators increasingly got the impression that Mujib was not interested in taking up the position of Pakistan's duly elected prime minister and that his goal was only to govern an independent Bangladesh. Some thought was given to the idea of a loose federation with Mujib as prime minister in the east and Bhutto in the west. But Bhutto, probably aware that the military was preparing to strike, raised various procedural and legal issues and avoided any agreement.

With the talks in deadlock Yahya lost his nerve. He was not convinced the National Assembly meeting could work and in true military fashion fell back on the view that a 'whiff of grapeshot' might force the Awami League back into line.[39] The military had first discussed the possibility of using force in February. Yahya stepped up his military preparations and, two days before it was due to meet, he called off the National Assembly session. It was a catastrophic decision. Bhutto fully supported Yahya's move and confidently predicted that since the Awami League was a

1. The founder of Pakistan, Mohammed Ali Jinnah.

2. Partition. Muslim refugees flee Delhi in September 1947.

3. The founder of Bangladesh, Mujibur Rahman.

4. Bengali freedom fighters beat men suspected of collaborating with the Pakistani army, December 1971.

5. General and later Field Marshal Ayub Khan (*top and above right*),
Pakistan's first military ruler.

I told him . . . since it was essential for him to be head and shoulders above
the others, it would be better if he elevated his own rank from that of a General
to that of a Field Marshal.

—Zulfikar Ali Bhutto

6. The military ruler who led Pakistan to defeat in 1971, General Yayha Khan.

He starts with cognac for breakfast and continues drinking throughout the day;
night often finding him in a sodden state.

—Zulfikar Ali Bhutto

7. Pakistan People's Party founder, Zulfikar Ali Bhutto.

He was the biggest dictator of Pakistan.

—General Musharraf

8. The military ruler who tried to Islamicise Pakistan, General Zia ul-Haq.

Each minute, each hour and every day of your despotic rule is a living testimony of your hatred and enmity towards me.

—Zulfikar Ali Bhutto

9. General Zia's civilian successor, Nawaz Sharif.

Nawaz Sharif was driven by insecurity, paranoia and the politics of revenge.

—Benazir Bhutto

10. Pakistan's first female prime minister, Benazir Bhutto.

She has been prime minister twice and she has completely mismanaged and corrupted the country.

—General Musharraf

11. Pakistani nuclear scientist, A.Q. Khan.

12. Pakistanis in Lahore celebrate the country's first nuclear test in May 1998.

13. Pakistani children play on a replica Ghauri missile.

14. (*below*) Pakistani soldiers climb the gates of Pakistan Television headquarters during the coup that brought General Musharraf to power.

15. General Pervez Musharraf and his dogs Dot and Buddy in their first photo opportunity, October 1999.

General Musharraf is a military dictator. When he speaks, others jump to attention. If they don't, they are locked away.
—Benazir Bhutto

16. A car burns after an explosion during continuing political unrest in Karachi, March 2000.

17. Pakistani soldiers at a forward position on the Siachin Glacier.

18. Pakistani troops pray during the Kargil conflict in Kashmir.

19. Pakistani troops in Kashmir fire artillery rounds across the line of control.

20. A young Talib, or religious student, learns the Quran in a Pakistani madrasa.

21. A member of Jaish-e-Mohammed in Peshawar calls for jihad, October 2001.

22. Pro-Taliban, anti-US protestors demonstrate in Peshawar, September 2001.

bourgeois party it would be quite incapable of launching a guerrilla struggle.[40] Yahya's military advisers on the ground in East Pakistan knew better and they repeatedly warned their chief that the reaction would be cataclysmic. They were right. Crowds armed with sticks surged onto the streets and enforced a total, nationwide strike. The final confrontation was rapidly approaching. Mujib was furious and threatened revenge. 'The Bengalis know how to shed blood,' he said.[41] And they did. There were strikes throughout East Pakistan and armed confrontations between protesters and troops. Denied their democratic rights inside Pakistan, the Bengalis strengthened their demands for full-blown independence. The Pakistani troops were overwhelmed. Students paraded through the streets waving Bangladeshi flags. The final push for independence had begun and Mujib was in control of events.

Fatally weakened, Yahya announced a new date, 25 March, for the Assembly meeting. Aware that he was running out of options, he also stepped up his preparations for a full-scale military campaign in East Pakistan. The announcement of a new date for the Assembly made nonsense of Yahya's first postponement. No genuine move towards a compromise was possible in three extra weeks. The regime was on the run. By the time Yahya returned to Dhaka on 15 March, West Pakistan's authority in the east was steadily ebbing away. Shortly after Yahya arrived, Mujib defied the martial law administration by announcing that he was taking over the administration of East Pakistan. It wasn't a declaration of independence but it came very close.

Civil War

At 8.00 p.m. on 26 March, General Yahya addressed the rapidly disintegrating Pakistani nation. The political negotiations, he said, had failed. Denouncing Mujib as an obstinate, obdurate traitor, he declared that it was the duty of the armed forces to ensure the integrity, solidarity and security of the country. The party that had won the overwhelming backing of the East Pakistani people, the Awami League, was banned. 'I should have taken action against Sheikh Mujib ur-Rahman and his collaborators weeks ago,' declared Yahya. 'He and his party have defied the lawful authority for over three weeks. They have insulted

Pakistan's flag and defiled the photograph of the Father of the Nation. They have tried to run a parallel government. They have created turmoil, terror and insecurity.'[42]

By the time he spoke, the Pakistan army had already moved into action. After the final breakdown of the negotiations with Mujib, Yahya had left Dhaka by plane. Operation SEARCHLIGHT began the moment he reached West Pakistani airspace. For weeks West Pakistani troops in Dhaka had been too afraid even to leave their barracks. Even to be seen in public risked violent attack from Bengali activists, and some soldiers had been killed in the city in broad daylight. The troops wanted revenge and, in the words of the Hamoodur Rehman Commission, 'It was as if a ferocious animal having been kept chained and starved was suddenly let loose.'[43] At midnight a commando unit raided Mujib's house and, after a brief fight, arrested the Awami League leader. The Pakistan army's next targets were any Bengalis with weapons.

While some in the Pakistan army were trying to gather weapons from their former colleagues, others headed for Dhaka University, long considered a hotbed of Bengali nationalism. At 2.00 a.m. Pakistani soldiers went to two student hostels and met strong resistance but two hours later the army had prevailed. It's impossible to say how many died – quite probably hundreds. By the morning freshly turned earth indicated that the Pakistani troops had dug mass graves.[44]

Dhaka was, more or less, under control, but outside the city it was a different story. With their obstinate refusal to understand East Pakistani opinion, the senior officers in West Pakistan predicted that the general population would remain largely neutral. It did not. The Bengali population stood full square behind their arrested leader, Mujibur Rahman. The West Pakistani troops responded to this defiance with furious aggression, raping, murdering and even massacring whole villages, women and children included. The man in charge of the campaign, General Tikka Khan, conceded that the West Pakistani troops killed as many as 30,000 people. Presumably the true figure was far higher.

Given what was happening, it was not surprising that Bengalis in the Pakistan army decided to make a run for it. All over East Pakistan Bengali soldiers headed for India where they formed the rapidly emerging Bengali resistance army – the Mukti Bahini, or freedom fighters. The Hamadoor Rehman Commission reckoned that out of 17,000 army personnel of Bengali origin, only 4,000 were successfully disarmed and all the rest made it to India.[45] The West Pakistani plans to take control of the radio stations also met with only partial success. In Chittagong, Bengali staff reacted to the army action by setting up their own Independent Bangladesh Radio station and broadcasting messages from Major Zia ur Rehman announcing the establishment of Bangladesh. For a week there were fierce battles in the city. The West Pakistanis had to deploy both the navy and air force to attack what used to be Pakistani military establishments but what had become rebel positions. Whenever West Pakistani soldiers travelled by road they were at risk of ambush. Some garrisons that came under rebel attack had to be evacuated by helicopter. The army also faced severe logistics and supply problems. Food supplies dried up and troops were deployed on hazardous missions to rural areas where they commandeered grain and other supplies from the civilian population.[46]

For all the difficulties it faced, though, the Pakistan army soon felt it was getting the upper hand. Even if they refused to acquiesce, the Bengalis suffered from a lack of arms, and by May the army had managed to establish control of all the major towns. The countryside, however, remained a much more difficult proposition. And, as the Bengalis became better organised, the Pakistan army's problems mounted. 'From June onwards,' Major General Shaukat Riza recalled, 'the Pakistan army was chasing ghosts. Every bush, every hut, every moving thing was suspect.'[47]

From their bases in India, the Mukti Bahini mounted hit-and-run attacks. Most were limited operations in which 10 to 15 men would slip across the border, strike at a defined target such as a bridge, and then move back to the safety of India. In some cases, though, groups of up to 250 men launched full-scale attacks on Pakistani military camps before melting away and beating a tactical retreat.

Most of these actions were in the border areas, but there was also considerable rebel activity in Dhaka – supposedly the most secure place of all. The atmosphere there has been captured by Hasan Zaheer, a senior West Pakistani civil servant, who in June 1971 attended a dinner for a visiting mission from the International Bank for Reconstruction and Development and the International Monetary Fund. It was a difficult evening:

> While drinks were being served in the drawing room of the Governor's House, sounds of bomb explosions, which did not seem to be very far off, were heard at regular intervals. This was while each one of us, the Pakistani officials, had got hold of one or two members of the mission and were arguing for our rehabilitation programmes and the bright future we envisaged for economic revival. By the time we had moved to the dining table, shooting had been added to the bomb explosions and the chatter of machine gun fire almost drowned the polite conversation and both we and our guests found it hard to keep up. We avoided looking at each other and tried to finish the meal as soon as possible. The incongruity of the situation was overwhelming: well dressed people eating in a civilised manner off the finest china and sparkling silver and crystal under the sound and fury of death and destruction. No one knew the location of these happenings but they were obviously timed for the benefit of the World Bank officials. The dinner was over at around 10.00 p.m. and all of us departed in a cacophony of howling dogs, explosion of bombs and rapid firing of machine guns.[48]

If senior civil servants were finding it difficult to hold a decent dinner party, the suffering of many others in East Pakistan was far more acute. The fighting grew ever more bitter. When killing Bengalis, the Pakistani soldiers used a euphemism: their victim, they used to say, 'was being sent to Bangladesh'. The following quotations are from Pakistani officers who gave evidence to the Hamoodur Commission report:

> There was a general feeling of hatred against Bengalis amongst the soldiers and officers including generals. There were verbal instructions to eliminate Hindus. In Salda Nadi area about 500 persons were killed. When the army moved to clear the rural areas and small towns, it moved in a ruthless manner; destroying, burning, killing.
>
> —Lt Col. Mansoor ul-Haq

> Many junior and other officers took the law into their own hands to deal with so-called miscreants. There have been cases of interrogation of

miscreants which were far more severe in character than normal and in some cases blatantly in front of the public. The discipline of the Pakistani army, as was generally understood, had broken down.

—Brigadier Mian Taskeenudin

General Niazi visited my unit at Thakurgaon and Bogra. He asked us how many Hindus we had killed. In May, there was an order in writing to kill Hindus.

—Lt Col. Aziz Ahmed Khan[49]

Of course, the Pakistan army was not alone in committing atrocities. The Mukti Bahini also carried out acts of terrible violence, particularly against the Biharis, Muslims who had moved from India to East Pakistan at the time of partition. Still loyal to Jinnah's vision of a united Muslim state on the subcontinent, the Biharis sided with the Pakistan army. There were many incidents of communal violence between them and the Bengalis. But the Mukti Bahini's main target was the Pakistan army itself. The Hamoodur Rehman Commission Report endorsed Pakistani claims that: 'Families of West Pakistani officers and other ranks serving in East Pakistan units were subjected to inhuman treatment, and a large number of West Pakistani officers were butchered by their Bengali colleagues.'[50] On General Niazi's account: 'In Bogra 15,000 persons were killed in cold blood. In Chittagong, thousands of men and women were bayoneted or raped. In Seraj Ganj women and children were locked in a hall and set on fire. The target of these brutalities were West Pakistanis . . .'[51]

Distracted by its effort to control the Bengali population, the Pakistani military command in Dhaka was perhaps insufficiently focused on what was happening in India. Although the Pakistan army believed that India was involved in instigating the Bengalis' belligerent attitude, few expected Delhi to intervene in East Pakistan directly. Once again it was a faulty judgement. After Mujib had been arrested, most of the Awami League leadership had dressed in peasants' clothing and slipped away across the border. Delhi helped the Awami League set up a government-in-exile in Calcutta. As the civil war intensified, an increasing number of Bengalis – especially the Hindus – fled to India as well. According to the Indian government, over 8 million people (7 million of them Hindus) had become refugees by the end of August. The precise numbers are contested but there were certainly several million. The refugee movement had an important impact on world opinion and drew attention to the Pakistan army's repressive measures.

Pakistan's international problems were not restricted to India. The United States, having always supported the unity of Pakistan, now started making contingency plans for a possible break-up. Much has been written about the splits in the US administration at this time: Henry Kissinger and Richard Nixon, in the White House, were generally more sympathetic than the State Department to General Yahya.[52] In the event, the divisions in Washington didn't make much difference: with Congress and the press complaining about the repression in East Pakistan, decisive US military intervention to keep Pakistan together was never a realistic possibility. The Indians, meanwhile, were reaching out to new allies. The signing of the Treaty of Friendship and Co-operation with Moscow in August 1971 had given the Indians the crucial assurance they wanted. True, it wasn't a security guarantee, but it did state that 'in the event that any of the parties is attacked or threatened with attack, the High Contracting Parties will immediately start mutual consultation with a view to eliminating the threat and taking appropriate effective measures to ensure peace and security for the countries'.[53] It was an effective counter to Pakistan's hopes of receiving military support from China. In the event, Beijing never delivered as much as Yahya wanted. China did speak of its commitment to Pakistani unity but never came close to military intervention. And if Pakistan was being outmanoeuvred at the regional level, things didn't look much brighter at the United Nations where opinion was increasingly swayed by press reports of atrocities in East Pakistan and of the suffering in the refugee camps.

It is not clear exactly when the Indian prime minister Indira Ghandi decided to go to war. Initially, Delhi believed that Operation SEARCHLIGHT would be a short-lived affair, followed by a negotiated settlement in which the East Pakistanis would accept the unity of the country. But as the Pakistani army's campaign continued, and refugees flowed into India, opinion in Delhi hardened. By June there was an emerging consensus that an independent Bangladesh was in India's interests and might even be worth fighting for. In July 1971, Lieutenant General Jagjit Singh Aurora was given the job of destroying the Pakistani forces in East Pakistan.[54] He was also given half a million men to complete the task.

International War

The first Indian attacks were limited to strikes on Pakistani forces followed by rapid withdrawals back to Indian territory. By 21 November, though, the Indians started digging in on East Pakistani soil. From the point of view of the military tacticians in Delhi, the timing could not have been better. The end of the monsoon meant that they would not be held up by torrential rain, while the arrival of snow in the passes on the Chinese–Indian border limited Beijing's military options should it want to get involved.

Yahya responded to the Indian incursions by opening up the western front. He launched air attacks on nine airbases in north-west India on 3 December. The attacks were futile: due to faulty intelligence, not one Indian aircraft was destroyed. Yahya then ordered some limited ground offensives intended to draw the Indian forces in the west into the open. Throughout the war, though, Yahya never launched a full-blown offensive on the western front. That is not to say there wasn't some fierce fighting on the borders of West Pakistan: there was. The two armies clashed in Kashmir and in Sindh, but these engagements were never on a big enough scale to affect the outcome of the war as a whole. On the many occasions when Yahya was urged to act more decisively in the west and commit more troops there, he always expressed reluctance to do so. Maybe he was afraid of defeat. For all the theorising, the defence of East Pakistan was to lie in the east.

After the Pakistani air strikes, Delhi could claim that Pakistan had dealt the first blow and India's full-scale invasion of East Pakistan, originally scheduled for 6 December, was brought forward. The Indian Air Force inflicted the first major damage by hitting Dhaka's military airport. Pakistan's squadron of Sabre fighter-jets were unable to take off and could play no part in the war. India enjoyed complete air superiority. It also had a significant manpower advantage, although its extent has been vigorously disputed. At one extreme Lieutenant General Niazi has claimed that, at most, he had 55,000 men under his command and that 'the ratio of troops between us and the Indians came to approximately one to ten'. The Hamoodur Rehman Commission report challenged these figures and estimated the Pakistani forces at between 73,000 and 93,000. The Indians have suggested a one to eight ratio.[55] The numbers are complicated by the fact that the Indians could rely on the highly motivated Mukti Bahini (generally estimated at 100,000) whilst Niazi had far less effective support from various irregular forces, including some 'Mujahid Battalions' and madrasa students.[56] India also had a clear advantage in terms of military equipment. Indeed, the Pakistanis were short of many basic items such as landmines. In some places they had to create lines of defence with nothing more than sharpened bamboo sticks stuck in the ground.[57]

Lieutenant General Niazi never stood a chance. When the Hamoodur Commission questioned Yahya Khan and other senior generals, they freely conceded that once India launched a full-scale invasion, defeat was 'inevitable'.[58] Niazi was outnumbered, outgunned and operating in territory with a hostile population. Despite his hopeless situation, many Pakistanis have been strongly critical of Niazi's strategy in East Pakistan and have blamed him for the Pakistan army's humiliation. The arguments about Niazi's record mainly concern his defensive strategy. He repeatedly claimed that he would defend Dhaka to the 'last man, last bullet'. But rather than concentrate his forces there, he spread them all along East Pakistan's 2,500-mile land border in small groups to hold up any Indian attack. Niazi said there was to be no withdrawal from these positions until 75 per cent casualties had been taken. One military historian described it as the most stupid order given during the whole war.[59] Under Niazi's plans, the surviving 25 per cent were then to regroup in over 30 strong points and fortresses that had been identified as crucial for the defence of East Pakistan. The fortresses were stocked with enough food and ammunition to hold out for a month.

Niazi's public relations officer Siddiq Salik recalls Niazi discussing his strategy with foreign correspondents in Dhaka shortly before the Indian attacks. Niazi said: 'My troops in the border outposts are like the extended fingers of an open hand. They will fight there as long as possible before they fold back to the fortresses to form a fist to bash the enemy's head.' Siddiq Salik went on to say: 'I was fascinated by the simile. But I recalled his latest decision prohibiting any withdrawals unless 75 per cent casualties had been sustained. When three out of four fingers are broken or wounded is it possible to form a fist?'[60]

In his assessment of the military campaign, Lieutenant General Aurora's chief of staff, General J.F.R. Jacob, has written that:

> Understandably this land with its huge rivers, swamps, mangroves and paddy fields and sparse roads and railways is very easy to defend. The very few bridges across the rivers add to the difficulties . . . Fortunately for us the Pakistanis had concentrated their troops in the towns. Had they chosen to defend approaches to the river crossing sites we would not have been able to cross the rivers and reach Dacca.[61]

Pakistani writers have generally used a different argument to criticise Niazi. In line with the findings of the Hamoodur Rehman Commission, they say Niazi should have concentrated his forces in Dhaka. The capital of East Pakistan, they argue, was always India's ultimate objective and the fact that it was surrounded by rivers on three sides rendered it a highly defensible city. Had Niazi concentrated his forces in Dhaka, the argument goes, he would have been able to hold up the Indians for longer. The reasoning, however, is unconvincing. The Indians would have been able to move through East Pakistan at will before besieging Dhaka. With a hostile population, and Indian air superiority, it is difficult to see how Niazi could have successfully defended the city. Furthermore, many of those who have criticised the fortress concept would have been the first to blame Niazi if he had let the Indians move through East Pakistan unopposed.

Niazi has rejected outright the argument that he should have concentrated his forces in Dhaka, but his book, *The Betrayal of East Pakistan*, includes some plainly ridiculous claims. He suggests, for example, that: 'All the efforts of Yahya's junta and Bhutto's coterie were directed towards losing the war.'[62] There is no evidence whatsoever that Yahya wanted to lose the war. But Niazi does have a point when he defends his fortress strategy. He believed he had to prevent the Indians,

or the Mukti Bahini, from establishing control of a large chunk of territory. Niazi had good reason to fear that, given the chance, the Awami
League would move its Bangladeshi government from Calcutta and,
furthermore, establish a military base on East Pakistani soil.

It is significant that when Niazi submitted his plans to GHQ in
Rawalpindi for approval, nobody objected to them.[63] He also has a
point when he blames Yahya for not opening up the western front. If
the long-standing strategy of 'the defence of the East lies in the West'
meant anything, then he had every right to have expected that to have
happened. Yet on 5 December Niazi received a message from
Rawalpindi stating that the Indian strategy was to take East Pakistan
and then to concentrate its forces for an assault on the west.

Niazi was asked to hold out as long as possible so that Yahya had
time to rustle up some international support. Pakistan's strategy had
been turned on its head. The defence of the west now lay in the
east. With Pakistan's strategists in disarray, Indira Gandhi told the
Indian Parliament on 6 December that her government recognised
Bangladesh as an independent and sovereign state. She was confident
of victory. General Niazi, meanwhile, seemed sure of defeat. He sent
the following message to GHQ in Rawalpindi:

> ... Indian air force causing maximum damage(.) have started using
> rockets and napalm against own defensive positions(.) internally rebels
> highly active, emboldened and causing maximum damage in all
> possible ways including cutting of means of communication(.) this
> including destruction of roads/bridges/rail ferries/boats etc.(.) local
> populations also against us(.) lack of communications making it diffi-
> cult to reinforce or replenish or readjust positions ... resorting to
> fortress/strong point basis(.) enemy will be involved though all methods
> including unorthodox action will fight it out to last man last round(.)
> request expedite actions vide your G-0235 of 5 Dec 1971.[64]

Niazi was alarmed because the Indians were moving through East
Pakistan with extraordinary speed. Rather than engage the fortresses
one by one, they simply bypassed them. The fact that they were
working closely with Mukti Bahini, who knew the territory of East

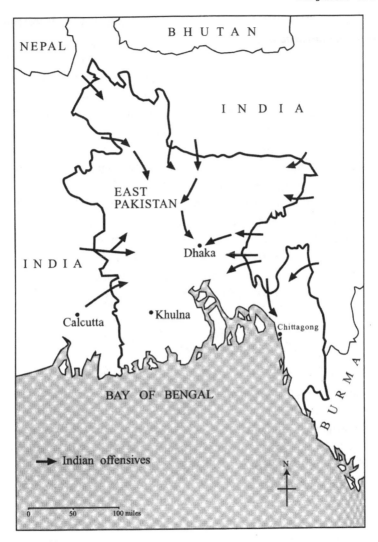

East Pakistan, 1971

Pakistan well, helped the Indian forces find routes that the Pakistanis had not anticipated.

Niazi was not helped by the fact that some of his men failed to put up much resistance. In its assessment of the 1971 war, the Hamoodur Rehman Commission bemoaned the performance of the Pakistan army, saying that many of the fortresses gave up without even making a fight of it. 'The only battle that was fought with any determination was in the Hilli sector . . .' Elsewhere, the Commission found, some senior Pakistani officers in the fortresses fled their posts and abandoned their troops as soon as the Indians came close.[65]

Although some Pakistani officers could well be accused of cowardice, others showed flamboyant bravery. At Jamalpur, near Dhaka, an Indian Brigadier, Hardit Singh Kler, surrounded a Pakistani unit led by Lieutenant Colonel Ahmed Sultan. On 10 December the two officers exchanged letters. The first, written by the Indian Brigadier, was taken across the front line by an elderly man who delivered it by hand.

To,
The Commander Jamalpur Garrison

I am directed to inform you that your garrison has been cut off from all sides and you have no escape route available to you. One brigade with full complement of artillery has already been built up and another will be striking by morning. In addition you have been given a foretaste of a small element of our air force with a lot more to come. The situation as far as you are concerned is hopeless. Your higher commanders have already ditched you.

I expect your reply before 6.30 pm today failing which I will be constrained to deliver the final blow for which purpose 40 sorties of MIGs have been allotted to me.

In this morning's action the prisoners captured by us have given your strength and dispositions, and are well looked after.

The treatment I expect to be given to the civil messenger should be according to a gentlemanly code of honour and no harm should come to him.

An immediate reply is solicited.

Brigadier HS Kler. Comd.

The reply was sent a few hours later.

Dear Brig,

Hope this finds you in high spirits. Your letter asking us to surrender had been received. I want to tell you that the fighting you have seen so far is very little, in fact the fighting has not even started. So let us stop negotiating and start the fight.

40 sorties, I may point out, are inadequate. Ask for many more.

Your point about treating your messenger well was superfluous. It shows how you under-estimate my boys. I hope he liked his tea.

Give my love to the Muktis. Let me see you with a sten in your hand next time instead of the pen you seem to have such mastery over,

Now get on and fight.

Yours sincerely

Commander Jamalpur Fortress.
(Lt Colonel Ahmed Sultan)[66]

The next morning the fight did indeed begin when Lieutenant Colonel Sultan tried to break out of his garrison. Over 230 of his men were killed. They died in vain. When the Indian Brigadier had written 'your higher commanders have already ditched you', he was absolutely right. The military and political leadership in Dhaka already knew the war was lost. Fully two days before Lieutenant Colonel Sultan led his men to their deaths, the governor of East Pakistan, Dr A.M. Malik, had sent this message to General Yahya:

From Governor East Pakistan(.) A-4660 of 091800(.) for the President(.) military situation desperate . . . Enemy likely to be at the outskirts any day if no outside help forthcoming. Secretary general UN's representative in Dacca has proposed that Dacca city may be declared as an open city to save lives of civilians specially non-Bengalis(.) am favourably inclined to accept the offer(.) strongly recommend this be approved(.) Gen. Niazi does not agree as he considers that his orders are to fight to the last and it would amount to giving up Dacca(.) this action may result in massacre of whole army, WP Police and all non-locals and loyal locals(.) there are no regular troops in reserve and once the enemy has crossed the Ganges or Meghna further resistance will be futile unless China or US intervenes today with massive air and ground support(.) once again urge you to consider immediate cease-fire and political settlement otherwise once Indian troops are free from east wing in a few days even west wing will be in jeopardy(.) understand local population has welcomed Indian army in captured areas and are providing maximum help to them(.) our troops are finding it impossible to withdraw and manoeuvre due to rebel activity(.) with this clear alignment sacrifice of West Pakistan is meaningless.

Five hours after sending his desperate message, the governor had Yahya's reply.

From President to Governor Repeated to Commander Eastern Command(.) your flash message A 4660 of 9 December received and thoroughly understood(.) you have my permission to take decisions on your proposals to me(.) I have and am continuing to take all measures internationally but in view of our complete isolation from each other decision about East Pakistan I leave entirely to your good sense and judgement(.) I will approve of any decision you take and am instructing Gen. Niazi simultaneously to accept your decision and arrange things accordingly(.) whatever efforts you make in your decisions to save senseless destruction of the kind of civilians that you have mentioned in particular the safety of our armed forces, you may go ahead and ensure safety of our armed forces by all political means that you will have to adopt with our opponent.[67]

Pakistan's hopeless military situation on the ground was matched on the diplomatic front. The Indians' diplomatic position would have been far worse if Yahya had acted with greater speed and determination to isolate Delhi for what was, after all, a blatantly illegal invasion of a foreign country. Amazingly, Yahya failed to raise the Indian invasion of Pakistan formally at the UN Security Council. He probably feared that any ceasefire resolution would include a provision that he had to negotiate with the Awami League – something he was determined to avoid. But whatever the rationale of the failure, it was an important blunder.

The Security Council did nevertheless discuss the situation in East Pakistan, but successive resolutions were vetoed by either Russia or China. The Russians, backing India, wanted any resolution to include commitments for a transfer of power to the Awami League; the Chinese, backing Pakistan, did not. In his capacity as foreign minister, Zulfikar Ali Bhutto went to New York but was unable to affect the course of events. With Pakistan's unity on the verge of destruction, and frustrated by the Russians' Security Council vetoes, Bhutto decided to make the best of a bad job and strengthen his own political position back home. On 15 December he told the Security Council that he would never address them again. As he ripped up some Security Council papers, he asked: 'Why should I waste my time here? I will go back to my country and fight.' It was the speech of a leader in waiting.

Despite the bleak communications emanating from Dhaka, Niazi has claimed that when the war came to a close Pakistan's position was not so bad:

> In fact when the time for an attack against Dhaka came, they [the Indians] were left with only four weak brigades. All the rest were fighting isolated battles against us and our well-stocked and well-prepared fortresses, and were having a tough time with heavy casualties. Aurora could not move his troops from these sectors to concentrate against Dhaka, his ultimate objective.[68]

Indian accounts of the war confirm many of Niazi's claims. General Jacob has described how he found himself in an increasingly awkward position. The Indian army chief, General Sam Manekshaw, had always made it clear that he did not consider Dhaka to be the primary objective for the Indian invaders. He argued that if the Indian forces took Chittagong and Khulna, then Dhaka would automatically fall. His officers on the ground, however, wanted the big prize and struck straight for Dhaka. As international pressure for a ceasefire built up, Manekshaw became ever more concerned that this focus on Dhaka was going to have disastrous consequences. He could foresee a ceasefire being imposed before India had taken any of East Pakistan's major towns. General Jacob recalls the situation as follows:

> On 13 December we received a signal from Gen Manekshaw ordering us to immediately capture all the towns in Bangladesh that we had bypassed. All the towns were named with the exception of Dacca. These included Dinajpur, Rangpur, Sylhet, Maynamati Cantonment and also Khulna and Chittagong.

Jacob was dismayed:

> We had reached the outskirts of Dacca and to me it was imperative that we capture Dacca rather than waste our efforts in going back and capturing those towns. Had we done so, our operations would have been bogged down. The only towns which we had been able to occupy were Jessore and Comilla from which the Pakistanis had withdrawn.[69]

General Jacob needed Pakistan to surrender as quickly as possible and he opted for some psychological warfare. He was greatly helped by the success of Indian intelligence operatives in intercepting the messages between Dhaka and Rawalpindi. Those messages indicated that morale in Dhaka was desperately low. Jacob then received another useful piece of intelligence. He was told that the East Pakistani governor had called a high-powered meeting in Government House on 14 December. Having looked up the location of the building on a tourist map, Jacob ordered an air strike on it.

It was a masterful tactic. Niazi's public relations officer, Siddiq Salik, was at the receiving end and described what happened. The Indian bombs, he recalled:

> ripped the massive roof of the main hall. The Governor rushed to the air raid shelter and scribbled out his resignation. Almost all the inmates of this seat of power survived the raid. Except for some fish in a decorative glass case. They restlessly tossed on the hot rubble and breathed their last.[70]

Jacob's air raid had finished off not only the fish but also the West Pakistanis' will. The governor, his cabinet and some West Pakistani civil servants headed to the safety of the Hotel Intercontinental. The Red Cross, which had declared the hotel to be a neutral zone, would not let them in unless they disassociated themselves from the Pakistani government. The terrified governor and his colleagues readily agreed.

On 14 December, President Yahya sent Niazi this message:

you have fought a heroic battle against overwhelming odds(.) the nation is proud of you and the world full of admiration(.) I have done all that is humanly possible to find an acceptable solution to the problem(.) you have now reached a stage when further resistance is no longer humanly possible nor will it serve any useful purpose(.) you should now take all necessary measures to stop the fighting and preserve the lives of all armed forces personnel from West Pakistan . . .'[71]

That evening Niazi went to see Herbert Spivack, the US consul general in Dhaka, to send a message to the Indian army chief requesting a cease-fire. By 16 December the negotiations on the ceasefire were sufficiently advanced for General Jacob to go to Dhaka. It was a difficult assignment. Niazi was still hoping to sign a ceasefire document and not a surrender. As Jacob recalled: 'Colonel Khara read out the terms of surrender. There was dead silence in the room as tears streamed down Niazi's cheeks . . . I asked him whether the document was acceptable. He handed it back without comment. I took this as acceptance.'[72] To Niazi's dismay Jacob then made it clear that his surrender would be in public.

Writing 25 years after the war, Niazi claimed that he had never wanted to give up fighting but was forced to by Yahya. 'I had to swallow my pride,' Niazi subsequently claimed, 'and make the supreme sacrifice of forfeiting reputation and honour, and the honour of my gallant troops, in the national interest.'[73] Niazi's account of his own defiance, however, is contradicted by a whole series of eyewitnesses who were in Dhaka during December 1971. One of Niazi's colleagues, General Rao Farman Ali, told the Hamoodur Rehman Commission that in fact Niazi's morale collapsed as early as 7 December. On that day Farman was present at a meeting between Niazi and the governor of East

Pakistan, A.M. Malik, who had asked for a formal briefing on the progress of the military campaign. General Farman described what happened: 'The Governor had hardly said a few words when General Niazi started crying loudly. I had to send the bearer out. The Governor got up from his chair, patted him, and said a few consoling words.'[74] This was a decisive moment after which the governor actively and repeatedly urged Rawalpindi to agree to a ceasefire. Whilst agreeing with the governor's approach, Niazi was reluctant to put his own name to such requests and demanded that any messages discussing the possibility of a ceasefire be sent from the governor's house and not his own military headquarters.

Niazi's surrender seemed all the more craven because, before the Indian offensive, he had repeatedly boasted about how brave he was going to be. Amidst all the talk of fighting to the last man and last round he even claimed that, to reach Dhaka, the Indian tanks would have to roll over his chest. In the event his conduct fell well short of such claims.

The surrender ceremony took place at the Ramna Racecourse, the place where Mujibur Rahman had held some of his mass political rallies. To the fury of the Pakistanis the most senior Indian officer present, Lieutenant General Aurora, brought his wife to witness the ceremony. Having met Aurora at the airport, Niazi drove with him to the racecourse. The two men then sat down in front of a rickety wooden table. With Indian officers crowding all around him and hundreds of thousands of Bengalis looking on, Niazi signed East Pakistan away: 'As I signed the document with trembling hands,' he later recalled, 'sorrow rose from my heart to my eyes, brimming them with unshed tears of despair and frustration.'

The document stated that: 'The Pakistan eastern command agree to surrender all Pakistani armed forces in Bangladesh to Lieutenant General Jagjit Singh Aurora General Officer Commanding in Chief of the Indian and Bangladesh forces in the Eastern Theatre. This surrender includes all Pakistan land air and naval forces . . .'[75] With the paperwork out of the way Niazi stood up, took out his revolver and handed it over to his Indian counterpart.

Niazi has subsequently claimed that he only agreed to Jacob's demands because he had been ordered to do so by President Yahya:

I never wanted, asked for or gave any indication for a ceasefire or surrender. My important signals ended with the assertion 'will fight to last man last round' . . . As a matter of fact Dhaka was so strongly held at this stage that it was impregnable and the Indians would have needed all their available troops to make an impression in it.[76]

Again, it is a bold claim and an implausible one. Close colleagues of Niazi have documented his collapse in morale in the last days of the campaign and confirmed that he was looking for a way out. Indeed, shortly after the surrender Niazi himself told a different story. Siddiq Salik recounts Niazi's comments soon after the two men arrived in Calcutta as prisoners of war. Niazi freely conceded that Dhaka had too few troops in it and he blamed Rawalpindi for failing to send more men.

'With what little you had in Dhaka,' suggested Salik, 'you could have prolonged the war for a few days more.' 'What for?' asked Niazi:

That would have resulted in further death and destruction. Dhaka's drains would have been choked. Corpses would have been piled up in the streets. Yet the end would have been the same. I will take 90,000 prisoners of war to West Pakistan rather than face 90,000 widows and half a million orphans there.[77]

When he eventually returned to West Pakistan, after 28 months as a prisoner of war, Niazi was greeted as an incompetent coward who had brought shame on his nation. Pakistan's official enquiry into the 1971 war was especially damning.[78] It accused Niazi of serial womanising, venal corruption and total military incompetence. It recommended a court martial charging him, amongst other things, with failure to appreciate the imminence of all-out war with India; failing to concentrate his forces; relying on strong points and fortresses that couldn't lend each other mutual support; and failing to plan the defence of Dhaka. Finally, the authors of the Commission's report concluded, somehow, that Yahya's communication of 14 December did not amount to an order to surrender:

there was no order to surrender. But in view of the desperate picture painted by the Commander, Eastern Command, the higher authorities only gave him permission to surrender if he in his judgement thought it necessary. General Niazi could have disobeyed such an order if he thought he had the capability of defending Dhaka . . . if General Niazi had done so and lost his life in the process, he would have made history and would have been remembered by the coming generations as a great hero and martyr but the events show he had already lost the will to fight . . .[79]

It is an unfair assessment written by civilians who were never near the fighting. However, defeated generals can expect little else. Few would claim that Niazi was either a saint or a brilliant general. But, surely, no one can believe that he ever had the remotest chance of defeating the Indian invaders or, indeed, that there was any point in leading his men to certain death so as to satisfy public opinion in West Pakistan. That such a high-powered committee should recommend such a futile course of action reflects the extent of Pakistan's humiliation. Twenty-four years after its creation, Pakistan was irreparably broken and its people distraught. For many of those who had witnessed the events of 1947 and who had had such high hopes of Pakistan, it was a devastating blow. Jinnah's Muslim nation no longer existed. Bangladesh was born.

The Bomb

If India builds the bomb, we will eat grass or leaves; even go hungry, but
we will get one of our own.

—Zulfikar Ali Bhutto, 1965[1]

Abdul Qadeer Khan is Pakistan's most decorated citizen. The official citation for one of his awards – the Hilal-i-Imtiaz – could scarcely have been more complimentary:

> The name of Dr Abdul Quadeer [*sic*] Khan will be inscribed in golden letters in the annals of the national history of Pakistan for his singular and monumental contribution in the field of nuclear science. Dr Khan has published more than 72 scientific research papers in the field of nuclear energy besides a well-known book on physical metallurgy.
>
> In 1976, imbued with the supreme spirit of patriotism, he returned to Pakistan to serve his motherland and gave up a most lucrative job in the West. In the face of all sorts of threats he stoically remained steadfast in his resolve to work for the strength and solidarity of Pakistan.
>
> His contribution in the field of nuclear physics has received national and international recognition by various agencies and organisations all over the world.
>
> In recognition of his epoch-making contributions in the field of science, the President of the Islamic Republic of Pakistan has been pleased to confer on Dr Abdul Quadeer [*sic*] Khan, the award of Hilal-i-Imtiaz. 23 March 1989.[2]

A hero at home, A.Q. Khan's international reputation could scarcely be worse. The Western press routinely describe him as a money-crazed fundamentalist, whose nuclear sales network was one of the most malevolent and dangerous organisations in the history of mankind. Both these depictions of A.Q. Khan are flawed. He was never a religious fundamentalist. His motivation lay in the sense of victimhood that was shared by Muslims all over the world. An angry man, he railed against Westerners who assumed Pakistan was too backward to build a bomb, and who tended to look on India as a relatively benign state despite the fact that it had tested a bomb. A Pakistani nationalist to the core, Khan despised the West as hypocritical and decadent. And as for the charge that he was driven by money, his lifestyle in Islamabad was more bourgeois than nouveau riche. But he was a man of some vanity, which made his televised confession of 4 February 2004 all the more surprising.

> My dear brothers and sisters, I have chosen to appear before you to offer my deepest regrets and unqualified apologies to a traumatized nation.
>
> The recent investigation was ordered by the Government of Pakistan consequent to the disturbing disclosures and evidence by some countries to international agencies relating to alleged proliferation activities by certain Pakistanis and foreigners over the last two decades.
>
> The investigation has established that many of the reported activities did occur, and that these were inevitably initiated at my behest.
>
> I also wish to clarify that there was never ever any kind of authorisation for these activities by the government.
>
> I take full responsibility for my actions and seek your pardon.
>
> In my interviews with the concerned government officials, I was confronted with the evidence and the findings. And I have voluntarily admitted that much of it is true and accurate.[3]

On the face of it, A.Q. Khan had plenty to confess. But confessions are inadmissible as evidence in a court of law for a good reason. Sometimes they are false. And for A.Q. Khan to suggest that the government had never authorised his activities and was by implication unaware of them stretched credibility to breaking point. Few who watched his performance thought they were being told the whole story. For many the question was not whether the army knew about the programme but rather whether the whole nuclear export network, far from being an illicit private business, was in fact an organisation created to implement state policy.

History of Pakistan's Nuclear Programme

The struggle to take credit for Pakistan's nuclear capability has lasted almost as long as the weapons programme itself. It's a story of personal rivalry and institutional division. On one side was the Pakistan Atomic Energy Commission (PAEC) headed, during the crucial years, by its urbane chairman, Munir Ahmed Khan. And on the other was A.Q. Khan.

A.Q. Khan's claim to be Pakistan's pre-eminent nuclear pioneer rests on the fact that, just six years after it was created, his Kahuta plant produced a vital bomb ingredient – enriched uranium. Dr Khan claims that the PAEC made just one contribution to the acquisition of the nuclear bomb – the production of uranium hexafluoride gas, a substance that is needed in the enrichment process. 'That's all they did,' he said. Indeed, he has gone so far as to claim that Munir Ahmed Khan was deliberately trying to undermine the programme and wanted to prevent Pakistan from acquiring nuclear capability because he had been influenced by the ideals of the UN's International Atomic Energy Agency, where he had been on the Board of Governors for ten years. It is a remarkable claim and demonstrates the depth of the bitter rivalries within Pakistan's nuclear establishment.[4]

Given his long-running campaign to claim credit for all aspects of the weapons programme, A.Q. Khan was disturbed when, in June 1998, one of the PAEC officials who had conducted the nuclear tests in the deserts of Balochistan, Samar Mubarakmand, returned home as a hero. A crowd of enthusiastic celebrants, who put garlands around his neck, feted him at Islamabad airport. International TV channels obtained the pictures and broadcast them. Within hours, A.Q. Khan's loyalists were ringing newsdesks complaining about the coverage. The real father of the bomb, they said, was A.Q. Khan himself. Suddenly the man who for decades had avoided Western journalists was available for on-the-record TV interviews in which he boasted about his role in the nuclear programme.

Samar Mubarakmand hit back and also started briefing the press. He said that building the bomb involved a chain with 25 separate links. The uranium had to be mined and refined. It had to be changed into uranium hexafluoride gas. Then there was the production of the warhead and the construction of the test site that had to be designed, built and monitored. A.Q. Khan, he argued, had provided one link in the chain – a golden link – but all 25 had been needed for success. To hit home his point, he added that although A.Q. Khan had indeed been at the test site in Balochistan on 28 May, he arrived only a few minutes before the tests, and that the invitation for him to attend had been extended by the PAEC as a 'courtesy'. The PAEC, he said (and not without a touch of condescension), thought he might like to 'see what a nuclear explosion looked like'.[5]

The controversies between A.Q. Khan and the PAEC continue, but both sides do agree on one point: that the man who first got the programme under way was Zulfikar Ali Bhutto. It was Bhutto who, in 1965, made the famous remark that 'we will eat grass' to get the bomb. And, in 1969, he wrote that Pakistan had to obtain a nuclear bomb to match that of India:

It will have to be assumed that a war waged against Pakistan is capable of becoming a total war. It would be dangerous to plan for less and our plans should therefore include nuclear deterrent ... If Pakistan restricts or suspends her nuclear programme, it will not only enable India to black-mail Pakistan with her nuclear advantage, but would impose a crippling limitation on the development of Pakistan's science and technology.[6]

Despite these statements of intent, Pakistan had still not yet seriously embarked on a weapons programme. By 1972, however, Zulfikar Ali Bhutto started taking more concrete steps. On 20 January he called a meeting of scientists in Multan. Beforehand he contacted Munir Ahmed Khan, who was with the International Atomic Energy Agency (IAEA) in Vienna at the time, and asked him to prepare a report about the status of Pakistan's nuclear programme. Munir Ahmed Khan conducted a survey and concluded that the progress had been slight. Many at Multan agreed and the meeting was turbulent. Some of the younger scientists expressed frustration and complained that Pakistan was lagging in the nuclear field because the bureaucracy would never allow decisions to be taken. The nuclear programme, they said, lacked leadership. Bhutto responded in typical fashion. He drew on his ample stock of charisma to motivate the men in front of him. Pakistan, he said, had to guard against the possibility of India becoming nuclearised and he wanted 'fission in three years'. 'We can do it,' came back the enthusiastic response: 'you will have the bomb!'[7]

The fact that the Multan meeting took place in 1972 – two years ahead of India's first nuclear tests – raises an interesting question. Pakistan has long argued that its programme was always entirely reactive to that of India, and that had Delhi not pursued nuclear capability then neither would Pakistan have done so. Such an assessment is probably fair. By 1972, even if India had not yet executed its tests, Bhutto was well aware that Delhi was trying to acquire a nuclear weapons capability. And despite Bhutto's rhetoric at Multan the issue was pursued with urgency only after the Indian test of 1974. As A.Q. Khan has put it: '1974 was the turning point. It was then Bhutto got really serious.'[8]

Bhutto's problem was that Pakistan was nowhere near being able to build a bomb. The country's first, tentative step along the road to nuclearisation had been taken in the late 1950s with the establishment of the PAEC. Its programme was focused on the peaceful use of nuclear technology and it immediately made plans to acquire an electricity-generating nuclear plant. But the process was painfully slow. Ten years after it was created, the PAEC had little to show for its efforts. There was just one very small research reactor that had been partly paid for by the United States under its Atoms For Peace programme.

In 1965 Pakistan's nuclear energy programme took a major step forward. The government reached an agreement with Canada to build a nuclear reactor outside Karachi. The Canadian plant became known by its acronym KANUPP (Karachi Nuclear Power Plant) and, by 1971, it was on stream. Since KANUPP produced not only electricity but also plutonium, which had potential military uses, the plant was put under international safeguards: to operate it Pakistan needed Canadian expertise, fuel and spare parts.[9] The dependence on Canadian co-operation proved to be critical. After the Indian test of 1974, international concerns about nuclear proliferation intensified. Pakistan complained bitterly that it should not be punished for India's test. But it was. Canada was worried that the safeguards on KANUPP were insufficient and it cut off all supplies of nuclear fuel to the plant.

With KANUPP's future in grave doubt, the PAEC focused on France. Back in 1972, Pakistan had made a formal request to France for the procurement of a reprocessing plant.[10] The French government had been enthusiastic and a contract was signed. The IAEA gave its approval in February 1976 but, ultimately, the plant was never built. Despite the fact that, like KANUPP, the French plant would have been under international safeguards, the Americans feared that Pakistan could use the reprocessing plant to develop a nuclear weapon. The US concerns were so acute that the secretary of state, Henry Kissinger, personally visited Pakistan in an attempt to persuade Bhutto to cancel the deal. Bhutto insisted that Pakistan's nuclear plans were entirely peaceful. Kissinger, in turn, dismissed such assurances as an insult to American intelligence. Since Bhutto remained defiant, Kissinger tried his luck in Paris. Initially, the French insisted that their contract with Pakistan would be honoured, but eventually, in 1977, President Giscard D'Estaing agreed to cancel it. A formal announcement was made in 1978. It was a huge blow to Pakistan which, once again, complained that the West was singling it out.

Given that the Canadian and French deals were always subject to international safeguards, it was never clear exactly how Pakistan planned to use them for a weapons programme. Both plants would have produced plutonium, but to have removed any of it from the site would have involved evading internationally administered monitoring systems. The cancellation of the French deal meant that even those hopes were dashed.

The extent to which Pakistan subsequently overcame these setbacks in producing plutonium for a bomb is uncertain. When the nuclear tests were conducted in 1998, the US Los Alamos National Laboratory concluded that plutonium had been released into the atmosphere, although other US agencies later contested that finding. In 2006 President Musharraf said, 'we do not have a plutonium bomb'.[11] Pakistan's plutonium programme is thought to have begun in earnest in the 1990s when, with Chinese assistance, a reactor was built at Khusab. In 1998, Pakistan announced that it was operational. US officials believe the reactor can produce 8 to 10 kilotons of weapons-grade plutonium every year – enough for three to five nuclear weapons.[12] In September 2008 satellite imagery showed that two more reactors being constructed at Khusab were near completion. Once completed, they would significantly increase Pakistan's plutonium production capacity.[13]

Back in the 1970s, however, the plutonium route seemed to be closed to Pakistan, and Islamabad decided to go for an alternative route to the bomb: enriched uranium. And A.Q. Khan was just the man to make it. Before he returned to Pakistan in 1976, A.Q. Khan had been in Europe for 15 years studying in Germany and Belgium. In 1973 he started work for the joint Dutch, German and British Urenco Consortium, which had access to a uranium enrichment facility at the Almelo Ultracentrifuge Plant in Holland. There are two main recognised methods of enriching uranium to the levels necessary for a weapon: in a diffusion plant or by using ultracentrifuge technology. Almelo specialised in ultracentrifuge and in 1974 A.Q. Khan wrote to Zulfikar Ali Bhutto saying that he not only had experience in uranium enrichment but would also be glad to return to Pakistan. His message provided Bhutto with hope that, despite the difficulties with Canada and France, the weapons programme could be resuscitated. In December of that year the two men met in Karachi and A.Q. Khan explained what he could do. On his return to Pakistan, he spent a few unhappy months within the PAEC structure, before persuading Bhutto that he needed to work alone if he was to succeed in making weapons-grade enriched uranium. The Kahuta laboratory was born.[14] A.Q. Khan had no doubts about his mission. Throughout the 1980s he issued indignant statements insisting that Pakistan's programme was a peaceful one and had no military purpose. But after the 1998 tests he became more sanguine. 'I never had any doubts,' he said. 'I was building a bomb. We had to do it.'[15]

But how did he do it? Even Pakistani authors have said that, during 1975, A.Q. Khan plundered the Almelo facility to provide Pakistan with 'blueprints of the enrichment plant, design and literature relating to centrifuge technology and lists of suppliers, equipment and materials.'[16]

In 1983 a Dutch court sentenced him, *in absentia*, to four years' imprisonment for attempting to obtain classified information. He was eventually cleared on appeal because of a technicality: he had not been properly served with a summons.[17] A.Q. Khan has always denied breaking any law and still strongly resents any suggestion that he was involved in espionage. Pressed on the point, he conceded that he was bound to pick up some knowledge at Almelo. 'As a technician I could understand how things there worked,' he said.[18] He has also said that the most useful knowledge he took away from Europe was not the technical data on ultracentrifuge techniques but information about European manufacturers in the nuclear sector. When Western governments tried to limit the supply of nuclear technology to Pakistan, A.Q. Khan was able to go directly to Western companies and make the purchases he wanted.[19]

And the Western governments did try. In 1975 the major powers had begun to coordinate their efforts. An international group was formed – the London Supplier's Group – which imposed an embargo on the supply of nuclear material and technology to any country that, like Pakistan, had not signed the Nuclear Non-Proliferation Treaty.[20] In 1976 the US Congress had approved the Symington Amendment, which meant that US economic aid, credits and training grants could be blocked if Pakistan showed any sign of frustrating the non-proliferation objectives of the US.[21] In April 1979, Washington did use the Symington Amendment to impose sanctions but later that year, on Christmas Day, something happened that effectively undermined the US non-proliferation efforts for the next decade: the Soviet invasion of Afghanistan. A new cold war front line had been created and Washington could not defend it without Pakistan's help. The National Security Adviser, Zbigniew Brzezinski, told President Jimmy Carter that 'our security policy cannot be dictated by our non-proliferation policy'.[22] Carter decided to lift the Symington-related sanctions.[23] A new reality – the need for Pakistani support in combating the Soviets – meant non-proliferation became a secondary concern. By 1981, Pakistan and the US were discussing a $3.2 billion aid package and the US secretary of state Alexander Haig told his Pakistani counterpart Agha Shahi that 'we will not make your nuclear programme the centrepiece of our relations'.[24]

Even so, many export controls remained in place and Pakistan's procurement programme had to rely on extraordinary methods. The Pakistanis used fake front companies in Europe and the Far East. Some staff in the Pakistani embassies in France and Germany worked full-time on the procurement of nuclear supplies. Diplomatic bags were used to evade the prying eyes of Western customs officials.[25] Pakistani buyers regularly claimed that the items they purchased were intended for civilian use when in fact they were destined for either the PAEC or Kahuta. It was a monumental – and costly – programme of clandestine activity, and it worked.[26] However hard Western governments tried to stem the flow of nuclear technology, Pakistani buyers always seemed to be one step ahead.

Inevitably, Pakistan's buying spree attracted attention. By the late 1970s books were written about it[27] and there was even a TV documentary.[28] The journalists and writers exposing Pakistan's nuclear programme insisted Western governments should step up their efforts to prevent nuclear proliferation. But what the journalists saw as a problem, Western companies considered an opportunity. A.Q. Khan has said that, as the publicity increased:

. . . we received several letters and telexes. Many suppliers approached us with the details of machinery and with figures and numbers of instruments they had sold to Almelo. In the true sense of the word they begged us to purchase their goods. And for the first time the truth of the saying 'they would sell their mother for money' dawned on me. We purchased whatever we required.[29]

Kahuta had started making serious progress. By 1978, A.Q. Khan had enriched uranium to 3 per cent: the concentration needed for generating electricity. Moving to the next stage – 90 per cent – was a huge task. It involved creating thousands of intricately engineered, high-speed centrifuges connected by a complicated pattern of pipe work. As well as combating Western export controls, the scientists at Kahuta had to contend with earthquakes that knocked the centrifuges out of alignment.[30] But by 1982, just six years after he returned to Pakistan, A.Q. Khan had succeeded. He could produce enough highly enriched uranium for a bomb.[31]

After the withdrawal of the Soviets from Afghanistan in 1989, the Americans once again stepped up their non-proliferation efforts. The US Congress passed the Pressler and Glenn Amendments, which outlined far-reaching sanctions to prevent Pakistan obtaining nuclear capability. Both were used: in 1990 Pressler sanctions were imposed, and after the 1998 tests the Glenn Sanctions kicked into effect. But it was all too late. Pakistan was a nuclear state before Pressler and Glenn were even on the statute books.

Pakistan has often argued that the Western effort to deny it nuclear technology was discriminatory and that similar efforts were not made in relation to India. Although it is fair to point out that Pakistan has indeed faced more international pressure over its nuclear programme, it is unreasonable to conclude that the West has simply been motivated by a desire to help India and harm Pakistan. Pakistan's programme was always likely to attract more international concern for two reasons. First, India began to develop its technology far earlier – before an international non-proliferation regime was in place. Second, Pakistan relied on outside technology to a greater extent than India. Even A.Q. Khan has admitted that Pakistan could not have done it alone. In 1990 he told a Pakistani audience that:

it was not possible for us to make each and every piece of equipment or component within the country. Attempts to do so would have killed the project in the initial stages. We devised a strategy by which we would go and buy everything we needed in the open market . . .'[32]

Having achieved the production of enriched uranium, Pakistan needed a warhead. It is on this point that the versions provided by A.Q. Khan and the PAEC clearly diverge.[33] Khan has said that he wrote to General Zia in 1982 saying he had enriched uranium and that he now wanted to build a warhead. Zia apparently gave him the go-ahead and two years later the job was done. But, A.Q. Khan maintains, there was a twist to the tale: Zia's deputy, General K.M. Arif, 'stole' the papers and handed them over to the PAEC. Overnight, the PAEC was able to claim it could produce warheads – but using Kahuta's designs. A.Q. Khan says that the nuclear bombs that eventually went off in 1998 were all of his design.

The PAEC presents a very different story. It maintains that while A.Q. Khan had been given the task of enriching uranium, the PAEC was told to design the warhead back in 1974. The first cold tests took place in 1978, but the device was too big and had to be miniaturised. By 1983 the task had been completed and the PAEC scientists were able to conduct a successful cold test on a usable design. But the PAEC was in for a shock. In 1984 it was told that Kahuta had also been working on a warhead and had also conducted a successful cold test. General Zia, perhaps afraid of penetration by foreign intelligence agencies, had embarked on a remarkably costly exercise – the creation of two warheads by two entirely separate parallel teams. The basic point of dispute is whether the PAEC tested before A.Q. Khan. The two sides present conflicting evidence but most neutral insiders believe the PAEC got there first.

So who is the father of the Pakistani bomb? Without A.Q. Khan, Pakistan would probably still not have the bomb. The PAEC would, more likely than not, have remained wedded to the plutonium route and been frustrated by a whole barrage of international restrictions and monitoring regimes. But A.Q. Khan's claim that he and his Kahuta colleagues developed the nuclear bomb with virtually no help from other institutions does not stand up to close scrutiny. However great his personal contribution, the fact remains that building the bomb was a task that involved not just one but thousands of people.

The Decision to Test

Late in the evening of 27 May 1998, Pakistan's director general of military operations in GHQ, Rawalpindi, made a series of urgent telephone calls. As well as contacting senior military colleagues he rang the prime minister's Secretariat and the Foreign Office in Islamabad. His message was extremely alarming. According to Saudi intelligence, he said, Israeli fighter jets were moving from Chennai in India towards the Pakistan border. He said the Israeli planes were tasked with destroying Pakistan's nuclear capability. The director general of military operations said that Pakistan was just seven hours away from conducting its first ever nuclear test – the Israelis and Indians wanted to ensure that the test would never take place.

Just two weeks before, on 11 and then 13 May, India had exploded five nuclear devices under the desert at Pokaran in Rajasthan. Pakistan was under huge international pressure not to follow suit. Whilst he weighed his options, Prime Minister Nawaz Sharif asked his nuclear scientists to prepare for a test as a contingency. Delighted that decades of research might at last bear fruit, they told him they would be ready by first light on 28 May.

The phone calls made by the director general of military operations had an immediate effect. Pakistan's chairman of the joint chiefs of staff, General Jehangir Karamat, scrambled F-16 fighter planes and sent them to protect the test site in Balochistan. Mirage aircraft and ground-based air defence units were tasked with preventing any attack on the Kahuta uranium enrichment plant just outside Islamabad. Pakistan also dispersed its missile arsenal so as to preserve its nuclear capability in the event of enemy attack. According to A.Q. Khan, the military also decided to arm Pakistan's intermediate-range Ghauri missiles with nuclear warheads.[34] It is, however, far from certain that Pakistan had the capability to mount a nuclear warhead on a Ghauri at this point, for the missile had been test-fired for the first time just one month before. But, armed or not, the Ghauris were moved out of the Kahuta plant. Within minutes the Indians responded by rolling out their own short-range Prithvi missiles. Pakistan and India had started climbing the escalatory ladder towards war with frightening speed.

Alerted by GHQ's phone call, Pakistan's Foreign Office swung into action. By midnight all its most senior diplomats – and the foreign minister himself – had gathered in the converted 1960s-style hotel in which they worked. They contacted the Pakistani embassies in Beijing, Tokyo, Moscow, many Western European capitals and, of course, Washington, warning of the impending attack. They also communicated, indirectly, with the Israeli ambassador in Washington. By 1.00 a.m. the Indian high commissioner to Islamabad had been called from his bed and summoned for a dressing down. Nawaz Sharif, backing up the Foreign Office's efforts, personally called President Bill Clinton in Washington and Prime Minister Tony Blair in London and told them that his intelligence reports were clear: Israeli planes were on the way.

In New York, Pakistan's permanent representative to the United Nations, Ahmed Kamal, received copies of the telegrams being sent from Islamabad. He informed the UN secretary general, Kofi Annan, and the Security Council about the threat. He then approached CNN and offered himself for an interview. Within a couple of hours he was live on air accusing Delhi of launching an attack. 'The world must understand that Pakistan is ready,' he said. 'The reaction would be massive and dissuasive and that it would lead us into a situation which would bode ill for peace and security not only in the region but beyond.'[35] Government spokesmen in Islamabad reinforced his message. Confusingly, they claimed the Israeli planes were coming not from Chennai but from Srinagar, the capital of Indian-controlled Kashmir.

The attack never happened. At the time Pakistan argued that its prompt diplomatic activity forced India and Israel to abandon the plan. Delhi said the whole story was a fabrication. As soon as they had received Pakistan's warnings, Western governments had started their own investigations. By the morning of 28 May they were able to assure the Pakistanis that no such attack was ever planned: the Americans arranged for the Israeli chief of staff to make a personal, categorical denial to the Pakistani ambassador in Washington.[36]

Some people within the Pakistani administration had also been sceptical about the possibility of an Israeli attack. Indeed, even some of those involved in the crisis management never really believed the Israeli planes were coming. They pointed out that if some F-16s were flying from Chennai to Kahuta, they would have to be refuelled three times – a process that would inevitably lead to their detection by Pakistani radar. But the dynamics of Pakistani politics are such that no one dared contradict the view from GHQ where many senior officers seemed convinced that the threat was real. For a civilian to challenge the military's assessment would open them up to the accusation of failing the country at a time of crisis. So, notwithstanding their doubts, senior officials and politicians acted on the basis that the threat was genuine. They knowingly responded to a non-existent threat. The inability of senior decision-makers openly to discuss the reality of the supposed danger raises serious questions about Pakistan's command and control capability. The most sobering comment was made by one of the most senior Pakistani officials involved in the events of that evening: 'Our radar stations were on high alert,' he said. 'If some Gulf State prince had been travelling unannounced in a private jet towards Karachi that night, the results would have been cataclysmic.'[37]

There were to be other moments of confusion. On 30 May, Pakistan conducted its second round of nuclear tests. Shortly after 1.00 p.m. the foreign minister, Gohar Ayub, announced that his country had success-fully detonated two nuclear devices under the Chagai mountains in Balochistan. Within seconds his statement was flashed around the world's international newsdesks. Then something strange happened. At 6.00 p.m. an official Pakistani spokesman issued a correction. The foreign minister had made a mistake. There had not been two detona-tions; there had been just one. The discrepancy was never explained, but it did raise more questions about command and control. If Pakistan's own foreign minister did not know how many nuclear bombs had gone off, then who did? Who was running Pakistan's nuclear programme?

There are various explanations for the events of 27 May 1998. Few now believe the threat of an Israeli attack was genuine. Some, however, believe it was a genuine mistake. Pakistan intelligence officials had been put on high alert ever since India's nuclear test. They were told to look out for any attempt to destroy Pakistan's nuclear facilities by methods such as an air strike, a helicopter raid or even a cruise missile attack. A Pakistani intelligence report from London straight after the Indian test said that ten Israeli planes had disappeared from an airfield in Israel. Ever distrustful of India and Israel's close defence relation-ship, the Pakistanis stepped up their surveillance of Indian airfields to see whether the planes could be seen there. Pakistan has long consid-ered the possibility of a joint Indian–Israeli strike. The former Pakistani army vice chief, General (retd) K.M. Arif, has said that in the mid-1980s he was made aware of possible Israeli attacks on three sepa-rate occasions.[38] The fact that the Israelis had used an air strike to destroy Iraq's Osirak nuclear plant just outside Baghdad in 1981 added to Islamabad's fears.

In reality, the Israelis never deployed any F-16s on 27 May. It is quite possible that some pro-test elements in Military Intelligence and the ISI were concerned that Prime Minister Nawaz Sharif, and for that matter the army leadership, might bow under the intense international pressure not to test and therefore decided to create a scare. To add credibility to the exercise they may have fed some of their information through contacts in Saudi intelligence. Many Western officials and a few Pakistanis involved in the events of 27 May believe this. Another piece of evidence suggesting that the Israeli scare was a deliberately planted false alarm is that a pro-test Pakistani journalist wrote about Israel's plans to attack Kahuta as early as 21 May. How he could possibly have known about the Israeli 'attack' one week in advance of its happening is far from clear.[39]

The pro-test hawks had good reason to doubt the prime minister's intentions. Immediately after the Indian tests, there was a vigorous debate in Pakistan as to how Islamabad should respond. Many argued that Pakistan should answer India in kind. But a substantial body of opinion disagreed. On the evening of 12 May, after India had conducted its first test, the army chief Jehangir Karamat called the navy and air force chiefs for an informal discussion at his house. The navy chief, Admiral Fasih Bokhari, argued against testing on the grounds that, for once, Pakistan would be able to claim the moral high ground. He pointed out that Pakistan still had nuclear capability whether it was tested or not, and recommended waiting to see how the world reacted to India's move.

He was not alone in that view. When Nawaz Sharif called a meeting of the Defence Committee of the Cabinet to discuss the issue, he arrived with the foreign minister, Sartaj Aziz, and one of his closest advisers, Chaudhry Nisar, who both urged restraint. Karamat took a middle course, arguing that Pakistan should 'take it easy' and not make any precipitate decision. He said that Pakistan not only did not need to test but might also be able to benefit from not doing so. Sharif did not commit himself but others did. The minister for religious affairs, Raja Zaffar ul-Haq, told Karamat that if he did not approve a test the army rank and file would think they had a leader who lacked the courage to stand up to India. At the end of the meeting Sharif ordered that appropriate preparations should be put in place while he considered the matter further.[40]

Nawaz Sharif was giving serious consideration to not testing. He told the Americans that he did not want to engage in tit for tat exchanges: 'The Indians were madmen,' he said, and he did not want to 'madly follow suit'.[41] It is noteworthy that the prime minister's close confidants wrote many of the press articles laying out the arguments for restraint. Take, for example, an article written by Mujeeb ur-Rehman Shami who was one of the closest advisers to, and a speechwriter for, the prime minister at the time. On 13 May he wrote:

> it will not be a wise thing to give a tit for tat response to India's nuclear explosions. We must wait and see what international opinion does to India . . . to accede totally to the demands being made by the Indian Vajpayees [Atal Behari Vajpayee was the Indian prime minister who authorised the Indian tests] would be tantamount to providing India with an umbrella. If Pakistan joins battle with India immediately, this would distract world attention from India.[42]

But if there was to be no test then Pakistan wanted something in return. The prime minister laid out his terms. He asked for an end to US sanctions, the extension of International Monetary Fund (IMF) loans and security guarantees. President Clinton did try to meet some of these demands. US officials said that Pakistan's $1.6 billion facility with the IMF could be trebled in size. They also offered to write off Pakistan's $3 billion dollars' worth of bilateral debt. More importantly, they said they were putting pressure on Japan to write off its bilateral debt that amounted to $9 billion. On sanctions, Clinton said that he would attempt to get them lifted but pointed out that the final decision rested with Congress. As for security guarantees, he could not even sound positive. Washington felt that any guarantee of Western military intervention in the event of an Indian attack on Pakistan would only encourage Islamabad to increase the level of the insurgency in Kashmir. Western diplomats in Islamabad tried to finesse the issue, but there was no hiding the fact that substantive security guarantees would not be forthcoming. Clinton, however, did make an offer that he hoped Pakistan could not refuse. He sent General Antony Zinni of the US Central Command to meet Karamat and offer him a huge conventional arms package in return for a no-test decision. Once again, however, there was always the risk that Congress could derail such a package and Clinton was in no position to make firm guarantees.

Taken as a whole, President Clinton's offer was substantial and could have resulted in a significant proportion of Pakistan's foreign debt being written off. But Nawaz Sharif was unimpressed. 'This is nothing,' he told a senior Finance Ministry official. 'If we test the whole world will give me money.' And if Sharif found the carrot unappetising, he was also unimpressed by the West's stick. The international response to India's tests was surprisingly muted. US sanctions were imposed but some European powers held back and no one really believed that the sanctions would be strong enough to make much impact in India. Sharif's foreign minister, Gohar Ayub, and his finance minister, Sartaj Aziz, assured the prime minister that Pakistan could easily withstand a similar level of sanctions. Commenting on his decision to conduct the test, Prime Minister Sharif made no secret of the fact that this was a factor in his decision-making:

> The pressure was irresistible at home. It was mounting on the government every day, every hour. The world outside is not aware of the emotional feelings of the people of this region. I have been holding on and exercising the utmost restraint. But we were disappointed that the world community really failed to take a strong action against India.[43]

By the evening of 27 May, Nawaz Sharif had made up his mind. Karamat agreed. First, and perhaps foremost, he was reluctant to cause a rift between the army and the civilian government. India's increasingly bellicose statements about Kashmir also concerned him. The Indian home minister, L.K. Advani, had caused great anxiety in Islamabad when he said India's tests had 'brought about a qualitatively new stage in Indo-Pakistani relations' and that India was 'resolved to deal firmly with Pakistan's hostile activities in Kashmir'.[44] But Karamat was not only guided by such matters of state. He had been stung by Raja Zafar ul-Haq's suggestion that he lacked courage: no army chief, least of all a Punjabi one, likes to be called a coward.

And so, with Karamat and Sharif agreed, the scientists who had decamped to Balochistan put the final process in motion. As dawn broke over the Chagai mountains, Pakistan became the world's seventh acknowledged nuclear state.

Nuclear Doctrine

In August 1999 Delhi's Strategic Policy Advisory Board set out India's post-test nuclear doctrine. It described Indian intentions in the clearest possible terms. Even though ministers touted it as a discussion paper, few doubted that Delhi would act on its recommendations to develop an 'effective, credible nuclear deterrence and adequate retaliatory capability should deterrence fail'. This, the document said, would require a 'triad of aircraft, mobile land-based missiles and sea-based assets'.[45] There were also plans to develop effective early warning systems.

Pakistan has not published any such document. Senior retired officials have, however, written articles that, with a degree of deliberate ambiguity, amount to much the same thing. The first came in October 1999 when three veterans of Islamabad's foreign policy, Agha Shahi, Zulfiqar Ali Khan and Abdul Sattar, co-authored a newspaper article. In it they argued that nuclear weapons in South Asia do have deterrence value, that Pakistan does not need to match India's nuclear arsenal bomb for bomb, and that Pakistan should not agree to no first use.[46]

General Musharraf subsequently confirmed that approach, saying that Pakistan would work out how many warheads it needed for a credible deterrence and not exceed that number, whatever India produced. It is also clear that unlike India, which has to consider both Pakistan and China as potential enemies, Pakistan's nuclear weapons are all pointed at one country and one country alone: India. There is ambiguity about the point at which Islamabad would decide to go nuclear.[47] It is not certain, for example, how Pakistan would respond to an Indian offensive across the line of control in Kashmir. It is likely that the nuclear threshold would not be reached until a limited, or full-scale, invasion was mounted across the recognised international border. Pakistani strategists point out that is not simply a question of when they would cross the nuclear threshold. Before launching a nuclear attack Pakistan could just threaten to do so. It might also decide to back up that threat by conducting another nuclear test. There are many options. But while many in the West are calling for greater transparency about these issues so as to reduce the risk of accidental nuclear conflict, many in Islamabad argue that openness and clarity about its intentions would be counterproductive as it would weaken the deterrent effect of its nuclear arsenal and lead to greater instability. Pakistan's reluctance to cooperate with the West on these issues has been reinforced by Washington's decision to reach a deal with India on nuclear cooperation whilst making it unambiguously clear that Pakistan could not expect similar treatment. The agreement between Washington and Delhi means that despite its nuclear military programme, the US can sell nuclear fuel, technology and reactors to India.[48] India secured the deal without giving any commitment to sign the Nuclear Non-Proliferation Treaty.

Pakistan knows that in the event of a conflict, India would try to deny Islamabad the opportunity to launch a first strike: Pakistan must have the ability to launch a retaliatory, second strike. For Pakistan, then, a minimum credible deterrence requires a first- and second-strike capability. The absence of missile silos means that Pakistan's nuclear arsenal must be dispersed in so many locations that some weapons would survive an Indian first strike. According to Agha Shahi, mobility, dispersal, camouflage and deception can provide assurance of the survival of at least a fraction of Pakistan's nuclear arsenal.[49] He is probably right. No Indian military commander is going to be able to tell the political leadership in Delhi that he can guarantee the destruction of Pakistan's nuclear capability in its entirety.

Pakistan says that it has already established the number of nuclear warheads it needs for a minimum nuclear deterrent, and that they will not exceed that number in an arms race with India.[50] Indeed, President Musharraf in 2005 said 'we have assessed the threat and . . . we quantified the minimum level. And today, I have been very pleased to announce that we have crossed that minimum deterrence level.'[51] Even if Pakistan feels it now has enough warheads, there is still uncertainty as to what the number is. The size of Pakistan's nuclear arsenal is constrained by a number of factors – not least the amount of fissile material produced in the country. According to the former army chief, General (retd) Aslam Beg, once it had built the bomb, Pakistan tried to create an arsenal around one third as large as that of India: 'India had fifty or sixty devices. We kept our stockpile in relation to that number.'[52] Many other sources confirm that kind of ratio, although the actual numbers vary considerably.[53] But in June 2000 reports emanating from the US gave a very different picture. Quoting unnamed US sources, the American TV network NBC reported that 'Pakistan's nuclear arsenal is vastly superior to that of India with up to five times the nuclear warheads, say US military and intelligence officials.'[54] The report said that the traditional understanding that Pakistan had around 10 to 15 nuclear weapons and India between 25 and 100 should be reversed: it was Pakistan that had the larger number. It was also claimed that Pakistan 'appears far more capable than India of delivering nuclear payloads'. The report was backed up by comments from General Antony Zinni of the US Central Command. 'Don't assume that the Pakistani capability is inferior to the Indians', he said. India, the Americans believed, 'has no nuclear-capable missiles and fewer aircraft capable of delivering a nuclear payload than Pakistan does'. The report, if accurate, may help explain General Musharraf's repeated statements that Pakistan did not want to match India bomb for bomb. He was, perhaps, speaking from a position of strength.

President Musharraf's statement that Pakistan has achieved its goal of a minimum deterrence level suggests that it is no longer building warheads. The resources going into the plutonium reactor at Khusab, however, suggest that this is not the case and that Pakistan is engaged in a nuclear arms race with India. One aspect of their competition is Pakistan's desire to match the Indian concept of a triad of delivery systems. Even though the Pakistani navy is relatively small, as early as 1999 some Pakistani writers were suggesting that Pakistan needs a submarine-based delivery system.[55] In 2004 a retired Pakistani general, Mahmud Ali Durrani, produced a semi-doctrinal document that picked up where Agha Shahi, Zulfiqar Ali Khan and Abdul Sattar had left off.[56] With the disclaimer that 'Pakistan has not formally announced any nuclear doctrine', he confirmed that the purpose of Pakistan's nuclear capability was to deter external aggression by means of a second-strike capability. He stressed that Pakistan had determined the size of its arsenal 'irrespective of the eventual size of the Indian arsenal'. However, he also wrote that Pakistan will try to match India's delivery systems: 'Pakistan will work towards the development of the triad by giving the Pakistan navy nuclear capability. The desire for naval nuclear capability will gain urgency if it is felt by the leadership in Pakistan that the ground-based systems do not provide assured second-strike capability. The primary reason for not developing a naval nuclear option would be an inability to resolve the technical problems.'

Missiles

Aside from a sea-based launch, there are two main methods of launching a nuclear attack: the air force has planes that can deliver nuclear payloads and the army has developed missile systems. The current aircraft of choice is a modified F-16. In 2006 the US enhanced the capability of the Pakistan Air Force by selling it 36 new F-16s, all of which could be modified to deliver nuclear weapons. Some Pakistani writers have suggested that Pakistan should continue to rely on aircraft to deliver nuclear weapons.[57] If India also agreed to forgo missile development, both sides would not only save money but also give each other a longer response time in the event of a nuclear conflict. Such arguments, however, stand no chance of prevailing. South Asia is already engaged in a missile race.

Pakistan has three different missile systems produced by different parts of the military-industrial complex. In February 1989, General Aslam Beg announced that two versions of the HATF had been successfully tested.[58] The most reliable version, built with Chinese cooperation, was HATF-1. First tested in April 1988, it was a relatively unsophisticated short-range (just 80 kilometres) rocket which provided too few options for the military planners. HATF-2, tested at the same time, could travel 200 kilometres but it was unreliable. Despite that, Pakistan pressed on with a HATF-3 missile which has a range of 290 kilometres. After some initial setbacks[59] the HATF-3, also known as the Ghaznavi, entered service in 2004.[60]

In addition to these missiles the PAEC worked on a separate programme based on Chinese M-11 missiles. The first of these, the Shaheen-1 (which, confusingly, is also known as the HATF-4), has a range, according to Pakistani officials, of 650 kilometres and was first tested in 1999. Shaheen-2 (or HATF-6) has a range of 2,200 kilometres, was first tested in 2004,[61] and looks set to become the mainstay of Pakistan's missile force. But, as ever, A.Q. Khan has provided an alternative. The development of missiles in Pakistan reflected the divisions that existed in the nuclear field. So, while the PAEC looked to China, A.Q. Khan approached North Korea. His Ghauri missiles are Pakistani-assembled versions of North Korea's Nodong missiles which have been supplied in parts by Pyongyang. In return, Pakistani officials said at the time that they sent money and rice to North Korea. The Ghauri-1 was test-fired in April 1998 when it was claimed that the missile could carry a warhead a distance of 1,300 kilometres.[62] Having acquired the basic technology, Kahuta characteristically made adaptations and improvements to the North Korean design. It devised, for example, a better guidance system – which was then shared with North Korea. The Ghauri-2 was meant to have a longer range – up to 2,000 kilometres – which would enable Pakistan to hit any target in India. However, the first test in April 1999 was a failure and the missile actually landed not in its intended spot but in Iran. Kahuta also has plans for a Ghauri-3 with a range of 3,500 kilometres.

The latest Pakistani research is concentrated on developing an equivalent of the US's cruise missiles. In 2007 Pakistan tested the HATF-7, which is thought to have been reverse engineered from some US Tomahawk cruise missiles, that were meant to hit a target in Afghanistan in 1998 but went astray and landed in Pakistan where they were recovered almost intact.[63] HATF-7 has ground-, sea- and air-launched versions. There is also a HATF-8, a low-altitude, terrain-following, radar-avoiding missile, which can be launched from a Dassault Mirage jet or an F-16.[64] According to the Pakistani military, it can carry a nuclear or conventional weapon.

Like Pakistan, India began its missile programme in earnest in the 1980s.[65] It has produced two nuclear-capable missiles: the Prithvi and the Agni. The Prithvi, based on Soviet designs, is a short-range weapon (150 kilometres) and was created with the target of Pakistan in mind. The Prithvi-1 was first tested in February 1988 and it went into production in 1994. According to Munir Ahmed Khan, it has already been deployed along the Pakistani border. Prithvi-2, which can reach 250 kilometres, was tested in 1996, with a naval version tested in November 2004. The Prithvi-3, which also has a naval version tested in 2004, can deliver a 1,000-kilogram payload up to 300 kilometres.[66]

The second missile system is the Agni which can take a bigger payload than the Prithvi and which has a much longer range of 1,500 to 2,500 kilometres. Agni-1 and Agni-2 were tested between 1989 and 1999. In April 2007, India finally overcame the technical problems that had delayed the Agni-3 and conducted what was said to be a successful test. An Agni-4 missile with a range of 5,000 kilometres is now under development.

The US has made efforts to control the proliferation of missile technology but seems to be having just as little success as it did with the bomb itself. Between 1991 and 1993, Washington imposed sanctions on Beijing on the grounds that M-11 technology had been transferred to Pakistan in breach of the Missile Technology Control Regime. But in the same way as the nuclear non-proliferation regime was undermined by the Soviet invasion of Afghanistan, different political considerations – in this case, the need to foster better relations with Beijing – came into play and the sanctions were dropped.

Does South Asia's Deterrence Work?

While many in the West deplored the 1998 nuclear tests and spoke of growing regional instability, the majority of Pakistanis and Indians said they felt more secure because of their nuclear capability. They see their weapons as a deterrent that will prevent nuclear attack and probably a conventional war as well. Those who want to establish that the nuclear weapon has been a deterrent point to four Indo-Pakistani disputes: Exercise BRASSTACKS in 1987, the Kashmir crisis of 1990 and Kargil in 1999, and the military build-up on the international borders in 2002.

In 1987 India began some ambitious, large-scale military exercises. Islamabad noticed the development and asked the Indian military for reassurances. They were not forthcoming. The Indian prime minister, Rajiv Gandhi, did tell his Pakistani counterpart, Mohammed Junejo, that the exercises were only for training purposes, but Pakistani suspicions were increased when they noticed the Indians creating arms and fuel dumps in forward positions. Pakistan's intelligence agencies warned the military leadership in Rawalpindi that Exercise BRASSTACKS could be transformed into Operation BRASSTACKS and advised the deployment of armoured formations in the border areas. The Pakistan army agreed. Having noticed that deployment, India, with unre-lenting inevitability, started planning its response. Rajiv Gandhi even discussed a pre-emptive ground attack on Pakistan, including a strike on Pakistan's nuclear facilities, to forestall any moves Islamabad might be planning. Eventually, the two countries managed to open direct communication and de-escalate the crisis.[67]

According to India's official report into the Kargil war, Pakistan did use a nuclear threat during BRASSTACKS: 'In 1987 Pakistan conveyed a nuclear threat to India at the time of Operation BRASSTACKS. This was officially communicated by Pakistan's Minister of State for Foreign Affairs, Zain Noorani, to the Indian ambassador in Islamabad.'[68] Pakistani officials have always denied this. General K.M. Arif, who was the vice chief of the Pakistan army throughout the BRASSTACKS episode, has said that nuclear weapons never came into play during the crisis. 'There was no operational deployment of nuclear weapons', he said.[69] But he also argues that since both sides knew about each other's nuclear capability there was added pressure to defuse the crisis. Some Indian sources take a similar view. In the crucial meeting when Rajiv Gandhi was considering a possible Indian pre-emptive strike, an adviser from the ministry of defence argued: 'India and Pakistan have already fought their last war, and there is too much to lose in contemplating another one.'[70] Although some of the evidence is contradictory, it is reasonable to conclude that nuclear weapons did have some deterrence value.

In 1990 another crisis emerged with both India and Pakistan step-ping up the rhetoric, and the level of military activity, in Kashmir. By this time the insurgency in Kashmir was well under way and the Indians were trying to suppress it. There was intense artillery shelling over the line of control and the Indians continued to pour troops into Kashmir. It has been argued that at this time the two countries came close to nuclear war. The US became convinced that during the crisis the PAEC was ordered to assemble at least one nuclear weapon. The US also believes that nuclear-armed F-16s were deployed in the south of Pakistan. The US assumed these moves were linked to the situation in Kashmir. According to General (retd) Aslam Beg, though, there was another aspect to the situation. Pakistani intelligence agents had reported that Israeli planes would take off from Israel, refuel in India and then strike Kahuta. India was to provide the coordinates. Pakistan sent a message to Delhi. It was blunt in the extreme: 'If Israel hits us, you shall be held responsible and Bombay will cease to exist.'[71]

The one point on which these accounts agree is that Washington had detected an escalation up the nuclear ladder. The US deputy national security adviser, Robert Gates, was dispatched to Islamabad. He urged restraint, revealed the US information about the nuclear weapons and threatened sanctions. He told Islamabad that the US had carried out extensive war-gaming exercises and that, in every one of them, Pakistan had lost. He then went to India and said that Pakistan had been persuaded to reduce the level of the insurgency in Kashmir by closing down militant training camps. The crisis passed. But afterwards a US official described it as 'the most dangerous nuclear situation we have ever faced . . . it may be as close as we've got to a nuclear exchange.'[72]

Since there is no definitive evidence that nuclear weapons were deployed in 1990, it is difficult to assess the deterrent effect they might have had. But, once again, they were certainly in the background and all the decision-makers on both sides were well aware of each other's capability. As he looked back on 1990, General (retd) Beg said: 'The fear of retaliation lessens the likelihood of war between India and Pakistan. I can assure you that if there were no such fear we would have probably gone to war in 1990.'[73] It is only fair to point out that many in Pakistan's military establishment believe that both Beg and the US have grossly exaggerated the extent of the crisis in 1990. One explanation that helps reconcile some of these differing perceptions is that Pakistan had for some years been working on modifications to the F-16 with a view to making them capable of carrying nuclear weapons. In 1990 it succeeded. Having noticed this development, the US misinterpreted it and mistakenly saw it as a deliberate threat linked to the deteriorating situation in Kashmir.

In 1999, in the midst of the Kargil crisis, Kashmir was once again causing international concern. Pakistani troops had crossed the line of control and were occupying territory on the Indian side. The Indians, humiliated by the failure to spot the incoming troops, and embarrassed by their difficulties in removing them, considered the possibility of a full-scale invasion across the international border. Another option was to cross the line of control elsewhere in Kashmir and hold it until nego-tiations returned the situation to the status quo ante. In the event, India relied on international diplomatic pressure to force a Pakistani with-drawal. This restraint won Delhi much international praise. Again, the nuclear issue was in the background. In the midst of the crisis, the reli-gious affairs minister and leader of the Pakistani Senate, Raja Zaffar ul-Haq, openly threatened the use of nuclear weapons. Even if it was a wild bluff, his statement had to be taken seriously: throughout the crisis he had attended all the meetings of Pakistan's Defence Committee of the cabinet. On 30 June he told his fellow senators: 'We made it [the nuclear weapon] for what? It is not something sacrosanct to be kept in an arsenal even if your own throat is cut by someone. It is our duty and right to defend ourselves with all the military might at our disposal.' Four days later, India responded in kind. Brajesh Mishra, a senior adviser to Prime Minister Vajpayee, said, 'we will not be the first to use nuclear weapons. But if some lunatic tries to do something against us, we are prepared . . .'[74] Again, it is difficult to claim that the nuclear issue did not play some role in the decision-making processes of the two sides.

Many of those involved in the Kargil affair insist there was no nuclear element to the crisis and certainly no nuclear deployment. But it is interesting to note that nuclear considerations were very much in the mind of the Pakistani prime minister, Nawaz Sharif. In the third week of June, with the Kargil crisis at its height, he told a Pakistani columnist of his fear that the conflict could lead to a nuclear war. He said that since the West was against Pakistan, India could be given high-technology defence equipment that could disable Pakistan's elec-tronic weapons systems and radar. He said the conflict could lead to the complete destruction of both countries, but that if it came to a matter of national survival, he would have to use the bomb.[75] And in his account of the Kargil conflict, the former special assistant to the US president, Bruce Riedel, has recorded how the Americans believed that the Pakistani military was preparing nuclear-tipped missiles – possibly without even telling the civilian leadership.[76] Speaking after the Pakistani withdrawal from Kargil, Pakistan's foreign minister, Sartaj Aziz, told the Senate: 'It was our nuclear deterrence that kept India at bay.'[77] For its part, the Indian leadership calculated that not extending the war to the international borders not only carried diplomatic benefits but also reduced the risk of the nuclear factor coming into play. Again it seems that the very existence of the nuclear arsenal did have a deterrent effect.

The fourth potentially disastrous conflict erupted in 2002 when India responded to a militant attack on its parliament building in Delhi by deploying hundreds of thousands of troops on its border with Pakistan. Pakistan responded in kind and for several months an estimated one million troops were in close proximity and on high alert. Eventually the forces were stood down and, speaking shortly afterwards in December 2002, General Musharraf claimed that the nuclear issue had been a factor. At an address to military veterans he said: 'I personally conveyed messages to Prime Minister Vajpayee through every international leader who came to Pakistan, that if Indian troops moved a single step across the international border or the Line of Control, they should not expect a conventional war from Pakistan.'[78]

A 2005 scholarly study of all the occasions on which Pakistan and India had nearly gone to war since acquiring nuclear capability found that the nuclearisation of South Asia had acted as a deterrent. Of course, the nuclear factor was by no means the only one influencing the political and military leaders. To varying degrees, depending on the circumstances, deterrence through conventional weapons and US mediation also played a role. But the main conclusion of the study was that, despite the strong possibility of conflict between India and Pakistan, 'nuclear-deterrence proposition provides the strongest explanation for the absence of major war in the region over the last two decades . . .'.[79]

Proliferation

It all began with Iran. In the 1970s the Shah of Iran had been interested in nuclear technology and ordered a reactor from Germany. It's not clear whether he was thinking of a possible weapons programme as well as nuclear energy but in any event his plans never reached fruition. After the Shah was swept from power by the 1979 Iranian revolution, the whole idea was put on hold: Ayatollah Khomeini saw nuclear weapons as a Western, un-Islamic invention. It wasn't until 1986 that

President, and later Supreme Leader, Ali Khamenei picked up where the Shah had left off. And it didn't take long for him to realise that foreign expertise would help speed up the process of going nuclear.

By 1987 Iran had made the necessary contacts. Businessmen with access to A.Q. Khan presented Teheran with a one-page handwritten list of prices for centrifuge designs, disassembled centrifuge machines and even an entire 2,000-machine centrifuge plant. At first Iran made relatively modest purchases, but in 1993 it wanted more. Despite efforts to create indigenous nuclear expertise, the Iranian leadership concluded that it needed to cut some corners with a bigger purchase from the network. This time Teheran opted for a package of centrifuge designs, a large number of components and possibly a nuclear weapons design.[80] According to the Iranians, this deal was completed by 1996, at which point their relationship with the A.Q. Khan network ended. Faced with evidence of further meetings, Iran has said they were set up only to complain about the poor quality of the materials the network had sent them.

The next big deal was with North Korea. During the 1980s North Korea had been working on a plutonium-based nuclear programme. Pyongyang's increasingly uncooperative attitude towards the IAEA, and its 1993 threat to pull out of the Non-Proliferation Treaty, led many to conclude that it was in fact trying to build a bomb. That concern led in 1994 to a diplomatic agreement under which the US agreed to supply North Korea with oil and civil nuclear energy reactors in return for a freeze of its other nuclear programmes.

Given the difficulty of negotiating with North Korea, the 1994 Agreed Framework was seen as something of a triumph by many in the US administration. It did, however, raise a difficult question. Had North Korea agreed to freeze its plutonium programme only because it had an alternative route to a bomb – the method that A.Q. Khan had mastered – namely, uranium enrichment?

In retrospect, that does indeed seem to have been the case. In fact, it now seems that Pyongyang's enrichment programme may have begun as early as the late 1980s. According to the journalist Shyam Bhatia, Pakistan was so heavily involved that the Pakistani prime minister, Benazir Bhutto herself participated in the transfers. Bhatia had known

Ms Bhutto from her Oxford University days and claims she told him that on a state visit to Pyongyang in 1993 she personally smuggled in some CDs with information about uranium enrichment. She hid the CDs in a specially purchased coat with suitably deep pockets. In return Pakistan was to get help with its missile programme. Bhatia published the story after her death.[81]

The claims about Ms Bhutto have not been verified, but from the mid-1990s rumours began to circulate that Pakistan had traded its knowledge of uranium enrichment for missile technology. Whether it paid with Nodong missiles or hard cash, there is now little doubt that nuclear technology was exported to North Korea. In his autobiography General Musharraf confirmed that nearly two dozen centrifuges were sent there as well as 'a flow meter, some special oils for centrifuges and coaching on centrifuge technology'.[82]

The third nuclear aspirant supplied by A.Q. Khan's network was Libya. Given that Libya had been an early supporter of Pakistan's fledgling nuclear programme, Colonel Gadaffi might reasonably have expected to have been amongst the first beneficiaries. Rather to his chagrin, however, that was not the case. His attempts to persuade General Zia not to hang Zulfikar Ali Bhutto led to something of a rupture in Pakistani–Libyan relations. But Gadaffi didn't give up on the idea of going nuclear and over the years made somewhat desultory attempts to train scientists and to buy materials on the international market. In the mid-1990s, though, he decided to get serious. Having established contact with the network he made some initial, small-scale purchases before, in 2000, placing a truly massive order. Libya wanted no fewer than 10,000 of A.Q. Khan's most advanced centrifuges along with some uranium hexafluoride feedstock.[83]

The Libyan deal raised the A.Q. Khan network to a new level and a decision was taken to produce many of the centrifuge parts in Malaysia. It was the Libyan deal that led to A.Q. Khan's downfall. For a whole variety of reasons, Colonel Gadaffi changed his mind about acquiring a nuclear weapon. Despite having spent a lot of money on his nuclear programme over a period of many years, Gadaffi was aware that it had produced remarkably little – and certainly not a bomb. Originally he had thought a nuclear weapon would protect Libya from attack.

Now, having seen what had happened to Saddam Hussein in Iraq, he began to wonder whether the very endeavour he had embarked upon – acquiring a weapon – might, contrary to his hopes, put Libya at greater risk.

In March 2003, Gadaffi sent his son to London to suggest that Libya might want to disarm. By this time the British and the Americans had penetrated the A.Q. Khan network. Gadaffi, though, did not realise just how much the Western powers knew about his programme. From the outset he was open about his relatively insignificant biological weapons programmes, but he tried to obscure parts of his nuclear facilities. The crucial breakthrough – undermining both Gadaffi and the A.Q. Khan network – came when the CIA got a tip-off about a shipment of centrifuge parts on board a ship called *BBC China*. The materials were seized on their way to Libya. Faced with this incontrovertible evidence of the Libyan programme, Gadaffi decided to let British and American inspectors see whatever they wanted. And for good measure he also handed over another of his purchases from the A.Q. Khan network: in a plastic bag from A.Q. Khan's favourite tailor were detailed plans, not just for building centrifuges, but also for a nuclear bomb.

In addition to the three governments to which nuclear sales were made, A.Q. Khan stands accused of trying to sell weapons to countries such as Iraq and Syria, which turned him down. The Iraqi case is well documented. In 1995 UN inspectors found documents at the farm of Hussein Kamel, Saddam Hussein's son-in-law, after he had defected to Jordan. They included a one-page memo from the Iraqi intelligence service, the Mukhabarat, dated October 1990, summarising a meeting between members of that organisation and a man who called himself Malik and claimed to represent A.Q. Khan. According to the memo, Khan was prepared to give Iraq designs for a nuclear weapon and provide help in enriching uranium. He would procure supplies from Europe via Dubai. Another document suggests that Malik was looking for an initial payment of $5 million. The proposal did not go anywhere. Saddam Hussein, with his remarkably consistent ability to miscalculate, reckoned it was a CIA sting operation.[84]

On the face of it then, A.Q. Khan was a traitor. Yet as soon as he had appeared on TV to make his confession in 2004, there was speculation that he had reached an understanding with the military. One of his claims in particular cast doubt on the credibility of his confession. 'I also wish to clarify', he had said, 'that there was never ever any kind of authorisation for these activities by the government.'[85] The claim that the military had known nothing about the nuclear transfers seemed highly implausible: after all, the military ran the programme and could hardly have missed planeloads of equipment being shipped around the world. Foreign governments were presenting ever more detailed evidence of Pakistani proliferation, and many Pakistanis wondered whether the army had offered A.Q. Khan a deal: house arrest and no international investigation in return for his televised confession.

After President Musharraf lost power in 2008, A.Q. Khan started telling a different story. He sensed that the mood in Islamabad was changing. When Benazir Bhutto had been courting the United States in 2007 to facilitate her return to Pakistani politics, she had called for A.Q. Khan to be handed over to the Americans. It was always an unpopular policy in Pakistan and her great political rival, Nawaz Sharif, by contrast, called for A.Q. Khan's release. After the 2008 elections were over, with Benazir Bhutto assassinated and Nawaz Sharif in the ruling coalition, Khan's house arrest conditions were eased and his telephone line was reconnected.

A.Q. Khan tested the waters with some press statements. Asked about his TV confession he recanted: 'I was never selling. This is the western garbage that uses the word selling. I never sold anything to anyone and I never got any money.'[86] He insisted that whatever he did do was part of Pakistani government policy. 'I did whatever my government wanted me to do. I gave them whatever they wanted.'[87] He said that he had been forced to confess and had gone along with the idea in the national interest. He also suggested that the businessmen in his procurement network may have acted independently and over-ordered equipment he was buying for Pakistan so that they could sell it on to others.[88]

For obvious reasons reliable information about the A.Q. Khan network is scarce, but there have now been a number of court cases and journalistic investigations. The overall picture that emerges is not of a hierarchically organised business that came up with sales plans and executed them. Rather, the businessmen involved, many of whom first established contact with Khan when he was buying for the Pakistani programme, were a group of around 50 mutually suspicious, self-interested and morally unscrupulous individuals, each working to maximise his own profits.[89]

There are some indications that the Americans are having second thoughts about their original understanding of the A.Q. Khan network. Back in February 2004, President George W. Bush had said that the network had been dismantled and he described Khan as 'the director of the network, its leading scientific mind, as well as its primary salesman. Over the past decade, he made frequent trips to consult with his clients and to sell his expertise.'[90] In July 2007, however, the US undersecretary for political affairs, Nicholas Burns, hinted at a more nuanced picture when he spoke to the Senate Foreign Relations Committee: although he thought the network had been fundamentally dismantled, he said, 'I cannot assert that no part of that network exists.'[91]

The possibility that, in some respects, elements of the network were acting independently should not obscure the fact that the nuclear sales to Iran, Libya and North Korea were all linked to Pakistan. The most important question is not whether some of A.Q. Khan's business associates made some extra money on the side but rather who in Pakistan was responsible. No one can seriously suggest that Khan did not know what was going on. The question rather is whether he was acting on his own initiative and for personal profit, or whether, as he now says, he was following government orders.

The evidence about A.Q. Khan's wealth is contradictory and unclear. According to a former officer at the National Accountability Bureau, a dossier prepared by Pakistan's intelligence agencies in 2000 found that he had $8 million in several bank accounts, a hotel worth $10 million in Timbuktu, Mali, and that he had given a house to the former army chief Aslam Beg.[92] For his part, A.Q. Khan insists that he lives nothing more than a middle-class lifestyle. Certainly, descriptions of his home in Islamabad as a palace are unfair; it is a typical house for a senior official in the city. He acknowledges having a few other properties in the capital, but says they belong to his wife and children. He has described his hotel in Timbuktu as 'an eight-bedroom mud brick house where the poor people reside.[93] The manager of the hotel has said that he met Hendrina, A.Q. Khan's wife, in 1999 when she hired him as a tour guide. She subsequently helped him get medical treatment in Islamabad in 2000 and then gave him the money to build the hotel as a 'gift'. He said that Hendrina Khan retains no stake in the hotel.[94]

So what did the Pakistan army know of the nuclear proliferation? In February 2009 President Zardari, apparently keen to win popular support by showing he could defy Washington on at least one issue, released A.Q. Khan from house arrest. But the scientist still did not give chapter and verse on his past activities, and the outside world was left guessing as to the extent of army involvement in the proliferation. In its report on A.Q. Khan the International Institute of Strategic Studies concluded that 'a careful analysis shows that most of A.Q. Khan's dealings were carried out on his own initiative'.[95] And yet, as the IISS acknowledged, the military has always controlled nuclear policy in Pakistan. The A.Q. Khan network had repeatedly exported large components, including fully constructed centrifuges, over a prolonged period, sometimes in military planes. Khan himself had made over a dozen visits to North Korea. By the time he was brought down, A.Q. Khan's activities were well known to Western intelligence agencies and an increasing number of customers. Even the IAEA had got hold of parts of the story. The Pakistan army is asking people to believe that it was in fact the last to find out what was happening in its own backyard.

Despite that prima facie case for military involvement, General Musharraf maintains that there are good reasons why the Pakistan army was in fact ignorant about the illicit nuclear trade. He has argued that A.Q. Khan's procurement network provided scientists with ready-made, clandestine arrangements that were difficult to penetrate. They simply had to reverse the flow: to use his network to sell rather than to buy. Furthermore, A.Q. Khan had almost complete operational autonomy: his hero status made it difficult for anyone to challenge him. General Musharraf has also offered the rather unconvincing argument that many of the nuclear exports took the form of hard-to-detect intellectual property transfers.[96]

Musharraf maintains that he acted against A.Q. Khan whenever there was evidence to do so. One of his problems, he insists, was that the US and others in the international community did not share their intelligence about Khan until a very late stage. US officials remember it differently. The State Department's Richard Boucher, for example, said in February 2004 that the US had 'discussed non-proliferation issues with Pakistan repeatedly, over a long period of time'.[97] He was referring to a whole series of meetings going back to the late 1990s. In August 1998 the US asked Islamabad to monitor A.Q. Khan's foreign activities – especially his dealings with North Korea.[98] In January 1999 the US deputy secretary of state, Strobe Talbott, told Nawaz Sharif that Washington believed the North Korean missile trade could involve the transfer of nuclear technology.[99] Again, in 2000 the US, claiming that tens of thousands of dollars had been deposited in the bank accounts of Khan Research Laboratory scientists, approached Pakistani officials with suspicions about their activities.[100]

After 9/11 the US deputy national security adviser, Stephen Hadley, went to Islamabad to raise concerns about proliferation, although this probably related to two retired nuclear scientists who had met Osama bin Laden and been asked the obvious question: 'Can you help me build a nuclear bomb?' The information about the meeting with bin Laden was gathered in Kabul after the fall of the Taliban and led to the arrest of the two men, Sultan Bashiruddin Mahmood and Abdul Majeed, in Pakistan.[101] It transpired that they were operating independently and there is no evidence of any links with A.Q. Khan. The US, however, provided further evidence in November 2000 and early October 2003.[102] The army had also had tip-offs from within Pakistan. As early as 1998 scientists working at Khan Research Laboratory had warned government officials that A.Q. Khan was involved in suspicious activities.[103]

General Musharraf's insistence that he always acted against A.Q. Khan in a timely way is unconvincing. Indeed it is more likely that he consistently did as little as possible, as late as possible. There are two ways of explaining Musharraf's reluctance. First, he wanted to avoid the political fall-out of a public humiliation of A.Q. Khan, and second, the military was nervous that its own role in sponsoring the nuclear trade would be made public.

If this view is correct, then Musharraf forced A.Q. Khan to retire as head of Khan Research Laboratory in 2001 only because he wanted to be able to tell the United States that he had acted. The scientist was told that he could retire with honour and there would be no more investigations and no charges.[104] To sweeten the pill Musharraf gave Khan a great send-off. At a formal dinner the Pakistani leader said: 'Dr Khan and his team toiled and sweated, day and night, against all odds and obstacles, against international sanctions and sting operations, to create literally out of nothing, with their bare hands, the pride of Pakistan's nuclear capability.'[105]

But to Musharraf's irritation the Western pressure didn't stop. The information coming out of Libya and Iran could be neither denied nor ignored. In October 2003, armed with these new facts, the US deputy secretary of state, Richard Armitage, and assistant secretary of state, Christina Rocca, went to Army House in Rawalpindi to give Musharraf very detailed evidence about proliferation. One Pakistani official described the briefing as 'mind boggling' in its detail of bank account transactions and travel movements, saying, 'it seemed that the Americans had a tracker planted on A.Q. Khan's body'.[106]

Despite finding themselves in an increasingly untenable situation, Pakistani officials continued in their efforts to limit the damage. In February 2004, just before A.Q. Khan's televised confession, officials were still trying to downplay the extent of his activities. They told journalists, for example, that the illicit cooperation with Iran only lasted from 1989 to 1991.[107] The statement directly contradicts overwhelming evidence that the trade in fact lasted from 1987 until 1996. There are similar discrepancies concerning the time frames of the cooperation with Libya and North Korea.[108] Most damningly of all, Pakistan has still refused to let US or IAEA investigators talk to A.Q. Khan.

It is impossible to draw a definitive conclusion about the military's involvement in the nuclear export programme. But it is worth examining the three deals separately: there may have been different levels of official involvement in each. To take the last first, there is little evidence of state involvement in the sales to Libya. Indeed, A.Q. Khan's own involvement may have been overshadowed by those of his associates who seem to have handled the business of actually sourcing the raw materials and then manufacturing parts for Libya.

The story of Iran is a different matter. Certainly the first contacts between Iran and Pakistan on the nuclear issue were on a state level.

The process seems to have begun in 1986 during a visit to Pakistan by President Khamenei, who asked his counterpart General Zia for military help. Nuclear experts from the two countries met and by the next year signed a cooperation agreement in Vienna, which set up programmes to train Iranian scientists.[109] These official channels paved the way for A.Q. Khan's involvement with Iran, although there is no evidence that General Zia or his deputy Aslam Beg wanted the cooperation to reach the point where Iran was able to build a bomb. Indeed Zia's aides say he specifically ordered that nothing of substance should be transferred to Iran.[110]

The first IAEA inspection of Iran was in 1992 but it revealed very little.[111] The breakthrough came 11 years later when nuclear inspectors went to a plant, Natanz, the existence of which had been revealed by some exiled Iranian opposition groups. The IAEA were stunned to discover that a building the Iranians had claimed was used for anti-desertification research was, in reality, a heavily fortified, well-advanced nuclear plant. Down in bunkers 75 feet deep, with walls 8 feet thick, was a cascade of 160 centrifuges and room for over 50,000 more. Unfortunately for Pakistan some of the centrifuge machines had traces of highly enriched uranium – a discovery that put the Iranians very much on the back foot. Fearing US attack, Teheran was desperate to establish that its own programme was entirely peaceful: Teheran said that the traces of highly enriched uranium must have come from Pakistan.

That news certainly rang a bell with Robert Oakley. Twelve years earlier, when he was US ambassador in Islamabad, he had had a conversation with the army chief of the time, General Aslam Beg. Beg remarked that he had reached an understanding with the head of Iran's Revolutionary Guards to help Teheran with its nuclear programme in return for oil and conventional weapons. Alarmed, Oakley raised the issue with the prime minister, Nawaz Sharif, who apparently informed the Iranian government that there would be no such deal.[112] There have been suggestions that Benazir Bhutto, like Sharif, also had to restrain generals keen to do a nuclear deal with Iran. According to one newspaper report quoting two 'former senior officials' in Pakistan, in 1991 President Rafsanjani, at a reception in Teheran, told Benazir Bhutto that some of her generals had proposed secretly transferring nuclear technology on a military-to-military basis. He wanted her political approval, which she declined to give.[113] Referring to approaches from senior officers, she later said: 'It certainly was their belief that they could earn tons of money if they did this. It was something that I was disabusing them of, that they could not get it. If they chose to sell it, only three countries would buy it because it wasn't like McDonalds hamburgers that would have a big consumer market.'[114]

The North Korean allegations are different. There is no doubt that the Pakistan army was directly involved with North Korea. The army chief, Jehangir Karamat, went there in 1997, apparently to purchase missile technology. The issue is whether the army paid for the missiles with hard cash or with nuclear technology. Musharraf claims that the army had no knowledge that A.Q. Khan had, not for the first time, exceeded the mandate given to him by the authorities and used the missile trading links to add some illicit deals of his own.

On the face of it there are many reasons to doubt that line. It suggests that not only A.Q. Khan but also the entire North Korean leadership was deceiving the Pakistan military. Khan flew to North Korea often – 13 times between 1997 and his house arrest.[115] Apparently the military did not ask why he was taking so many materials to, rather than from, North Korea. In 2008 Khan confirmed that a transfer had taken place. He said that some used P-1 centrifuges had gone to North Korea but that the exercise had been supervised by the army who had 'complete knowledge' of what was happening.[116] It sounds like a reasonable claim.

The cases of Iran, North Korea and Libya are now relatively well known and have been investigated with some vigour. But there is also increasing evidence emerging about Pakistan's nuclear cooperation with China. According to Simon Henderson, a Western writer with unmatched access to A.Q. Khan, China and Pakistan were proliferating nuclear materials to each other. He has written that a British official told him in the 1980s that China had given Pakistan the plan for an atomic bomb and in return Pakistan had provided China with an enrichment plant. That plant, Henderson believes, is at Hanzhong in Sichuan province. The Pakistanis made more than a hundred C-130 Hercules transport flights to supply the plant.[117] The design provided by the

Chinese is thought to have been for a bomb first tested in a series of explosions at Lop Nor between 1964 and 1966, and copies of the Chinese documents were amongst those found in Libya. They were annotated with names of Chinese ministers who, presumably, were involved in the original Pakistani–Chinese deal.[118] A.Q. Khan implicitly acknowledged that Pakistan was in possession of a tested bomb design when he said in 1998 that there was no need for another test because Pakistan already had a design of 'proven reliability'.[119] As it emerges as a superpower, China will presumably lose interest in its nuclear relationship with Pakistan. The Pakistanis, though, will try to keep their contacts with Beijing's nuclear establishment for as long as possible: officials in Islamabad now see it as the best way of countering the ever closer nuclear relationship between the US and India. But whatever realignments take place in the future there is little doubt that, based on what has already happened, the idea that A.Q. Khan could have such a critical and close relationship with China without the military's knowledge does not hold water.

Indeed, some Pakistani politicians and officials have confirmed the existence of a state-level nuclear relationship between Pakistan and China. The former Pakistani foreign secretary, Agha Shahi, recalled that in 1965 'we made a pact with Beijing that ushered in decades of assistance we could not have got elsewhere'.[120] Indian officials believe Zulfikar Ali Bhutto was referring to the Chinese decision to hand over a bomb design when he wrote in his prison cell shortly before being hanged: 'My single most important achievement which I believe will dominate the portrait of my public life is an agreement I arrived at after an assiduous and tenacious endeavour spanning over eleven years of negotiations. In the present context the agreement of mine, concluded in June 1976, will perhaps be my greatest achievement and contribution to the survival of our people and our nation.'[121]

For years Pakistan used to dismiss suggestions that it was a source of nuclear proliferation with some contempt, insisting that its record was impeccable. That assertion is now totally discredited. Pakistani nuclear know-how and nuclear components were sold or bartered to a number of different customers over many years. The army and now A.Q. Khan both profess their innocence. Neither is convincing.

Command and Control

Given his role in creating Pakistan's nuclear device, and indeed his consistent defence of the value of nuclear weapons to Pakistan, it is surprising that one of the clearest possible warnings of the risk of an accidental nuclear detonation came from none other than A.Q. Khan:

> ... there is a real danger of nuclear war by accident due to technical failure or malfunctioning, or due to accidental detonation or launching of a nuclear weapon. Nuclear war can also be started by unauthorised action, human error or sheer madness. There is moreover, a great danger of a person or a group of persons responsible for launching nuclear weapons going insane and deciding to launch a nuclear attack on the enemy, eliciting immediate retaliation and a real holocaust.[122]

A former Pakistani foreign minister, Agha Shahi, has raised similar concerns:

> Pakistan may well be confronted with a hair trigger alert situation. Neither country [India and Pakistan] has an effective early warning system against missile attack to detect intruding aircraft carrying nuclear devices. The flight time of their [India's] nuclear-armed short and medium range missiles is only three to less than ten minutes. Hence a 'launch-on-warning' system (launching missiles before incoming missiles arrive) that existed between the United States and the former Soviet Union – 25 minutes of warning time in the case of ICBM's and 15 minutes in that of their SLBM's from deployed submarines – would elude Pakistan and India. The risk of nuclear strike by miscalculation or unauthorised use therefore cannot be but high, as the respective command and control systems cannot ensure real-time instructions for alerting and launching nuclear forces.[123]

These warnings come from Pakistanis. Yet government officials and nuclear scientists in Islamabad tend to become indignant if Western officials or journalists express doubts about the efficacy of their command and control systems. To suggest that the systems might need improvement is to invite an accusation of racism.[124] 'Are you saying,' the argument runs, 'that only white Europeans and Americans are capable of looking after nuclear devices? Are you claiming that Pakistani (or for that matter Indian) scientists and strategists are less capable or less responsible than their counterparts in the five declared nuclear states?' For all such rhetoric, there are serious issues at stake.

There are three routes to a nuclear holocaust in South Asia. First, either India or Pakistan might take a deliberate decision to use nuclear weapons. Second, the two countries might blunder into an accidental nuclear war. Finally, there is the possibility that the nuclear arsenal in either country could be the subject of unauthorised use.

In assessing the likelihood of a deliberately executed nuclear conflict, the crucial issue is whose finger is on the button. In April 1999 – before the coup – a number of press reports stated that the chairman of the joint chiefs of staff was to be the strategic commander of the nuclear forces, but that the final decision to use the bomb would be the prime minister's, acting on the basis of consultations with the National Command Authority.[125] The release of this information may have been intended to soothe Western fears about the role of the military. In the context of Pakistani politics, however, although there would doubtless be a search for consensus, few in the army, and for that matter, few outside of it, believe that any civilian prime minister would be able to face down the military chief on such a crucial question at a time of crisis. Furthermore, it is difficult to imagine any Pakistani officer accepting an order to use the bomb from the prime minister without first clearing the instruction with the army chief.

Serving Pakistani officers are tight-lipped about their command and control structure, but it is widely believed that the country's nuclear weapons are stored unassembled with the fissile core separated from the non-nuclear explosives. The delivery vehicles are kept in a third location.[126] As for the mechanisms for firing the nuclear device, a senior retired officer, General Durrani, in his semi-doctrinal document, stated that: 'Based on information provided by officialdom, Pakistan is using a three-man rule, a variant of the two-man rule for security. The code to arm a weapon is divided between three people, rather than two people. ... The Pakistani system is not as sophisticated as the US

Permissive Action Link (PAL) system but it appears that attention is being given to security issues.'[127]

Apart from the initial years under Zulfikar Ali Bhutto, the army has always enjoyed more control over the nuclear programme than civilians. Senior Pakistani analysts accept this. The deputy head of a government-sponsored think tank, the Islamabad Policy Research Institute, for example, has said: 'It's always been a military programme. If it came to it, the civilian prime minister would have to do as he's told by the military.'[128] Similarly, a veteran of Pakistan's nuclear programme, the former foreign minister, Agha Shahi, has written: 'Control over Pakistan's nuclear capability has always remained with the military.'[129]

Benazir Bhutto famously complained that when she was prime minister she wasn't even allowed to visit a nuclear facility. Senior military officers who were serving when she was prime minister have insisted that had she wanted to go to any site she could have done so but that she never asked. They have also pointed out that civilians have taken some of the key decisions relating to the programme. Zulfikar Ali Bhutto got the programme under way. As prime minister, his daughter Benazir decided to continue with it and, in 1998, it was Nawaz Sharif who opted for the nuclear tests.[130] But all these decisions were in line with the military's wishes and, like Benazir Bhutto, Nawaz Sharif has also complained of being excluded from some aspects of nuclear decision making. The real question is: would the military have ever accepted decisions that they didn't agree with? Few believe that they would have done so.

While the ultimate decision, then, is likely to lie with the army chief, there is one body that might act to restrain him: the National Command Authority (NCA). The establishment of the organisation was announced in February 2000 and in May of that year officials spoke publicly about the 'inaugural, first meeting of the NCA'.[131] The body, it was stated, would include civilian members, and the foreign minister (a post always held by a civilian) would not only sit on the NCA by right but would also act as its deputy chairman.[132]

For all the talk of a 'new' body holding its 'inaugural' meeting, the NCA had in fact existed, without any official acknowledgement, for a quarter of a century: it was set up in 1975 by Zulfikar Ali Bhutto to oversee the creation of Pakistan's bomb.[133] After the 1998 tests the military ordered a review of the NCA and completely overhauled it. The military's pre-eminent role in nuclear policy was institutionalised: six of the nine places on the NCA were given to military officers. The NCA was given control of all aspects of Pakistan's nuclear programme, including the Kahuta plant. It was also given authority over a new body with 50 officers,[134] the Strategic Plans Division, which was established in the military's General Headquarters and put in charge of all financial issues relating to the nuclear programme and managing the command and control system. It is responsible not only for ensuring that a nuclear weapon can be used when so ordered by the proper authority, but also for creating a system that will prevent unauthorised or accidental use.

There are good reasons for believing that a nuclear South Asia poses new, genuine threats that did not exist during the cold war. India and Pakistan have a disputed border, a history of armed conflict and no early warning systems.[135] The case of the non-existent Israeli 'attack' cited in this chapter demonstrates that, at best, false intelligence or, at worst, deliberate misinformation have already been fed into the decision-making process at a time of nuclear crisis.

There are many stories about moments during the cold war when the United States and the Soviet Union nearly launched nuclear missiles on the basis of false intelligence. Reliable information on these near-disasters is scarce: the governments in Washington and Moscow have never wanted to advertise their intelligence failures. Nevertheless, it is clear that some serious lapses in command and control did occur. A US early warning system, for example, once mistook a flock of geese and, on another occasion, the moon, for incoming Soviet missiles.[136]

In South Asia the risks are greater. Pakistan's nuclear decision-makers could have just three minutes to respond to an incoming attack. That timescale puts pressure on both India and Pakistan to have operationally capable weapons ready to fire at all times. The extent to which this has already taken place is unclear. India's nuclear doctrine envisages: 'assured capability to shift from peacetime deployment to fully employable forces in the shortest time . . .'[137] Pakistani scientists have said that they do not keep fully assembled nuclear weapons in times of peace. Asked whether it would take 'days or hours' to render the bombs operationally deployable, one senior Pakistani scientist replied: 'Less than that. Minutes.'[138] Having both sides ready to fire in such a short period of time clearly enhances the risk of a misinterpretation of the other side's intentions leading to a deliberate but unnecessary nuclear detonation. There is little indication that Pakistan and India are ready to agree not to have weapons ready to fire, but such an agreement could clearly reduce the nuclear danger. Agha Shahi has estimated that if nuclear weapons were not deployed in forward positions then the warning time would increase from three minutes to between seven and ten minutes.[139]

An accidental detonation of a nuclear device cannot be ruled out but what, finally, of unauthorised use? The fact that Pakistan could suffer a devastating surprise attack opens up the possibility of the military chief, the civilian prime minister, or both, being killed or rendered incommunicado before any decision on retaliation could be taken. In the event of such decapitation, who would have the authority to launch a retaliatory strike? Pakistani officials say the Strategic Plans Division has drawn up contingency plans but that they will not be announced publicly. There are two possibilities. The fall-back authority could follow the traditional pattern and rest with the longest-standing service chief (army, navy or air force) who is formally considered the next most senior officer after the chairman of the joint chiefs of staff. Alternatively, the chain of command could be restricted to the army, in which case the authority would presumably be passed on to the longest-serving corps commander. There is a similar lack of clarity in India. The August 1999 Indian nuclear doctrine stated that: 'The authority to release nuclear weapons for use reside in the person of the prime minister of India, or the designated successor(s).'[140] Again, the identity of the 'designated successor(s)' is not revealed.

Even if the Strategic Plans Division has laid down contingency plans, there is no escaping a tension between protecting a nuclear arsenal against a first strike and ensuring that it is sufficiently tightly controlled to prevent unauthorised use. A policy of dispersing the nuclear arsenal in a time of crisis is bound to weaken command and control and put weapons in the hands of relatively junior officers. PAEC sources insist that all Pakistan's nuclear weapons have codes without which the warheads cannot be armed. In the case of airborne missiles, for example, the codes would not be given to an aircraft crew until the plane was outside Pakistani airspace. But, as some Pakistani analysts have acknowledged, the command and control structure has to take into account the possibility that an Indian first strike would disable at least some elements of the nuclear leadership. Consequently, not only the authority to launch an attack but also the technical know-how for doing so must be passed down the chain of command. That plainly increases the possibility of unauthorised use.[141]

But succession planning could be the least of Pakistan's problems. The growing strength of militant Islam poses two new threats. First, as the director general of the International Atomic Energy Agency, Mohamed el Baradei, has put it, 'nuclear weapons could fall into the hands of an extremist group in Pakistan or Afghanistan.'[142] It is a disturbing fact that many of Pakistan's nuclear facilities are located near the part of the country that is now most affected by militancy: North West Frontier Province. The dangers are obvious: either an Islamist group could physically capture enough nuclear materials to make a dirty bomb or Islamists could at some point take over the central government and get complete control of the whole arsenal. It is quite possible that further Taliban advances in the northwest will persuade the US that the nuclear arsenal is under threat and that it should be destroyed. Needless to say an attack on the only nuclear weapons possessed by a Muslim state would have highly unpredictable consequences.

The other danger is that a senior member of staff in one of the nuclear facilities becomes more fervently religious late on in his (or her) career. Such personal transformations are by no means uncommon and the risk of unauthorised transfer of nuclear materials to an extremist group is real. It is very difficult for the Pakistani authorities to guard against the risk – but they are trying. Since 2005, Pakistan has introduced a Personnel Reliability Programme which attempts to vet people's religious sentiments and to distinguish between the devout and the dangerous.[143] Personnel are screened every two years with checks by at least three intelligence or security agencies which look into family background and political affiliations.[144] Retired scientists are given jobs within Pakistan to prevent them being recruited by foreign companies or governments. The programme was set up with the help of the United States which since 2001 has spent $100 million of classified funds to help secure Pakistan's nuclear weapons.

The money has paid for the training of Pakistani personnel in the US and the construction of a nuclear security training centre in Pakistan. Equipment ranging from helicopters to night-vision goggles were given to the Pakistani authorities for use in securing nuclear material and facilities.[145]

Yet, for all the dangers, many Pakistanis are remarkably relaxed about command and control issues. Senior figures in Pakistan, such as the retired army chief Aslam Beg, have argued that the risks are exaggerated:

> The presidents of Russia and America carry a black box and are in a constant state of alert: that is not the case with us. We don't need that kind of elaborate command and control system and state of readiness. In our context we have a period of tension and confrontation; a period of conventional forces deployment. At that stage there may be a need to activate the National Command Authority. But that comes at the last stage.

And in any case, he said: 'I don't think India would be stupid enough to take advantage by attacking facilities without any reason, just to damage our programme.' It is a breathtakingly casual assessment.[146]

6

Democracy

Democracy is the best revenge.
    —Bilawal Bhutto Zardari, the son of Benazir Bhutto and Asif Ali
        Zardari, speaking after her funeral on 30 December 2007

Asif Ali Zardari's election victory was testament to the strength of dynastic politics in Pakistan. Just nine months earlier his wife had been buried in the Bhutto's vast family mausoleum in Sindh. People from all over Pakistan braved the civil unrest that followed her assassination and travelled hundreds of miles to pay their last respects. And on one point they were unanimous. Asked who should take over the party following her death, the mourners all gave the same answer. It was none of their business. It was the family's job to choose someone and it was the people's job to vote for that person.[1] Many had strong reservations about Asif Zardari both because of his reputation for being corrupt and because he was only a Bhutto by marriage. But when the time for voting came, the PPP's electoral base knew what to do.

That democracy has failed to take root in Pakistan is indisputable. The army has been in power for more than half the country's existence, and it is commonplace for senior officers to complain that the politicians are too incompetent and corrupt to govern. 'The Western type of parliamentary democracy,' Ayub Khan once wrote, 'could not be imposed on the people of Pakistan.'[2] Many civilians share his jaundiced view. The feudal landlords, the bureaucrats, the intelligence agencies and the judiciary have all shown a reluctance to accept, never mind promote, the rule of law. So have the country's Islamic radicals: 'It's a good thing,' said Lashkar e-Toiba's spokesman, Abdullah Muntazeer, speaking of Musharraf's 1999 coup, 'the parliament was un-Islamic and he's got rid of it.'[3]

Besides the Zardari presidency there have been three periods of civilian rule in Pakistan. The first, between 1947 and 1958, began at the time of independence and ended when the chief of army staff, Lieutenant General Ayub Khan, mounted Pakistan's first military coup. The second period, between 1971 and 1977, belonged to Zulfikar Ali Bhutto and was ended by General Zia's military takeover. The third, dominated by Bhutto's daughter Benazir and her rival Nawaz Sharif, began after General Zia's death in a plane crash in 1988 and ended in October 1999 when Musharraf grabbed power. Many Pakistanis explain the failure of democracy in their country by bemoaning the poor quality of their elected leaders. In reality, there are deeper reasons for the fact that no elected leader in the country's entire history has ever completed his or her term in office.[4]

1947–1958

Mohammed Ali Jinnah wanted Pakistan to be a constitutional, parliamentary democracy informed by Muslim values. Many Pakistanis believe that had he lived longer he would have been able to transform his vision into reality. Yet, for all his ideals, Jinnah never behaved democratically. From the moment of independence he assumed control of all the levers of power in Pakistan. He was not only the governor general, but also the president of the Muslim League and the head of the Constituent Assembly. As the founder of the nation, Jinnah had such massive personal authority that few dared challenge him and, even if they did, a momentary scowl was enough to silence his most determined opponent. Arguably, the new country, lacking any political institutions, needed a strong leader. But even Jinnah's most ardent supporters concede that the concentration of power in his hands set an unfortunate precedent.[5] When Jinnah died, 13 months after Pakistan was born, there was no one capable of filling the vacuum he left behind.

Pakistan's first generation of politicians were inexperienced men faced with truly daunting challenges. As well as being confronted by fundamental national issues such as the demand for provincial rights, the status of the Urdu language and the role of Islam in the new state, they had to deal with the millions of new arrivals in Pakistan at a time when

an economy barely existed. It was perhaps inevitable that power inex-
orably slipped into the hands of the only people capable of delivering any
semblance of governance: Pakistan's small group of highly educated civil
servants. As Jinnah's aide-de-camp Ata Rabbani wrote:

> . . . our senior politicians had little experience of the running of a
> government for they had spent most of their lives criticising govern-
> ments in power. Now saddled with the responsibility they took the easy
> way out. Instead of applying themselves to the task and working hard to
> learn the ropes they relied on the advice of senior bureaucrats.[6]

Masters of the new nation, the bureaucrats had little interest in organising
elections, and political developments following Jinnah's death can only be
described as chaotic. There were no fewer than seven prime ministers in
ten years. Liaquat Ali Khan (50 months in office) was assassinated. His
successors – Khwaja Nazimuddin (17 months), Mohammed Ali Bogra
(29 months), Chaudri Mohammed Ali (13 months), Shaheed Suhrawardy
(13 months), I.I. Chundrigar (2 months), and Firoz Khan Noon
(11 months) – all became victims of palace intrigues. Of the seven only
two, Liaquat Ali Khan and Suhrawardy, could claim to have any substantial popular support. Throughout the 1950s two archetypal unelected
powerbrokers, Ghulam Mohammed and Iskander Mirza, both governor
generals, brazenly abused their powers to make or break governments. In
April 1953, Ghulam Mohammed set an unfortunate trend when, citing
the government's failure to resolve 'the difficulties facing the country', he
dismissed Khwaja Nazimuddin and installed Bogra in his place. When
Bogra responded by trying to limit the governor general's power, Ghulam
Mohammed simply dismissed him. And so it went on.

As the politicians and bureaucrats bickered and quarrelled, the military became increasingly involved in political decisions. This was
partly a result of the civilians' failure to govern effectively: the military
was frequently called upon to fulfil functions that should have been
performed by the police. Indeed, the army soon became the only
organisation capable of keeping order on the streets, and in 1953 the
relative power and competence of the military and the civilians became
plain for all to see. In February law and order in Lahore started to dete-

riorate when some Islamic-based parties demanded that the Ahmedis be declared non-Muslims. Within a matter of days a frenzied anti-Ahmedi campaign spread throughout Punjab. By March the civilian government had to admit that it had lost control of events and it asked the army to take over Lahore. The martial law administrator in the city, General Azam Khan, soon managed to restore calm. Before he relinquished his martial law powers he undertook a number of other initiatives, including the highly popular 'Cleaner Lahore Campaign'. In the eyes of many, martial law in Lahore proved that, whereas the civilian politicians consistently failed to provide effective government, the military could deliver. By asking the army to manage a political crisis the civilians had undermined their own authority. When Ayub Khan took over in 1958 few were surprised, and many were relieved, that the failed democratic experiment was over.

Heads of state, 1947–present

Name	Title	Dates
Mohammed Ali Jinnah	governor general	Aug 1947 – Sept 1948
Khwaja Nazimuddin	governor general	Sept 1948 – Oct 1951
Ghulam Mohammed	governor general	Oct 1951 – Aug 1955
Iskander Mirza	governor general/president	Aug 1955 – Oct 1958
Mohammed Ayub Khan	chief martial law administrator/president	Oct 1958 – Mar 1969
Mohammed Yayha Khan	chief martial law administrator/president	Mar 1969 – Dec 1971
Zulfikar Ali Bhutto	chief martial law administrator/president	Dec 1971 – Aug 1973
Chaudhry Fazal Elahi	president	Aug 1973 –Sept 1978
Mohammad Zia ul-Haq	chief martial law administrator/president	July 1977 – Aug 1988
Ghulam Ishaq Khan	president	Aug 1988 – July 1993
Wasim Sajjad	acting president	July 1993 – Nov 1993
Farooq Leghari	president	Nov 1993 – Dec 1997
Rafiq Tarar	president	Dec 1997 – June 2001
Pervez Musharraf	president	June 2001 – August 2008
Mohammed Mian Soomro	acting president	August 2008 –Sept 2008
Asif Ali Zardari	president	Sept 2008 –

Chief executives, 1947–present

Name	Title	Dates
Liaquat Ali Khan	prime minister	Aug 1947 – Oct 1951
Khwaja Nazimuddin	prime minister	Oct 1951 – Apr 1953
Mohammed Ali Bogra	prime minister	Apr 1953 – Aug 1955
Chaudhri Mohammed Ali	prime minister	Aug 1955 – Sept 1956
H.S. Suhrawardy	prime minister	Sept 1956 – Oct 1957
I.I. Chundrigar	prime minister	Oct 1957 – Dec 1957
Firoz Khan Noon	prime minister	Dec 1957 – Oct 1958
Zulfikar Ali Bhutto	prime minister	Aug 1973 – July 1977
Mohammed Khan Junejo	prime minister	Mar 1985 – May 1988
Benazir Bhutto	prime minister	Aug 1988 – Aug 1990
Ghulam Mustafa Jatoi	caretaker PM	Aug 1990 – Oct 1990
Nawaz Sharif	prime minister	Oct 1990 – Apr 1993
Balkh Sher Mazari	caretaker PM	Apr 1993 – May 1993
Nawaz Sharif	prime minister	May 1993 – July 1993
Moeen Quereshi	caretaker PM	July 1993 – Oct 1993
Benazir Bhutto	prime minister	Oct 1993 – Nov 1996
Meraj Khalid	caretaker PM	Nov 1996 – Feb 1997
Nawaz Sharif	prime minister	Feb 1997 – Oct 1999
Pervez Musharraf	chief executive	Oct 1999 – Nov 2002
Mir Zafarullah Khan Jamali	prime minister	Nov 2002 – June 2004
Chaudhry Shujaat Hussain	caretaker PM	June 2004 – Aug 2004
Shaukat Aziz	prime minister	Aug 2004 – Nov 2007
Mohammed Mian Soomro	caretaker PM	Nov 2007 – Mar 2008
Yousaf Raza Gilani	prime minister	Mar 2008 –

Zulfikar Ali Bhutto

In 1963 Zulfikar Ali Bhutto met President J.F. Kennedy in Washington. After a day of talks Kennedy looked at Bhutto and said: 'If you were American you would be in my cabinet.' 'Be careful Mr President,' Bhutto replied. 'If I were American you would be in my cabinet.'[7] Bhutto was a deeply ambitious man whose undoubted abilities were matched by his massive ego. Had he been operating in the American environment he might have fulfilled his potential. But in Pakistan, with no checks on his executive power, he ran amok. His choice of role model told it all. Bhutto's bookshelves were filled with biographies of

Napoleon Bonaparte, a man who rose to power by appealing to the people over the heads of the ruling establishment and who invited personal disaster because he overreached himself. The parallels between Bhutto and his hero are striking.

The radical programme put forward by Bhutto's Pakistan People's Party (PPP) in the 1970 elections genuinely inspired many Pakistanis. But its heady mix of socialist and Islamic idealism was an illusion. Even before the elections it was clear to PPP insiders that the party was little more than a vehicle for Bhutto's personal ambitions. He demanded complete loyalty from even the most senior party officials. By the time Bhutto had come to power, those who dared disagree with him found they were not only removed from their party positions but, in many cases, thrown into prison as well.[8] Bhutto had little difficulty in replacing them with sycophants who could be relied upon to do his bidding. Having dealt with the party, Bhutto moved on to the civil service. Arguing that he wanted to make the bureaucracy more responsive to the wishes of the government,[9] he swept away legal provisions that gave civil servants job security. The consequent politicisation of the civil service has remained one of Bhutto's most damaging legacies.

Like his predecessors (and his successors) Bhutto resisted demands for greater provincial autonomy. But the force with which he did so was unusual. Within months of taking over he provoked a fierce clash between Islamabad and the provinces. When the provincial government in Balochistan insisted on its right to take local decisions, Bhutto brushed it aside and installed a PPP administration. He then deployed the army, ordering it to open fire on any 'miscreants' who continued to resist the authority of the Pakistani state. It was the start of a four-year campaign in which 80,000 troops were deployed in Balochistan. The army's presence there served clear notice to all Pakistan's provinces: those who challenged Zulfikar Ali Bhutto would pay the price.

While Bhutto relied on the army to assert his authority in the provinces, he simultaneously undermined it by creating a new paramilitary outfit, the Federal Security Force (FSF). It was widely seen as Bhutto's personal army and the generals in Rawalpindi bitterly resented it. That Bhutto used the FSF to scare his opponents is beyond dispute, but establishing the extent of the force's excesses is difficult. Certainly, at the time, many Pakistanis believed that the organisation was routinely carrying out murders. Leading independent historians have concluded that the FSF was involved in several incidents in which Bhutto's political enemies were harassed and even killed.[10]

Bhutto's regime consistently relied on heavy-handed tactics. When, in 1972, he decreed that the state should nationalise plants in the iron and steel, chemical, cement and energy sectors, there was inevitably bitter resentment amongst those who lost their property. Characteristically, Bhutto met their opposition with brute force. Leading industrialists were imprisoned or asked to surrender their passports.[11] Opposition politicians met the same fate. The memoirs of a former Pakistani air chief, Mohammad Asghar Khan, give a flavour of Bhutto's authoritarian tendencies.[12] When, after his retirement, Asghar Khan went into politics and opposed Bhutto's government, the FSF responded with characteristic force. Virtually every time Asghar Khan tried to organise a political rally he faced violent mobs who, together with the local police, would try to prevent the meeting from taking place. On some occasions Asghar Khan and his party workers were fired on and one party worker was killed in such an incident. Asghar Kahn himself received death threats and was repeatedly arrested. The treatment meted out to him revealed not only Bhutto's intolerance but also his insecurity: at no stage did the former air chief enjoy significant levels of popular support and he never posed a serious political threat to the government.

Bhutto's downfall came after the 1977 elections. Despite being the favourite to win, the election was rigged in Bhutto's favour. Many methods were used to influence the result. Local government officials managed to remove the names of many opposition candidates from the ballot paper by citing various technical breaches of the election law. In constituencies where there was a contest, the police and FSF routinely disrupted opposition campaign rallies. Although such tactics were not unexpected, the actual rigging of the result did cause surprise and widespread anger. Independent analysts have pointed out that since 63 per cent of the electorate had voted in Pakistan's first national elections of 1970 (for which there had been considerable public enthusiasm), the 1977 turnout of 80 per cent was implausibly high.[13] The extent of the rigging remains uncertain, but it is clear that Bhutto or his supporters not only tried to influence the result but also, to a considerable extent, succeeded.

The aftermath of the 1977 elections brought out the worst in Zulfikar Ali Bhutto. Anti-government protestors who were demanding a new poll were shot dead and opposition politicians were arrested. As the public protests grew out of control, Bhutto tried to shore up his increasingly vulnerable position by reaching out to the Islamic parties, decreeing that alcohol, gambling and nightclubs would be banned. The public pressure on Bhutto to step down became so overwhelming that he was forced to call in the army to keep control of the major cities. But the army sided with the protestors, and General Zia ul-Haq took over.

The execution of Bhutto at 2 a.m. on 4 April 1979, on a charge of attempted murder, has been described as the final blow to democracy in Pakistan. In truth, democracy was already in serious trouble before Zia decided that the only way to neutralise his most formidable political opponent was to have him killed. Like many other politicians in post-colonial countries, Zulfikar Ali Bhutto wanted to govern for life. As a young man he never doubted that he would become Pakistan's leader and once he had fulfilled his destiny he did not believe that anyone else in the country was able to match him. His failure to hang on to power is one of the clearest indications of just how difficult it is to govern Pakistan. The nationalists in the provinces, the pro-democracy campaigners and, most importantly, the army were strong enough to frustrate Bhutto's ambitions.

The Return of the Civilians

On 17 August 1988, General Zia's Hercules C-130 plummeted to the ground shortly after taking off from Bahawalpur airport. Remarkably little is known about the crash. The Pakistani investigation produced no information of any value but concluded that Zia was probably the victim of sabotage. According to Sardar Muhammad Chaudhry, who at the time was the head of Special Branch in Lahore, the enquiry established just one point of value: the plane's debris was spread over a very restricted area. That suggested that the Hercules had neither exploded in the air nor been hit by a missile. The Pakistani investigators wondered whether the crew had been debilitated by a nerve gas.[14] One rumour about the crash that refuses to go away is that a box of mangoes, loaded onto the plane at the last moment, was in fact packed with explosives, but there is no evidence to substantiate the story.

Zia's death ushered in the third period of democratic rule in Pakistan and many in the country had high hopes that they were embarking on a new era. There was to be no shortage of elections in the post-Zia period: the people were called upon to vote in 1988, 1990, 1993 and 1997. But it is surely significant that the turn-out figures for those elections steadily declined, from 50 per cent in 1988 to 45 per cent in 1990 and then to 40 per cent in 1993. The official figure for 1997 was 35 per cent although the true figure was probably closer to 26 per cent. By 1999 disillusionment with democracy had reached such a depth that General Musharraf's coup was welcomed as a blessed relief.

Most Pakistanis believe that the post-Zia civilian politicians have been self-seeking, corrupt and unprincipled. They have a point. Two leaders, Benazir Bhutto and Nawaz Sharif, dominated the 1990s. There were important differences between them. As the daughter of Zulfikar Ali Bhutto and heir to a large estate in Sindh, Benazir Bhutto had her roots in the traditional feudal system. Nawaz Sharif, by contrast, was from a self-made industrial family that had steadily accumulated wealth ever since 1947. By the end of the twentieth century, Nawaz Sharif and his family owned one of the biggest industrial empires in the country. There were other dissimilarities. Bhutto, bitter about her father's execution, was always afraid of, and hostile to, the military. Sharif, who had served as General Zia's chief minister in Punjab, was initially far closer to the military establishment, although his attitudes naturally changed after the 1999 coup removed his government. And while Bhutto was educated in the West and well aware of secular liberal ideas, Sharif was, as his image-makers put it, 'made in Pakistan' and far more sympathetic to the religious parties. As prime minister he made a point of paying his respects to Zia's memory by visiting his grave on each anniversary of his death. It is also worth remembering that the rivalry between the Sharifs and the Bhuttos had a history. In 1972 Zulfikar Ali Bhutto nationalised the Sharif family's Ittefaq Foundry. It was a bitter blow to the Sharifs and they have never forgotten it.

There were also dissimilarities in the way the two leaders governed. Although both encouraged state-owned radio and television to broadcast blatant pro-government propaganda, Benazir Bhutto was generally more tolerant of press criticism than Nawaz Sharif. She also showed more interest in human rights issues and never attacked the non-governmental organisations in the way that Sharif did. On religious matters, Bhutto clearly had a more modernist outlook than Sharif, but, like her father, she was always willing to pander to the religious lobby for short-term political advantage.

For all these differences, however, the similarities of the Sharif and Bhutto administrations are striking. Neither pushed through any significant reforms. In national policy terms, their most important shared characteristic was their ability to run up huge levels of foreign debt. By the time General Musharraf took over in 1999, Pakistan owed foreign creditors over $25 billion and debt servicing had become the largest component of the annual budget. Most of this debt had been run up in the 1990s. Between 1947 and 1970 Pakistan ran up a modest foreign debt of just $3 billion and the country was widely cited as one of the developing world's best users of foreign loans.[15] By the time General Zia was killed in 1988 that foreign debt had increased substantially – to $13 billion.[16] General Zia, and to a lesser extent Zulfikar Ali Bhutto, may have been profligate but their appetite for foreign loans was dwarfed by that of Nawaz Sharif and Benazir Bhutto.

Between 1988 and 1999 Pakistan borrowed, and failed to repay, $13 billion.[17] Of course, nobody knows how much of that money was stolen, but Pakistan has remarkably little to show for it. Major spending projects in the 1990s included the Lahore-Islamabad motorway and the opulent Prime Ministerial Secretariat in Islamabad. A substantial amount was also spent on Nawaz Sharif's 'Yellow Cab' scheme in which tens of thousands of taxis were distributed to towns and villages throughout the country. Theoretically, the beneficiaries were meant to pay back the cost of the taxis but few have ever done so. Taken together these projects cost around $3 billion. That leaves $10 billion unaccounted for. Some of that money went towards the provision of electricity and irrigation projects, but it is difficult to argue that the democratic governments used their foreign loans with even a modicum of prudence. Indeed, these figures do not reveal the full extent of their profligacy. In 1998, after the Sharif government froze all the foreign-currency bank accounts in the country, it transpired that the democratic governments had also spent several billion dollars of foreign exchange that had been lying in personal bank accounts in the domestic banking sector.

Both Nawaz Sharif and Benazir Bhutto faced corruption cases in Pakistan's courts. Both claimed that their trials were politically motivated and, in a sense, they were right. Ever since 1947, Pakistani governments have used selective accountability to target and discredit political opponents. Nevertheless, many Pakistanis believed that both Bhutto and Sharif were indeed guilty of corruption. They pointed out that despite all the rhetoric about improving the lot of the poor, both lived in considerable luxury. Sharif's opulent estate at Raiwind near Lahore and Benazir Bhutto's ancestral home in Larkana, Sindh, both boasted private zoos. Both also purchased valuable foreign properties. The extent of the Sharif family's foreign holdings has never been clear. Throughout his second term in office Sharif was embarrassed by the revelation that, among many other foreign properties, he owned some luxury flats on London's Park Lane. Asif Zardari, according to the National Accountability Bureau, owned several properties in the UK, Belgium and France as well as a stud farm in Texas.

That the Sharifs and the Bhuttos are multi-millionaires is beyond dispute. The methods used to acquire their wealth are far less apparent. The Sharifs made most of their money in the 1980s and 1990s. After his companies were nationalised, Nawaz Sharif's father, Mohammed Sharif, realised that to protect his business interests he would need political as well as financial muscle. Once Zulfikar Ali Bhutto had been removed from power in 1977 the possibilities opened up and Mohammed Sharif's youngest son Nawaz (who showed no interest in, or much aptitude for, business) joined the Zia administration. In June 1979 the Sharifs were rewarded for their services to the Zia regime by having their company denationalised and handed back to them. From that moment the Sharif family fortunes soared.

Many of the Sharifs' assets had been acquired through bank loans. As early as 1991 the Pakistani press was printing detailed stories alleging that senior politicians were pressurising banks into giving them multi-million-dollar bank loans.[18] In 1998 Nawaz Sharif acknowledged that he did have many outstanding loans. Hoping to underpin his huge popularity following his decision to conduct Pakistan's nuclear tests, he vowed to pay back everything he owed. In a televised address to the nation in June 1998, he said that the Ittefaq group of companies would offer its assets to the banks so that all the loans could be recovered.[19] The credibility of the pledge was hardly helped by another promise he made in the same speech. He said that his family would eat only one meal a day as a contribution to the austerity campaign necessitated by the post-test economic sanctions. Aware of their prime minister's penchant for earthy Punjabi food, most Pakistanis were sceptical.

They were right to be so. Although the Sharif family did surrender over 33 industrial units to the state, subsequent investigations established that most of them were inoperative and worthless. Pakistani press reports claimed that the total value of the units given up by the Sharifs would not cover the amount owed to the banks. The precise amount of that debt remains contested, but when General Musharraf's military regime published a list of major loan defaulters in November 2001 it put the total amount owed by politicians and businessmen at 211 billion rupees (over $3 billion) and claimed that the Sharif family owed over 3 billion rupees ($50 million).[20] The Pakistani press generally quotes figures of two or three times that amount.[21] The situation is complicated by internal disputes within the Sharif family, various members of which have taken each other to court because it is not clear which branches of the family own which parts of the empire. Consequently, when Nawaz Sharif announced that he would pay off his loans, it was far from obvious which debts were his direct responsibility and which fell to his relatives.[22]

Despite being an extremely rich man, Nawaz Sharif showed little enthusiasm for paying tax. According to his 1996 nomination form for National Assembly elections, he paid under $10 in income tax between 1994 and 1996.[23] Sharif's supporters argued that this was entirely legal and pointed out that in the same period he had paid nearly $60,000 in wealth tax. Nevertheless, even if Sharif had the best accountants money could buy, the sums were remarkably small for a man whose family controlled assets worth hundreds of millions, if not billions, of dollars.

Benazir Bhutto and her husband Asif Zardari were also accused of using their political power for personal gain. The most serious charges against them concerned kickbacks. In Benazir Bhutto's first term, Zardari was widely known as Mr 10 Per Cent. By the second term Zardari, like the Pakistani people, was suffering from the effects of inflation: he had become known as Mr 20 Per Cent. The first case to reach some sort of conclusion was the SGS Cotecna case. It concerned a Swiss-based company that, in 1994, was hired by Benazir Bhutto's government (in which Zardari was a minister) to improve the system for collecting customs duties on imports. Determined to discredit his most popular political opponent, Nawaz Sharif ordered his second government to investigate the SGS Cotecna case. His enquiry concluded that Bhutto and her husband had been paid millions of dollars' worth of bribes as kickbacks for awarding the contract. Some of the most damning evidence against the Bhuttos came from a Geneva magistrate, Daniel Devaud. He said he had found Swiss bank accounts in the name of offshore Virgin Islands companies, which were in fact controlled by Asif Zardari. Furthermore, he said that Benazir Bhutto had used money from one of the accounts to buy a diamond necklace worth $175,000. Devaud convicted the couple, although they appealed and secured a retrial which the Swiss abandoned when Asif Zardari became president.

In 1999 the Lahore High Court heard the SGS Cotecna case, convicted Bhutto and Zardari of corruption, fined them over $8 million and sentenced the couple to five years in prison. But in March 2001 the conviction was overturned because a British newspaper, the *Sunday Times*, had printed transcripts of some audio tapes which suggested the outcome of the trial was fixed.[24] The source of the tapes was Abdul Rahim, a senior official in the Intelligence Bureau, who claimed that he had been ordered to tap the phone of Abdul Qayoom, the judge hearing the case. The tapes suggested that Qayoom had come under heavy pressure from senior officials in the Sharif administration. In one passage, recorded two days before he gave his verdict, the judge was heard discussing the outcome of the case with Sharif's most senior anti-corruption investigator, Senator Saif ur Rehman:

> Justice Qayoom: 'Now you tell me what punishment do you want me to give her?'
>
> Saif ur Rehman: 'Whatever you have been told by him.'
>
> Justice Qayoom: 'How much?'
>
> Saif ur Rehman: 'Not less than seven years.'
>
> Justice Qayoom: 'No, not seven. Let us make it five years. You can ask him. Seven is the maximum punishment and nobody awards maximum.'
>
> Saif ur Rehman: 'I will ask, and tell you.'

According to Abdul Rahim, the Intelligence Bureau then recorded a second conversation that took place after Saif ur Rehman had discussed the matter with Nawaz Sharif:

> Saif ur Rehman: 'When I enquired about five or seven he said I should ask you why you would not like to give them the full dose.'
>
> Justice Qayoom: 'It is not like this. You know it is never done like this by anybody. It would look odd.'
>
> Saif ur Rehman: 'OK if you think five. But whatever he said I have told you.'

When the tapes were published Justice Qayoom issued a statement saying he believed they were 'doctored'.[25] His credibility, however, was severely undermined by the revelation that in 1998 Nawaz Sharif had given explicit orders that Qayoom and his wife be provided with diplomatic passports despite the fact that, technically, high court judges did not qualify for them. Musharraf's military regime accepted the quashing of the verdict but indicated that it still wanted to pursue the case and would start another trial afresh.[26] Both Nawaz Sharif and Benazir Bhutto consistently denied the corruption charges they faced.

It is, perhaps, only fair to point out that neither Bhutto nor Sharif governed in easy circumstances. Having enjoyed a decade of unrestrained power under Zia ul-Haq, the army and the civil service resented the democratic governments. Aitzaz Ahsan, the interior minister in Benazir Bhutto's first administration, has related how the senior bureaucrats in his ministry exhibited their disdain for the Pakistani public. Whenever Ahsan had constituents visit him in his office he noticed that, as soon as the meeting was over and the guests had departed, the three most senior civil servants working under him developed a habit of spraying his room and the corridors with air freshener.

The Pakistani establishment had other, more serious methods of displaying their disdain for the politicians as well as their voters. In the first place the president was able to use General Zia's notorious Eighth Amendment, which allowed him to dismiss a sitting government. The amendment was employed to get rid of two of Benazir Bhutto's governments and one of Nawaz Sharif's. Throughout the 1990s the judiciary consistently failed to stand up to these displays of executive power. Indeed, Pakistan's judiciary has never provided a strong defence of civilian rule. In 1955, following the decision of governor general Ghulam Mohammed to dissolve the Constituent Assembly and remove the government of Mohammed Ali Bogra, the Supreme Court declared: 'That which otherwise is not lawful, necessity makes lawful.'[27] The doctrine of necessity has been used on many subsequent occasions to justify the removal of various governments retrospectively. Generals Ayub Khan, Yahya, Zia and Musharraf all browbeat the courts into validating their coups.

Musharraf's contemptuous attitude to the judiciary, however, did eventually rebound against him. In March 2007 he dismissed the chief justice of the Supreme Court, Iftikhar Muhammad Chaudhry. It was one of his biggest mistakes. Tension between the two men had been building for some months. In June 2006 the Supreme Court had blocked a major deal to privatise the Pakistan Steel Mills, which many believed would benefit government cronies. The Court also irritated Musharraf by raising a series of other issues, including that of people who had gone missing in government custody. Iftikhar Muhammad Chaudhry directed the Ministry of the Interior and the representatives of the military agencies to release prisoners who had not been given due process. It was a highly controversial decision and, as far as Musharraf was concerned, a direct encroachment on his powers. In March 2007,

President Musharraf responded: he suspended the chief justice, accusing him of misconduct.

Chaudhry, however, refused to go quietly. And for millions of Pakistanis he became a symbol of the rule of law versus a military leader. In May 2007 Chaudhry travelled from Islamabad to Lahore to address the Lahore High Court Bar Association. It became a triumphal procession. The journey should have taken four to five hours, but there were so many demonstrators along his route that it took him 25 hours to reach his destination. The row between Chaudhry and Musharraf dragged on for months and involved, at various points, the chief justice's reinstatement and his dismissal again as a result of the November 2007 state of emergency. But the chief justice won the day: Musharraf had to resign in part because his struggle with lawyers sapped his authority. Just like Musharraf, the new president, Asif Zardari, had no interest in an independent-minded chief justice who might once again defy the government, and Iftikhar Chaudhry was restored to office only when further mass demonstrations led by Nawaz Sharif gained real momentum. The army chief General Kayani intervened and told Zardari that in the interests of national stability the chief justice had to be given his job back. Even if there were genuine questions about some aspects of Iftikhar Chaudhry's past, including allegations of nepotism, his restoration was significant: for the first time Pakistan's judiciary was led by a genuinely independent figure whose popular support would allow him to challenge those in power.

Even if the judiciary played a big part in undermining President Musharraf, the fact remains that it is the army which remains the single most significant obstacle to the survival of elected governments. Throughout Benazir Bhutto's first administration the chief of army staff, General Aslam Beg, repeatedly sought credit for his decision that following Zia's death the civilians would be 'allowed' to rule again. Bhutto never showed any willingness to challenge this utterly undemocratic and presumptuous attitude.[28] Given that the army had executed her father, it was perhaps understandable that she decided, in her own words, 'to give them whatever they wanted.'[29] Asked in one news conference whether she intended to cut the defence budget she replied, 'Not unless we want the army to take over again'.[30] Bhutto's foreign affairs adviser, Iqbal Akhund, witnessed her first administration at first hand

and concluded that: 'On Afghanistan, Kashmir, and India the government was faced with very complex and thorny issues, but the decision-
making in all of these had been taken over by the army and the
intelligence agencies in Zia's time and there, in the ultimate analysis, it
remained.'[31] This is a fair assessment; Bhutto was neither sufficiently
confident nor strong enough to take the generals on.

Sharif, particularly during his second administration, showed greater
determination to establish control over the military. Indeed, from the
moment he was re-elected in 1977, he concentrated on making his
political position impregnable. He began by undermining the parliamentarians by forcing through a Constitutional Amendment that
required all members of the National Assembly to vote according
to party lines. He bullied the press by arresting journalists who wrote
against him and ordering tax investigations into those editors who
continued to print critical articles. He also tackled the judiciary, and
with far more brutality than Musharraf. When the Supreme Court tried
to hear a contempt of court case in which Sharif was a defendant in
1997, a mob of his supporters, led by some cabinet members and close
advisers, ransacked the Supreme Court, disrupting proceedings and
smashing furniture. The terrified judges caved in and the contempt of
court case was dropped. Sharif then moved on to tackle the president,
Farooq Leghari. As soon as the latter voiced support for the embattled
judiciary, Sharif had him replaced by an old family friend from Lahore,
Rafiq Tarar. A former Supreme Court judge, Tarar had a reputation
both as a pious Muslim and a man who had a huge repertoire of
dirty jokes. He was not, however, known for his ability to stand up to
authority. As soon as he became president, Tarar readily agreed to
Sharif's proposal that the presidency be stripped of its power to remove
a sitting government. By 1998 the only significant power centre that
remained untouched was the army.

On 6 October 1998, General Musharraf's widely respected predecessor, General Jehangir Karamat, despairing of the sustained corruption and incompetence of the Sharif administration, had voiced the
frustration felt by countless officers. In a speech to Lahore Naval
College he called for the establishment of a National Security Council
that would give the military a formal role in the political decision-

making process: 'A National Security Council,' he said, 'or similar committee at the apex would institutionalise decision-making.'[32] Sharif responded ruthlessly. Within two days Karamat was forced to resign and Sharif replaced him with General Pervez Musharraf. It may have seemed like a good idea at the time, but he quickly came to regret the decision. The origin of the two men's mutual antagonism lay in Kargil. Whilst General Musharraf had sent the troops in, Prime Minister Sharif was left with the unenviable task of getting them out. For three decades the Pakistani people had absorbed a steady flow of vitriolic propaganda about the Kashmir issue: Sharif's decision to withdraw seemed incomprehensible and humiliating. As the man who had defied world opinion and tested Pakistan's nuclear bomb in 1998, Sharif had been acclaimed as a national hero. As the man who pulled out from Kargil in 1999 he was denounced as a supine coward. Sharif's sense of resentment was acute.

The soldiers, though, were also unhappy. They believed that by deciding to pull out of Kargil without negotiating any Indian concessions in return, Sharif had squandered a militarily advantageous position and caused a crisis of confidence within the Pakistan army. After the Kargil withdrawal, Musharraf faced a surge of discontent within the army. As he toured a series of garrisons he repeatedly faced the same question: 'If Kargil was a victory then why did we pull back?' Musharraf told his men that it was the prime minister's fault and the army had had no choice but to obey his order. It was a disingenuous response. Musharraf had been fully consulted on the withdrawal order and had raised no serious objection to it.

After Kargil the relationship between the prime minister and army chief was severely damaged. By early September 1999, GHQ was buzzing with rumours that Sharif would sack Musharraf. It was clear that a crisis was imminent. Recalling that time, the former navy chief Admiral Fasih Bokhari has said: 'The two men could not work together and both were preparing to take some action. I could see that there were now two centres of power on a collision course.'[33]

Bokhari was not the only one to notice the tension between the two men. On 8 and 9 September, Sharif and Musharraf travelled together to the Northern Areas. They were to preside over a ceremony to reward the

Northern Light Infantry (NLI) for its role in the Kargil campaign. Previously a paramilitary force answerable to the Ministry of the Interior, the NLI was being inducted into the regular army. On the evening of 8 September, General Musharraf was in the lobby of the Hotel Shangri-La outside Skardu, showing off a new Italian laser-guided pistol to the information minister, Mushahid Hussain. As Musharraf was explaining how the pistol could never miss its target, the prime minister walked into the lobby. Aware of his prime minister's fondness for high-tech gadgets, Mushahid Hussain called Sharif over. 'Have you seen this new pistol?' he asked Sharif. 'It's remarkable.' Uncharacteristically, Sharif did not ask how the pistol worked. But he did put one question to the army chief. 'General,' he asked, 'who are you aiming it at?'[34] A month later the guns were pointing at Sharif for real as he was led in handcuffs to a prison cell.

The Intelligence Agencies

The civil service, the army, the judiciary and the politicians have all played their part in undermining Pakistani democracy. But so, too, have Pakistan's many intelligence agencies. The most important civilian agency is the Intelligence Bureau (IB), which is run by the Ministry of the Interior and is answerable to the prime minister or the president. Officially, it is responsible for counter-intelligence but in reality it spends most of its time monitoring and disrupting the activities of the political opponents of the government of the day. It is the organisation that, for example, is responsible for bugging the phones of leading Pakistani journalists. There are also two military agencies. Military Intelligence or, as it is more usually known, MI, is almost entirely focused on internal army matters. Run by a major general, it is formally charged with gathering information that the armed forces might require to wage war. In practice the MI is the ears and eyes of the army chief who uses it to gauge morale within the armed forces, to ensure discipline is maintained and to get early warning, for example, of any attempt by serving personnel to assassinate the army chief.

All three of these organisations are dwarfed by Pakistan's premier agency, the Inter Services Intelligence (ISI). The ISI was created in 1948 by a British officer, Major General William Cawthorne,[35] and was initially charged with collecting military intelligence – mainly from India – for the army, air force and navy. Since then the ISI has broadened its remit. The process began under Ayub Khan who asked the ISI to monitor his opponents and sustain military rule.[36] Indeed, the ISI became so concentrated on internal politics that even semi-official histories of Pakistan concede that it lost focus on its main task. In the 1965 war the ISI proved incapable of identifying the location of an entire Indian armoured division.[37] Keen to control the ISI, Zulfikar Ali Bhutto substantially increased the organisation's funding.[38] He wasn't just after information on regional and international politics; he also wanted the ISI to spy on his political opponents.[39] After Bhutto's removal from power, General Zia in turn did not hesitate to use the organisation to harass Bhutto's party, the PPP. Indeed, under Zia the ISI flourished. The organisation took over management of the anti-Soviet struggle in Afghanistan and was given responsibility for distributing the billions of dollars pumped into the conflict by the United States and Saudi Arabia. The Mujahideen's campaign to force a Soviet withdrawal transformed the ISI into one of the best financed, self-confident and most powerful of all Pakistan's state institutions.

After the Soviet retreat from Afghanistan, the ISI turned its attention once again to domestic politics, actively conspiring against Benazir Bhutto. A former director general of the ISI, Lieutenant General (retd) Azad Durrani, has recorded in a Supreme Court affidavit that he was instructed by the then chief of army staff, General Aslam Beg, to provide 'logistic support' to the disbursement of funds to Benazir Bhutto's opponents in the Islami Jamhoori Ittehad (IJI) coalition led by Nawaz Sharif. According to Durrani, the ISI opened some cover bank accounts in Karachi, Rawalpindi and Quetta, and deposited money into them. The sums were not small. One account in Karachi was credited with over $2 million and smaller amounts were then transferred to other accounts on the instruction of the chief of army staff and the election cell in the presidency. The recipients of the money included Nawaz Sharif ($58,000), the Jamaat-e-Islami ($83,000) and a whole series of anti-PPP politicians based in Sindh.[40]

When this activity came to light, General Aslam Beg brazenly told the Supreme Court that: 'It would be in the fitness of things that further

proceedings on this matter are dropped.' As to the substance of the allegations, he did not deny that the ISI had been involved in disbursing
the funds. Rather, he argued that such activity was quite normal,
proper and lawful: 'A full account was maintained of all the payments
made by the DG ISI and no amount was misappropriated or misused.'[41]

The ISI also got involved in foreign policy, helping create the Taliban
movement. When Mullah Omar took the city of Kandahar in 1994, his
Taliban forces were joined by Pakistani fighters. Some were religious
students from madrasas in Balochistan and NWFP who went to
Afghanistan with the support of the ISI. It is also quite possible that the
ISI not only organised the deployment of some regular Pakistani troops
to back up the Taliban's offensive but also paid off the Taliban's opponents
in Kandahar to ensure that it fell without much of a fight.[42] By the time
the Taliban took Kabul in 1996, the ISI was making little secret of its
involvement in installing a new Afghan government. According to one
reliable eyewitness in the city, a senior ISI officer was openly performing
basic command and control functions on behalf of the Taliban.[43]

The ISI also became a significant power in Kashmir. From the very
start the Kashmiri insurgency was encouraged, and to some extent,
organised, by the ISI. It grew close to many of the militant groups
that fought, in Kashmir, and there were also deep links between the ISI
and the militant organisations active within Pakistan itself. Indeed,
the ISI helped to create much of the Islamic militancy that General
Musharraf later tried to combat.

The question of who controls the ISI is one of the most controversial
in Pakistani politics. There are two issues. First, does the ISI work only
for the military or can civilian governments control it? Secondly, does
anyone in fact control the organisation or is it a largely independent
body full of rogue agents determined to foster Islamic revolution at
home and abroad?

In 2008 a row between the army and President Zardari helped answer
the first question. Theoretically, the ISI is meant to be answerable to the
prime minister. But the extent of the prime minister's control has always
been limited because the senior ranks of the ISI are filled with serving
military officers appointed by, and answerable to, the chief of army staff.
Senior ISI officers have generally felt that their first loyalty is to their

military colleagues, so, whilst nominally being under the authority of the prime minister they have, in practice, worked for the army. In July 2008 the incoming government of the Pakistan People's Party tried to change those arrangements. Responding to US concerns that the ISI was helping rather than hindering Islamic militants, the government issued a notification stating that the ISI would come under the direct control of the Interior Ministry. To outside observers the switch from oversight by the prime minister's office to the Interior Ministry might have seemed like a diminution of civilian control. In fact, the intention was the opposite. The prime minister's office was staffed by a small number of civil servants mainly handling protocol matters. The Interior Ministry, by contrast, was better placed to control the ISI. 'No one will now be able to say that this agency is not under the elected government's control,' said Zardari.[44]

The army reacted to the decision with fury and insisted the government back down. As the army spokesman General Athar Abbas euphemistically put it: 'When we realised that the decision had been taken, we discussed the issue with the government and are thankful that there was a realisation of ground realities and our position was accepted.' Within 24 hours the government issued a clarification that its earlier statement had been 'misunderstood' and the ISI would 'continue to function under the prime minister' – which meant, in practice, the army.[45]

The second issue concerns the extent to which the ISI is a rogue agency. It is often claimed that the ISI, because of the private sympathies of its staff, fuels Islamic militancy in Kashmir, Afghanistan and even within Pakistan. Indeed, in private briefings with western interlocutors Pakistani ministers and civil officials often suggest that the ISI is a law unto itself.

The reality is very different. Whenever it has backed Islamic militants, the ISI has been following orders and implementing Pakistani state policy. For years Pakistani officials claimed that any ISI links with militants fighting in Kashmir were uncontrolled, freelance operations. It's now widely accepted, however, that the ISI was supporting the Kashmiri insurgency because Islamabad, or more accurately the army command in Rawalpindi, ordered it to do so. More recently, the US has complained that the ISI has secret links with the Taliban. In 2008 the CIA chief Michael

Hayden, for example, complained about the 'double game played by Pakistan's spy agency'.[46] The Americans argued that improved government control of the agency would solve the problem. But that missed the point. The reason the ISI was supporting some elements of the Taliban was because the government ordered it to do so. The impression that the ISI is out of control has offered successive Pakistani governments a welcome degree of plausible deniability. Western officials have often been gullible when accepting such denials. If the US intelligence agencies were correct, for example, in claiming that the ISI was involved in the 2008 bombing of the Indian Embassy in Kabul, then it is reasonable to conclude that the army leadership ordered that attack. No ISI staff member would dare to organise such a major incident without being ordered to do so.

The ISI is headed by a lieutenant general and its senior positions are filled by officers who are seconded to the organisation for two to three years before being transferred back to the army. This clearly limits the extent to which they will dare defy their senior officers. Having said that, many ISI officers, both secondees and permanent staff at mid-ranking levels, are hardline nationalists.[47] Many take it as read, for example, that the Indian government is helping Al Qaeda secure its sanctuary in Pakistan and encouraging it to attack targets within Pakistan; that the United States is an unreliable, hypocritical ally and bound to lose in Afghanistan; that Pakistan is a victim of outside powers and, if it can use radical Islam as a way of asserting itself, it should not hesitate to do so. Such views, however, are by no means unusual: most military officers and many other Pakistanis would agree with them.

Feudalism

As they contemplate the failure of democracy in their country, many Pakistanis are apt to blame the country's major landowners. The 'feudals', as they are known, are routinely denounced as pretentious, self-interested, unprincipled, reactionary snobs who constitute a major obstacle to social and democratic development. The Pakistani historian and political scientist, Iftikhar H. Malik, for example, argues that, having been given land and power by the British, the feudals have managed to hang onto both ever since by using a combination of cunning and brute force. 'A new generation of aristocrats,' Malik writes, 'with degrees from privileged Western universities have seen to it that their near monopoly of national politics and the economy remains unchallenged. In lieu of political support to a regime, whether military or quasi democratic, feudalists exact favours through ministerial positions, loans and property allocations.'[48] Malik argues that in periods of both military and civilian rule the feudals have been the power behind the throne.

It is certainly true that many major landholders in Pakistan have remained close to the seat of power and that some continue to command extraordinary degrees of loyalty in their own communities. One story about a leading Sindhi feudal, Pir Pagaro, helps make the point. When Pakistan's military ruler, Ayub Khan, visited the pir in the 1960s, the latter advised the field marshal to walk one step behind him. Otherwise, he warned, my followers may think you consider yourself equal to me and they could harm you. It was not an idle comment. His devotees would have been quite capable of mounting a frenzied attack on anyone who insulted their pir by challenging his supremacy.

Throughout Pakistan the rural elite carries out a number of functions that would, in most other countries, be seen as the responsibility of the courts, police or other administrative bodies. Local notables dispense justice in their own areas. Typically, a feudal lord will make himself available once a week to anyone in his area who wishes to see him. Many of the petitioners ask for jobs for themselves or their children. Others will have had a problem with the police and want the feudal to intervene to get the case dropped. But on many occasions the requests go further than that. The feudal will be asked to resolve divorce settlements or claims that a neighbour was guilty of theft or even rape and murder. Having heard the evidence from all sides of any particular dispute, the feudal will make a judgement on the spot. Given that the whole procedure takes a few minutes and is free, it is hardly surprising that many people prefer it to the slow, expensive and notoriously corrupt courts. Many feudal leaders order punishments – such as a physical beating – for those they consider guilty of a crime. Some feudals have private prisons.

In some areas feudal lords and their tribal equivalents have extraordinary powers. Before his death in 2007, Nawab Bugti in Balochistan used to order trials by fire. Anyone forced to undergo this ordeal had to wash his feet in the blood of a goat and then walk seven paces along some burning embers. If his feet blistered the nawab declared him to be guilty. The nawab ordered a trial by fire only if he was presented with a dispute and could not decide which party was telling the truth. He insisted that the trials by fire (they happened about once a month) never failed to identify the guilty and exonerate the innocent.

Defining the feudals with any precision is not easy. By most accounts the 'classic' feudals are the major landowners in southern Punjab and Sindh. Many of these grandees derive their power not only by virtue of the sheer size of their estates but also by claiming spiritual powers. Typically they are the direct descendants of a pir, or saint. After the pir's death, often several centuries ago, his grave became a shrine visited by devotees. The descendants took on the task of maintaining the shrine and were considered to have inherited spiritual powers. Since the devotees often donated money to the shrine, being a pir's descendant was a highly profitable business, allowing the family to buy land. Some analysts differentiate between the feudal leaders of Sindh and Punjab and the tribal leaders who hold sway in Balochistan and, to a lesser extent, NWFP. They point out that the tribal leaders do not have unquestioned title over all their tribe's lands and, unlike the feudals, they cannot be certain that their power will be passed down to their sons.

For some analysts, however, such distinctions are largely irrelevant. S. Akbar Zaidi, for example, maintains that the mode of production in the agricultural sector is, for the most part, no longer feudal but capitalist. He argues that Britain's imperial government in Delhi introduced a number of reforms such as the recognition of private property and the establishment of agricultural commodity markets and that, as a result, 'capitalist agriculture has been the leading trend and it is not possible to label Pakistan or Pakistani agriculture today as feudal'.[49] Such arguments, however, miss the point. When Pakistanis speak out aganist the feudals they are complaining about the fact that the rural elite is able to ignore the state institutions and use religion, their landholdings and the tribal system to wield huge amounts of power.

Nevertheless, those who insist on a strict definition of feudalism do make one important point. Many of those described as feudals in reality have quite small landholdings and enjoy very limited authority in their home area. Take the case of Ghulam Mustafa Khar, one of the founders of the Pakistan People's Party, a close political ally of Zulfikar Ali Bhutto and, at one stage, his chief minister of Punjab. Khar's conduct has often been described as classically feudal and one of his wives, Tehmina Durrani, wrote a book about him entitled *My Feudal Lord*.[50] She recounts how Khar, in his personal as well as his political life, was a violent tyrant. For many, Khar provides a good example of everything that is wrong with feudalism. But Khar was never a major landowner. Even if his family was powerful in his hometown of Muzaffargarh, he never enjoyed the same kind of loyalty or adoration as some of the major religious landowners in Sindh. The source of Khar's power was initially his close relationship with Zulfikar Ali Bhutto and, in later years, his status as a national political leader. Khar, in short, behaved like the worst kind of feudal lord even though he was little more than a Punjabi farmer.

For all the definitional difficulties, it is indisputable that successive Pakistani parliaments have been filled with landowners and tribal leaders who have not hesitated to use their seats to protect their own interests. Despite considerable pressure from the International Monetary Fund, for example, no Pakistani government has ever been able to impose a tax on agriculture. It is also beyond dispute that some feudal landowners have held onto their authority by preventing social and economic development in their areas. In his memoirs Lieutenant General (retd) Attiqur Rahman recalled a visit he made to the nawab of Dir, a major landowner in NWFP:

When the government sent him an educationalist to offer all help and provide schools the Nawab said nothing. He changed the subject and said they would go for a duck shoot the next morning. This was in the middle of winter and it can be very cold in the early mornings. The Nawab shot a duck and told his followers to collect it, at which about thirty jumped into the water. The Nawab then turned to the education-alist and said: 'If I educated my people, not one of these men would have gone into the water to fetch the duck.'[51]

Although the nawab of Dir never aspired to much more than having a steady supply of people to fetch his ducks, many other feudals have participated in national politics. Amir Mohamed Khan, the nawab of Kalabagh, provides a good example. At the age of 14 he became the undisputed master of the family estate in a remote part of southern Punjab. Like many feudals he was initially doubtful about the creation of Pakistan.[52] But once he realised that Pakistan was going to happen he sought to protect his interests first by joining the Muslim League and then by becoming one of its major financial contributors. By the time of independence he had ingratiated himself with the new ruling establishment and used his solid vote bank of tenants to secure seats in both the Punjab and West Pakistan Assemblies. When military rule was imposed in 1958, the nawab of Kalabagh was well placed: Ayub Khan was a regular guest at his partridge shoots. Within months the nawab was a federal minister and in 1965 he became the governor of West Pakistan. The nawab was a feudal and he ruled like one. His orders were delivered verbally and all civil servants and police officers in Punjab were told that they owed their loyalties not to the Pakistani state but to the nawab alone. Even his defenders, such as his military secretary Jahan Dad Khan, concede that the nawab could never outgrow his origins:

> He had inherited his full share of the negative traits of feudalism which included commitment to the maintenance of the status quo and an authoritarian outlook. He strongly believed in breeding, family background and the caste system . . . he resisted every change which posed a threat to his interests as a feudal landlord.[53]

Although he had good relations with many feudals, Ayub Khan did recognise that they were a brake on social and political development. In his memoirs he recorded that in 1958 in West Pakistan 'more than 50 per cent of the available land in the Punjab, a little less than 50 per cent in NWFP and over 80 per cent in Sindh was in the possession of a few thousand absentee landlords'.[54] In 1959 Ayub Khan announced a land reform programme under which no one would be allowed more than 500 acres of irrigated land or 1,000 acres of non-irrigated land. Ayub subsequently claimed that this policy had far-reaching effects: 'The disappearance of the class of absentee landlords, who exercised great political influence under the previous land-holding system, marked the beginning of a new era in West Pakistan.'[55]

In reality, however, Ayub's land reforms never worked. In the first place his limits of 500 and 1,000 acres were not especially stringent. The feudals managed to get around the law by, for example, transferring ownership to close relatives and even farm workers. In some cases illiterate peasants were told to put their thumbprint on a piece of paper. Technically, the land now belonged to them but since they were illiterate they did not even know it. The feudals also made liberal use of an exemption that allowed them to hold onto hunting grounds and orchards in excess of the stipulated limits.

Recognising that Ayub's efforts had been thwarted, Zulfikar Ali Bhutto made another attempt to introduce land reform in 1972. He reduced the ceilings to 150 acres of irrigated and 300 acres of non-irrigated land. The land would be taken, he said, without compensation and handed to landless peasants without payment. Although Bhutto did close down some of the loopholes that undermined Ayub's programme, others remained in place. It was still possible, for example, for landowners to transfer ownership to relatives and, for all Bhutto's rhetoric, the amount of land handed over to the government was insignificant.

Neither Ayub Khan nor Bhutto was serious about land reform. Only a small percentage of the country's cultivable land was taken from the feudals. But even if the major landowners have shown great resilience, a number of election results suggest that although they enjoy great authority in their local areas they are not always able to count on people's votes. The feudals' electoral difficulties began in 1970 when Zulfikar Ali Bhutto's campaign slogan of 'Bread, Clothing, and Shelter' gave him a resounding victory in Punjab and Sindh. Many feudal landowners lost their seats. Those who were defeated included representatives of major families such as the Chandios, Khuhros and Legharis. The results of 1970 were not a one-off. In 1988 a number of other feudal leaders such as Pir Pagaro, Mohammed Khan Junejo and Ghulam Mustafa Jatoi also lost their seats. The nawab of Kalabagh's sons have experienced similar difficulties. As all these men now know, party affiliation has become a more important determinant of voting behaviour.

It would be wrong, however, to conclude that the feudals are a spent force. Their cynical ability to adjust to the various political dispensations in Pakistan means that they are seldom far removed from the seat of power for long. This enduring trait in their conduct was apparent even before partition. Many major landowners, especially in Punjab, spent many years opposing the creation of Pakistan. Some feared that the division of Punjab would leave them with property on both sides of the new border and that they would consequently be forced to abandon some of their lands. But as soon as they realised that Mohammad Ali Jinnah's appeal to the Muslim masses had resonated they switched sides, joined his Muslim League and promptly rose to high positions in the party. Their success can be gauged by the fact that following independence major landowners were given the chief ministerships in Punjab, Sindh and NWFP. (At that stage Balochistan did not have a chief minister.)

Many of the feudals defeated in the 1970 election performed a similar manoeuvre, deciding that if they could not beat the PPP they would join it. By the time of the next elections in 1977 many had become PPP candidates. As Andrew Wilder has put it: 'The PPP's slate of 1977 election candidates read like a Who's Who of Punjab's rural elite.' And having penetrated the party, the feudals did not hesitate to influence PPP policy so as to protect their interests. By 1977 Bhutto had dropped his anti-feudal rhetoric and instead issued a manifesto, which made the implausible claim that there was no need for more land reform as the PPP's policies had already 'brought an end to feudalism in Pakistan'.[56] By 1985, after Bhutto had been hanged, the feudals had switched sides once again. In the partyless elections of that year they had a field day. Rural notables secured over three-quarters of the 875 positions on the national and provincial level at stake in the elections.[57]

Take, as an example, the pir of Ranipur, Abdul Qadir Shah. The pir is both a religious leader and major landowner in the Khaipur district of Sindh. In 1970 he opposed the PPP and lost. In 1977 he stood for the PPP. Under General Zia, with the PPP at its lowest ebb, he abandoned the party and stood in the 1985 non-party elections. In 1988, after Zia's death, he patched up his differences with Benazir Bhutto and became a PPP candidate once more.[58] The arrangement works both ways. The feudal wants to be on the winning ticket and the parties want the candidate most likely to deliver a substantial personal vote bank. As one PPP official admitted in 1988: 'The main consideration for the allotment of party tickets was that the candidate should belong to the influential and affluent families.'[59]

The feudals employ other strategies to remain in powerful positions. Many have formed marriage alliances to senior figures in the army or bureaucracy. Both sides gain from the arrangement: the civil servant or army officer wins some of the social respectability associated with landownership; the feudals gain access to corridors of power. Another tactic is for close relatives to join different political parties and contest elections against each other. Whoever wins the election, the family will have someone in the National Assembly. In the 1988 elections, for example, the Makhdooms of Rahim Yar Khan put up two candidates for Nawaz Sharif's IJI and one for Benazir Bhutto's PPP. Similarly the Shahs of Nawabshah covered their options by having two candidates for the IJI and another two for the PPP.

The feudals, of course, deploy many arguments to justify their preeminent position. 'People have lost faith in the police, the judiciary and the parliament,' Benazir Bhutto's first cousin Mumtaz Bhutto once said. 'We are doing the job that the administration should be doing.'[60] Some feudals also complain, with some justification, that their critics make far too many sweeping generalisations about them. The Sindhi landowner Abdul Ghaffar Jatoi, for example, has complained about 'city-bound pseudo intellectuals and armchair experts sitting hundreds of miles away from the countryside offering utopian solutions to the complex and deep rooted problems of the country dwellers.'[61]

Jatoi argues that a more equitable distribution of land would do little to improve agricultural productivity. Experience elsewhere in East Asia and beyond suggests he is wrong. If Pakistani farmers cannot get enough credit to buy the tools they need to cultivate small plots of land, then the state should provide them with what they lack. If Pakistan is to enjoy higher economic growth and social development, then it needs a middle class. Although the feudals might not like to admit it, there can be little doubt that Pakistan would benefit if people were able to rise to the top of the system on the basis of merit rather than land titles handed out often by the British decades ago. Those who believe that the feudals' powers are overrated argue that they have less authority than they used to and the trend is against them. Increased labour mobility, the private TV channels and the (albeit woefully slow) processes of spreading education and providing micro-credit are undermining the feudals' power bases. Nonetheless, despite the gradual process of change, it is a remarkable fact that men like Pir Pagaro and many others are still able to lock people up in private prisons, dispense justice and own bonded labourers. There are few countries, and no successful ones, where local landlords wield such power.

General Musharraf's regime, like that of Ayub Khan, stated its concern about the feudals. In February 2000 it announced plans to carry out a massive land-reform programme to remove what one official described as 'centuries-old feudalism'.[62] In October it issued a report, 'Decentralisation and the Devolution of Power', which called for rapid land redistribution so as to empower landless peasants. 'This is being done,' the report said, 'to stop the rural elite from dictating their terms and conditions and getting their own candidates elected. ... These power holders have traditionally controlled and even subverted the electoral process at the national and provincial levels.'[63] As in so many other policy areas, the rhetoric sounded fine but in the event little happened. Musharraf could not afford to take on some of Pakistan's most astute and powerful politicians. The events of 11 September further reduced the chances of Musharraf tackling the feudal issue. As some of the most pro-Western and conservative elements of Pakistani society, the feudals became an indispensible part of his campaign against the forces of radical Islam.

7

The Army

Throughout the whole world, yes throughout the world, no armed force is so irrevocably devoted to Islam as the Pakistani armed forces.
—Editorial in the armed forces' weekly journal *Hilal*, 1996[1]

The story of Pakistan is the story of ambitious and adventurist generals denying the people their rights.
—Former air force chief, Mohammad Asghar Khan, 1983

Soldiers of Allah?

Brigadier Nusrat Sial, the commander of Pakistan's 62nd Infantry Brigade, was sitting in his office in Skardu when the news came through. 'Allahu Akbar!' a young officer yelled down the line. 'We've shot down two Indian jets.'[2] It was in the midst of the Kargil campaign and just two days earlier, on 25 May 1999, the Indian prime minister had authorised the use of air power to help to repel Pakistani troops who had crossed the line of control. The brigadier could not suppress his delight and within hours was escorting a group of international journalists to see the wreckage of one of the planes, an Indian MiG-27. Scraps of twisted metal lay all around the steep mountainside where it had hit the ground. The brigadier smiled broadly as he surveyed the scene and contemplated Pakistan's success in shooting down the plane. He then dilated on a subject close to his heart: Islam. 'I have seen something of the world,' he said. 'I spent two years in Germany and do you know the fastest growing religion there? It is Islam. Yes, even Germany could become an Islamic state. And the United States too.'[3] The more the brigadier spoke it, the more it became clear that his whole world-view was defined by Islam. He may have been a soldier but he considered himself to be serving a divine purpose.

If the Pakistan army can be characterised as an Islamic army then the implications are profound. Should there ever be a massive social upheaval in Pakistan it would inevitably be suffused with Islamic values and led by radical clerics. And the outcome of such a challenge to the existing order would depend in large part on the army. A modernist army leadership, sure of its orders being obeyed, could prevent the Islamic radicals from riding a popular movement to grasp power. An ambivalent or divided military leadership, unsure of the willingness of its men to do battle with the Islamists, might take a different attitude. So, if an Islamic revolution ever did get under way, what would the army do?

Had that question been asked in 1947 there would have been no doubt as to the answer. At that time Pakistan did not have an Islamic army: it had an army with an overwhelming majority of Muslims. Trained in the British system, Pakistan's leading officers were more interested in modern military theory than theology and were committed to a national as opposed to a religious project. They took their orders from their military superiors, not from the mosques. They were soon put to the test. In a report on partition-related violence in Lahore, Field Marshall Sir Claude Auchinleck described how the nascent Pakistan army performed when communal riots seemed likely to sweep the city:

> There is very strong evidence that the police are taking little notice of their officers (all the remaining European officers left yesterday) and that they have actually joined hands with the rioters in certain instances. But for the presence of the army there would by now be a complete holocaust in the city. Local Muslim leaders are trying to persuade the Muslim soldiers to follow the bad example of the police – so far without success.[4]

The military faced a not dissimilar challenge during the 1953 anti-Ahmedi riots in Lahore. When the army intervened there was not the slightest suggestion that it would side with the religious extremists who were persecuting the Ahmedis. Officers involved in the operation saw their mission as the restoration of law and order and the suppression of the Islamic leaders' destabilising campaign.

A story told by Major General (retd) Shahid Hamid further illustrates the attitudes of senior officers during this period. In 1950 the general was given command of a brigade stationed on the Afghan border and he decided to hold regular open meetings with his men. In one of these sessions an army mullah stood up to ask a question:

> He came to stand at the head of the queue expecting me to give him preference above the troops. I did not like this and made him wait his turn. He said that he wanted me to issue an order that the troops should attend all the five prayers in the mosque. Thereupon I repeated his request on the loudspeaker and added that the orders on the subject already existed from the Holiest of the Holiest and required no further directive. Later I told the centre commander to get rid of him as he was a potential troublemaker.[5]

Such actions would probably have won the approval of Mohammed Ali Jinnah. In the run-up to the transfer of power he fought hard to persuade the British that their cherished India Army should be dismantled. Eventually he succeeded in securing agreement for a separate Pakistan army but there is no reason to believe that he ever envisaged an Islamic army. In the few months he had to effect the development of the military forces in Pakistan, Jinnah concentrated not on the army's religious sentiment but on its professionalism. Indeed, the first two commanders in chief, General Sir Frank Messervy and General Sir Douglas Gracey, were British Christians. Speaking to officers at the Staff College in Quetta in February 1948, Jinnah characteristically laid emphasis on national rather than religious concerns. 'Every officer and soldier,' he said, 'no matter what the race or community to which he belongs, is working as a true Pakistani.'[6]

Like Jinnah, the first Pakistani commander-in-chief, Ayub Khan, was no religious zealot. On the contrary, Sandhurst-educated and strongly pro-American, he consistently downplayed the role of Islam in the Pakistani state. The views of Jinnah and Ayub reflected those of the vast bulk of the officer corps at the time. They wanted to create an effective modern military machine that could match the Indian armed forces. They took as their role models not the Muslim commanders of times past but rather the American generals who had stormed to victory in the Second World War.

The first Pakistan army chief to play on religious sentiment was General Zia ul-Haq. His Islamicisation campaign affected Pakistani society as a whole, but he made a special effort to reform the military and to create a more puritanical, devout army. He made it clear that the alcohol ban imposed during the last days of Zulfikar Ali Bhutto's government was to apply in officers' messes where, previously, drink had flowed very freely. Greater emphasis was laid on organising prayer times and religious fasts for army personnel. He also allowed some religious groups to operate in the army with relative freedom. In particular, Zia encouraged the largest Islamic organisation in Pakistan, the Tablighi Jamaat, to become active within the army and he became the first army chief to attend the Tablighis' massive annual conventions in Raiwind near Lahore.[7] Although the Tablighis were known to hold some extreme opinions, it should also be said that they were not generally regarded as a potential source of instability. The organisation had always advocated 'Jihad through conscience' rather than 'Jihad through the sword' and promoted a policy of non-intervention in politics.

Zia also wanted Islam to be integrated into the syllabus of the Staff College and he encouraged the study of Islam's teaching regarding the conduct of war. All the Quranic passages relevant to war were printed and distributed in military circles. One article published in Pakistan's *Defence Journal* in 1979 was typical of the debate that Zia encouraged. It argued that the Muslim laws of war contained more extensive humanitarian provisions than the Geneva Convention. The Quran and subsequent Islamic teaching, the article argued, required Pakistani soldiers to refrain from committing excess cruelty; to respect the sanctity of non-combatants; to refrain from taking hostages (unless for the purpose of freeing Muslims) and so on.[8] Similarly, Zia supported the publication in 1979 of Brigadier S.K. Malik's *Quranic Concept of War*. Starting from the premise that: 'As a perfect divine document, the Holy Quran has given a comprehensive treatment to its concept of war', the brigadier went on to apply Quranic principles to modern military strategy. In a signed foreword to the publication, General Zia wrote:

This book brings out with simplicity, clarity and precision the Quranic philosophy on the application of military force within the context of the totality that is JEHAD. The professional soldier in a Muslim army, pursuing the goals of a Muslim state, CANNOT become 'professional' if in all his activities he does not take on 'the colour of Allah'.[9]

General Zia also took religion into account when making senior military appointments. In 1982 Cecil Chaudhry, one of Pakistan's leading fighter pilots, who had been decorated for his bravery in the 1965 war, was up for promotion. The Air Board approved his appointment as a staff officer, a post of such seniority that it had to be approved by the president, General Zia. But he rejected the Air Board's recommendation. 'No reason was given,' Chaudhry later recalled, 'but I attribute it to my being a non-Muslim. Before the Zia era a Christian did make it to the number two post in the Air Force. But after Zia took over no non-Muslim was able to make it even to group captain. It was the same in the army.'[10]

The high levels of discipline within the Pakistan army meant that Zia's campaign made it difficult for secular-minded officers to resist his ideas. But some tried. One of Zia's generals, for example, was faced with a mullah who insisted that it was un-Islamic to wear shorts. His edict led to the cancellation of afternoon sports. The general responded by saying that since the mullah was technically a full member of the regiment, he would be expected to take part not only in the physical training but also in all combat operations.[11]

Despite such attempts to keep the mullahs in their traditional place, Zia's ideas left a deep mark on the army and seven years after his death some senior officers tried to build on his legacy. On the morning of 26 September 1995, Brigadier Mustansir Billah was driving from Pakistan's tribal areas when he was stopped at a police checkpoint. Inside his car the police found a cache of Kalashnikovs and rocket launchers that had been purchased by a member of Harkat ul-Ansar, Qari Saifullah Akhtar (who was later named by Benazir Bhutto as the provider of weapons for the bomb attack on her in Karachi in October 2007). The brigadier, eager to get away, pulled rank and called GHQ in Rawalpindi demanding help to get his car released. His pleas fell on deaf ears. The brigadier had just walked into a trap.

The police who made the discovery had been tipped off and, far from helping Billah, the officers at GHQ ordered his immediate arrest.

The brigadier had been transporting the weapons prior to a coup attempt. The leader of the plot was a major general, Zahir ul-Islam Abbasi, who had first tasted popular acclaim in 1988 when he was serving as Pakistan's military attaché in Delhi. In the course of his work he had acquired some sensitive security documents from an Indian contact. When Indian intelligence agents found out, they beat him up and threw him out of the country. He returned to Pakistan a national hero. Seven years later, the ambitious major general, disenchanted by the failure of Zia's successors to press on with Islamic reform, decided to take matters into his own hands.

When Abbasi and his co-conspirators were later put on trial, it emerged that he had planned to storm the GHQ during a meeting of corps commanders, kill the participants, arrest other prominent personalities and impose sharia, or Islamic law. In an earlier version of the plan the general had considered the possibility of killing some generals while they were playing golf. Eventually, though, he settled on the corps commanders' meeting because all the military leadership would be in the same place at the same time. He planned to have a staff car lead a bus-load of 30 Harakat ul-Ansar militants dressed in commando uniforms into the military headquarters. Once inside the perimeter they would storm the building and establish control. Abbasi planned to proclaim himself not only the chief of the army staff but also the leader of the faithful, or Amir ul-Momineen.[12]

The major general's intended address to the nation left no doubt as to the kind of administration he had in mind: 'We are thankful to almighty Allah and, with complete confidence, after declaring Pakistan a Sunni state, we announce the enforcement of the complete Islamic system.' The draft speech also announced bans on films, music, interest payments, contraception and photographs of women. It stated that Islamic scholars would be invested with the power to take any decisions they considered necessary.[13]

In army circles Abbasi had long been known as a religiously minded man, not least because he had established a Quranic study group in the officers' mess. Even if most senior officers viewed the intensity of Abbasi's religious views with some misgivings, they did not want to create an incident by limiting his activities. Nor did they consider him a serious threat. He was known to have links with Tablighi Jamaat, but ever since the Zia period that was seen as quite acceptable.

Had the army delved deeper, however, they would have discovered that the general was also associated with other religious groups. The investigation that followed his arrest revealed that he had established close links with many civilian Islamic leaders who openly called for Islamic revolution. Not only did Abbasi invite these leaders to preach to his troops, he also frequently attended political meetings in the clerics' homes. In these meetings the general, together with Brigadier Billah, openly advocated an Islamic-inspired military takeover. Once the general was arrested it turned out he was well known to all the major Islamic-based parties in Pakistan. Jamaat-e-Islami and the Sipah-e-Sahaba both rallied to his defence saying that he was a man known for his 'love of Islam' and 'patriotism'.[14]

The Abbasi coup attempt can be read in two ways. It can be argued that it demonstrated the weakness of Islamic forces in the army. Neither General Abbasi nor any of his fellow plotters occupied key positions. All had been passed over for promotion and none had any direct command over any troops.[15] That may have been, in part, because they were known to hold strong religious views. It was surely significant that in his planned coup the general was going to rely on Harakat ul-Ansar militants rather than disaffected troops. Furthermore, Abbasi's desire to kill all the corps commanders indicates that he was far from impressed by his colleagues' religious credentials. And the fact that the coup was thwarted demonstrated that discipline within the Pakistan army remained strong enough to withstand internal Islamic-based challenges.

On the other hand, there are good reasons for believing that Abbasi was not representing an isolated bunch of fanatics. After his arrest, Islamic elements in the army, far from being cowed into submission, were emboldened. The appointment of a new, secular army chief, General Jehangir Karamat, brought matters to a head. Embittered by the failure of Abbasi's coup attempt and frustrated by Karamat's appointment, Islamists sought to project their views in *Hilal*, a weekly magazine produced by the army and distributed to all soldiers. In January 1996 the journal published an article that first of all caricatured the suspected attitudes of the new army chief. Under the headline 'Expulsion of Islam from Pakistan Armed Forces', *Hilal* claimed that:

> An order had been received that:
> a) Armed forces of Pakistan should be secularised;
> b) Armed forces of Pakistan should be reorganised along the lines of certain countries of the Middle East and Africa;
> c) All officers possessed of Islamic thought and action should be scrupulously weeded out of the armed forces;
> d) Promotion of bearded officers already shortlisted must be stopped. No bearded officer or *jawan* [regular soldier] should be seen in the armed forces in the future.

It was obvious that such a crude, provocative order would never have been given, but having described this implausible 'order' *Hilal* went on to defend the army's religiosity:

> By Allah's grace no other official, semi-official or non-official institution of Pakistan has been so attached and devoted to Islam in thought and action as the armed forces of Pakistan. Throughout the world, yes throughout the world, no armed force is so irrevocably committed to Islam as the Pakistani armed forces.[16]

Hilal was a magazine with official status: it would have been quite impossible for the magazine's editor to publish such material without senior support. Despite Karamat's attempts to moderate the views being expressed in *Hilal*, the articles kept on coming. In March 1996, for example, *Hilal* ran an article that described the proper role of 'The Soldiers of Allah'. It was clear to all those who read *Hilal* that, while some elements of the army remained as modernist as ever, others had the passion and the confidence to advance a radical Islamist agenda.

The Pakistan army, obsessed with secrecy, has always refused to disclose any figures about its recruitment patterns or indeed the attitudes of its men. Western defence attachés in Islamabad are so short of information that they are reduced to conducting 'beard counts' at the annual ceremony to induct new officers into the army. They also rely on anecdotal evidence. Two stories related by Colonel (retd) Brian Cloughley, an author (and former defence attaché in Islamabad) who has had considerable access to the Pakistan army, help reveal the attitudes of some members of the military:

> During an exercise I crawled 100 metres to a dug-in artillery observation post where a young officer showed me a laser range-finder with which I busied myself. After congratulating him on this device I was treated to an exposition on how, in fact, there is no need for advanced technology providing one believes in Allah. On another occasion I was informed gravely by a junior officer that the beard of one of his soldiers (the luxuriance and shade of which had attracted my admiration) had turned red of its own accord because of the piety displayed during his Hajj. His commanding officer buried his head in his hands, but made no comment.[17]

In his classic account of the Pakistan army, the American academic Stephen Cohen identifies three generations of officers.[18] First, he argues, there was the British generation. When Pakistan's army was established its men were all products of Britain's India Army. Many of its officers had served in the Second World War and in some cases had been trained at Sandhurst. The British had selected most of these men because they came from loyal, westernised families and for the most part they did not hold strong religious views.

Impoverished by the Second World War, Britain was in no position to provide the kind of aid that the young Pakistan army so badly needed. Ayub Khan instead looked to the United States for support and thereby spawned the second, American generation of Pakistani officers. Many Pakistani military personnel officers went to the US for training and their US counterparts came to live in Pakistan. In general terms, the Pakistani officers of this generation were marked by modernist, even secular, attitudes and their leading figures had distinctly un-Islamic lifestyles. In its examination of the causes of the 1971 defeat in East Pakistan, the Hamoodur Rehman Commission came to the view that in the run-up to the war 'a considerable number of senior Army officers had not only indulged in large-scale acquisition of lands and houses and other commercial activities but had also adopted highly immoral and licentious ways of life which seriously affected their professional capabilities'. The report went on to accuse the most senior officer in East Pakistan, General Niazi, of having relations with two prostitutes, adding that 'he came to acquire a stinking reputation owing to his association with women of bad repute and his nocturnal visits to places also frequented by several junior officers under his command'.[19]

If some officers serving in East Pakistan were living it up, then so too were their military superiors. General Yahya, even when he was chief of army staff, regularly drank himself into a stupor. A senior Pakistani police officer, Sardar Muhammad Chaudhry, has described the atmosphere in the army high command when Yahya was president. As the Special Branch superintendent of police in Rawalpindi he was responsible for President Yahya's security. When he first saw President House (known to his policemen as 'the whore house') he was surprised to find that it was filled with prostitutes, pimps and drunks. Yahya's staff and friends were endlessly covering up for the president's excesses. On one occasion:

> The Shahinshah of Iran, on a state visit, was getting late for his departure but the president would not come out of his bedroom. A very serious protocol problem had arisen but nobody could enter his bedroom. General Ishaq, military secretary to the president, requested Rani (one of Yahya's lovers) to go in and bring him out. When she entered the room, she claims she found the most famous female singer of the country performing oral sex on Yahya. Even Rani found it abhorring. She helped the President dress and brought him out.

Chaudhry even considered Yahya's activities a security risk. 'The armed guards intensely resented such behaviour by the head of a Muslim state. I was afraid they could harm him in a fit of frenzy.'[20]

After the 1971 defeat in Bangladesh, the rakish American generation of officers was totally discredited and came to be replaced by the third generation identified by Stephen Cohen: the Pakistani generation (or as he later described it, the Zia generation). Writing in 1998, Cohen rejected the view that the Zia generation was driven by radical Islamic ideals. Zia, he pointed out, would have opposed the Abbasi coup:

> The idea of a coup followed by the Islamic transformation of Pakistani was *not* [original italics] one that Zia subscribed to, nor were his close associates cut from this cloth . . . Even the officers who pushed Zia into his own coup were not 'Islamic' types – in that sense Zia, his colleagues and the Zia experience did not promote a 'Zia Generation.'[21]

Many Pakistani liberals do not accept this. Those who believe that the army is becoming increasingly Islamic argue that ever since the 1960s, and especially after the defeat of 1971, the army has been forced to recruit a different kind of soldier. The shortage of jobs in the civilian sector and the diminished prestige of the army meant that a military career became less attractive to the elite and more attractive to people from lower-middle class, urban families. Consequently, the army became more representative of Pakistani society as a whole. As one retired officer has put it: 'These young men were basically conservative in their views, hostile to western ideas and far more receptive to religious ideas.'[22]

During the 1980s and 1990s there was another factor at play: the close relationship between the military and various Islamic militant groups or jihadis. Pakistani soldiers became used to fighting alongside the Mujahideen in Afghanistan. Similarly, in Kashmir, army regulars and civilian Islamic militants cooperated closely. During the Kargil campaign, for example, the army coordinated its actions with jihadis, just as it had in 1965. At least one of the militant groups, Tehrik-e-Jihad, fought in Kargil using army maps and on the basis of briefings from military officers. As the relationship between the army and the militant organisations grew closer, mutual trust was established to the point that, in the 1990s, some officers used militants to carry out limited operations on the line of control in Kashmir. The officers said the tactic worked because the Indian soldiers were more frightened of the militants than regular Pakistani troops. And while the militants' willingness to die for their cause frightened the Indian troops, it simultaneously impressed the soldiers from Pakistan who increasingly admired their more glamorous compatriots from the radical groups.

The various plots against General Musharraf revealed that some serving military personnel did harbour radical Islamist views. When the man who organised the 9/11 plots, Khalid Sheikh Mohammed, was arrested in 2003, he was found in a safe house in Rawalpindi provided by a serving military officer, Major Adil Qaboos. In August of the same year the military arrested at least three officers, including a lieutenant colonel, Khalid Abbassi, on suspicion of having links with Islamic extremists.[23] In December 2003 two assassination attempts against Musharraf also involved serving personnel, and at least one soldier, Islamuddin Siddiqui, was later executed for his role in the plot.[24] In October 2006, as many as 40 young air force officers were arrested for conspiring to kill Musharraf. They were discovered because one of them was careless enough to use his cell phone to activate a rocket aimed at the president's residence in Rawalpindi. The rocket was recovered, and its activating mechanism revealed the officer's telephone number.[25] Given the reluctance of the Pakistani military to speak publicly about internal discipline, it is safe to assume that there have been many other cases which never made it into the media.

It is not only officers who have held strong Islamist views. Broader trends within Pakistani society have affected the religiosity, particularly, of the lower ranks. The militant groups and the army draw their recruits from the same pool of young men, many of whom hold deep resentments against the West. The increasingly radical views of many Pakistani soldiers have given the army leadership real problems. As we have seen in the Introduction, for example, when the military was fighting militants in the Swat Valley and Waziristan in 2007 some of its men simply refused to fight militants, whom they considered admirable, selfless and pious defenders of Islam. It is worth noting that the number of desertions was highest in the relatively ill-trained and predominantly Pukhtoon Frontier Corps.

The Zia era, the Abbasi coup attempt, the subsequent *Hilal* articles and the desertions in Swat and Waziristan all indicate that the question of Islam's role in the army should be taken seriously. But discussing this subject is a hazardous exercise. Many Pakistani officers become highly defensive whenever the subject is raised. They accuse Pakistani liberals and Western observers alike of harbouring anti-Islamic prejudices that distort reality and exaggerate the importance of Islam in the army. Captain (retd) Ayaz Amir, for example, writing in 1995, dismissed claims that the nature of the officer corps was changing: 'There has been little difference between the drinking and club-going General of old and his more outwardly pious successors. The continuities of the Pakistan army accordingly are stronger than its discontinuities.' He went on to argue that the army 'has never been a breeding ground of radical ideas', and that the idea of revolution, whatever its motivation, was anathema to most officers.[26] Speaking in 2001, another retired officer, Brigadier Shaukat Qadir, made a similar point:

> If five per cent of the population could be described as extremist, then in the army they will number only three per cent. The recruitment policies weed them out. And the more senior you get, the more difficult it is for an extremist to survive. At the top of the army only a tiny percentage could be described as having strong religious views.

Furthermore, Qadir argued, if Zia did have an impact then it did not last: 'Under Zia many in the officer corps tried to join the ranks of the religious in search of advancement. After his departure most reverted to a more secular way of life.'[27]

The process of returning to the army's secular traditions was strongly encouraged by General Musharraf. In many ways he saw his task as dismantling the Zia legacy. Within months of the 1999 military coup, Musharraf was overlooking strongly religious senior officers and promoting those who shared his more worldly attitudes. His decision in 2002 to ban Lashkar-e-Toiba and Jaish-e-Mohammed gave a clear lead to army officers who could see that Zia's policies were being unravelled. Of course, General Musharraf was acutely aware of the constraints of modern Pakistani society. While he was known to enjoy a glass of whisky himself, he did not feel able, for example, publicly to reverse General Zia's ban on alcohol in the mess room. At the same time, the Zia days when an officer would jeopardise his prospects if he drank in the company of fellow officers were well and truly over. Undoing Zia's Islamicisation of the army took many years. He had promoted so many religious officers (and civil servants) that his policies outlived him. But much the same was true for General Musharraf. When he stood down as army chief in 2007, he did so in the knowledge that the relatively secular officers he had promoted would, for at least a decade, constitute one of the most important parts of his political legacy.

So, which side of the debate has the upper hand? What would the Pakistan army do if there was a serious attempt to mount an Islamic revolution? Clearly, some in the army would support such a movement and, probably, a far greater number would oppose it. But it is worth considering one final point. Even if the supporters of an Islamic revolution were in the minority, that might not matter. Faced with street protests inspired by Islam, especially if they were in the main cities of Punjab, the army leadership could find itself facing an awkward dilemma. An order to fire on such a crowd could well be disobeyed by soldiers, some of whom could well consider the protesters to be more devout than their officers. The army has always considered the maintenance of national unity as one of its highest priorities, and creating conditions in which the army might be split would be anathema. In those circumstances it would not be surprising if, despite its misgivings, the army leadership let events take their course.

The Fighting Army

From the day of its creation Pakistan's army has struggled to keep up with its Indian counterpart. Most of the arms production facilities and training centres established under British rule were located on land that became part of India. To a large extent this was a matter of chance. But the Indians also took deliberate steps to ensure that the Pakistan army was weak and ill-equipped. In the run-up to partition it was agreed that India should receive about two-thirds of the ammunition, weapons and other stores left behind by the British. The rest was meant to go to Pakistan and plans were drawn up to move 160 trainloads of military equipment from southern India to Pakistan. India, however, reneged on the deal and the trains never arrived.

Faced with an acute military imbalance, Pakistan's first politicians made military expenditure their top priority. Between 1947 and 1959 up to 73 per cent of Pakistan's total government spending was devoted to defence. The average for the period was 60 per cent. By the 1960s the figure had fallen to between 46 per cent and 61 per cent with an average for the decade of 48.7 per cent.[28] Spending dipped in the years before 9/11 but then accelerated again. According to its own conservative figures, which exclude major items such as pensions, Pakistan spent $4.5 billion on defence in 2007, a sum that accounted for 17.5 per cent of the national budget.

Defence expenditure in India and Pakistan, 1987–2007

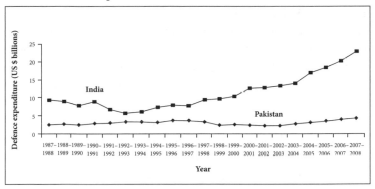

Source: Defence expenditure as quoted by the annual federal budgets of India (covering 1 April–31 March) and Pakistan (1 July–30 June). PKR/USD converted at spot price coincident with each budget, INR/USD conversion according to annual average exchange rates provided by the Reserve Bank of India.

Defence expenditure in India and Pakistan as a percentage of national budget, 1987–2007

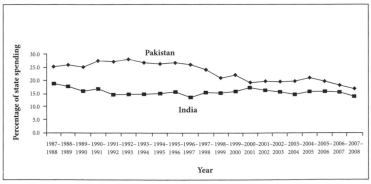

Source: Defence expenditure as a percentage of the total budgetary outlay quoted by Indian and Pakistani finance ministers in federal budgets.

High as they are, Pakistan's levels of defence spending have failed to match those of India. Between 2000 and 2007 India doubled its defence expenditure from $10.5 billion to $23.2 billion per annum. Over the same period Pakistan's military expenditure rose from $2.7 billion to $4.5 billion. India is totally committed to the South Asian arms race and the gap is likely to become even wider. In the first seven years of the twenty-first century, Delhi spent a staggering $133 billion on its military. Plainly, Pakistan is unable to keep up. The relative figures for defence expenditure as a percentage of the national budget reveal the extent of Pakistan's difficulty. In 2007 Pakistan spent 17.5 per cent of the national budget on defence, resulting in a far lower total figure than India's allocation of 14.1 per cent of its national budget. The different absolute spending levels are reflected not only in the number of men in the two countries' armed forces but also in the amount of military hardware available to those men.

That India has always managed to maintain its military lead over Pakistan has never been in doubt. The hard numbers, however, do not tell the whole story. Factors such as the quality of leadership and the levels of training are also important, as are strategic considerations. Even if some of Ayub Khan's advisers did harbour dreams of a drive for Delhi in 1965, no Pakistani army chief has ever given serious consideration to the conquest of India. Although Pakistan wants to maintain the capability to go on the offensive in Kashmir, the main purpose of its military is to deter or counter an Indian attack over the international borders. This defensive objective requires fewer resources than any offensive goals. The situation has been further complicated by the two

Comparison of men and hardware in India and Pakistan

	Pakistan	India
Armed forces personnel	619,000	1,316,000
Paramilitaries and reservists	302,000	1,120,000
Tanks	2,491	4,168
Submarines	8	16
Combat aircraft	352	864

Source: *The Military Balance, 2007*, International Institute of Strategic Studies, Oxford University Press, London, 2007.

countries' acquisition of a nuclear capability: Pakistan hopes that its nuclear arsenal will make up for its conventional inferiority and deter a full-scale war between the two countries.

Bad Strategy

There is no doubt that, compared to India, Pakistan's army has a resource problem. But many of its difficulties can be attributed to another factor: bad strategy. The army's most humiliating defeat came in 1971. And with the exception of the Rann of Kutch campaign (a relatively minor affair in early 1965), the Pakistan army has consistently failed to achieve its military objectives. This is not the place to attempt a comprehensive military history of Pakistan, but it is worth expanding on one point: Pakistan's record in developing military strategies is atrocious.

It would perhaps be unfair to refer to the conflict of 1947 and 1948 in support of this contention. The Pakistan army, after all, barely existed at the time and some of its problems were a result of the reluctance of its British commander to deploy his men for fear that British officers in the new Indian and Pakistan armies could end up fighting each other. By 1965, however, the Pakistan army had managed to equip itself and its main problems were self-inflicted. First, despite being the initiators of the conflict, the army was unprepared. As Major General S. Shahid Hamid has recorded: 'The army was not trained or ready for the offensive; some 25 per cent of the men were on leave.'[29] Secondly, the army was over-confident. During the Rann of Kutch campaign in early 1965, the Pakistani forces were generally considered to have acquitted themselves well. Ayub Khan apparently drew the conclusion that all his efforts to train the army and to secure good, modern equipment had paid off. As one senior Pakistani officer wrote:

The success of arms in the Rann of Kutch skirmish and the subsequent settlement of the dispute appears to have had a profound effect on Ayub. . . . It was in the euphoric aftermath of the short-lived conflict in the salt marsh that Ayub's senior advisors [sic] found a sudden change in his thinking on the Kashmir issue.[30]

Ayub Khan should have known better. The fighting in the Rann was localised and on a small scale. It was clearly a mistake to think that victory in the Rann would mean victory in Kashmir.

Thirdly, and crucially, the Pakistani leadership thought the fighting could be restricted to Kashmir. It was an absurd assumption. When the Indians came under serious pressure they did not hesitate to extend the fight to the international borders. Fourthly, Ayub Khan miscalculated the international reaction to the fighting. His stated aim was to bring India to the conference table to discuss Kashmir. During the conflict he repeatedly called for US support. It should, however, have been clear to Ayub that ever since the 1962 Sino–Indian war, Washington, fearful of Chinese expansionism, was never going to abandon its relationship with India for the sake of Pakistan. Pakistan had started a war that it was in no position to win.

Much the same can be said of 1971. The loss of East Pakistan was the subject of a major government enquiry in Pakistan. The Hamoodur Rehman Commission's findings could scarcely have been more critical. Perhaps the most damning criticism of the military high command in 1971 is the way in which it drifted towards a war without contemplating the consequences. The Hamoodur Rehman Commission was especially unforgiving on this point:

> It is remarkable that, even in the critical months after March 1971, when war was clearly a probability, if not an imminent certainty, the question seems to have bothered the general staff very little. It does not appear that even the chief of staff, much less the commander in chief, ever showed any interest in this all-important question.[31]

It was like 1965 all over again and many of these flaws re-emerged during the Kargil campaign of 1999. Speaking after the campaign a former director of the ISI, Lieutenant General Durrani, made this comment on Pakistan's performance. 'Tactically,' he said 'it was a brilliant operation. But we had not set our strategic priorities and failed in the diplomatic and political preparations to back it up.'[32] It's a fair assessment. In operational terms, the Kargil campaign was one of the most successful ever mounted by the Pakistan army. The infiltration of Indian-held territory was executed without any serious setback. Admittedly, Kargil was a relatively small-scale affair: the number of Pakistani troops who crossed the line never exceeded 2,000. Nevertheless, the military could claim for once that they had lived up to their own high opinion of themselves.

But at a strategic level, Kargil also revealed that Pakistan had failed to learn from its previous mistakes. Just as in 1965 and 1971, the generals did not think through the consequences of their actions. The high levels of distrust between the political and military elites hampered the planning process. The failure to factor in the diplomatic and international consequences of the Kargil campaign is partly explained by the military's reluctance fully to consult all the relevant civilian officials. The military was afraid of leaks, but its desire for secrecy was so great that it undermined the quality of the decision-making process.

Another consistent weakness in Pakistani strategy has been the Pakistan high command's heavy reliance on volunteer fighters outside of the formal military structure. It has tried to fight its battles by proxy. This practice began in 1947, when tribal forces from NWFP marched into Kashmir. Even if one accepts the Pakistani argument that they did so on their own initiative, there is no doubt that the army was soon working with the tribals, and that, by 1948, Pakistani army officers in Kashmir were coordinating their military actions with the militants. The relationship between regular and irregular Pakistani forces in Kashmir has remained close ever since. In 1965 Ayub Khan hoped that Kashmir could be secured by Operation GIBRALTAR in which armed militants would cross into Indian-held Kashmir and instigate a general revolt. Since 1988 Pakistan's military establishment has employed similar tactics. Its support for the insurgency in Kashmir has demonstrated a continuing faith in militant groups. And in Kargil, too, the military high command used irregular troops together with civilian volunteers.

Pakistani strategists seem to believe that the element of deniability afforded by the use of irregular forces works to Pakistan's advantage. In reality, the use of irregulars has proved counterproductive. In 1947, just as during the Kargil campaign 52 years later, Pakistani spokesmen had to perform an impossible balancing act. On the one hand, they wanted to justify the tribals or militants in their battle against the Indians. On the other, they had to issue unconvincing statements insisting that the Pakistan government had no connections with the irregulars – especially when they committed human rights atrocities. The duplicity required to advance these two positions has fooled nobody and has undermined Pakistan's diplomatic standing. Perhaps more importantly from Pakistan's point of view, the tactic has consistently failed in military terms. The gains secured by irregular forces in Kashmir and Afghanistan have continually fallen short of the hopes invested in them. Pakistan's repeated reliance on irregular forces in Kashmir reflects a basic lack of confidence. The Indians have never suffered from this problem. Ever since 1947, if the leadership in Delhi thought there was a national objective that had to be secured, it showed no hesitation in using the army to do it. The invasions of Junagadh, Hyderabad and East Pakistan all prove the point.

No assessment of the Pakistani armed forces' military performance would be complete without consideration of the most hostile of all its battlegrounds: the Siachin Glacier. Ever since 1984 the Pakistani and Indian armies have fought on the highest battlefield on earth. Some of the forward posts are located at a bone-chilling 20,000 feet above sea level. Temperatures on Siachin drop to minus 50 degrees Celsius and blizzards can exceed 100 miles per hour. Before the troops can fire a gun they have to thaw it on a kerosene stove. The air is so thin and the winds so violent that the artillery shells which the two sides lob at each other follow unpredictable trajectories. In some places the opposing troops are just 1,000 feet apart, but the extreme cold, the crevasses and the avalanches claim more lives than any fighting.

However brave the men who fight on Siachin may be, there is no escaping the fact that they are engaged in a futile and outrageously expensive battle. Although there are no reliable figures, it is conservatively estimated that both sides commit more than half a million US dollars to the conflict each day. What is Pakistan hoping to achieve by this lavish use of scarce resources? When General Musharraf was asked why Pakistan was fighting on the Siachin Glacier, he gave the following reply: 'We have the upper hand here. It costs the Indians more to fight on Siachin than us. It's all about the degree of difficulty we can create for the other side.'[33] Factually, the general was quite correct. But for Pakistan to think that it can reduce India to bankruptcy is clearly absurd. Morally, it's difficult to see how either India or Pakistan can justify expending so many lives and so much money on such a useless conflict.

In 2007 there were hopes that the increased levels of dialogue between India and Pakistan could result in an agreement about the Siachin Glacier as a first step, leading to a more general agreement on Kashmir as a whole. In May 2007 Pakistan's foreign office spokesman, Mohammad Sadiq, said that a deal on Siachin was 'very near'.[34] It was an overly optimistic assessment. The Indian army dug in its heels, insisting that the (advantageous) positions it held in Siachin should be authenticated by Pakistan before any withdrawal of forces could take place.[35] The Pakistani side had agreed to the demand but only on the condition that such an authentication should not become a final endorsement of India's claim over the glacier.[36]

A Political Army

The Pakistan army has repeatedly shown a greater willingness to grasp power than to give it up. None of the country's four military rulers gave up power voluntarily – and they all started in strikingly similar ways. After taking over, the first task of any military ruler is to address the nation on radio and television. It has happened in Pakistan four times and on each occasion the coup leaders have summoned as much sincerity as they could muster and delivered carbon-copy speeches.

> This is a drastic and extreme step taken with great reluctance but with the deepest conviction that there was no alternative to it except the disintegration and complete ruination of the country.
>
> – Ayub Khan, 8 October 1958

> The armed forces could not remain idle spectators of this state of near anarchy. They have to do their duty and save the country from utter disaster.
>
> – Yahya Khan, 26 March 1969

> I was obliged to step in to fill the vacuum created by the political leaders.
>
> – Zia ul-Haq, 5 July 1977

I wish to inform you that the armed forces have moved in as a last resort
to prevent any further destabilisation.

                                          – Pervez Musharraf, 13 October 1999

The four addresses have other passages in common. Ayub Khan
pledged: 'Our ultimate aim is to restore democracy.' His successor Yahya
insisted: 'I have no ambition other than the creation of conditions
conducive to the establishment of a constitutional government.'
Ironically, the least democratically minded of the lot, Zia ul-Haq, gave
the clearest assurance of all: 'My sole aim is to organise free and fair
elections which would be held in October this year.' Most recently,
Pervez Musharraf claimed that: 'The armed forces have no intention to
stay in charge any longer than is absolutely necessary to pave the way for
true democracy to flourish in Pakistan.'

A few days after the 1999 coup Musharraf's spokesman, Brigadier
Rashid Qureshi, insisted that while 'Others may have tried to hang on
to power, we will not. We will make history.'[37] Musharraf agreed. 'All I
can say,' he assured a television interviewer in January 2000, 'is that I
am not going to perpetuate myself. . . . I can't give any certificate on it
but my word of honour. I will not perpetuate myself.'[38] Later in 2000
Musharraf went a stage further and said he would respect a Supreme
Court judgement that stated he should remain in office for just three
years. In June 2001, however, Musharraf performed a complete U-turn.
Following the examples of Ayub, Yahya and Zia, he had himself made
president and in May 2002 held a referendum that allowed him to
remain in power for a further five years. In 2007, when he was still the
all-powerful leader of Pakistan, in charge of both the army and the
civilian cabinet, he was challenged in an interview about his failure to
keep his promise to step down after three years. In response, he was
reduced to saying that he had forgotten his previous pledges: 'Did I say
I would step down? I don't know whether I said I would step down. . . .
I don't remember these words.'[39]

Pakistan's military leaders have had other traits in common. All of
them have placed great emphasis on devising institutional arrangements
for the better governance of the country. Ayub Khan was particularly
enthusiastic about constitutional reform. During a sleepless night in a

London hotel in 1954 (four years before he took over), he set down his political views on paper. The document he produced, entitled 'A Short Appreciation of Present and Future Problems of Pakistan',[40] was filled with the kind of mess-room 'common sense' that has characterised the thinking of all Pakistan's military rulers.

Ayub started from the premise that Pakistan wasn't ready for Westminster-style democracy and needed some form of controlled or guided democracy. The system he devised was called Basic Democracies and it was introduced on the first anniversary of his coup. At the lowest, district level there were constituencies of approximately 1,000 people, which each elected a representative or Basic Democrat. These Basic Democrats would then elect some of their number to participate in the next tier of government. In all there were five tiers (although this was later reduced to four). At the higher levels, however, the elected representatives were joined by appointed civil servants. Ever the paternalist, Ayub Khan believed that although the Basic Democrats might be able to articulate the people's wishes and needs, only bureaucrats would be capable of devising and implementing policies to address those needs.

By January 1960, 80,000 Basic Democrats had been elected and the next month Ayub Khan held a referendum to ask them whether they had confidence in his leadership. Since all the representatives owed their positions to Ayub Khan, there was never any doubt about the result. Over 95 per cent voted for the military leader and three days later he was sworn in as president. Ayub insisted the result gave his regime democratic legitimacy but few were convinced. The vast majority of the traditional politicians always rejected the Basic Democracies scheme as nothing more than a device to prop up Ayub Khan.

The field marshal, however, apparently never realised that he was attempting the impossible. He wanted to combine an authoritarian system, in which he made all the decisions, with a democratic process. The two goals were incompatible. Ayub Khan's political naivety was fully exposed when the Basic Democrats were called upon to elect the National Assembly in 1962. During the run-up to the vote, Ayub refused to allow political parties to operate, insisting that independent individuals should be elected on merit. As soon as the National Assembly started functioning, however, its members inevitably began to organise themselves into factions. Within weeks, Ayub Khan was forced to back down and sanction the functioning of political parties. By December the irreconcilable tensions between democracy and military rule were plain for all to see. Completely abandoning all he had previously stood for, Ayub Khan himself became a party leader, accepting the presidency of a faction of the Muslim League. The man who took over to rid Pakistan of scheming politicians had joined their ranks.

When he was in power, the Western press lavished praise on Ayub Khan, referring to him as the 'Asian de Gaulle'. In retrospect such plaudits seem far too complimentary. Ayub Khan cannot be faulted for boldness: he tried to create a new kind of political system in Pakistan. The fact remains, however, that he failed.

No one has ever described Ayub's successor, General Yahya Khan, as an Asian de Gaulle. A more typical assessment was made by one of his colleagues, Lieutenant General Jahan Dad Khan:

> It is generally felt that his highest ceiling was a divisional commander. His rise beyond that level was disastrous for the country and also unfair to the General who was a happy-go-lucky person without the stamina or the intellectual discipline to undertake the rigours of a higher appointment. It was unfortunate for Pakistan that Ayub decided first to appoint Yahya as the Army C-in-C and then hand over power to him.[41]

For all his detractors, however, Yahya Khan's constitutional reform programme was in many respects far more convincing than Ayub's. Within 24 hours of taking over, Yahya Khan had promised 'the smooth transfer of power to the representatives of the people elected freely and impartially on the basis of adult franchise'.[42] For a military leader to make such a pledge was not unusual, but Yahya actually meant it.

The 1970 elections are widely accepted to have been among the fairest that have ever occurred in Pakistan. During the campaign Yahya allowed the political parties to operate freely and encouraged the political leaders to broadcast their views on national radio and television. The campaign was fought on genuine issues. In East Pakistan the electorate was effectively asked to give its verdict on Mujibur Rahman's six-point programme for regional autonomy. In West Pakistan, Zulfikar

Ali Bhutto's secular-leaning Pakistan People's Party slugged it out with the Islamic-based parties. True, it was never clear how or when Yahya would step down and it is also indisputable that, once the election results became known, Yahya proved incapable of controlling events. Nevertheless, it would be churlish to ignore the fact that, for the first time since 1947, Pakistan had a leader who not only was genuinely committed to free and fair elections but also actually delivered them.

General Zia ul-Haq, by contrast, was never sincere about restoring democracy. Whenever pressure for some form of democratic representation became irresistible, Zia consistently gave as little as he could, as late as he could. Arguing that Western-style democracy was un-Islamic, in 1981 he announced the creation of the Majlis-e-Shoora. Zia himself chose all the members of this body and, although he described it as a legislature, it was no such thing. It had only advisory powers: Zia made the laws. The Majlis convinced nobody and by 1984 Zia realised he would have to give more concessions to the politicians. Before doing so he wanted to make his own position impregnable and he consequently put the following, utterly fatuous, question to the Pakistani electorate in a referendum:

Whether the people of Pakistan endorse the process initiated by General Mohammad Zia ul-Haq, the President of Pakistan, for bringing laws of Pakistan in conformity with the injunctions of Islam as laid down in the Holy Quran and Sunnah of the Holy Prophet (PBUH) and for the preservation of the ideology of Pakistan, for the continuation and consolidation of that process for the smooth and orderly transfer of power to the elected representatives of the people?[43]

Despite a low turn-out Zia declared that, since most people had answered in the affirmative, he would be the president for the next five years. National elections on a non-party basis followed in February 1985. The new parliament enjoyed more powers than the Majlis-e-Shoora and Zia's hand-picked prime minister, Mohammed Khan Junejo, did try to assert his independence. As a result, he was sacked shortly before Zia died. General Zia's main objective was always to hang on to power. His 'parliaments' were nothing more than fronts and they were dismantled as soon as the general was killed in 1988.

Eleven years after Zia's death Pakistan had another military ruler: General Pervez Musharraf. The parallels between him and Ayub Khan are striking. Both were Pakistani nationalists and modernisers who argued that their country was not yet ready for Western-style democracy. Although both were believing Muslims, they shared a disdain for radical clerics whose knowledge of the world consisted of little more than the Quran. Both wanted to be the sole decision-maker in the country while simultaneously claiming to have installed a democratic system. The two men railed against corruption, but ended up working with the corrupt. They also ended their careers in very similar ways: surrounded by sycophants and consequently unaware that they were discredited and unpopular.

For all his constitutional theorising, Ayub Khan could never conceal the fact that the Basic Democracies system was designed to bolster his rule. Musharraf, by contrast, realised that there was no alternative to full-blown elections in which the political parties would participate. But having made that decision he did his utmost to keep the politicians under control. Most of the methods he used had a long pedigree in Pakistan. If politicians were recalcitrant he could open corruption cases against them. For obvious reasons most Pakistani politicians live in fear of having their financial affairs investigated. Musharraf manipulated the membership of parliament by redrawing parliamentary constituencies and by decreeing that the National Assembly would include 25 appointed technocrats and 60 appointed women. At a stroke the army had put in place a voting bloc that, it hoped, would hold the balance of power.

Musharraf was fatally undermined by political and ideological contradictions. He insisted that he was not a politician: indeed he was insulted by the idea that he could be considered in the same category as people he viewed, with some justification, as venal and self-serving. Yet, like Ayub, he ended up leading a parliamentary faction – as in his case, the Pakistan Muslim League (Q). He also claimed to be a legitimate leader with the support of the people, yet he never stood in an election unless he had manipulated the situation so that he could be sure of victory.

The first time Musharraf put himself to the test was in a referendum, which was about as worthwhile as General Zia's. In the traditional fashion, government workers were bussed in to answer a fatuous question:

For the survival of the local government system, establishment of democracy, continuity of reforms, end to sectarianism and extremism, and to fulfil the vision of Quaid-e-Azam [Great leader – i.e. Pakistan's late founder, Mohammed Ali Jinnah], would you like to elect President General Pervez Musharraf as president of Pakistan for five years?[44]

That was the only time Musharraf faced the Pakistani people. The general claimed a 98 per cent win on a 70 per cent turn-out. His opponents estimated turn-out at 5 per cent. Had Musharraf stood in free and fair elections immediately after his coup, he would have won with an overwhelming majority. But he failed to do so and as his legitimacy and authority gradually ebbed away he became increasingly concerned, not with implementing his programme, but merely with staying in power. And yet in many ways he fell short of being a dictator. In 2002, for example, when he held parliamentary elections, he gave up martial law. Like many Pakistani leaders he tended to seek consensus and to work through established institutions, however flawed they may have been.

Like Ayub Khan, Musharraf lost power not through a single cataclysmic event but by a steady draining of authority as increasing numbers lost faith in his ability to bring real change and improvement to the country. His consistent support for the US 'war on terror' put him at odds with his own people who, not surprisingly, objected to the fact that US aircraft were regularly killing Pakistani civilians in air raids on the tribal areas. The economic growth that Musharraf oversaw, and the many billions in aid he secured from the US, helped him. But as time passed it became increasingly clear that these were not enough to save a man who, as we shall see in the next chapter, failed to achieve any of the objectives he had set himself when he took over in 1999.

Civil–Military Relations

It is often said that Pakistan has been ruled by the military for a little over half the country's existence. That is a serious underestimate: even in times of civilian rule, the military has interfered in foreign and domestic policies and intervened in the political process. The peculiar circumstances of Pakistan's creation have meant that from the very outset the army has had a large degree of influence. During the country's first decade, the politicians and the senior officers did not have a particularly adversarial relationship and there was a sense in which both groups believed they were working together to get Pakistan established. After Ayub took over that changed. His coup not only led officers to believe they had a right to be involved in the country's governance but also meant that all future civilian leaders were nervous that they, too, could be thrown out of office.

Should any prime minister, for example, make a serious attempt to pursue nuclear disarmament in Pakistan, it would certainly result in a coup. A leading scholar of the Pakistan army, Hasan Askari Rizvi, has identified six other areas in which he believes the army will not tolerate civilian interference. They are: Kashmir; weapons procurement and related foreign policy issues; internal military personnel decisions; cuts in defence expenditure; and any moves to curtail the perks associated with high military office. Rizvi also argues that the military would tolerate a government only if it proved capable of delivering social and political stability.[45] In fact, the military considers any issue of 'strategic national importance' to be within its domain.

The first civilian leader to suffer as a result of the army's post-Ayub confidence was Zulfikar Ali Bhutto, who was always alive to the risk of a coup. He appointed Zia ul-Haq as chief of army staff precisely because he thought that the general would be pliant and controllable. It was, of course, a monumental misjudgement, but the 1977 coup cannot be explained by Zia's personal ambition alone. Throughout Bhutto's period in power there was a lack of stability in civil–military relations. The difficulty of establishing a stable working relationship between the military and the civilian politicians re-emerged in the period after Zia's death. During the campaign that followed her father's hanging, Benazir Bhutto launched vitriolic attacks on the Zia regime, but when she became prime minister she adopted a much more conciliatory position. It was a futile effort. Zia's successor, General Mirza Aslam Beg, with the connivance of President Ghulam Ishaq Khan, played an active political role. The two men, and their successors, repeatedly used their powers under the Eighth Constitutional Amendment to dismiss a sitting government. In 1990, 1993 and 1996 the army influenced and fully supported presidential decisions to remove civilian governments. As long as the Eighth Amendment was in place, democratically elected leaders knew that their fate depended on the army leadership.

When Nawaz Sharif came into office for the second time he was determined to cut the army down to size. He overturned the Eighth Amendment: no longer could an army chief, working through the president, use constitutional means to remove a government. The army, however, still believed it had the right to be involved in the governance of the country. In April 1999 Musharraf spoke at a seminar in Karachi and compared Pakistan to a boat full of trained soldiers waiting for the enemy. Their boat, Musharraf said, had started to develop holes: 'So what should these trained soldiers do? Should they keep on waiting for the enemy ship and let their own boat sink? Or should they try and plug the leakage?'[46] Six months later he plugged the leak and established once again that the Pakistan army is not only a military machine but also a political organisation.

The Army and the Economy

The army is also a major player in the Pakistani economy. Taken together, the military's enterprises account for nearly 3 per cent of Pakistan's gross national product.[47] The two biggest army businesses – in fact, they are two of the biggest conglomerates in the country – are the Fauji Foundation and the Army Welfare Trust. The Fauji Foundation's assets include sugar mills, chemical plants and fertiliser factories. In the energy sector it owns a gas company and power plants. As well as generating funds, the Fauji Foundation runs its own welfare programmes. It owns over 800 educational institutions and more than 100 hospitals. The Army Welfare Trust has assets worth nearly one billion dollars, including one of Pakistan's biggest financial institutions, the Askari Bank. It also owns farms, real estate business, sugar mills and plants which produce petro-chemicals, pharmaceuticals and shoes. Unlike the Fauji Foundation, the Army Welfare Trust does not run any charitable projects: all its profits are sent to GHQ and about half its income is used to pay army pensions.

These and some other national-scale military businesses are for all practical purposes run from GHQ. On the second tier, beneath the Fauji Foundation and Army Welfare Trust, are the Frontier Works Organisation, the National Logistics Cell and the Special Communications Organisation. The Frontier Works Organisation is a road construction company which, since 1966, has undertaken the vast bulk of the government's road projects. It has a subsidiary business sending mine clearers around the world – an activity that during the 1990s earned around 10 million dollars a year. The Special Communications Organisation is responsible for supplying telecom-munications services to the people of Pakistani-held Kashmir. The National Logistics Cell is a transport company which has also been involved in road and bridge construction and, for some reason, the control of locusts and other pests. It has 7,279 staff including 2,549 serving military personnel.[48]

Another group of companies includes the Pakistan Ordnance Factory at Wah and the Heavy Defence Industries and the Heavy Rebuild Factories at Taxila. These are technically controlled by the government but in practice work for the military, which appoints the officers who run them and which buys most of their products.[49] Although the army enjoys the lion's share of the military's economic activities, the air force and navy have tried to get involved as well. They have a number of commercial operations including, most notably, the air force's Shaheen Foundation (activities include Pay TV, knitwear and air cargo) and the navy's Bahria Foundation (amongst many other things, activities include paints, fishing, bakeries, ship-breaking and a university). At a local level, military units run smaller enterprises such as road toll collection operations, fuel stations and even shopping malls. In all these cases serving personnel are used to make money which does not get counted in the defence budget.

In a good example of Musharraf's failure to rise above his military background and of his inability to understand the wider interests of all

Pakistanis, he dismissed all criticism of these activities as close to unpatriotic:

> Then, we have the Army Welfare Trust, we have the Fauji Foundation. Yes they are involved in banking. . . . So what is the problem if these organisations are contributing and being run properly? We have the best banks. Our cement plants are doing exceptionally well. Our fertilizer plants are doing exceptionally well. So why is anyone jealous? Why is anyone jealous if the retired military officers or the civilians with them are doing a good job of contributing to the economy of Pakistan and doing well.[50]

What Musharraf failed to acknowledge is that the army's economic businesses employ serving as well as retired personnel and that they are so profitable in part because they are in a good position to lobby for tax exemptions and subsidies. The military's enterprises also benefit from free start-up capital and the fact that Pakistani consumers favour organisations such as banks which have army backing because they calculate that they will never be allowed to go bankrupt.

While a select few military men manage to secure very desirable sinecures in these institutions (providing the army chief with a significant source of patronage to buy off disgruntled colleagues), there is another commercial activity that corrupts far larger numbers of senior officers: they receive generous, personal allocations of plots of land, both urban and rural. It is a perk that is entirely legal but considered by most Pakistanis to be plainly immoral. Officers also use insider information and tax breaks to benefit from Defence Housing Authority schemes. These arrangements, which boomed in the final Musharraf years, involve many scams that have one thing in common: the most senior and best connected officers take the largest profits. In fact, the profits have been so vast that, inevitably, the military started acquiring desirable land, saying it was needed for military purposes, and then using it for commercial development.[51]

When Musharraf took over in 1999 the majority of Pakistanis considered, with some justification, that most senior military officers were less corrupt than most civilian politicians. By the time he left office they had lost faith, again with some justification, in the military's ethical standards. Junior officers who would have been too frightened to take a bribe in 1999 were by 2007 routinely demanding pay-offs from contractors and other businesses with which they had contact. During his time in power Musharraf placed more than 1,000 active and retired officers in civilian jobs in the various ministries.[52] No doubt he saw it as a way of increasing efficiency and getting his policies implemented. But once the military men were in place, the opportunities for making money proved irresistible for many. Musharraf's successor, General Ashfaq Kayani, recognised the problem. One of his first acts as army chief was to recall many army officers from civilian job assignments.

In 2007 the Pakistani academic, Ayesha Siddiqa, published the most comprehensive study to date of the army's role in the economy.[53] She advanced a number of arguments: that the military's business activity encouraged independence from, and even disdain for, the country's civilian political and economic structures; that the military's repeated coups could be explained in part by the profit motive; that the great lack of transparency surrounding military enterprises allows senior officers, rather than the most deserving, to receive most of the benefits from the welfare organisations; and that the military's leading economic role has stunted the growth of the private sector. She makes a convincing case.

Conclusion

Pakistan's army enjoys a better reputation than it deserves. Both on the field of battle and in periods of military rule its record has been far from glorious. If Pakistan is, as many Pakistanis believe, a failed state, then the army must take its fair share of the blame. As well as governing the country for nearly half its existence, it has consumed a disproportionate amount of government expenditure. No Pakistani military officer can credibly argue that the army has played a positive role in the country's political development. And it is arguable that the army's performance has been more damaging to Pakistan in times of civilian rather than military rule. Under military regimes, Pakistan has at least achieved a level of stability, but no civilian government has been able to operate free of army interference.

The Pakistani public, though, tends to direct its invective and vitriol at the country's civilian leaders. With good reason, the politicians are routinely denounced as corrupt, self-interested and incompetent. There is a genuine belief that while the civilian institutions have become tarnished, the army retains some glitter. Even the politicians share this perception. Ever since 1947 the military has frequently been called upon to carry out tasks that the politicians felt unable to manage themselves. But the keenest advocates of the view that the army is a cut above the rest of Pakistani society are its own officers. They have genuine pride in their institution, which they believe to be the only major organisation in the country that works. And yet whenever the army has been in government, the generals have found Pakistan's problems less easy to resolve than they imagined.

In 1976 a Pakistani lieutenant general, M. Attiqur Rahman, wrote a devastating critique of the Pakistan army. His book, *Our Defence Cause*,[54] lifted the veil on an institution that had hitherto conducted its business behind a tight wall of secrecy. His complaints were legion. Under Ayub Khan's period of military rule, he argued, army officers had been exposed to opportunities for making money. Many had become corrupt but would go unpunished for fear that the morale of the army would suffer. Rahman was also unimpressed by the criteria for promoting senior officers. In some cases, he wrote, officers' careers were advanced on the basis of nepotism or regional affiliation. There was also a tendency to favour 'yes men' who would not rock the boat. Rather than raising genuine problems, junior officers soon learnt that they were better off writing positive reports which reflected well on the army high command. In the prevailing atmosphere of smug self-satisfaction, discipline slackened and too much time was spent on staging ceremonial events to impress the public. Attiqur Rahman described how military setbacks would inevitably be followed by attempts to restore damaged reputations. He even claimed that after the 1965 war some officers went to the extent of altering the record by fraudulently writing orders that they should have issued during the conflict. Attiqur Rahman made his criticisms over three decades ago but many of them remain valid.

None of Pakistan's military rulers have left office in happy circumstances. After the 1965 presidential elections Ayub Khan became increasingly unpopular and isolated. By early 1968 he was also sick and exhausted. A year later his administration ended amid a wave of popular protest and rancour. This reduced the field marshal to crisis management in the face of an increasingly active opposition. However bold his vision, Ayub Khan had failed to realise his dreams. When Yahya Khan took over and imposed martial law, Ayub was harsh about his own achievements. Shortly before he stepped down he remarked to a group of ministers: 'I am sorry we have come to this pass. We are a very difficult country structurally. Perhaps I pushed it too hard into the modern age. We were not ready for reforms. Quite frankly I have failed. I must admit that clearly.'[55]

By the time he was forced out of office, the loss of East Pakistan meant that Yahya Khan was even more thoroughly discredited than Ayub. But of all Pakistan's military rulers it is General Zia who left the most damaging legacy. Most of Zia's major policy initiatives went wrong. Pakistan's political development was retarded by his fear that if he ever handed power back to the civilians, the Pakistani People's Party would avenge Bhutto's death. His Islamicisation campaign never enjoyed popular support and gave rise to one of Pakistan's most debilitating scourges: sectarian violence. His support of the Afghan Mujahideen may have pleased Washington, but the impact on Pakistan was disastrous. Millions of Afghan refugees settled in Pakistan; drugs and guns became ever more widely available.

In many ways General Musharraf was the opposite of Zia. But he too failed Pakistan. It was perhaps understandable that in his address to the nation after the 1999 coup Musharraf concluded with the thought that 'we have reached rock bottom'. Sadly, as we shall now see, despite all his bold pronouncements he did not prove any more capable than his military predecessors of leading the country to a higher level.

8

The Musharraf Years

I shall not allow the people to be taken back to the era of sham democracy, but to a true one. And I promise you I will Inshallah.
—Pervez Musharraf, 17 October 1999

You can't achieve 100 per cent success. With martial law, then maybe I would have achieved much more.
—Pervez Musharraf, 12 October 2007

The 1999 Coup

On 12 October 1999, Nawaz Sharif finally made up his mind. His army chief, General Pervez Musharraf, would have to go. In his place Sharif would appoint a man in whom he had more trust, the head of the Inter Services Intelligence (ISI), Lieutenant General Ziauddin. As the prime minister told his officials to process the paperwork, Musharraf was just leaving Colombo where he had attended the fiftieth anniversary celebrations of Sri Lanka's army. As the general's flight, PK805, climbed into the sky, Sharif's principal secretary Saeed Mehdi had completed drafting the official notification. It stated that:

> It has been decided to retire General Pervez Musharraf, Acting Chairman, Joint Chiefs of Staff Committee and Chief of the Army Staff with immediate effect. Lt. Gen. Ziauddin has been appointed as the Chief of Army Staff with immediate effect and promoted to the rank of General.
>
> Before orders to this effect are issued, the President may kindly see.

By 4.30 p.m. Sharif had signed the document. The deed was done and Sharif told PTV to broadcast the news. It did so on the 5.00 p.m.

bulletin. PTV was also told to take pictures of Ziauddin receiving his badges of rank.

Ziauddin was now the *de jure* army chief, but he knew that he would have to move fast. Two men in particular were Musharraf loyalists: the chief of the general staff, Lieutenant General Aziz Khan, and the commander of the 10th corps, Lieutenant General Mehmood Ahmed. Ziauddin decided to remove both of them and started calling other senior generals to try to win their support. As he did so, Aziz and Mehmood were playing tennis. They realised that there was a problem when both their mobile phones started ringing on the side of the court. The second they were told what was happening, Aziz and Mehmood held a brief conversation and decided to act. As one eyewitness put it: 'I have never seen two senior officers move so fast.' Their first priority was to get the news off the television and they despatched Major Nisar of the Punjab Regiment, together with 15 armed men, to the PTV building in Islamabad. He was ordered to block any further announcement about Musharraf's sacking. As the major set off, Aziz called a meeting of all available corps commanders and other senior officers at army head-quarters in Rawalpindi. And with Mehmood and Aziz determined to resist Ziauddin's appointment, the corps commanders decided to implement a decision they had already taken in September.

At that time Musharraf had realised that his relationship with Sharif was reaching breaking point. He had called together his corps commanders and raised the question of Sharif's competence. Although there had been wide agreement that Sharif was not performing well, the meeting decided that the army could not intervene without clear justification. But if Sharif tried to sack Musharraf, the corps commanders had agreed they would act. Musharraf had been in place for only 11 months and to lose two army chiefs in the space of a year would be unacceptable. Musharraf's preparations paid off. Mehmood and Aziz knew what to do.

Unaware of the growing crisis, PTV continued to put out the news of Ziauddin's appointment. The station's managers first knew there was a problem when Major Nisar stormed into the control room and ordered the PTV staff to block the news of Musharraf's dismissal. 'Take it off! Take it off!' he yelled. Faced with 15 armed men and a screaming major, the staff complied.

At 6.00 p.m. Nawaz Sharif was sitting in the TV lounge of his official residence waiting for the news bulletin. But when it came on he found there was no mention of Musharraf's sacking. He told his military secretary, Brigadier Javed Iqbal, to go straight to the TV headquarters to investigate. Sharif was now convinced that he had to prevent General Musharraf's plane from landing. Ziauddin agreed. He advised Sharif that if Musharraf were kept out of the country then the army would have to accept his removal.

The prime minister picked up the phone and spoke to Aminullah Choudhry, the Karachi-based director general of the Civil Aviation Authority. A classic civil servant, Choudhry could be relied upon to execute the prime minister's orders without hesitation. Sharif told Choudhry that flight PK805 should not be allowed to land in Pakistan. Choudhry immediately called the air traffic control tower at Karachi: 'Which international flights do you have coming in at this time? Is there any coming in from Colombo?' he asked.[1] Having learnt that PK805 was due to land within an hour, he ordered the closure of Karachi airport. Minutes later the runway lights were switched off and three fire engines were parked on the landing strip: one at each end and a third in the middle. Choudhry also ordered the closure of PK805's alternate destination: a small rural airport in Nawabshah, 200 miles east of Karachi.

Back in Islamabad, meanwhile, Brigadier Javed Iqbal had reached PTV headquarters at 6.15 p.m. and he had gone straight to the control room where he found Major Nisar with his 15 men. 'Disarm yourself immediately!' the Brigadier yelled.[2] Major Nisar refused. The Brigadier then drew a pistol and pointed it at Nisar's chest. Nisar blinked first and told his men to lay down their weapons. Within minutes the major and his men were locked in a room with an armed guard at the door. The jubilant military secretary headed back to report his success to the prime minister. (Later, Brigadier Iqbal was to rue his actions. On 13 October he was arrested and charged with drawing a pistol on a fellow officer.)[3]

With the TV station back under civilian control, the news about Musharraf's retirement was rebroadcast at the end of the 6.00 p.m. bulletin. Sharif was encouraged but in fact his government was all but over. When army officers at GHQ saw the news of Musharraf's sacking at the end of the 6.00 p.m. news bulletin, they despatched a second army unit to PTV and by 7.15 p.m. the station was off-air. By then the coup was well under way. The first soldiers from 111 Brigade to reach the prime minister's residence had arrived at around 6.30 p.m. Having secured the gatehouse, a major took 15 men over the extensive lawns and headed for the building's main entrance. As the porch came into view, the major saw General Ziauddin on the steps with six plain clothes ISI officers. The major ordered the ISI men to lay down their weapons. They refused and General Ziauddin tried to persuade the major to back down. The major started trembling. He was, after all, disobeying an order from the duly appointed army chief. Beads of sweat poured down his forehead. 'Sir,' he threatened Ziauddin, 'it would take me just one second.' Ziauddin, reckoning that resistance was futile, told his men to lay down their weapons.

But if developments on the ground were reaching a conclusion, the same could not be said for the events in the air. The pilot of PK805, Captain Sarwat Hussain, was becoming increasingly agitated. Despite his misgivings, Aminullah Choudhry was still trying to implement the prime minister's order to prevent the plane landing in Pakistan. As the recordings from the air traffic control tower reveal, Choudhry's staff knew that there could be a disaster. 'If it crashes, then?' asked one. 'We cannot take the blame if it crashes,' responded another. To add to their woes, the air traffic controllers now had the military coming on the line. GHQ in Rawalpindi had already ordered the troops in Karachi to take over the airport there so that Musharraf's plane could land. The chief of Pakistan's Air Defence, Lieutenant General Iftikhar Hussain Shah, called the air traffic controller in person. He took a paternalistic but uncompromising approach. 'Son, do this,' he told the hapless controller, 'it must not be diverted.' This admonition came just five minutes after Aminullah Choudhry had repeated his order to divert the flight. The tape recorder in the air traffic control tower captured the controller's reply. It's best transcribed as 'Uuuuhn!'

These were critical minutes. The air traffic controllers were caught between two authorities. They decided to obey their immediate boss, Aminullah Choudhry. The pilot's situation, meanwhile, was now desperate. He could not land in Pakistan but he did not have enough fuel to reach the Middle East. The air traffic controllers, however, would not back down.

18.59:
ATC: 'PK805. It's up to you. You have to decide what you have to do. Proceed as per your decision.'
PK805: 'We understand that Karachi very well. The point is we have limited fuel. Either we run out of fuel and that's the end of the story or you allow us to land . . .'
ATC: 'PK805. You cannot land at any airport in Pakistan and you can proceed outside Pakistan.'

Captain Sarwat realised that his unenviable predicament had something to do with General Musharraf's presence on board his plane.[4] He called Musharraf to the cockpit and told him that air traffic control had denied permission to land. The pilot said the plane had just enough fuel to land in Ahmedabad in India. 'We are actually now left with forty-five minutes of fuel,' the pilot said, 'and we can only go to India.' 'Over my dead body,' replied Musharraf.

Unaware that troops loyal to him had by this time taken over Karachi airport, Musharraf was in fact reluctant to land anywhere. In an attempt to coax Captain Sarwat down a senior colleague of Musharraf's, Lieutenant General Iftikhar went to the air traffic control tower in person:

19.26:
ATC (Iftikhar): 'PK805. This is Karachi ATC. Over.'
PK805 (crew): 'Go ahead. Over.'
ATC (Iftikhar): 'This is General Iftikhar. You are hereby directed to land at Karachi airport. The Karachi control tower will guide you. There is no need to divert anywhere. Is that clear? Over.'

The message was relayed to Musharraf who still refused to comply. He told Captain Sarwat that he wanted to hear from one man and one man alone, his friend and trusted colleague, the Karachi corps commander, General Usmani.

19.30:

PK805 (crew): 'I have been directed by the chief that the corps commander should come on the line.'

ATC (Iftikhar): 'Please convey to the chief: this is General Iftikhar. I would like to speak to him.'

PK805 (crew) 'Stand by, we will get the general.'

(Musharraf): 'Iftikhar this is Pervez. Where is Usmani?'

ATC (Iftikhar): 'PK805, go ahead.'

PK805 (Musharraf) 'This is Pervez. Message for Iftikhar. General Iftikhar where is Usmani?'

ATC (Iftikhar): 'Sir, this is Iftikhar on the set. General Usmani is in the VIP lounge. He is waiting at the gate for you. I am in the control tower.'

PK805 (Musharraf): 'Where is Iftikhar now? Is that Iftikhar speaking?'

ATC (Iftikhar): 'Affirmative.'

PK805 (Musharraf): 'Iftikhar, what is the problem?'

ATC (Iftikhar): 'I am sure you would not know. About two hours back your retirement was announced and you were to be replaced by Zia. The army has taken over and they were trying to divert your plane, so that it does not land here. We have taken over the airport and you are coming in now.'

PK805 (Musharraf): 'Iftikhar thank you. Tell Mehmood and Aziz nobody will leave the country.'

When the plane landed at 7.47 p.m., Musharraf said it had just seven minutes of fuel to spare. At 10.15 p.m. PTV came back on air to announce the dismissal of Nawaz Sharif's government. General Musharraf, PTV said, would address the nation shortly. He did so the next day at 2.50 a.m.:

I was in Sri Lanka on an official visit. On my way back the PIA commercial flight was not allowed to land at Karachi but was ordered to be diverted to anywhere outside Pakistan. Despite acute shortages of fuel, imperilling the lives of all the passengers, thanks be to Allah, this evil design was thwarted through speedy army action. My dear countrymen, having briefly explained the background, I wish to inform you that the armed forces have moved in as a last resort to prevent any further destabilisation.[5]

Another period of military rule had begun. Although he had not given the final order to launch the coup, General Musharraf found himself in charge. Most Pakistanis were delighted. Tired of the corruption and incompetence of the democratic governments, they were more than willing to give the army a chance. Musharraf, though, insisted that he was not a politician: his failure to submit himself to the electorate was one of his first big blunders. Although he did retain considerable popular support for some years, for many at home and abroad he always lacked the legitimacy that comes from a genuine election victory.

Nonetheless, there were still reasons for believing Musharraf could buck Pakistan's rather negative trends. He did at least have an agenda. Throughout the 1990s Pakistan had been led by politicians who never had a comprehensive reform programme. Neither Nawaz Sharif nor Benazir Bhutto had even tried to dismantle Zia's legacy. Sharif didn't particularly want to and Bhutto didn't dare. Musharraf had a vision: he wanted a modern, liberal, prosperous, tolerant Pakistan. After 9/11 he also had considerable international support. Not for the first time Afghanistan's chronic instability had benefited a Pakistani military leader. During the 1980s General Zia had used the Soviet occupation of Afghanistan to enhance his international legitimacy: 9/11 enabled General Musharraf to pull off the same trick. The aid flowed in. Partly because of their profligacy, but also because of the nuclear-related economic sanctions imposed on Pakistan, the civilian governments of the 1990s were distracted by repeated financial crises. Musharraf never had that problem.

Nor did Musharraf have the army breathing down his neck. Civilian governments have failed in Pakistan for a number of reasons: the politicians have been corrupt and listless; the civil service has proved incompetent and ineffective. But the army's habit of intervening in policy decisions and removing elected politicians from power has also been a significant factor. Musharraf never had to worry about such interference. His control of the army allowed him to do things that no civilian leader would ever risk attempting. Neither Benazir Bhutto nor Nawaz Sharif, for example, was allowed to formulate their own policies regarding India. During her first administration Benazir Bhutto had wanted to go to India to meet Rajiv Gandhi, but the military establishment was so strongly opposed to the idea that she gave it up. It was much the same story a decade later when, in February 1999, Nawaz Sharif invited his Indian counterpart Atal Behari Vajpayee to Lahore. General Musharraf (who at the time was chief of army staff) undermined Sharif's diplomatic effort by refusing to go to the Wagah border point to welcome Vajpayee to Pakistan. He maintained that it would have been unacceptable for Pakistan's military leaders to be seen shaking the hand of the prime minister of an enemy state. But just two years later, after his coup, Musharraf not only shook Vajpayee's hand but also visited him in India for the Agra summit.

There were good reasons, then, for believing that Musharraf could achieve something. He was to have nearly a decade in power: so, what had he achieved by the end of it? When he resigned in 2008 he claimed that 'everything I have done will have long-term benefits for Pakistan'. But Pakistanis only had to look at the promises he had made back in 1999 to see that in fact the military ruler had not managed to achieve many of the goals he had set for himself.

Democracy

Musharraf came into power with a bold promise: 'I shall not allow the people to be taken back to the era of sham democracy, but to a true one.'[6] And when he gave up power nine years later he said he had achieved his goal by incorporating the 'essence of democracy into the system'.[7] In one respect, Musharraf was more democratic than many of his predecessors. His liberalisation of the media sector marked a genuine change from the past. It is true that in the dwindling days of his administration Musharraf, desperate to hang on to power, tried to impose limits on the private TV stations he had created. Nevertheless, any fair assessment must conclude that, on balance, he did more for press freedom than any Pakistani leader before him. In 1999 Pakistanis had no choice but to watch the stodgy, state-controlled monopoly provider, PTV. By the time Musharraf left office there was a plethora of lively, controversial, hard-hitting 24-hour news channels.

In most other respects, however, Musharraf failed to change the political system in the way that he hoped. The main political parties remained vehicles for the promotion of a tiny elite. Despite Musharraf's considerable efforts to loosen the stranglehold of Pakistan's leading politicians, in 2008 he handed over power to the very same families he had originally kicked out. The Pakistan People's Party had replaced Benazir Bhutto with her widower and her son; all power within the Muslim League still lay with Nawaz Sharif and his brother Shabaz. Altaf Hussain remained the leader for life of the Muttahida Qaumi Movement (MQM), and in NWFP there was no sign of Asfandyar Wali letting control of the Awami National Party (ANP) slip from his family. It was not just the party leaders who remained entrenched. Initially, Musharraf was critical of the feudal leaders who held sway in so many of Pakistan's villages and rural towns. But in most parliamentary rural constituencies the feudal landlords remained unassailable. The only change some of them have complained about is that the growing political awareness led by the private TV stations has meant that, although they can still count on their constituents' votes, they are now expected to travel to towns and villages and ask for support.

Like the Pakistani military rulers before him, General Musharraf faced a fundamental contradiction. He was all in favour of democracy – for others. That is not to say he was an omnipotent dictator. Arguably, he would have been able to achieve much more had he been more authoritarian and simply implemented his programme. Fearful of public opposition to unrestrained military rule, he worked with an elected parliament from 2002. As a result, from December 2003 he was forced to rely on the support of the Muttahida Majlis e-Amil (MMA), a six-party alliance of hardline religious parties which consistently undermined his reforms. Yet there were also distinct limits to Musharraf's democratic instincts. Whenever his own political survival was at stake he did not hesitate to break the law. The 1999 coup set a precedent of illegality which culminated in the November 2007 suspension of the constitution.

Corruption

Straight after the 1999 coup Musharraf had stated that the elimination of corruption was one of his top priorities. But even at the outset there were indications he would compromise on that commitment if it were politically expedient to do so. The judiciary managed to secure an undertaking that, in return for its retrospective validation of Musharraf's coup, judges would not be investigated for corruption. Mindful of the need for positive press coverage, the military also let it be known that journalists would not be investigated. By 2002 the regime's commitment to the anti-corruption drive had disappeared without trace, as was amply demonstrated by the case of the former navy chief, Mansur ul-Haq.

Admiral Mansur ul-Haq was chief of the navy between 1994 and 1997. Shortly after he took up his post there were rumours that he was taking kickbacks on defence contracts. The civilian government of the time (probably wishing to conceal its own involvement in the scandal) accepted the view of the other service chiefs that formally charging the admiral would undermine the prestige of the armed forces.[8] After Musharraf's coup the authorities said they were determined to pursue the case and, in May 2001, they had gathered sufficient evidence to secure Mansur ul-Haq's extradition from the United States so that he could face charges in the Pakistani courts. By the end of the year, however, the military's commitment to the anti-corruption drive had weakened. The National Accountability Bureau struck a deal with Mansur ul-Haq in which he secured his freedom by promising to pay back $7.5 million to the state. No one in authority even attempted to explain why, if he admitted misappropriating the money, the admiral did not remain in jail. As one Pakistani journalist pointed out, the amount Mansur ul-Haq promised to return was the equivalent of 1,270 years of an admiral's salary or twice the annual salary bill for the navy's entire personnel.[9]

The admiral's case was part of a pattern. By the start of 2002 several politicians also found that their corruption cases had been dropped. The military attempted to excuse itself on the grounds that finding solid evidence of white-collar crime is extremely difficult and time-consuming. But the real reason for the softened approach was that the army saw the legal cases as useful levers with which they could control politicians. If any politicians transgressed the line of 'acceptable' criticism of the military, they could expect to have their corruption cases revived. By the same token, politicians who accommodated themselves with the military regime could expect to have their cases dropped.

The climax of Musharraf's failure to confront corruption was reached in 2007 when he was under increasing US pressure to allow Benazir Bhutto, who was in self-imposed exile, back to Pakistan. The evidence of corruption against her was strong. Three of the cases she faced had an international dimension. In 2003 a Geneva magistrate had found her and her husband, Asif Zardari, guilty of money-laundering. The couple had appealed the judgement and the Swiss had said there would be a retrial. In the UK there was a case in which the Pakistani government had alleged that Benazir Bhutto and Asif Zardari had bought a country home, the so-called Rockwood palace, using money from kickbacks. Ms Bhutto and Mr Zardari denied owning the estate for eight years. But in 2004 Mr Zardari admitted that it was his. In 2006 an English judge, Lord Justice Collins, said there was a 'reason-able prospect' of the government of Pakistan proving that the couple bought and refurbished Rockwood with 'the fruits of corruption'. The case was endlessly postponed, in large part because Bhutto and Zardari used a whole array of methods to put off a verdict for as long as possible. One of their delaying tactics, which later proved to be somewhat embarrassing, was to have Asif Zardari declared mentally ill. His lawyers filed documents from doctors saying he was suffering from severe psychiatric problems including dementia, major depres-sive disorder and post-traumatic stress disorder.[10] When he became president his aides were quick to say that, even if dementia was an irreversible illness, he had fully recovered.[11]

Ms Bhutto also faced allegations concerning the United Nations oil-for-food scandal. In 2005 the Independent Inquiry Commission led by former US Federal Reserve head Paul Volcker found that more than 2,000 companies breached UN sanctions by making illegal payments to Saddam Hussein's government in Iraq before 2003. Among them was a company called Petroline FZC, based in the United Arab Emirates. Mr Volcker's inquiry found that it had traded $144 million of Iraqi oil, and made illegal payments of $2 million to Saddam Hussein's regime. Documents from Pakistan's National Accountability Bureau appear to show that Ms Bhutto was Petroline FZC's chairwoman.

Many of these international cases were the subject of charges within Pakistan as well. And there were many more cases in the country including allegations about kickbacks. To give just a few examples, these included deals involving gold import licenses, Polish tractors and French fighter jets.

General Musharraf was never in any doubt that Bhutto was corrupt and at first he vowed to convict her. 'Legal action will be taken against her, certainly', he said in 2001. 'She is accountable to this nation for her misdeeds.'[12] But it was easier said than done. Both at home and abroad Benazir Bhutto's lawyers managed to prevent the courts making any progress. And as each month passed and Musharraf's popularity declined, he found himself in increasing need of support from the political parties.

Benazir Bhutto offered a deal. She would tell her national assembly members not to block Musharraf's election as president in October 2007 in return for an amnesty. The Americans enthusiastically backed the plan. They believed that Benazir Bhutto's return to Pakistani politics would give them the dream ticket of a democratic, legitimate leader determined to combat Islamic radicalism working with the man who could carry the army and get it done – Musharraf. It was a hopelessly naive view: the two leaders never trusted each other and were bound to fall out. However, Musharraf, increasingly weak and isolated, eventually went along with it. After a series of secret meetings with Benazir Bhutto in Dubai, the terms of the 2007 National Reconciliation Ordinance were negotiated. The wording was such that Benazir Bhutto and Asif Zardari were let off their cases, but Nawaz Sharif could still be put on trial should the need arise. Most Pakistanis were disgusted. The man who had won their support in 1999 by promising speedy justice had ended up, in blatant disregard of the law, making a secret deal with one of the politicians he had once denounced.

The Economy

When General Musharraf seized power, Pakistan was technically bankrupt. Both remittances and export income were falling. The International Monetary Fund (IMF) and the World Bank had suspended their programmes with Pakistan.[13] Pakistan did not default only because both Islamabad and its creditors had a mutual interest in avoiding the use of a term that would have made a bad situation worse. By the time General Musharraf left office the situation had improved significantly. His most striking achievement was to increase Pakistan's foreign exchange reserves from $1.6 billion when he took over to $14.3 billion when he left power. An annual growth of 4.2 per cent had increased to 7 per cent by the time he resigned.[14] Foreign direct investment reached a record level of over $5 billion in 2006–07.

In its 2007 assessment the IMF concluded that the Musharraf administration's 'sound macroeconomic management and wide-ranging structural reforms have contributed to high real GDP growth, a reduction in the debt burden and an improved business climate'.[15] Per capita income doubled under Musharraf, bringing genuine relief to tens of millions who lived on the breadline. Good management, no doubt, was a part of it, but there were other factors. During the 1990s, before Musharraf took over in 1999, there were no fewer than nine different governments or caretaker administrations. The political upheavals were especially disruptive because both Nawaz Sharif and Benazir Bhutto used the government's economic patronage, or the withdrawal of it, to reward loyalists and punish opponents. Each change of government would throw countless private sector investment projects off course. Musharraf, merely by dint of remaining in power, was able to provide a more stable environment. As a military ruler he was also better placed to take some unpopular decisions such as increasing fuel and utility prices.

Economic trends, 1999–2008

	1999/ 2000	2000/ 01	2001/ 02	2002/ 03	2003/ 04	2004/ 05	2005/ 06	2006/ 07	2007/ 08*
GDP growth %	3.9	2.2	3.4	4.7	7.5	9	6.6	7	6.8
Debt (% GDP)	98.9	109.8	100.8	74.5	67.8	62.9	57.3	54.6	56
Gross reserves	916	1679	4330	9,529	10,564	9,805	10,760	14,287	12,344
Foreign direct investment	471	368	576	798	951	1525	3521	5140	5150
Inflation %	3.6	4.4	2.7	3.1	4.6	9.3	7.9	7.8	12

Source: IMF Staff Reports 2001–07; * Pakistani official figures. All monetary figures in $m.

Musharraf also managed to attract significant amounts of foreign aid. Indeed, the aid flows have been so big that no one knows how much aid the US has given to Pakistan. The sheer number of programmes, many of them classified, makes it virtually impossible to obtain an accurate overview. Overt US aid to Pakistan between the 9/11 attacks and 2009 amounted to $12.3 billion.[16] That figure is made up of four funding streams for which there are published accounts: Coalition Support Funds, Budget Support, Security Assistance and Development Aid. The most detailed and comprehensive study of US aid programmes to Pakistan since 9/11 found that its estimate of $10 billion in overt or declared funding 'has likely been matched, if not exceeded, by classified funds that have gone toward intelligence and covert military action'.[17] The real figure for US aid to Pakistan since 9/11, then, may be closer to $20 billion.[18] Covert funding streams have included support to the ISI, training Pakistani officers in nuclear safety and cash payments to tribal leaders hired to fight Al Qaeda elements in their areas.[19]

Pakistani officials, however, insist that the levels of covert funding have been relatively small and do not amount to anything like $10 billion. They also argue that some of the funds should be seen as reimbursement rather than aid and point out that between one-third and one-half of funds leaving the US never reach Pakistan because of US consulting fees and administrative overheads.[20]

Of the four declared funding streams, the Coalition Support Funds have been the most significant and have totalled approximately $6 billion since 9/11. This money reimbursed Pakistan for operational and logistical costs incurred in counter-terrorism operations. The US, to put it another way, was paying for the conflict in Waziristan. The sums were huge: Coalition Support Funds equal more than a quarter of Pakistan's total military expenditure.[21] A separate category of aid, Security Assistance, paid for capital military expenditure. The money was spent on items such as maritime patrol aircraft, Cobra attack helicopters, roads in the tribal areas and night vision equipment.[22] The remaining funds – approximately $2.5 billion – were split into two categories. The largest proportion ($1.6 billion) went into budgetary support to Pakistan. The idea was that these funds could be used to pay off foreign debts, thus freeing up money to be spent on social security. The relatively free hand that Pakistan has had in disbursing these funds, however, has meant that much of the money ended up in military-related expenditure. The remaining money ($0.9 billion) was more specifically earmarked for social spending projects such as the relief effort for the Kashmir earthquake of 2005.

For as long as General Musharraf's stock in Washington was high, the money flowed with remarkably few questions being asked. By 2007, however, with Musharraf clearly impeding a return to democracy in Pakistan, US policymakers started articulating concerns that the generals in Rawalpindi were equipping themselves to defeat not Al Qaeda but their traditional enemy, India. Senator Robert Menendez, who was chairing a Senate Foreign Relations Sub-Committee on US aid to Pakistan, made the point quite bluntly: despite the lavish spending, he said, 'al Qaeda and the Taliban have a safe haven in the FATA region, Osama bin Laden is still on the loose in the region, anti Americanism remains high and Pakistan's President has repeatedly exercised the powers of a dictator. Do we dare to call our policies in that respect a success? . . . My concern is that we may be spending money to simply prop up a dictatorial ruler with a poor and worsening record.'[23] Similar concerns were expressed in the House of Representatives. Congressman Gary Ackerman complained that despite the US aid, 'there has been neither success against terrorism nor a return to democracy'.[24]

Despite Al Qaeda having neither an air force nor a navy, the critics complained, Pakistan had used the Foreign Military Finance funds to purchase, amongst other things, maritime patrol aircraft and surveillance radars.[25] The concerns in Congress became more acute when it became known that Pakistan was planning to spend over 5 billion dollars (of its own money) buying 18, possibly 36, newly built advanced F-16 combat aircraft. Unconvinced that these huge outlays were targeting terrorism, the US Congress responded in December 2007 by making some funds conditional on progress both in the war on terror and in restoring democracy.[26]

Under pressure from Congress, the State Department announced it would take control of the budgetary support funds and disperse them through the development agency, USAID.[27]

The aid flows undoubtedly bolstered the Musharraf regime but arguably they allowed him to delay much-needed structural reform of the economy. There was one area of the economy, for example, in which Musharraf failed to achieve the radical changes he had hoped for in 1999. When he came to power fewer than 1 per cent of Pakistanis paid tax. He knew it was a big problem. An official report commissioned by General Musharraf found that:

Tax receipts are insufficient to pay even for debt service and defence and there is hardly any net foreign assistance for development. Simultaneously there is a crisis of confidence between the taxpayer and the government. If taxes relative to GDP do not increase significantly, without new levies, Pakistan cannot be governed effectively, essential public services cannot be delivered and high inflation cannot be avoided. The reform of tax administration is the single most important economic task for the government.[28]

It was not difficult to work out why Pakistan had such a dire tax collection rate. Since 1947 no one had served a prison sentence for income tax evasion. Pakistan's tax-raising body, the Central Board of Revenue, frequently announced crackdowns on tax evaders. But the threats of stern action and declarations of 'final' deadlines were bluffs and made no difference. Few Pakistanis believed the state institutions were strong enough to force them to pay tax. And even when taxpayers did pay their share, there was little guarantee that the money would end up in the state's coffers. In 2001 a former senior World Bank official claimed that almost 50 per cent of the money paid by Pakistani taxpayers went straight into the pockets of tax officials.[29]

In May 2000, shortly after he took over, General Musharraf announced that improving the tax collection system was one of his main priorities. He focused on a tax that he thought would be relatively easy to raise: a General Sales Tax (GST). It was by no means a new idea. The IMF had long championed GST. Initially, General Musharraf showed considerable determination to make people register for GST. When the country's traders went on strike to oppose the tax, he stood firm. After the strike collapsed, small businessmen in all Pakistan's major cities reluctantly participated in a National Survey and filled out forms giving key data about their businesses.

In the event, though, the traders had little to fear. In 2001 an official from the Central Board of Revenue admitted that most of the survey forms gathered by the government had not been processed and had consequently 'not yielded a single penny'.[30] By April 2001 – a year after Musharraf's stand-off with the traders – there were still only 62,000 registered sales-tax payers in all of Pakistan.[31] The National Survey data had been collected, but the whole initiative got bogged down in Pakistan's notoriously lethargic bureaucracy. In January 2002 the finance minister, Shaukat Aziz, said that the National Survey had yielded data that meant there were another half a million 'potential taxpayers'.[32] Even if those potential taxpayers were transformed into real ones, only 1.5 per cent of the population would have been registered taxpayers. Meanwhile tax collectors remained so hopelessly underpaid that even senior government officials conceded that they had no choice but to supplement their income through corrupt practice.

It was hardly surprising that the IMF was once again complaining that Pakistan's rate of tax collection was hopelessly inadequate.[33] Six years into Musharraf's period in power, the total tax collected had increased significantly in line with the growth of the economy but as a proportion of GDP had remained static. Although the IMF said in 2008 that there had been improvement in tax administration, it still found that 'little progress has been made in broadening the tax base'.[34] Henri Lorie, the senior resident representative of the IMF in Pakistan, said that income tax was the lowest-performing tax of all and that the

Total tax collections as a proportion of GDP, 1998–2006

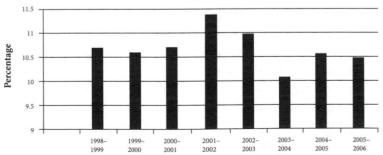

Source: http://www.finance.gov.pk/survey/sur_chap_06-07/05-Fiscal.PDF

solution lay in stronger tax enforcement.[35] Even the head of the Central Board of Revenue conceded that tax compliance was still too low and that the tax: GDP ratio was well below that found in comparable economies.[36]

Militancy

When Musharraf first came into power some commentators in India tried to portray him as a religious extremist.[37] Although never remotely convincing, the case rested on two facts: Musharraf had backed Mullah Omar's Taliban regime and he had always supported Islamic militants who were active in Kashmir. But the Indian writers had missed the point. Musharraf's policies towards Afghanistan and Kashmir were driven by nationalistic, not religious, concerns. He had never supported the Taliban's interpretation of Islam, but he did believe that with Mullah Omar running a friendly Pukhtoon government in Kabul, Pakistan had strategic depth. Musharraf's army could concentrate on guarding the border with India and had no reason to fear an attack from the northwest. As he said in May 2000: 'Afghanistan's majority ethnic Pashtuns have to be on our side. That is our national interest. . . . The Taliban cannot be alienated by Pakistan. We have a national security interest there.'[38] Similarly, his support for Islamic-based Kashmiri militants was driven by a desire to advance Pakistan's long-standing national claim rather than one to promote radical Islam.

After the 1999 coup, Islamabad's formidable rumour machine came up with a more realistic view of Musharraf's world-view. Stories circulated about his penchant for whisky and the general himself freely recounted how he had gambled in casinos.[39] His relatives made little effort to conceal their attitude to religion. Shortly after the 1999 coup a BBC interviewer asked the general's father: 'Does your son pray five times a day?' 'If the father doesn't', came the deadpan reply, 'I don't see why the son should.'[40]

Musharraf himself gave an early indication of his thinking when he described the Turkish secularist Mustafa Kemal Atatürk as his hero. And in his first major policy speech Musharraf included a passage on Islam:

And now for a few words on exploitation of religion. Islam teaches tolerance not hatred; universal brotherhood and not enmity; peace and not
violence; progress and not bigotry. I have great respect for the Ulema
and expect them to come forth and present Islam in its true light. I urge
them to curb elements which are exploiting religion for vested interests
and bring bad name to our faith . . .[41]

Even if he chose his words carefully, in the context of Pakistani political
discourse, the general's meaning was clear: he was distancing himself
from the Islamic radicals. Whereas Zia ul-Haq had used his military
might to try to Islamicise Pakistan, Musharraf was indicating that he
wanted to modernise the Pakistani state. In some respects he would
succeed. In 2005, for example, he at least held the line by ensuring that
the Supreme Court declared as unconstitutional an attempt by the
Provincial Assembly in NWFP to set up a Taliban-style vice and virtue
department. And in some respects he managed to reverse measures
introduced by Zia. In 2006 he overturned General Zia's Hudood
Ordinance, which among other things meant that rape cases were
dealt with in sharia courts and that victims had to have four male
witnesses or else face prosecution for adultery. Musharraf introduced a
new system in which civil courts could try rape cases and use DNA
samples as evidence. It was a hard-fought victory which the religious
parties fiercely opposed. Khurshid Ahmed from Jamaat-e-Islami, for
example, described the bill as 'an attempt to promote an alien culture
and secularism in Pakistan'.[42]

That Musharraf did have moderate views on religion should not be
in doubt. In June 2001 he made a major speech to leading Pakistani
Islamic scholars and clerics who had been transported to Islamabad for
the purpose. It was one of the clearest statements of Islamic modernism
ever articulated by a Pakistani leader. 'How does the world look at us?'
he asked:

The world sees us as backward and constantly going under. Is there any
doubt that we have been left behind although we claim Islam will carry
us forward in every age, every circumstance and every land. . . . How
does the world judge our claim? It looks upon us as terrorists. We have

been killing each other. And now we want to spread violence and terror abroad. Naturally the world regards us as terrorists. Our claim of toler-ance is phoney. . . . We never tire of talking about the status that Islam accords to women. We only pay lip service to its teachings. We do not act upon it. This is hypocrisy.[43]

The June speech was a major political event in Pakistan. Since the 1950s, no Pakistani leader had dared speak to the clerics in this way. But there were still strict limits on how far Musharraf was prepared to go. When he spoke of terrorism he was not referring to the Taliban or to the Kashmiri militants. His target rather was the increasing of sectarianism in Pakistan.

It was a big and growing problem. In August 2001 Musharraf signalled that he meant to confront it: he banned the Shia's most powerful militant organisation, Sipah-e-Mohammad Pakistan (SMP), and its Sunni coun-terpart, Lashkar-e-Jhangvi. He also put two hardline political organisa-tions, which had close links with the militants, on the watch list: the Shias' Tehrik-e-Jafria Pakistan (TJP) and the Sunnis' Sipah-e-Sahaba Pakistan (SSP). In 2002 he banned them as well. Officials insisted that the bans enabled the authorities to capture or kill the most significant sectarian leaders.[44] But, as ever, there were questions about implementa-tion. The TJP reformed under a new name, Tehrik-e-Islami while the SSP became Millet-e-Islami (although it is still often referred to as SSP).[45] Although the SSP has been weakened by internal splits, the bans have not achieved their main goals – reducing the numbers killed. Since many activists from the two organisations were already wanted for murder, they were used to keeping a low profile and were capable of operating clandestinely.

The nature of the sectarian violence in Pakistan changed over the course of Musharraf's period in power. During the 1990s most of the killings were in Punjab. Under General Musharraf there were two significant changes. First, most sectarian attacks shifted from Punjab to NWFP, Balochistan and the tribal areas, especially Kurram. It is a particularly grim development as sectarian clashes there can morph into very violent tribal disputes.[46] Secondly, the scale of the problem increased. By 2007 there was an average of more than one victim

Number of deaths from sectarian conflict, Punjab and Pakistan, 1989–2007

	Punjab	Pakistan
1989	10	10
1990	32	32
1991	47	47
1992	44	58
1993	38	39
1994	73	73
1995	58	59
1996	86	86
1997	90	193
1998	75	157
1999	53	86
2000	29	149
2001	65	261
2002	23	121
2003	3	102
2004	74	187
2005	33	160
2006	4	201
2007	7	441

Punjab Figures: 1989–93: Muhammad Qasim Zaman, 'Sectarianism in Pakistan: The Radicalisation of Shi'e and Sunni Identities', *Modern Asia Studies*, 32: 3, 1998, pp. 689–716. These are based on official figures and are likely to be low estimates. **1994:** *Schinan Times*, an anti-sectarian website, www.schinan.com. **1995 and 2000:** Interview with senior police official, Lahore, February 2002. **1996:** Institute of Conflict Management, www.satp.org/satporgtp/countries/pakistan/database/sect-killing.htm. **1997:** *State of Human Rights in 1997*, Human Rights Commission of Pakistan, Lahore, 1998. **1998:** *State of Human Rights in 1998*, Human Rights Commission of Pakistan, Lahore, 1999. **1999 and 2001:** I.A. Rehman of the Human Rights Commission of Pakistan, February 2002. **Pakistan Figures: 1989–2007:** Institute of Conflict Management, www.satp.org/satporgtp/countries/pakistan/database/sect-killing.htm.

of sectarian violence every day. Although most suicide bombers in Pakistan have tended to be portrayed by the Western media as almost invariably Taliban members targeting the Pakistani state, it's estimated that in fact a majority of them are motivated by sectarian hatred[47] and target either Sunni or Shia civilians. A new twist on sectarian violence since 2004 has been the fighting between different Sunni groups, especially in the Khyber tribal agency.

After the 9/11 attacks Musharraf apparently broadened his challenge to Islamic militancy from the sectarian groups to jihadis more generally. He discovered he had greater room for manoeuvre than he had previously thought. When the US bombing of Afghanistan began in October 2001, there were protests in which effigies of President Bush and General Musharraf were burnt. Western journalists and politicians thought that the Musharraf regime was at risk, but the general himself drew precisely the opposite conclusion. The demonstrations were far too small to pose a threat, and they soon petered out. By November 2001 the best the radical clerics could do was to muster a few hundred anti-US protesters after Friday prayers each week. For years the radicals' trump card had been their ability to organise 'street power' but now they stood exposed: their trump card was weak. As Musharraf later said, 'I thought ten times about putting my hand in the beehive of religious extremism. But I realised that this was the maximum they could do and the vast majority of people were with me.'[48]

Musharraf was also pushed into action. The December 2001 attack on the parliament building in India forced his hand. Many Indians believed that their government should respond with just as much force as the Americans had deployed after the 11 September attacks on the World Trade Center in New York. The Indian government seemed to agree. It recalled the Indian high commissioner from Islamabad, cut rail and other transport links with Pakistan and moved missiles, fighter aircraft and tens of thousands of troops to the Pakistani border. Musharraf was in a corner and under pressure from Washington, not only to denounce those responsible for the attack, but also to act against them. Musharraf concluded that he had little choice but to reverse Pakistan's long-standing policy of backing the Kashmiri insurgency. On 12 January 2002 he delivered a landmark speech. For too long, he argued, Islamic militants had been allowed to flout the authority of the central government and, he declared, he was going to take them on. 'The day of reckoning,' he said, had come. 'Do we want Pakistan to become a theocratic state? Do we believe that religious education alone is enough for governance or do we want Pakistan to emerge as a progressive and dynamic Islamic welfare state? The verdict of the masses is in favour of a progressive Islamic state.' Complaining that the religious extremists had created a 'state within a state,' he vowed that the writ of the government would be established. He banned two of the most prominent Pakistan-based militant groups, Jaish-e-Mohammed and Lashkar-e-Toiba.[49]

It is interesting to note that although he banned Lashkar and Jaish, Musharraf did not abandon the insurgency altogether. He made no move against the most prominent of all the militant groups active in Kashmir, Hizb ul-Mujahideen, despite the fact that the group had many close links with Pakistan. That is probably explained by the fact that Musharraf was able to persuade the Americans that there was a distinction between Lashkar and Jaish, which have both always been first and foremost Islamic organisations, and Hizb ul-Mujahideen, which never required its new recruits to be strongly religious and which, for all its links with Pakistan, had a greater claim to being an indigenous Kashmiri national organisation.

Having done the difficult thing – banning groups involved in the Kashmiri insurgency – Musharraf did not hesitate to announce a whole series of other modernist reforms and to launch a number of other broadsides against the radicals. In the week after the January speech he arrested thousands of Islamic activists. He announced measures to control the construction of mosques and introduced limits on their use of loudspeakers.

Throughout the time General Musharraf was in power, Western and Pakistani commentators debated whether or not he was serious about tackling his country's jihadis. The rhetoric was there and the policy on Kashmir clearly changed, but there were many reasons for doubting his sincerity. To give just one example, the activists arrested after the January speech were within a few months quietly released. So was it all for show? For Washington it was a crucial question: the US Treasury was paying billions of dollars a year for Pakistan's cooperation. Was Musharraf keeping his end of the bargain? The case for doubting Musharraf was perhaps most clearly expressed by Frederic Grare, a former French diplomat in Pakistan turned public policy analyst with the Carnegie Endowment. As late as 2006 Grare stated that:

the risk of an Islamist takeover in Pakistan is a myth invented by the Pakistani military to consolidate its hold on power. In fact, religious political parties and militant organisations are manipulated by the Pakistan army to achieve its own objectives domestically and abroad. The army, not the Islamists, is the real source of instability on the subcontinent.[50]

Grare argued that, far from being a threat to the Pakistani state, the militant groups were in fact a creation of the state to advance policy goals such as winning control of Kashmir and installing a friendly regime in Kabul. The assassination attempts against senior army officers were, Grare conceded, signs that the military could not keep total control of the militants. But even then the army was able to manipulate such incidents to persuade the West that the threat posed by the Islamic radicals was a clear and present danger. Although the sectarian and jihadi groups had nuisance value, he concluded, 'the army is the problem'.[51]

Grare's analysis was always open to challenge: even if the army and the ISI had played a leading role in creating some of the jihadi groups, there was surely a risk of blowback. The tribal insurgency, the army's difficulties in Swat and the inability to stop the suicide bombing campaign all suggested that, towards the end of his time in power, President Musharraf was in fact too weak to control the militants. Nevertheless, in underestimating the strength of the jihadis, Grare was in good company: Musharraf himself failed to see the extent of the challenge he faced.

To explain Musharraf's ambivalence towards the jihadis, it is necessary to understand two widespread perceptions within the Pakistan army. First, senior Pakistani officers consistently underestimated the effectiveness of the militants, believing that having created the militant groups, the army could equally well cut off the funding and watch them wither away. Over-confident in their own military prowess, senior officers perceived militants as potentially useful but as wild, undisciplined fighters who could never even compare with regular army soldiers. Secondly, within a few months of Mullah Omar's regime being toppled in Afghanistan, the Pakistani senior military leadership believed that the Afghan Taliban would eventually stage a comeback and that a US-backed regime in Kabul had no chance of long-term success. The US and the UK repeatedly sent senior officials, ministers and military officers to Islamabad to try to persuade their Pakistani counterparts that the Western troops would remain in Afghanistan, if necessary, for decades. The Pakistanis simply did not believe them.

On the face of it, these assessments were contradictory. They simultaneously played down the power of the militants whilst arguing that they were capable of defeating the Western powers. In fact, Pakistani officers believed that only they were capable of defeating the jihadis. These considerations, coupled with a desire to avoid a confrontation that could undermine his ruling coalition in the parliament (that included the MMA religious party alliance), led Musharraf to adopt a nuanced policy towards militants after 9/11. Having signed up to the US 'war on terror', he had little choice but to take on Al Qaeda. In fact, it was not just that he felt compelled by US pressure to act against the organisation. Far from advancing any Pakistani state policies, the Al Qaeda elements on Pakistani soil were damaging the country's international image. Furthermore, Al Qaeda espoused a view of Islam that Musharraf believed to be outdated and wrong-headed. When he told the state authorities to tackle Al Qaeda, he meant it. And as he revealed in his memoirs, he was more than happy to collect the reward money the US offered when Pakistan handed over senior Al Qaeda captives.

The Kashmiri militant groups, however, were a different proposition. For years they had been funded and organised by the Pakistan army. Many Pakistanis respected their bravery in opposing India's repressive tactics in Kashmir. As we have seen in chapter 3, Musharraf, for various reasons, decided from 2002 to cut back his support for the insurgency in Kashmir. In the case of some of the smaller militant groups he went so far as to offer cash to fighters who demobilised. But he knew that such an approach would never work with the major groups such as Jaish-e-Mohammed and Lashkar-e-Toiba. Although he did ban these organisations, he understood that their independent funding streams, largely from mosque collections, and their sheer size meant they could not be dismantled overnight. And one way of getting them out of Kashmir was to divert them to Afghanistan. Many officers and men in the Pakistan army had grave misgiving about winding down the Kashmiri insurgency: by redirecting the biggest jihadi outfits to the Afghan front, Musharraf had found a way to assuage those critics.

Musharraf's attitude to Al Qaeda, then, was quite different to his approach to the Kashmiri militant outfits. The Taliban posed a third set of considerations. While he could not be seen to support the Afghan Taliban, Musharraf did not want to alienate them. It wasn't just that he thought that the Taliban would eventually win in Afghanistan. To some extent he also wanted them to do so. However obscurantist their world-view, the alternative, after all, was a hostile non-Pukhtoon government with deep ties to India. Western observers consistently underestimated the depth of Pakistan's fears about India's involvement in Afghanistan. Yet concerns about Delhi's links to, and investment in, the Karzai regime were one of the main reasons that President Musharraf was so steadfastly hostile to his counterpart in Kabul. And certainly India did emerge as a significant donor to Afghanistan, pledging over $1.2 billion in reconstruction funds.[52] The result of these various factors was a policy of passive support for the Afghan Taliban. With a massive income from the poppy crop, Mullah Omar had little need of money or weapons. But he did need a place for his fighters to find sanctuary. And while Musharraf had to deploy troops on the Durand Line to satisfy the West, he was content to let the Afghan fighters move back and forth across the border, and even through Pakistani army checkpoints.[53]

Musharraf's policy options, however, became more complicated when the Pakistani Taliban emerged as a significant force. To the extent that they supported the Afghan Taliban and fought in Afghanistan rather than Pakistan, Musharraf could tolerate them. Indeed, many in the military establishment saw them as assets, potentially useful at some point in the future.[54] But the Pakistani Taliban also forced Musharraf to overcome his hubris and recognise the limits of state power. In 2007 Baitullah Mehsud humiliated the Pakistan army. The ease with which he captured over 200 soldiers and then held them for months exposed the army's weakness and made it quite clear that, even if it wanted to, the state could not dismantle the Pakistani Taliban. Similarly, Musharraf's inability to slow the rate of sectarian killings in the country revealed his limitations. No one seriously disputes that Musharraf opposed sectarian killings. Not only did he repeatedly denounce them but he also had no strategic interest in allowing the sectarian killers to be so active on Pakistani soil. And yet, as we have seen, the number of sectarian killings quintupled between 2000 and 2007.

For a whole series of reasons, then, General Musharraf tolerated some militants and opposed others. That he managed to do so while simultaneously taking billions of dollars in US aid was in itself a remarkable achievement. But the policy was flawed and carried huge risks for Pakistan. By 2008 some Pakistani officials were conceding that they had lost control of the organisations they had once nurtured. The very high levels of anti-Americanism in Pakistan meant that many in the population gave the jihadis the benefit of the doubt. And after the siege of the Red Mosque in 2007, the threat posed by the jihadis became increasingly clear. By the time he left office in 2008, it was indisputable that Musharraf's failure to back his desire for enlightened moderation with a consistent approach towards the jihadis had been one of his biggest mistakes.

Education

No assessment of the Musharraf years would be complete without considering one other policy area and arguably the single most important long-term issue facing the country: education. Pakistan's disastrous illiteracy rate of around 45 per cent is probably the main obstacle to the country's economic and social development. Education was something Musharraf did not even mention in his first TV speech after the 1999 coup. In fact, he never took the issue seriously enough. There are two big problems facing those trying to improve the education system in Pakistan. First, how can government schools be improved? Second, what can be done about the religious seminaries or madrasas? It is worth looking at Musharraf's record in these two areas in some detail, not only because they are so important but also because they are good examples of what went wrong in his administration more generally. As we shall see, his inability to set clear policy goals and to stick to them, his need to appease the religious political parties, his desire for consensus and his resentment of simplistic Western analyses, all combined to undermine reform.

At the time of Pakistan's independence there were just 250 madrasas in the country. The Soviet invasion of Afghanistan, however, had transformed the situation. The madrasas won a well-deserved reputation for producing highly motivated anti-Soviet fighters. As a result, foreign funds, chiefly from the US and Saudi Arabia, flowed into the madrasa system. By 1987 there were an estimated 2,862 madrasas producing around 30,000 graduates each year.[55] Having received this boost, the madrasa movement went from strength to strength. In 2001 General Musharraf said that there were 7,000 or 8,000 madrasas in Pakistan.[56] In 2005–06 the Ministry of Education managed to organise the first ever complete national survey counting the number of schools in Pakistan, including the madrasas. It found that the true number was far higher than previous official estimates: there were 12,979 madrasas in Pakistan. The province with the highest number was Punjab with 5,459; NWFP was in second place with 2,843.[57] The census found that 1.5 million children attended madrasas, which equated to 4.6 per cent of all children in education.[58]

General Musharraf, then, could not afford to ignore the madrasas: the clerics who staffed them were educating a significant number of Pakistani children. For some years, though, he had been ambivalent about these institutions. Irritated by repeated lectures from Western politicians who saw all madrasas as jihadi universities, Musharraf often defended them on the grounds that they provided a valuable social service for families who were not served by a state school and who could not afford private school fees. In 2002, for example, he said: 'These schools are excellent welfare set ups where the poor get free board and lodge. In my opinion no NGO can match their welfare aspects. Many of the madaris [madrasas] are imparting excellent education. In addition to religious teaching, other subjects such as science, education and computer-training are also being imparted there.'[59]

Many Pakistani officials and a few Western experts echo this argument, dismissing concerns about madrasas as prejudiced and arguing that radical reform could lead to a dangerous backlash. Alexander Evans, for example, has argued that, although there are a few 'problem' madrasas in Pakistan, for many orphans and children from poor rural families 'madrasas provide essential services: education and lodging for children who could well find themselves the victims of forced labour, sex trafficking or other abuse'.[60]

It's a very generous assessment. Many madrasas are Dickensian institutions in which children are subjected to cruelty and in some cases sexual abuse.[61] Fear of retribution means that few cases come to public attention, but recent examples of child abuse have included a seven-year-old blind boy being hung upside down from a ceiling fan and then beaten to death for failing to learn the Quran,[62] and a 17-year-old boy being blinded and disfigured by having acid poured onto his face for refusing to have sex with his religious teacher.[63]

Although many Muslims (particularly those that have never visited a madrasa) may consider the children at madrasas to be pious and devout, the fact remains that their education is a woefully inadequate preparation for life in the rest of society. The top priority in all of them – even the most liberal and progressive – is to get the children to learn the Quran by rote in Arabic despite the fact that most pupils do not speak the language. Pupils do nothing else but repeat the verses, eight hours a day, six days a week, for as long as it takes. The clever ones can learn the text in 18 months; others can take four or five years. Most madrasas that teach non-religious subjects do so absurdly badly. In some, for example, medicine is taught through texts written in the eleventh, thirteenth and fifteenth centuries.[64] Indeed, most madrasa students receive such a limited, useless education that the only jobs they can get are within the madrasa system. The more controversial issue, however, is how many go on to become jihadis.

There has been a debate both in Pakistan and in the West about just how much of a threat the madrasas pose. Many Western journalists have argued, or perhaps assumed, that madrasa graduates are filled with hatred of America, Hindus, Jews and Christians (probably in that order), and have been so starved of female company that they positively seek the heavenly virgins that they believe will follow their martyrdom. Some scholarly studies of suicide bombers have found, however, that people who carry out attacks are more likely to have been educated in Western universities than madrasas. Marc Sageman has found that in a sample of 137 jihadis only 17 per cent had attended Islamic primary and secondary schools: 83 per cent had been to secular schools.[65]

In the most thorough study of madrasas to date, Christine Fair reconciles these apparently contradictory viewpoints with a crucial distinction. Although there is indeed little evidence of madrasa students being involved in international attacks, she argues that there is plenty of evidence to suggest that they have been responsible for many of the suicide attacks within Pakistan and Afghanistan.[66] One explanation for this disparity is that most madrasa students are so poorly educated and have so little idea about the world that they are only capable of mounting attacks within their own communities. Anyone who has visited many madrasas might agree that few of their alumni could be relied upon to carry out anything but the simplest attack. Even when they try to hit targets close to home, there are many examples of their murderous missions failing because of stupid errors such as wandering around towns, primed and ready to explode, but unsure of how to find a target.

There were occasions when General Musharraf acknowledged that the radical madrasas were indeed a problem. In his January 2002 speech he accepted that some madrasas 'are under the influence of politico-religious parties or have been established by them. I know that some promote negative thinking and propagate hatred and violence instead of inculcating tolerance, patience and fraternity'.[67] Musharraf went on to announce a programme of $113 million for madrasas that were willing to teach maths, science, English and Pakistan studies as well as the standard religious topics. In June 2002 the cabinet approved a draft law under which any foreign student or teacher who wanted to attend a madrasa would have to get permission from his or her own government and inform the Pakistani authorities. Musharraf announced that all those attending madrasas would have to register, and there would be restrictions on foreign grants and donations. Finally, he vowed that any madrasa involved in subversion or militant activity would be closed down.[68]

All these policies failed for the usual reason: they were never implemented. General Musharraf never signed the draft law because he needed the support of the hardline religious parties in parliament: he was not willing to antagonise them for the sake of madrasa reform. For their part the madrasas simply refused to register students. Most strikingly, they also turned down the $113 million. Needless to say, they feared that it would come with strings attached in the form of government encroachment on their autonomy.

Aware that his initiatives were making little headway, General Musharraf appointed an education minister whom he hoped could force change. A former director general of the ISI, Lieutenant General Javed Ashraf Qazi was not only secular in outlook but also knew how to cope with Islamabad's bureaucrats. But having appointed a man willing and able to reform the education system, Musharraf failed to back him. The madrasas were immediately aware that they faced a formidable opponent and tried to undermine him by insisting that their dealings with the government should be through the Ministry of Religious Affairs rather than the Ministry of Education. In a disastrous decision Musharraf agreed to the request. The madrasas' leaders now negotiated with the most senior civil servant in the Ministry of Religious Affairs and managed to drag out even the simplest matters – such as whether or not they should be registered – for several years. They even managed to challenge the idea of signing a pledge not to teach sectarianism and not to promote militancy. The prohibition on sectarianism, they argued, would undermine their teaching of comparative religion, and to say they would not promote militancy would be a tacit admission that they had done so in the past.[69] They also successfully resisted a government demand that they declare the sources of their funding.

The siege of the Red Mosque in 2007 gave the madrasa leaders the excuse they needed to break off dialogue with the government altogether. At last, General Musharraf could see that if he was to achieve change within the madrasa system he would need to consider more radical options. Back at the Ministry of Education, Javed Ashraf Qazi had one such option ready and waiting. He proposed identifying the most hardline radical madrasas in the country and then undermining them by building especially well-resourced government schools very close by. He was confident that, given a choice between a good government school and a radical madrasa, the vast majority of parents would opt for the government school. The method had been tried in Algeria with some success. But it was too late; Musharraf approved the plan just as his authority was dwindling. It never happened.

Musharraf's education policies also fell short in another crucial respect: under his management the government schools remained inadequate, moribund institutions. Arguably, reform of the government schools should have been an even higher priority than dealing with madrasas. Indeed, Pakistani officials tend to get frustrated with Western critics who concentrate on the madrasa system to the exclusion of the other parts of the Pakistani education system. And they have a point. If 4.6 per cent of Pakistani schoolchildren attend madrasas, then 95.4 per cent are going to the other two types of school available: government schools and private schools.

Unregistered, unmonitored and largely unnoticed, the private schools in fact constitute a very significant part of Pakistan's education system and can now be found in quite remote villages. Of children enrolled in school, 36 per cent now attend private schools.[70] The fact that families who can ill afford the fees still use the private sector is a demonstration, first, of the utter failure of the government school system to provide the service people need and, second, of the moderation of most Pakistanis. Many families would prefer to make a significant financial sacrifice to get their children into an English-medium private school rather than send them free to a madrasa.

The reason that the private sector is flourishing is obvious: the Pakistani state spends far too little on the government schools. During the 1990s under the democratic governments, education spending had declined from 2.1 per cent of GDP in 1991–2 to 1.7 per cent around the time of the military coup.[71] Under Musharraf, spending remained stagnant.[72] That there are not enough government schools is clear, but that is just one problem. Another is their low standards. Many government school teachers are political appointees who, sure in the knowledge that they will never be sacked, often fail to turn up for work. Random checks on government schools reveal very high levels of absenteeism.[73]

There are also problems with the syllabus. Most Western criticisms of the curricula in Pakistani schools have focused on the madrasas. But even within government schools the textbooks are often filled with highly controversial material. Hindus are regularly demonised and their role in achieving independence on the subcontinent is ignored.[74] In 2004 a Pakistani think tank, the Sustainable Development Policy

Institute (SDPI) examined textbooks in Urdu, English, social sciences and civics, and found all of them to contain 'falsehoods, distortions and omissions' as well as repeated incitements to 'militancy and violence, including encouragement of holy war and martyrdom'.[75] The SDPI concluded that: 'The textbooks tell lies, create hate [and] incite jihad'.[76]

Partly as a result of US pressure, in 2002 General Musharraf made an attempt to reform the syllabus. The Ministry of Education was asked to undertake a comprehensive review of what children were being taught. The timing, however, was unfortunate. The crucial meetings on the issue happened in 2003 and 2004 just as General Musharraf was relying on support in parliament from the hardline religious parties. In the course of those negotiations he agreed to stop any changes to the textbooks. There was, however, some limited progress on the issue in 2007 when the government published a liberal-leaning consultative white paper soliciting views on what the curriculum should include.[77]

Musharraf hasn't been alone in failing to give due attention to education. After 9/11 there were indications that the US understood the dangers of allowing another generation of uneducated Pakistanis to emerge. The 9/11 Commission identified the issue as a top priority: 'The United States should support Pakistan's government in its struggle against extremists with a comprehensive effort that extends from military aid to support for better education'.[78] In line with those sentiments, the US State Department spokesman Richard Boucher said in March 2002: 'A lot of US aid money that's going to Pakistan will be used to help with the education system'.[79]

In fact, that has not been the case. Depending on how the figures are calculated, of the US aid spent in Pakistan since 9/11, education has received as little as 1.3 per cent of the total.[80] Despite the obvious importance of education in Pakistan, the planned aid expenditure in the education sector for 2008 was less than that in 2004.

Conclusion

Musharraf had an unusually good opportunity to transform his country. His two civilian predecessors, Benazir Bhutto and Nawaz Sharif, were never given a chance to govern. The machinations of the army and the bureaucracy (and, it should be said, the corruption of their governments) meant that neither got a full term in office and, even when they were in power, significant areas of policy were beyond their authority.

Musharraf, by contrast, enjoyed the power that comes with being a military ruler. He also enjoyed the support of the people. The Pakistani people's disillusionment with the civilian governments was so profound that Musharraf was very popular when he first took over. For the first couple of years of his administration he ruled without constraint. Sadly, he lacked the vision or capability to use his power wisely. The corrupt remained unpunished, the education sector remained unreformed, the tax was uncollected. And then, as the years went by, his political objectives were subsumed by the sheer difficulty of staying in office.

Yet some Pakistanis were sorry to see him go. Artists, writers and musicians flourished under Musharraf and they fear that with him gone the civilian politicians will bend to Islamist pressure to limit their freedom of expression. And although, by the end, Musharraf had alienated the press, there is no denying that without his bold media reforms all the new private TV stations would not exist. His attempts to find a settlement to the Kashmir problem may have been spurned by India, but he went further than any previous Pakistani leader had dared to go in making concessions to try to get forward movement. Even if some of the economic improvements on his watch could be put down to the foreign aid, there was also an acknowledgement among the business community that the army had provided them with a relatively stable environment.

At the time of the 1999 coup Musharraf was politically naive. Frustrated by the incompetence and corruption of the civilian politicians, he thought that he and his military colleagues had the common sense, patriotism and honesty to put Pakistan on a different track. But it was not so easy. He had to face an obstructive and inefficient bureaucracy, militants who tried to assassinate him more than a dozen times, courts that would not convict the guilty and civilian politicians who wanted to get back into power. He wasn't helped by being surrounded by sycophants who left him out of touch and unaware that his authority was draining away. He was neither dictatorial enough to impose his will nor democratic enough to be legitimate.

The remorseless, familiar cycle of Pakistani politics has turned once more. As democracy returned, however, there was more of a sense of relief that Musharraf had gone than jubilation about his successors. To many Pakistanis the idea that the civilian politicians could deliver what they most want – jobs, decent schools and the rule of law – was simply ludicrous. They had not done so before and there was no reason to believe that anything had changed. I ended the first edition of this book with the comment that, far from being the solution, the army had not realised that they were in fact part of the problem. This is still true. But exactly the same can be said of the 'democratic' politicians as well.

Notes

INTRODUCTION

1. National Intelligence Council, 'Global Trends 2015: A Dialogue about the Future with Nongovernment Experts', Washington DC, 2000, pp. 64–6.
2. BBC News, 'US Warns Pakistan on Taliban Link', 28 March 2009, http://news.bbc. co.uk/1/hi/world/south_asia/7969450.stm.
3. Bill Roggio, 'Pakistani troops retreat after Taliban onslaught in Bajaur', *The Long War Journal*, http://www.longwarjournal.org/archives/2008/08/pakistani _troops_ret.php.
4. This story was told to me in May 2009 by retired civil servant and Sufi scholar Riaz Naqvi, who heard it first hand from Miangul Abdul Wadud Badshah himself.
5. Rahimullah Yusufzai, 'Violence Returns to Swat', News International Pakistan, 2 November 2007.
6. Agence France Presse, 1 November 2001.
7. Ashfaq Yusufzai, 'Impotence Fears Hit Polio Drive', BBC News Website, 25 January 2007, http://news.bbc.co.uk/2/hi/south_asia/6299325.stm.
8. *Daily Times*, 8 August 2006.
9. *The News*, 24 May 2007.
10. http://online-rmnp.tripod.com/paknews/index.blog?end=1153092481.
11. Text of report by Iqbal Khattak, 'Swatis Torch TVs Under TNSM Spell', BBC Monitoring, 9 August 2006.
12. 'Pakistan Militants End Truce Deal', BBC News Website, 15 July 2007, http://news.bbc.co.uk/2/hi/south_asia/6899621.stm.
13. Jane Perlez and Ismail Khan, 'Militants Gain Despite Decree by Musharraf', *New York Times*, 16 November 2007.
14. Hamid Mir, 'Taliban Has Responsibility to Arrest Musharraf', Rediff Website, www.rediff.com/news/2007/nov/06taliban.htm.
15. BBC Urdu Service, 2 November 2007.
16. Nicholas Schmidle, 'Next-Gen Taliban', *New York Times*, 8 January 2008.
17. Riaz Khan, 'Pakistan Free pro-Taliban Leader, Makes Peace With Group', Associated Press, 22 April 2008.
18. Rahimullah Yusufzai, 'Time to Rethink Swat', *The News*, 4 October 2008.
19. 'Pakistan Will Retake Swat', BBC News 28 January 2009, Website, http://news.bbc. co.uk/1/hi/world/south_asia/7856866.stm.
20. 'Pakistan to Probe Girl's Flogging', BBC News website, 4 April 2009, http://news.bbc.co.uk/1/hi/world/south_asia/7980899.stm.
21. Pervez Hoodbhoy, 'Five Year Forecast: Whither Pakistan', 12 June 2009, http://pakteahouse.wordpress.com/2009/06/12/five-year-forecast-whither-pakistan.
22. Mahboob Mahmood, 'A New Beginning for Pakistan: America's strategy for success', March 2009, available on www.spearheadresearch.org.

CHAPTER ONE: THE INSURGENCY

1. Interview with author, 24 August 2008, Islamabad.
2. See, for example, http://uk.youtube.com/watch?v=vvBs-zwoxUg.
3. Having repeatedly seen a series of various mobile-phone pictures showing the event from different angles in ultra-slow motion on a big screen, I believe that she was shot. The pictures were collected by Aaj TV.
4. Sherry Rehman interview with author, Naudero, rural Sindh, 30 December 2007.
5. British High Commission, Islamabad, Press Release, P-455, 8 February 2008.
6. Benazir Bhutto interview with author, Karachi, 19 October 2007.
7. Syed Faisal Shakeel, 'PPP Demands Probe Based on Benazir's Letter', *Dawn*, 30 December 2007.
8. Benazir Bhutto, *Reconciliation: Islam, Democracy and the West*, Simon & Schuster, London, 2008, p. 221
9. 'Significance of Qari Saifullah Akhtar's Arrest', *Daily Times*, 9 August 2004.
10. Amir Mir, 'HUJI Chief Still at Large', *The News*, 23 September 2008.
11. Text available at http://www.telegraph.co.uk/news/worldnews/1573885/Text-of-alleged-al-Qa%27eda-phone-call.html, 29 December 2007.
12. Author interviews with two people who had met Baitullah Mehsud and who frequently spoke with him on the phone, Islamabad, January 2007.
13. 'CIA Boss Names Bhutto "Killers" ', BBC News Website, 18 January 2008, http://news.bbc.co.uk/1/hi/world/south_asia/7195591.stm.
14. 'Bhutto's Alleged Killers Detained for 10 More Days,' Asian News International, New Delhi, 3 February 2008.
15. 'Suspect of Bhutto's Assassination Identifies Bomber', Xinhua News Agency, Beijing, 29 January 2008.
16. 'Baitullah, Ambassador Azizuddin and BB's Assassins', Editorial, *Daily Times*, 22 April 2008.
17. BBC Urdu Service, 20 April 2008.
18. 'Baitullah, Ambassador Azizuddin and BB's Assassins', Editorial, *Daily Times*, 22 April 2008.
19. 'Troops Storm Pakistan Red Mosque', Associated Press, 10 July 2007. Also see 'Army Shows Huge Cache of "Recovered" Arms', *The News*, 13 July 2007.
20. 'Madrassa Registers to Clear Ambiguity' *Gulf Times*, 18 July 2007.
21. 'Al-Qaida Video Calls for War against Pakistan and Musharraf', *Guardian*, 12 August 2008.
22. Matthew Lee, 'US State Department Says Terror Attacks Increase in Afghanistan, Pakistan as Al-Qaida Gains', Associated Press, 30 April 2008.
23. International Crisis Group, 'The State of Sectarianism in Pakistan', Asia Report, no. 95, April 2005.
24. Interview with the author, July 1999.
25. Rahimullah Yusufzai, 'Islami Jirga Sets TV and VCRs on Fire in Mardan', *The News*, 19 February 2001, p.10.
26. International Crisis Group, 'The State of Sectarianism', April 2005.
27. Richard Kurin, 'A View from the Countryside', pp. 115–27 in Anita M. Weiss (ed.), *Islamic Reassertion in Pakistan*, Vanguard, Lahore, 1987.
28. Mohammed Hanif, BBC, 'From Our Own Correspondent', 8 November 2008
29. Joshua T. White, *Pakistan's Islamist Frontier: Islamic Politics and US Policy in Pakistan's North-West Frontier*, Religion & Security Monograph Series, no.1, Center on Faith & International Affairs, Arlington, VA, 2008, p. 39.
30. After 9/11 the MMA won sufficient support to form the provincial government in NWFP. Its electoral base, however, became increasingly disillusioned. As well as two factions of the JUI, the other parties in the MMA were Jamaat-e-Islami, the Barelvis'

Jamaat Ulema-e-Pakistan, the Wahabi Jamiat Ahl e-Hadith and the Shias' Islami Tehrik-e-Pakistan. Joshua T. White, *Pakistan's Islamist Frontier: Islamic Politics and US Policy in Pakistan's North-West Frontier*, Religion & Security Monograph Series, no.1, Center on Faith & International Affairs, Arlington, VA, 2008, p. 48.

31. Khalid Rahman et al. (eds), *Jama'at-e-Islami and National and International Politics*, vol. 2, Bookmakers, Islamabad, 1999, p. xviii.

32. There are many ways to spell Maududi's name. I am using the spelling preferred by Jamaat-e-Islami in its own website.

33. Afzal Iqbal, *Islamisation of Pakistan*, Vanguard, Lahore, 1986, p. 25.

34. Akbar S. Ahmed, *Jinnah, Pakistan and Islamic Identity: The Search for Saladin*, Routledge, London, 1997, p. 175.

35. Hamid Khan, *Constitutional and Political History of Pakistan*, Oxford University Press, Oxford, 2001, p. 100.

36. Ibid., p. 92.

37. Mohammed Ayub Khan, *Friends Not Masters*, Oxford University Press, Karachi, 1967, p. 209.

38. Ibid., p. 203.

39. White, *Pakistan's Islamist Frontier*, p. 28.

40. Ibid., p. 37.

41. Ibid., p. 106.

42. Hamid Ali, *Martial Law Orders & Regulations*, Ideal Publishers, Karachi, 1980.

43. Anita M. Weiss (ed.), *Islamic Reassertion in Pakistan*, Vanguard, Lahore, 1987, p. 11.

44. Interview with the author, London, September 2007.

45. Interview with the author, Lahore, April 2008.

46. Quoted in Hasan-Askari Rizvi, *The Military and Politics in Pakistan: 1947–1986*, Progressive Publishers, Lahore, 1987, p. 40.

47. Lawrence Ziring, *Pakistan in the Twentieth Century: A Political History*, Oxford University Press, Karachi, 1997, p. 86.

48. Ainslie T. Embree (ed.), *Pakistan's Western Borderlands*, Vikas, New Delhi, 1985, p. 24.

49. The Oxus river marks Afghanistan's northern border with the former Soviet Union (now Tajikistan). Attock is a town on the Indus river just 100 kilometres west of Islamabad.

50. Quoted in Selig S. Harrison, *In Afghanistan's Shadow: Baloch Nationalism and Soviet Temptations*, Carnegie Endowment for International Peace, New York, 1981, p.144.

51. Imtiaz Gul, 'Pakistan Army Told to Plan Fence and Mines along Afghan Border', *Guardian*, 27 December 2006.

52. 'Durand Line Serves as Line of Hate: Karzai', *Frontier Post*, 18 February 2006.

53. The incoming government of Yousaf Gilani in 2008 said it would review the FCR with a view to abolishing it.

54. International Crisis Group, 'Pakistan's Tribal Areas: Appeasing the Militants', *Asia Report*, no.125, 11 December 2006, p. 9.

55. Francis (Tim) Stockdale, *Walk Warily in Waziristan*, Arthur H. Stockwell Ltd, Devon, 1982.

56. Norwegian Refugee Council, *Pakistan*, Global IDP project, 3 September 2004, p. 2.

57. International Crisis Group, *Pakistan's Tribal Areas*, p. 15.

58. Sami Yousafzai and Ron Moreau, 'A Jihad Between Neighbours', *Newsweek*, 2 June 2008.

59. International Crisis Group, *Pakistan's Tribal Areas*, p. 23.

60. Hassan Abbas, 'Increasing Talibanization in Pakistan's Seven Tribal Agencies', *Terrorism Monitor*, vol. 5, issue 18, Jamestown Foundation, 27 September 2007.

61. Hassan Abbas, 'Is the NWFP Slipping out of Pakistan's Control?', *Terrorism Monitor*, vol. 5, issue 22, Jamestown Foundation, 26 November 2007.

62. Jane Perlez, 'Frontier Insurgency Spills into Peshawar', *New York Times*, 18 January 2008.

63. Munir Ahmed, 'Taliban Leader Urges Halt to Attacks', *Fortnightly Khaleej Islamabad*, 25 April 2008.

64. Yousaf Raza Gilani, 'Pakistan's Moment', *Washington Post*, 30 April 2008.

65. Paul Tighe and Khalid Qayum, 'Pakistan Will Use Army to Combat Terrorism Threat Gilani Says', *Bloomberg*, 27 May 2008.

66. Eric Schmitt and Mark Mazzetti, 'Bush Said to Give Orders Allowing Raids in Pakistan', *New York Times*, 11 September 2008.

67. *National Intelligence Estimate: The Terrorist Threat to the US Homeland*, Office of the Director of National Intelligence, Washington DC, July 2007, http://www.dni.gov/press_releases/20070717_release.pdf.

68. Ismail Khan and Carlota Gall, 'Battle of Bajur: A Critical Test of Pakistan's Daunted Military', *New York Times*, 23 September 2008.

69. Simon Cameron-Moore, 'Pakistan Says 1,000 Militants Killed in Bajur Campaign', Reuters, 26 September 2008.

70. Khan and Gall, 'Battle of Bajur'.

71. 'Kayani Vows to Eliminate Militants from Bajur', *The News*, 29 September 2008.

72. 'Pakistani Tribesmen Stand Up Against Militias', Associated Press, 11 October 2008.

73. See, for example, '18 Militants Killed in Bajur', *Dawn*, 14 October 2008.

74. 'Dir Jirga Agrees to Raise Lashkar Against Militants', *The News*, 22 September 2008.

75. Saeed Shah, 'Pakistani Tribesmen Organize to Fight Taliban Insurgents', *McClatchy Newspapers*, 26 September 2008.

76. 'Pakistani Tribesmen Stand Up Against Militias', Associated Press, 11 October 2008.

77. Qazi Jawadullah and Pir Zubair Shah, 'Bomber Strikes Anti-Taliban Meeting, Killing More Than 40', *New York Times*, 11 October 2008.

78. Jane Perlez, 'Widower of Bhutto Takes Office in Pakistan', *New York Times*, 10 September 2008.

79. Fasih Ahmed, 'Can Pakistan Stay Afloat?', *Newsweek*, 10 October 2008.

80. 'President Zardari Calls for $100 bn Grant from World Community', *The News*, 5 October 2008.

81. BBC News Pakistan asks IMF for rescue loan. http://news.bbc.co.uk/1/hi/world/south_asia/7730943.stm

82. Syed Shoaib Hasan, 'Changing Ways of Pakistan's Militants', BBC News Website, 6 February 2008, http://news.bbc.co.uk/1/hi/world/south_asia/7228864.stm.

83. Kathy Gannon, 'Al Qaeda Influence Apparent in Groups in Pakistan', Associated Press, 26 October 2008.

84. Author interview with senior military officer, Peshawar, April 2008.

85. Ismail Khan, 'Omar Threatens to Intensify War: Talks with Karzai Govt Ruled Out', *Dawn*, 4 January 2007.

86. B. Raman, 'After Baitullah What?', Rediff.com, 2 October 2008.

87. Hassan Abbas, 'A Profile of Tehrik-i-Taliban Pakistan', *CTC Sentinel*, vol. 1, issue 2, West Point, January 2008.

88. Bernard Gwertzman, 'Is a Pakistan Truce Good for the United States?', Interview with David Markey, Council for Foreign Relations, New York, 22 May 2008.

89. Ahmed Rashid, *Descent into Chaos: How the War Against Islamic Extremism is Being Lost in Pakistan, Afghanistan and Central Asia*, Allen Lane, London, 2008.

90. Ahmed Rashid, 'Taking Back the Frontier', *Washington Post*, 4 May 2008.

91. White, *Pakistan's Islamist Frontier*, p. 60.

CHAPTER TWO: NATIONALISM

1. The quotation comes from an interview Altaf Hussain gave to the *Herald* in October 2000. The numbers are somewhat wayward but his point is nonetheless clear. His description of partition as a great mistake was first made in his speech at Acton Hall, London, 17 September 2000.

2. This remark, made by Akbar Bugti Khan in an interview with the author in March 1999, is similar to one made by the prominent Pukhtoon leader, Wali Khan. Wali Khan's comment is quoted in Akbar S. Ahmed, 'Tribes, Regional Pressures and Nationhood', in Victoria Schofield (ed.), *Old Roads and New Highways: Fifty Years of Pakistan*, Oxford University Press, Karachi, 1997, p. 141.

3. Strictly, all those who moved to Pakistan at the time of partition can be described as Mohajirs – the word means refugee.

4. Quoted in Akbar S. Ahmed, *Jinnah, Pakistan and Islamic Identity: The Search for Saladin*, Routledge, London, 1997, p. 236.

5. These are the opening words of Ayub Khan's memorandum entitled 'A Short Appreciation of the Present and Future Problems of Pakistan', written on 4 October 1954. It is reproduced in full in Hasan Askari Rizvi, *The Military and Politics in Pakistan: 1947–1986*, Progressive Publishers, Lahore, 1987, p. 265.

6. Rizvi, *Military and Politics*, p. 283.

7. Quoted in Selig S. Harrison, *In Afghanistan's Shadow: Baloch Nationalism and Soviet Temptations*, Carnegie Endowment for International Peace, New York, 1981, p.156.

8. Ibid., pp. 150–51.

9. International Crisis Group, 'Devolution in Pakistan: Reform or Regression?', *Asia Report*, no. 77, Islamabad and Brussels, 22 March 2004.

10. Mohammed Ayub Khan, *Friends Not Masters*, Oxford University Press, Karachi, 1967, p. 93.

11. Andrew Wilder, *The Pakistani Voter*, Oxford University Press, Karachi, 1990, p. 59.

12. Tariq Rahman, *Language and Politics in Pakistan*, Oxford University Press, Karachi, 1996, p. 111.

13. G.M. Syed, *A Case for Sindu Desh*, Sorath Publication, Bombay, 1985, p. 11.

14. Feroz Ahmed, *Ethnicity and Politics in Pakistan*, Oxford Pakistan Paperbacks, Oxford University Press, Karachi, 1999, p. 110.

15. Rahman, *Language and Politics*, p. 114.

16. Syed, *A Case for Sindu Desh*, pp. 4, 5, 38.

17. Tahir Amin, *Ethno-National Movements of Pakistan*, Institute of Policy Studies, Islamabad, 1988, p. 75.

18. Anita M. Weiss and S. Zulfiqar Gilani (eds), *Power and Civil Society in Pakistan*, Oxford University Press, Karachi, 2001, p. 200.

19. Ahmed, 'Tribes, Regional Pressures and Nationhood', p. 147.

20. *Herald*, September 1987, p. 131.

21. See front-page stories in *Dawn* from 8 to 17 July 1972.

22. Syed, *A Case for Sindu Desh*, p. 77.

23. Ian Talbot, *Pakistan: A Modern History*, Vanguard Books, Lahore, 1999, p. 254.

24. See Seyyed Vali Reza Nasr, 'State, Society, and the Crisis of National Identity', chapter 5 in Rasul Bakhsh Rais (ed.), *State, Society and Democratic Change in Pakistan*, Oxford University Press, Karachi, 1997, p. 122.

25. Roedad Khan, *A Dream Gone Sour*, Oxford University Press, Karachi, 1998, pp. 89–90.

26. Ahmed, *Ethnicity and Politics*, p. 123.

27. *Herald*, September 1987, p. 130.

28. Altaf Hussain has himself given the date of March 1984 for the founding of the MQM, although the party could not be formally registered until January 1986 after General Zia lifted martial law. See his interview in the *Herald*, September 1997, p. 32.

29. This account of 14 December 1986 is drawn from contemporaneous accounts in the Pakistani press. The fullest is in the *Herald*, January 1987, pp. 38–52 and 60.
30. Rahman, *Language and Politics*, pp. 121 and 130.
31. *Herald*, March 1987, p. 30.
32. *Herald*, September 1997, p. 32.
33. *Herald Annual*, January 1993, pp. 129 and 130.
34. *Herald*, November 1989, p. 51.
35. Amnesty International, *Pakistan: Human Rights in Karachi*, ASA, 33/01/96, February 1996.
36. At the time of writing, July 2009, he is still there.
37. *Herald Annual*, January 1996, p. 54.
38. *Herald*, August 1995, p. 25.
39. 'Karachi Resurgent', a *Herald* handout, June 2000. The *Herald* got its figures from the Sindh Home Department.
40. International Crisis Group, 'Elections, Democracy and Stability in Pakistan', *Asia Report*, no. 137, 31 July 2007.
41. Mian Ata Rabbani, *I Was the Quaid's ADC*, Oxford University Press, Karachi, 1996, p. 150.
42. See, for example, Lt Colonel Syed Iqbal Ahmed, *Balochistan: Its Strategic Importance*, Royal Book Company, Karachi, 1992.
43. For Z.A. Bhutto's account of this affair see Roedad Khan (ed.), *The American Papers: Secret and Confidential Documents India–Pakistan–Bangladesh, 1965–1973*, Oxford University Press, Karachi, 1999, p. 888.
44. Harrison, *In Afghanistan's Shadow*, p. 3. Ian Talbot also estimates the Pakistani force at 80,000 – Talbot, *Pakistan*, p. 224.
45. Harrison, *In Afghanistan's Shadow*, p. 38.
46. Brian Cloughley, *A History of the Pakistan Army: Wars and Insurrections*, Oxford University Press, Karachi, 2000, p. 361.
47. Talbot, *Pakistan*, p. 226.
48. Carnegie Endowment for International Peace, *Pakistan: The Resurgence of Baluch Nationalism*, Carnegie Paper no. 65, January 2006, p. 5.
49. *Herald*, December 2000.
50. Carnegie Endowment for International Peace, *Pakistan*, p. 4.
51. Owais Tohid, 'Will Rising Baloch Nationalism Undermine Pakistan's War on Terror?', *Christian Science Monitor*, 26 January 2005. www.csmonitor.com/2005/0126/p07s01-wosc.html.
52. International Crisis Group, *Pakistan: The Forgotten Conflict in Balochistan*, Asia Briefing, no. 69, Islamabad and Brussels, 22 October 2007.
53. Interview with the author, November 2004.
54. Interview with Ataullah Mengal available on http://www.paklinks.com/gs/pakistan-affairs/209696-interview-sardar-mengal.html.
55. Human Rights Commission of Pakistan, *Fact Finding Mission December 2005–January 2006, Conflict in Balochistan*, p. 10.
56. Carnegie Endowment for International Peace, *Pakistan*, p. 3.
57. BBC News, 12 January 2005, http://news.bbc.co.uk/1/hi/world/south_asia/4167299.stm.
58. Human Rights Commission of Pakistan, *Fact Finding Mission*, p. 30.
59. Aamer Ahmed Khan, 'Balochistan "peace has collapsed"', BBC News, Karachi, 10 May 2005, http://newswww.bbc.net.uk/1/low/world/south_asia/4534219.stm.
60. Human Rights Commission of Pakistan, *Fact Finding Mission*, p. 32.
61. Tarique Niazi, 'Baloch Insurgents Escalate Attacks on Infrastructure', *Terrorism Focus*, Jamestown Foundation, 23 May 2006.
62. Human Rights Commission of Pakistan, *Fact Finding Mission*, p. 35.

63. Saleem Shahid, 'Bugti Killed in Operation: Six Officers Among 21 Security Personnel Dead', *Dawn*, 27 August 2006.

64. Interview with Ataullah Mengal, June 2004, available on http://www.paklinks.com/gs/pakistan-affairs/209696-interview-sardar-mengal.html.

CHAPTER THREE: KASHMIR

1.   *Throughout this chapter I shall use the word Kashmir to refer to the State of Jammu and Kashmir. I shall make it clear when I am referring to the more limited area of the Vale of Kashmir or Kashmir Valley.*

2.   Chaudri Muhammed Ali, *The Emergence of Pakistan*, Research Society of Pakistan, Lahore, 10th impression, 1998 p. 297.

3.   Karan Singh, *Autobiography*, Oxford University Press, Delhi, 1994, p. 31.

4.   Larry Collins and Dominique Lapierre, *Freedom at Midnight*, HarperCollins, London, 1997, p. 191.

5.   Patrick French, *Liberty or Death: India's Journey to Independence and Division*, HarperCollins, London, 1997, p. 373.

6.   Alastair Lamb, *Kashmir: A Disputed Legacy 1846–1990*, Oxford University Press, Karachi, 1991 p. 88.

7.   Sumantra Bose, *The Challenge in Kashmir: Democracy, Self-Determination and a Just Peace*, Sage, New Delhi, 1997, p. 24.

8.   Singh, *Autobiography*, p. 20.

9.   Collins and Lapierre, *Freedom at Midnight*, p. 257.

10. Ali, *Emergence of Pakistan*, p. 286.

11. Prem Shankar Jha, *Kashmir 1947: Rival Versions of History*, Oxford University Press, Delhi, 1998, p. 38.

12. He also had to demarcate the new boundary in Bengal.

13. Ali, *Emergence of Pakistan*, p. 202.

14. Christopher Beaumont, interview with BBC Radio 4, in the programme *Document: A Judge Remembers*, 22 September 1994.

15. See for example Jha, *Kashmir 1947*, pp. 74–82.

16. Ali, *Emergence of Pakistan*, p. 216.

17. Lamb, *Kashmir*, p. 111.

18. Collins and Lapierre, *Freedom at Midnight*, p. 355.

19. His testimony is reproduced in Jha, *Kashmir 1947*, p. 143.

20. Lamb, *Kashmir*, p.110.

21. Singh, *Autobiography*, p. 80.

22. Akbar S. Ahmed, *Jinnah, Pakistan and Islamic Identity: The Search for Saladin*, Routledge, London, 1997, p. 116.

23. Hasan Zaheer, *The Rawalpindi Conspiracy 1951*, Oxford University Press, Karachi, 1998, p. 63.

24. Victoria Schofield, *Kashmir in Conflict: India, Pakistan and the Unfinished Conflict*, I.B. Taurus, London, 2000, p. 46.

25. Ijaz Hussain, *Kashmir Dispute: An International Law Perspective*, Quaid-e-Azam University, Rawalpindi, 1998, p. 112. For a very full account of who in Pakistan knew what about the tribal invasion, see Andrew Whitehead, *A Mission in Kashmir*, Penguin, Delhi, 2007, pp. 52–64.

26. Schofield, *Kashmir in Conflict*, p. 51.

27. Singh, *Autobiography*, p. 57.

28. Sherbaz Khan Mazari, *A Journey to Disillusionment*, Oxford University Press, Karachi, 1999, pp. 11 and 12.

29. Jha, *Kashmir 1947*, pp. 133–8.

30. This is now accepted by historians from both sides of the debate. See Jha, *Kashmir 1947*, pp. 133–8.

31. Lamb, *Kashmir*, p.135.
32. Andrew Whitehead, *A Mission in Kashmir*, Penguin, Delhi, 2007, pp. 108–21.
33. Jha, *Kashmir 1947*, p. 62.
34. Whitehead, *A Mission in Kashmir*, pp. 255 n29.
35. Stanley Wolpert, *Jinnah of Pakistan*, Oxford University Press, New York, 1984, p.13.
36. Whitehead, *A Mission in Kashmir*, p.120.
37. Schofield, *Kashmir in Conflict*, p. 63.
38. Zaheer, *Rawalpindi Conspiracy 1951*, p. 149.
39. Ali, *Emergence of Pakistan*, p. 299.
40. Zaheer, *Rawalpindi Conspiracy 1951*, pp. 55 and 56.
41. Ali, *Emergence of Pakistan*, p. 305.
42. Lamb, *Kashmir*, p.189.
43. Mohammad Ayub Khan, *Friends Not Masters: A Political Autobiography*, Oxford University Press, Karachi, 1967, p. 242.
44. Roedad Khan (ed.), *The American Papers: Secret and Confidential India- Pakistan- Bangladesh Documents, 1965-1973*, Oxford University Press, Karachi, 1999, p. 82.
45. Stanley Wolpert, *Zulfi Bhutto of Pakistan: His Life and Times*, Oxford University Press, New York, 1993, p. 78.
46. Major General (retd) Shaukat Riza, *The Pakistan Army War 1965*, Services Book Club, Lahore, 1984, p. 19.
47. Riza, *Pakistan Army War 1965*, p. 82.
48. Wolpert, *Zulfi Bhutto*, p. 88.
49. Brigadier (retd) Z.A. Khan, *The Way it Was*, Ahbab, Karachi, 1998, pp. 155 and 156.
50. Wolpert, *Zulfi Bhutto*, p. 90.
51. Brian Cloughley, *A History of the Pakistan Army: Wars and Insurrections*, Oxford University Press, Karachi, 2000, pp. 70 and 71.
52. Khan (ed.), *American Papers*, p. 35.
53. Riza, *Pakistan Army War 1965*, p. 192.
54. Lamb, *Kashmir*, p. 267.
55. Schofield, *Kashmir in Conflict*, p. 118.
56. Hussain, *Kashmir Dispute*, p. 157. Some Pakistani versions of the Simla Agreement – strangely, including the one given in Ijaz Hussain's index – omit this part of the text.
57. Lamb, *Kashmir*, p. 307.
58. Interview with JKLF leader Amanullah Khan, 12 October 2001.
59. ICG, 'Kashmir: The View from Srinagar', *ICG Asia Report*, no. 41, 21 November 2002, footnote 4.
60. 'Alliance Closes on Key City', *Guardian*, 9 November 2001.
61. US Department of State, *India: Country Report on Human Rights Practices for 1996-2000*.
62. US Department of State, *India: Country Report on Human Rights Practices for 1998*.
63. Bose, *The Challenge in Kashmir*, p. 71.
64. For a good analysis see 'Kashmir: The View from Srinagar', *Asia Report*, no. 41, 21 November 2002.
65. 'Karnal Sher Revives Spirit of Martyrdom', *The News*, 18 July 1999.
66. www.rediff.com/news/1999/jul/16akd1.htm.
67. 'Enemy Mounting Pressure', *Dawn*, 4 October 2001.
68. Executive Summary of the Kargil Review Committee Report, p. 4. Available at http://alfa.nic.in/rs/general/25indi1.htm.
69. Syed Ali Dayan Hasan, 'Double Jeopardy', *The Herald*, July 2000, p. 26.
70. Hassan Abbas, *Pakistan's Drift into Extremism*, M.E. Sharpe, New York, 2005, p. 170.
71. Cabinet minister interview with the author, December 1999.
72. Rajeev Sharma, *Pak Proxy War: A Story of ISI, Bin Laden and Kargil*, Kaveri Books, Delhi, 1999, p. 9.

73. Vinod Anand, *India's Response to the Kargil Aggression*, Institute for Defence Studies and Analyses, www.idsa-india.org.
74. Quotes and details of back-channel diplomacy from an interview with Niaz Naik, January 2000.
75. Sharma, *Pak Proxy War*, p. 30.
76. Major General Y. Bahl (ed.), *Kargil Blunder: Pakistan's Plight, India's Victory*, Manas Publications, Delhi, 2000. See chapter 11 by Air Commodore (retd) N.B. Singh, p. 162.
77. M.J. Akbar, *Kargil: Cross Border Terrorism*, Mittal Publications, Delhi, 1999, p. 179.
78. Yadav, interview with *Hindustan Times*, 17 August 1999.
79. For an account of the fighting see the Indian press on 5 July – for example, *Indian Express*, 5 July 1999.
80. Bruce Riedel, *American Diplomacy and the 1999 Kargil Summit at Blair House*, Policy Paper Series, 2002. Center for the Advanced Study of India, University of Pennsylvania.
81. Ibid.
82. Anand, *India's Response to the Kargil Aggression*.
83. Cloughley, *A History of the Pakistan Army*, p. 388.
84. Interview with Brigadier (retd) Shaukat Qadir, November 2001.
85. Hasan, *Double Jeopardy*, p. 36.
86. Sharma, *Pak Proxy War*, p. 49.
87. Ibid., p. 24.
88. Interview with the author, October 2001.
89. Interview with the author, March 2001.
90. 'Kashmir Only Dispute between India and Pakistan', *The News*, 5 February 2002.
91. Robert G. Wirsing, *Kashmir in the Shadow of War*, M.E. Sharpe, New York, 2003, p.29.
92. 'The Agra Summit and Thereafter', *The Hindu*, 31 July 2001.
93. Pervez Musharraf, *In the Line of Fire*, Free Press, New York, 2006, p. 301.
94. From the President's Desk, http://generalpervaizmusharraf.com.
95. A.G. Noorani, 'The Truth about Agra', *Frontline*, issue 15, July 2005.
96. 'Musharraf to Blame for Summit Failure', *The Hindu*, 27 September 2006.
97. Steve Coll, 'The Stand Off: A Reporter at Large', *New Yorker*, 13 February 2006.
98. '12 Dead in Attack on Indian Parliament', *Guardian*, 13 December 2001.
99. 'A Decisive Battle Has to Take Place', *The Hindu*, 14 December 2001.
100. Excerpts from Musharraf's speech can be found on http://news.bbc.co.uk/2/hi/south_asia/1757251.stm.
101. The acid attack was actually claimed by an organisation calling itself Lashkar e-Jabbar, but previous to the attack Lashkar e-Toiba had put up posters warning women to wear the burqa or face the consequences. Interestingly, Hizb ul-Mujahideen ordered the posters to be removed. It was widely believed in militant circles that Lashkar e-Jabbar was a cover name for Lashkar-e-Toiba.
102. 'Inside Jihad', *Newsline*, February 2001, p. 32.
103. See Musharraf's speech highlights, http://news.bbc.co.uk/2/hi/south_asia/1757251.stm.
104. Coll, 'The Stand Off'.
105. Glenn Kessler, 'A Defining Moment in Islamabad', *Washington Post*, 22 June 2002.
106. 'Kashmiri Militants Angry at being Blocked from India', *New York Times*, 9 June 2002.
107. 'Pakistan Allows Kashmir Raids, Militants Say', *New York Times*, 19 September 2002.
108. MORI, *Kashmir's Political Future: Survey of Opinions of the Adult Population of Jammu and Kashmir*, May 2002, MORI/16827.LMV.
109. ICG, *Kashmir: the View from Srinagar*, p. 1.
110. Strobe Talbott, *Engaging India*, Brookings Institution, Washington, 2006, p. 106.
111. ICG, 'Kashmir: The View From Islamabad', *ICG Asia Report*, no. 68, 4 December 2003, p. 19.

112. *The Independent*, 19 December 2003.
113. ICG, *India, Pakistan and Kashmir: Stabilising a Cold Peace*, Asia Briefing, no. 51, Islamabad/Brussels, 15 June 2006, pp. 2 and 4.
114. Robert Wirsing, *Pakistan and the United States 2004–2005: Deepening the Entente*, Asia Center for Security Studies, February 2005, p. 3.
115. Author interview with a senior Pakistani military official, January 2007.
116. Author interviews with former militants, Rawalpindi, January 2007.
117. General Musharraf interview with ND-TV, December 2006.
118. All of Kasuri's remarks about a possible deal on Kashmir are taken from CNBC-TV, Khurshid Kasuri interview with Karen Thapar. The full transcript is on www.moneycontrol.com/india/news/politics/india-pak-had-almost-agreed-kashmir-khurshid-kasuri/386235.
119. Musharraf, *In the Line of Fire*, p. 304.
120. 'The Times of India Officials Dismiss Kasuri's claims on Kashmir, Sir Creek', 20 February 2009.
121. CNBC-TV Omar Abdullah interview with Karen Thapar. Full transcript is on http://ibnlive.in.com/news/independence-not-viable-for-kashmir-omar-abdullah/73068-3-single.html.
122. Steve Coll, 'The Back Channel', *The New Yorker*, 2 March 2009.
123. Coll, *The Stand Off*.
124. Baroness Nicholson of Winterbourne, *Draft Report on Kashmir: Present Situation and future prospects*, Committee on Foreign Affairs of the European Parliament, 2 November 2006.
125. 'Soldiers Killed in Kashmir Blast', http://news.bbc.co.uk/1/hi/world/south_asia/7515458.stm.
126. 'Rivals Trade Blame over Kashmir', http://news.bbc.co.uk/1/hi/world/south_asia/7529432.stm.
127. Bret Stephens, 'The Most Difficult Job in the World', *Wall Street Journal*, 4 October 2008.

CHAPTER FOUR: BANGLADESH

1. *Hamoodur Rehman Commission Report*, part IV, chapter XII, para. 16, *Dawn*, 24 January 2001, p.23. The Commission was set up by Zulfikar Ali Bhutto to investigate the events of 1971, and in particular, why the Pakistan army surrendered. The Commission's report came in two stages. The main report was finished by July 1972 but not published until 2000. The supplementary report, which relies on evidence from some of the main Pakistani participants such as General Niazi, was completed in 1974 and also published in 2000. For both, see successive copies of *Dawn* from 8 January to 1 February 2001 inclusive.
2. Interview with an eyewitness, June 2001.
3. Major General (retd) Shaukat Riza, *The Pakistan Army 1966–1971*, Army Education Press, Lahore, 1990, p. 83.
4. Richard Sisson and Leo E. Rose, *War and Secession: Pakistan, India and the Creation of Bangladesh*, Oxford University Press, Karachi, 1990, p. 57.
5. Hasan Zaheer, *The Separation of East Pakistan: The Rise and Realization of Bengali Muslim Nationalism*, Oxford University Press, Karachi, 1995, p. 6.
6. K.K. Aziz, for example, argues that under the All Indian Muslim League Constitution, the All India Muslim League Legislators' Convention had no such right. Any amendment could only be made by a full session of the All India Muslim League itself. See K.K. Aziz, *The Murder of History: A Critique of History Textbooks Used in Pakistan*, Vanguard, Lahore, 1993, p. 147.
7. Anwar Dil and Afia Dil, *Bengali Language Movement to Bangladesh*, Ferozons, Lahore, 2000, p. 62.

8. Hasan Zaheer, *The Separation of East Pakistan, The Rise and Realization of Bengali Muslim Nationalism*, Oxford University Press, Karachi, 1995, p. 10.
9. Dil and Dil, *Bengali Language Movement*, p. 68.
10. Strictly speaking Pakistan's eastern wing should be referred to as East Bengal until 1956 when it was renamed East Pakistan. For the sake of clarity, however, I shall use the term East Pakistan throughout the text. Similarly I shall refer to the western wing as West Pakistan.
11. Dil and Dil, *Bengali Language Movement*, p. 82.
12. Ibid., p. 82.
13. For an account of the riots see Lawrence Ziring, *Pakistan in the Twentieth Century: A Political History*, Oxford University Press, Karachi, 1997, p. 130.
14. Dil and Dil, *Bengali Language Movement*, p. 92.
15. Zaheer, *Separation of East Pakistan*, p. 35.
16. It is quoted in full in Riza, *Pakistan Army*, p. 215.
17. This figure and those that follow have been collated by Hasan-Askari Rizvi. See Hasan-Askari Rizvi, *The Military and Politics in Pakistan: 1947–1986*, Progressive Publishers, Lahore, 1987, p. 137ff.
18. Sisson and Rose, *War and Secession*, p. 10.
19. Riza, *Pakistan Army*, pp. 32 and 33.
20. This is a summary. A full version can be found in *Hamoodur Rehman Commission Report*, part I, chapter V, para. 18, *Dawn*, 10 January 2001 p. 24. In subsequent years there were revised versions of the Six Points, but the essential demands always remained the same.
21. Zaheer, *Separation of East Pakistan*, p. 144.
22. G.W. Choudhury, *The Last Days of United Pakistan*, Oxford University Press, Karachi, 1993, p. 15.
23. Larry Collins and Dominique Lapierre, *Freedom at Midnight*, HarperCollins, London, 1997, p. 159.
24. Siddiq Salik, *Witness to Surrender*, Oxford University Press, Karachi, 1977, p. 3.
25. Roedad Khan (ed.), *The American Papers: Secret and Confidential India–Pakistan–Bangladesh Documents, 1965–1973*, Oxford University Press, Oxford, 1999, p. 274.
26. Herbert Feldman, *The End and the Beginning: Pakistan 1969–1971*, Oxford University Press, Karachi, 1976, p. 67.
27. Choudhury, *Last Days*, p. 85.
28. *Hamoodur Rehman Commission Report*, part I, chapter VI, para 96, *Dawn*, 13 January 2001, p. 21.
29. *Hamoodur Rehman Commission Report*, part I, chapter VI, para. 26, *Dawn*, 11 January 2001, p. 22.
30. Salik, *Witness to Surrender*, p. 32.
31. Zaheer, *Separation of East Pakistan*, p. 134. See also Sisson and Rose, *War and Secession*, p. 63.
32. Choudhury, *Last Days*, p. 149.
33. Ibid., p. 146.
34. Lieutenant General A. A. K. Niazi, *The Betrayal of East Pakistan*, Oxford Pakistan Paperbacks, Karachi, 1999, pp. xxiv and xxv.
35. Salik, *Witness to Surrender*, p. 36.
36. Khan (ed.), *American Papers*, p. 466.
37. Ziring, *Pakistan in the Twentieth Century*, p. 334.
38. Sisson and Rose, *War and Secession*, p. 81.
39. Zaheer, *Separation of East Pakistan*, p. 41.
40. Sisson and Rose, *War and Secession*, p. 85.
41. Khan (ed.), *American Papers*, p. 497.
42. *Dawn*, 27 March 1971, p. 1.

43. *Hamoodur Rehman Commission Report*, part VI, chapter VI, para. 81, *Dawn*, 13 January 2001, p. 22.
44. Salik, *Witness to Surrender*, p. 76.
45. *Hamoodur Rehman Commission Report*, part I, chapter VI, para. 11, *Dawn*, 19 January 2001, p. 21.
46. *Hamoodur Rehman Commission Report*, supplement, part V, chapter 1, para. 11, 6 February 2001, p. 15.
47. Riza, *Pakistan Army*, p. 103.
48. Zaheer, *Separation of East Pakistan*, p. 201.
49. *Hamoodur Rehman Commission Report*, supplement, part V, chapter II, paras 12–17, *Dawn*, 6 February 2001, p. 16.
50. *Hamoodur Rehman Commission Report*, supplement, part V, chapter II, paras 2–6, *Dawn*, 6 February 2001, p. 16.
51. Niazi, *Betrayal of East Pakistan*, p. 42.
52. See, for example, Henry Kissinger, *The White House Years*, Weidenfeld & Nicolson and Michael Joseph, London 1979, and Zaheer, *Separation of East Pakistan*, pp. 237–73.
53. Rizvi, *Military and Politics*, p. 190.
54. Brian Cloughley, *A History of the Pakistan Army: Wars and Insurrections*, Oxford University Press, Karachi, 2000, p. 183.
55. For the various estimates see Niazi, *Betrayal of East Pakistan*, p. 112; *Hamoodur Rehman Commission Report*, part I, chapter II, para. 1, *Dawn*, 8 January 2001, p. 15; and Lt General J.F.R. Jacob, *Surrender at Dacca: Birth of a Nation*, Manohar Publishers, Delhi, 1997, p. 157.
56. Niazi, *Betrayal of East Pakistan*, p. 78.
57. Ibid., p. 85.
58. See, for example, *Hamoodur Rehman Commission Report*, part IV, chapter IV, para. 22, *Dawn*, 18 January 2001, p. 21.
59. Cloughley, *History of the Pakistan Army*, p. 208.
60. Salik, *Witness to Surrender*, p. 128.
61. Jacob, *Surrender at Dacca*, p. 56.
62. Niazi, *Betrayal of East Pakistan*, p. xxv.
63. Ibid., pp. 198–200.
64. *Hamoodur Rehman Commission Report*, supplement, part II, chapter IV, para. 8, *Dawn*, 4 February 2001, p. 24.
65. *Hamoodur Rehman Commission Report*, supplement, part V, chapter III, para. 7, *Dawn*, 7 February 2001, p. 23.
66. The letters are reproduced in Riza, *Pakistan Army*, pp. 160–61.
67. *Hamoodur Rehman Commission Report*, supplement, part IV, chapter II, paras 19–20, *Dawn*, 4 February 2001, p. 24.
68. Niazi, *Betrayal of East Pakistan*, p. 211.
69. Jacob, *Surrender at Dacca*, p. 129.
70. Salik, *Witness to Surrender*, p. 206.
71. *Hamoodur Rehman Commission Report*, supplement, part IV, chapter II, para. 38, *Dawn*, 5 February 2001, p. 24.
72. Jacob, *Surrender at Dacca*, p. 142.
73. Niazi, *Betrayal of East Pakistan*, p. 235.
74. *Hamoodur Rehman Commission Report*, supplement, part IV, chapter II, para. 11, *Dawn*, 4 February 2001, p. 24.
75. Full text in Jacob, *Surrender at Dacca*, p. 176.
76. Niazi, *Betrayal of East Pakistan*, pp. 194 and 211.
77. Salik, *Witness to Surrender*, p. 213.
78. *Hamoodur Rehman Commission Report*, supplement. There are references to Niazi throughout the supplement.

79.   *Hamoodur Rehman Commission Report*, supplement, part V, chapter IV, para. 33, *Dawn*, 8 February 2001, p.8.

CHAPTER FIVE: THE BOMB

Many of those who know about Pakistan's nuclear weapons programme are unable to speak about it openly. Both in Pakistan and in the West many interviewees requested anonymity. Unless otherwise stated in subsequent footnotes, this chapter relies on interviews with these Western and Pakistani officials conducted between April 1998 and February 2001.

1.   As so often with famous quotations, there is some uncertainty as to the actual words used by Z.A. Bhutto in 1965. The version given here has appeared many times in Pakistani literature. George Perkovich, however, has found a contemporaneous account, in the *Manchester Guardian*, which reported Bhutto saying that if India got the bomb, 'then we should have to eat grass and get one, or buy one of our own'. George Perkovich, *India's Nuclear Bomb: The Impact on Global Proliferation*, University of California Press, 1999, p. 108.
2.   The citation is quoted in S. Shabbir Hussain and Mujahid Kamran (eds), *Dr A.Q. Khan on Science and Education*, Sang e-Meel Publication, Lahore, 1997. The publication also reproduces a (longer) citation for the Nishan e-Imtiaz award.
3.   'I Seek Your Pardon', *Guardian*, 5 February 2004.
4.   Interview with A.Q. Khan, July 2000.
5.   BBC News, 3–4 June, 1998.
6.   Zulfikar Ali Bhutto, *The Myth of Independence*, Classic, Lahore, 1995, p. 153.
7.   An account of the Multan meeting can be found in Shahid ur-Rehman, *Long Road to Chagai: Untold Story of Pakistan's Nuclear Quest*, Print Wise Publication, Islamabad, 1999, pp. 16–19. Also see Zahid Malik, *Dr A.Q. Khan and the Islamic Bomb*, Hurmat Publication, Islamabad, 1992, p. 128.
8.   Interview with A.Q. Khan, July 2000.
9.   Munir Ahmed Khan, 'Nuclearisation of South Asia and its Regional and Global Implications', Regional Studies, autumn 1998, Institute for Regional Studies, Islamabad, p. 7. The article has histories of both the Indian and Pakistani nuclear programmes.
10.   Malik, *Dr A.Q. Khan*, p. 185.
11.   'Nuclear Black Markets: Pakistan, A.Q. Khan and the Rise of Proliferation Networks', International Institute for Strategic Studies (IISS), May 2007, p. 34.
12.   Pakistan Nuclear Weapons, http://www.fas.org/nuke/guide/pakistan/nuke/index.html.
13.   David Albright and Paul Brannan, 'Second Khusab Plutonium Production Reactor Nears Completion', Institute for Science and International Security, 18 September 2008.
14.   When it was founded, the laboratory went under the name of Aviation Development Workshop. In July 1976 it was renamed the Engineering Research Laboratory. Then, in May 1981, after a visit by General Zia, it was given its current name of Khan Research Laboratory. Many refer to the plant as Kahuta – the name of a nearby village. Interview with A.Q. Khan, July 2000.
15.   Ibid.
16.   ur-Rehman, *Long Road to Chagai*, p. 51. The charge is also made in Steve Weissman and Herbert Krosney, *The Islamic Bomb: The Nuclear Threat to Israel and the Middle East*, Times Books, New York, 1983, 2nd edition.
17.   Simon Henderson, 'Pakistani Scientist Cleared', *Khaleesh Times*, 19 July 1986. See also 'Court Quashed Nuclear Spying Conviction', *Gulf News*, 29 March 1985.
18.   Interview with A.Q. Khan, July 2000.
19.   Hussain and Kamran (eds), *A. Q. Khan*, p. 117.
20.   Khan, *Nuclearisation*, p. 15. See also Jorn Gjelstad and Olav Njolstad (eds), *Nuclear Rivalry and International Order*, Sage Publications, 1996, p. 163.

21. The details of the sanctions imposed on Pakistan are based on interviews in June 2000 with officials from the Pakistani Foreign Office and the US Embassy in Islamabad.
22. Richard Cronin, Alan Kronstadt and Sharon Squassoni, 'Pakistan's Nuclear Proliferation Activities', Congressional Research Service, 25 January 2005.
23. Perkovich, *India's Nuclear Bomb*, p. 221.
24. Interview with Agha Shahi, July 2000.
25. Malik, *Dr A.Q. Khan*, p. 76.
26. The activity is documented in great detail in Weissman and Krosney (eds), *Islamic Bomb*.
27. For example, ibid.
28. 'Project 706 – The Islamic Bomb' was broadcast by the BBC's 'Panorama' programme in 1980.
29. Quoted in Malik, *Dr A.Q. Khan*, p. 83.
30. Letter from the former Pakistani president Ghulam Ishaq to Zahid Malik, editor of the *Pakistani Observer* and biographer of Dr A.Q. Khan.
31. Interview with A.Q. Khan, July 2000.
32. Speech to the Pakistan Institute of National Affairs, 9 September 1990, quoted in Hussain and Kamran (eds), *Dr. A.Q. Khan*, p. 117.
33. Interviews with A.Q. Khan and a former PAEC official, July 2000.
34. Interview given by A.Q. Khan to *Al-Akbar*, 13 July 1998. Khan subsequently said that, although he had given an interview to the newspaper, he had not made any remark about the Ghauris being armed with nuclear warheads.
35. www.cnn.com/WORLD/asiapcf/9805/27/pakistan.nuclear.pm/index.html
36. Bruce Riedel, *American Diplomacy and the 1999 Kargil Summit at Blair House*, Center for the Advanced Study of India, University of Pennsylvania, 2002.
37. Interview with the author, 1998.
38. Interview with General (retd) K.M. Arif, June 2000.
39. See Dr Zafar Iqbal Cheema, 'How to Respond?', *The News*, 21 May 1998, p. 6.
40. Interview with a participant at the meeting of the Defence Committee of the cabinet, July 2001.
41. Strobe Talbott, *Engaging India*, Brookings Institution Press, Washington, DC, 2006, p. 70.
42. *Jang*, 13 May 1998.
43. *Time*, 8 June 1998.
44. Craig Baxter and Charles H. Kennedy (eds), *Pakistan 2000*, Oxford University Press, Karachi, July 2000, p. 120.
45. Kamal Matinuddin, *The Nuclearisation of South Asia*, Oxford University Press, Karachi, 2002, pp. 340–44.
46. 'Responding to India's Nuclear Doctrine', *Dawn*, 5 October 1999.
47. Agha Shahi, Address to seminar organised by Islamabad Council of World Affairs and Institute of Strategic Studies held in Islamabad, February 2000.
48. See Peter Baker, 'Senate Approves Indian Nuclear Deal', *New York Times*, 1 October 2008.
49. Ibid.
50. Paul Kerr and Mary Beth Nikitin, *Pakistan's Nuclear Weapons: Proliferation and Security Issues*, Congressional Research Service, 9 November 2007, p. 4.
51. IISS, *Nuclear Black Markets*, p. 41, n. 67.
52. Interview with General (retd) Mirza Aslam Beg, July 2000.
53. See E.A.S Bokhari, 'India-Pakistan: The Nuclear Option', *Defence Journal*, March 1998, 2:3, pp. 49–52, p. 51; Shahi, Address to seminar, Islamabad, February 2000.
54. 'Pakistan Nukes Outstrip India's, Officials Say', 6 June 2000, see www.msnbc.msn.com/id/3340687/.
55. Anon., 'Nuclear South Asia: Opportunities and Challenges for Pakistan', *Air War College Journal*, 1999, pp. 19–37, p. 29.

56. Major General Mahmud Ali Durrani, *Pakistan's Strategic Thinking and the Role of Nuclear Weapons*, Occasional Paper 37, Rawalpindi Cooperative Monitoring Center, Sandia National Laboratories, July 2004.

57. See, for example, Syed Akhtar Ali, 'Towards a Safe and Stable Nuclear Environment in South Asia', *National Development and Security*, November 1999, pp. 1–26, p. 8 (published by the Foundation for Research on International Environment, National Development and Security, Rawalpindi, Pakistan).

58. Leonard S. Spector with Jacqueline Smith, *Nuclear Ambitions: The Spread of Nuclear Weapons 1989–1990*, Farda Publishing Company, Karachi, 1990, pp. 102–3.

59. Carnegie Endowment for International Peace, 'Non-Proliferation', fact sheet, 15 April 1999. Western officials have confirmed this assessment of the intermediate-range HATF.

60. Kerr and Nikitin, *Pakistan's Nuclear Weapons*, p. 3.

61. http://www.state.gov/r/pa/prs/ps/2004/30302.htm.

62. Carnegie Endowment for International Peace, 'Non-Proliferation', fact sheet, 15 April 1999.

63. www.janes.com/extracts/extract/jsws/jswsa305.html.

64. 'Cruise Missile Fired from Aerial Platform', *Dawn*, 8 May 2008.

65. Khan, 'Nuclearisation', p. 9. For an account of Pakistan's and India's missile programmes see also, Anon., 'Nuclear South Asia: Opportunities and Challenges for Pakistan', *Air War College Journal*, 1999, pp. 19–37.

66. http://yearbook2005.sipri.org/files/yb05ap12a.pdf, p. 597.

67. This account of BRASSTACKS is partly based on an interview in July 2000 with General (retd) K.M. Arif, who was at the time vice chief of the Pakistan army. There is a much fuller account of the BRASSTACKS episode in Perkovich, *India's Nuclear Bomb*, p. 280.

68. Executive Summary of the Kargil Review Committee Report, section III, 'The Nuclear Factor', http://nuclearweaponarchive.org/India/KargilRCB.html.

69. Interview with General (retd) K.M. Arif, July 2000.

70. Perkovich, *India's Nuclear Bomb*, p. 280.

71. Interview with General (retd) Mirza Aslam Beg, July 2000.

72. Perkovich, *India's Nuclear Bomb*, p. 280.

73. Quoted in ibid., p. 312.

74. For coverage of these two comments see Press Trust of India, 30 June and 4 July 1999.

75. The columnist was Naseem Zehra who made a typewritten record of Nawaz Sharif's remarks immediately after their conversation.

76. Riedel, *American Diplomacy*.

77. Reuters, 14 August 1999.

78. Zahid Hussain, 'Pakistan Issued Nuclear Threat', *The Times*, 31 December 2002.

79. Sumit Ganguly and Devin T. Hagerty, *Fearful Symmetry: India–Pakistan Crises in the Shadow of Nuclear Weapons*, University of Washington Press, Seattle, 2005, p. 10.

80. Gordon Corera, *Shopping for Bombs*, Hurst & Co., London, 2006, p. 70.

81. Glenn Kessler, 'Bhutto Dealt Nuclear Secrets to N. Korea, Book Says', *Washington Post*, 1 June 2008.

82. Pervez Musharraf, *In the Line of Fire*, Free Press, New York, 2006, p. 296.

83. Cronin, Kronstadt and Squassoni, *Pakistan's Nuclear Proliferation Activities*, p. 12.

84. David Albright and Corey Hinderstein, *Documents Indicate A.Q. Khan Offered Nuclear Weapon Designs to Iraq in 1990: Did He Approach Other Countries?* Institute for Science and International Security Press, 4 February 2004. www.isis-online.org/publications/southasia.

85. 'I Seek Your Pardon', *Guardian*, 5 February 2004.

86. 'Why Should I Talk to the IAEA?', *Guardian*, 30 May 2008.

87. 'Father of Pakistan's Bomb Stands Defiant', *Washington Post*, 5 June 2008.

88. William J. Broad, David Rohde and David E. Sanger, 'Inquiry Suggests Pakistanis Sold Nuclear Secrets', *New York Times*, 22 December 2003.

89. The number comes from Bruno Tertais, *Pakistan's Nuclear Exports: Was There a State Strategy?*, Nonproliferation Policy Education Centre, Washington, DC, 23 October 2006.

90. Speech at Fort Lesley J. McNair, National Defense University, 11 February 2004, available on www.whitehouse.gov.

91. Kerr and Nikitin, *Pakistan's Nuclear Weapons*.

92. Farah Stockman, 'Pakistan Had Case Against Scientists', *Boston Globe*, 13 February 2004.

93. A.Q. Khan Interview excerpts, *Guardian*, 30 May 2008.

94. John Lancaster and Kamran Khan, 'Pakistan Fires Top Nuclear Scientist', *Washington Post*, 1 February 2004.

95. IISS, *Nuclear Black Markets*, p. 93.

96. Gaurav Kampani, *Proliferation Unbound: Nuclear Tales from Pakistan*, Center for Nonproliferation Studies, Monterey, 23 February 2004, pp. 4–6.

97. 'US Confirms Illicit Nuclear Activity in Pakistan has Stopped', *Daily Times*, 11 February 2004.

98. IISS, *Nuclear Black Markets*, p. 96.

99. Strobe Talbott, *Engaging India: Diplomacy, Democracy, and the Bomb*, p. 150.

100. Cronin, Kronstadt and Squassoni, *Pakistan's Nuclear Proliferation Activities*, p. 13.

101. Corera, *Shopping for Bombs*, p. 162.

102. 'Islamabad Received CIA Report on Dr Qadeer in Oct', *The News*, 8 February 2004.

103. 'Pakistan Warned on Nuke Scientist in 98', *USA Today*, 10 February 2004.

104. Kamran Khan, 'Dr Qadeer Linked to N-Black Market', *The News*, 28 January 2004.

105. Cronin, Kronstadt and Squassoni, *Pakistan's Nuclear Proliferation Activities*, p. 19.

106. 'Islamabad Received CIA Report on Dr Qadeer in Oct', *The News*, 8 February 2004.

107. Cronin, Kronstadt and Squassoni, *Pakistan's Nuclear Proliferation Activities*, p. 12.

108. Kampani, *Proliferation Unbound*, p. 2.

109. Corera, *Shopping for Bombs*, p. 64.

110. IISS, *Nuclear Black Markets*, p. 67.

111. Corera, *Shopping for Bombs*, p. 68.

112. Kampani, *Proliferation Unbound*, p. 4.

113. 'Iran Closes in on Ability to Build a Nuclear Bomb', *LA Times*, 4 August 2003.

114. 'Military Officials Sought my Permission to Sell N-Tech', *Daily Times*, 25 February 2004.

115. By the late 1990s Western agencies were sufficiently suspicious of A.Q. Khan's movements to be tracking him closely. See Corera, *Shopping for Bombs*, p. 94.

116. 'Pakistani Says Army Knew Atomic Parts Were Shipped', *Associated Press*, 5 July 2008.

117. Simon Henderson, 'Pakistan's Dr Nuke Bids for the Presidency', *Sunday Times*, 24 August 2008.

118. William J. Broad and David E. Sanger, 'As Nuclear Secrets Emerge in Khan Inquiry More are Suspected', *New York Times*, 26 December 2004.

119. IISS, *Nuclear Black Markets*, p. 32.

120. Adrian Levy and Catherine Scott-Clark, *Deception: Pakistan, the United States and the Global Nuclear Conspiracy*, Penguin India, 2007, p. 61.

121. Levy and Scott-Clark, *Deception*, p. 60.

122. Quoted in Hussain and Kamran (eds), *A. Q. Khan*, p. 28. A.Q. Khan has confirmed that he wrote this address, but since Western European countries were denying visas to him at the time, it was delivered by somebody else who read it out in his name.

123. Shahi, address to seminar, Islamabad, February 2000.

124. See, for example, Ashok Kapur, 'Western Biases', *Bulletin of Atomic Scientists*, Educational Foundation for Nuclear Science, 1 January 1995.

125. See, for example, *The News*, 10 April 1999, and 'Pakistan Expected to Announce Nuclear Command Authority Soon', *Press Trust of India*, 11 April 1999. See also *Khabrain*, 13 May 1999.
126. Kerr and Nikitin, *Pakistan's Nuclear Weapons*, p. 4.
127. Major General Mahmud Ali Durrani, *Pakistan's Strategic Thinking and the Role of Nuclear Weapons*, Occasional Paper 37, Rawalpindi Cooperative Monitoring Center, Sandia National Laboratories, p. 33.
128. Interview with Brigadier (retd) Shaukat Qadir, vice president, Islamabad Policy Research Institute, July 2000.
129. Shahi, address to seminar, Islamabad, February 2000.
130. Interview with General (retd) Mirza Aslam Beg, July 2000.
131. *Pakistani Observer*, 27 May 2000, p. 1, and *The Nation*, 27 May 2000, p. 1.
132. Radio Pakistan, 4 February 2000.
133. Interview with General (retd) Mirza Aslam Beg, July 2000.
134. IISS, *Nuclear Black Markets*, p. 112.
135. See Steven Erlanger, 'India's Arms Race Isn't Safe Like the Cold War', *New York Times*, 12 July 1998.
136. Shaun Gregory, 'Nuclear Command and Control in South Asia', *Strategic Issues*, March 2000, issue entitled 'The Nuclear Debate', Institute of Strategic Studies, Islamabad, p. 77.
137. Kamal Matinuddin, *The Nuclearisation of South Asia*, Oxford University Press, Karachi, 2002.
138. Interview with Pakistani scientist, July 2000.
139. Shahi, address to seminar, Islamabad, February 2000.
140. Matinuddin, *Nuclearisation*.
141. Interview with Brigadier (retd) Shaukat Qadir of the Islamabad Policy Research Institute, July 2000.
142. 'Atomic Chief Fears for Security of Pakistan's Nuclear Arsenal', *AFP*, 8 January 2008.
143. Alan Kronstadt, *Pakistan-US Relations*, Congressional Research Service, updated 11 January 2008, p. 42.
144. Durrani, *Pakistan's Strategic Thinking*.
145. David E. Sanger and William J. Broad, 'US Secretly Aids Pakistan in Guarding Nuclear Arms', *New York Times*, 18 November 2007.
146. Interview with General (retd) Mirza Aslam Beg, July 2000.

CHAPTER SIX: DEMOCRACY

1. Author interviews, Naudero, December 2007.
2. Mohammad Ayub Khan, *Friends Not Masters: A Political Autobiography*, Oxford University Press, Karachi, 1967, p. 208.
3. Interview with the author, 13 October 1999.
4. I do not count Shaukat Aziz, 2002–2007, because he was prime minister during a period of de facto military rule.
5. See, for example, Akbar S. Ahmed, *Jinnah, Pakistan and Islamic Identity: The Search for Saladin*, Routledge, London, 1997, p. 133.
6. Ata Rabbani, *I Was the Quaid's ADC*, Oxford University Press, Karachi, 1996, p. 142.
7. Stanley Wolpert, *Zulfi Bhutto of Pakistan: His Life and Times*, Oxford University Press, New York, 1993, p. 76.
8. Lawrence Ziring, *Pakistan in the Twentieth Century: A Political History*, Oxford University Press, Karachi, 1998, p. 380.
9. Lieutenant General Jahan Dad Khan, *Pakistan: Leadership Challenges*, Oxford University Press, Karachi, 1999, p. 51.

10. Ziring, *Pakistan*, p. 381, and Ian Talbot, *Pakistan: A Modern History*, Vanguard Books, Lahore, 1999, p. 219.

11. Shahid ur-Rehman, *Who Owns Pakistan?*, Mr Books, Islamabad, 1998, p. 15.

12. Mohammad Asghar Khan, *Generals in Politics: Pakistan 1958–1982*, Vikas, Delhi, 1983.

13. Andrew Wilder, *The Pakistani Voter*, Oxford University Press, Karachi, 1990, p. 26.

14. Sardar Muhammad Chaudhry, *The Ultimate Crime*, Quami Publishers, Lahore, 1997, p. 393.

15. Mohammad Uzair, 'Foreign Aid and Indebtedness in Pakistan', in Mehrunnisa Ali (ed.), *Readings in Pakistan Foreign Policy 1971–1998*, Oxford University Press, Karachi, 2001, p. 369.

16. *Economic Survey of Pakistan 2000–2001*, Economic Advisors Wing, Finance Division, Government of Pakistan, Islamabad, Table 9.3.

17. Ibid.

18. See, for example, Zahid Hussain, 'The Great Loan Scandal', *Newsline*, September 1991.

19. *Dawn*, 13 June 1998.

20. 'Nawaz Sharif Tops Defaulters List', *Associated Press*, 14 November 1999.

21. See, for example, Amir Mir, 'The Great Repayment Scandal', *Newsline*, October 1998.

22. See Amir Mir, 'Slipping Through the Net', *Herald*, August 1988, p. 34.

23. Nawaz Sharif's nomination paper for the National Assembly elections, 1996.

24. *Sunday Times*, 4 February 2001.

25. 'Justice, Lies and Audio Tapes', *Newsline*, March 2001, pp. 32–7.

26. 'Benazir Zardari Ordered to Appear in Court on Sept 7', *Nation*, 11 August 2001.

27. Rafi Raza (ed.), *Pakistan in Perspective 1947–1997*, Oxford University Press, Karachi, 1997, p. 8.

28. Iqbal Akhund, *Trial and Error: The Advent and Eclipse of Benazir Bhutto*, Oxford University Press, Karachi, 2000, p. 118.

29. Interview with the author, summer 1999.

30. Akhund, *Trial and Error*, p. 119.

31. Ibid., p. xiii.

32. Azhar Abbas, 'The Creeping Coup', *Herald*, May 1999, p. 28.

33. Admiral (retd) Fasih Bokhari, interview with the author, 13 July 2001.

34. Mushahid Hussain, interview with the author, 12 July 2001.

35. Shaun Gregory, 'The ISI and the War on Terrorism', *Studies in Conflict & Terrorism*, 30:12, December 2007, p. 1,013.

36. Ibid., p. 1,014.

37. Gregory R. Copley and Purvis, *The Defense and Foreign Affairs Handbook on Pakistan, Pakistan: The Global Strategic Lynchpin*, International Strategic Studies Association, Alexandra, USA, November 2008.

38. Abbas Nasir, 'The Inside Story', *Herald Annual*, 1991, p. 29.

39. Wolpert, *Zulfi Bhutto*, p. 279.

40. Lieutenant General Durrani's affidavit to the Supreme Court.

41. Reply to the Supreme Court by Mirza Mohammad Aslam Beg.

42. Illyas Khan, 'The ISI Taliban Nexus', *Herald*, November 2001, p. 22.

43. Ibid., p. 24.

44. Syed Irfan Raza, 'Govt Forced to Withdraw ISI Decision', *Dawn*, 28 July 2008.

45. Ibid.

46. 'Pakistanis Rise Up', editorial, *Washington Times*, 2 October 2008.

47. I had an opportunity to see this for myself in July 2007 at an off-the-record briefing at ISI headquarters.

48. Iftikhar H. Malik, *State and Civil Society in Pakistan: Politics of Authority, Ideology and Ethnicity*, Macmillan, Basingstoke, 1997, pp. 81–93.

49. S. Akbar Zaidi, *Issues in Pakistan's Economy*, Oxford University Press, Karachi, 1999, p. 18.

50.　Tehmina Durrani, *My Feudal Lord*, Corgi, London, 1994.
51.　M. Attiqur Rahman, *Back to the Pavilion*, Ardeshir Cowasjee, Karachi, 1989, p. 142.
52.　Anita M. Weiss and S. Zulfiqar Gilani (eds), *Power and Civil Society in Pakistan*, Oxford University Press, Karachi, 2001, p. 126.
53.　Lieutenant General Jahan Dad Khan, *Pakistan: Leadership Challenges*, Oxford University Press, Karachi, 1999, p. 82.
54.　Khan, *Friends Not Masters*, pp. 86–7.
55.　Ibid., p. 90.
56.　Wilder, *The Pakistani Voter*, p. 77.
57.　Zahid Hussain, 'House of Feudals', *Herald*, April 1985, p. 41.
58.　*Herald Election Special*, 1988, p. 109.
59.　*Herald*, November 1988, p. 48.
60.　*Far Eastern Economic Review*, 20 May 1999.
61.　*Dawn*, 11 May 2000.
62.　'System of Absentee Landlords to be Abolished', *Dawn*, 21 February 2000.
63.　'Provinces Asked to Expedite Land Reforms', *Dawn*, 26 October 2000.

CHAPTER SEVEN: THE ARMY

1.　Quoted in Brigadier (retd) Abdul Rahman Siddiqi, 'Army and Islam: An Appraisal', *Defence Journal*, 21, May–June 1996, 3–11, p.5.
2.　Jason Burke, 'India Walks into Kashmir Trap', *Observer*, 30 May 1999.
3.　Interview with the author, May 1999.
4.　Quoted in Major General S. Shahid Hamid, *Early Years of Pakistan*, Ferozons, Lahore, 1993, p. 212.
5.　Hamid, *Early Years*, p. 30.
6.　Stephen Cohen, *The Pakistan Army*, Oxford University Press, Karachi, 1998, p. 89.
7.　Anita M. Weiss and S. Zulfiqar Gilani (eds), *Power and Civil Society in Pakistan*, Oxford University Press, Karachi, 2001, p. 207.
8.　Dr Marcel A. Boisard, 'Islamic Conduct of Hostilities and the Protection of the Victims of Armed Conflicts', *Defence Journal*, 5: 1–2, January–February 1979, p. 18.
9.　Brigadier S.K. Malik, *The Quranic Concept of War*, Wajidalis, Lahore, 1979, p. xi.
10.　Interview with the author, May 2001.
11.　Shuja Nawaz, *Crossed Swords: Pakistan, its Army, and the Wars Within*, Oxford University Press, Karachi, 2008, p. 408, n. 66.
12.　See 'Maj. Gen. Abbasi's Intended Address to the Nation', *Defence Journal*, 21, May–June 1996, pp. 53–4.
13.　*The Frontier Post*, 15 March 1996.
14.　Zaffar Abbas, 'Defenders of the Faith', *Herald*, November 1995, p. 34.
15.　Zaffar Abbas, 'The Coup that Wasn't', *Herald*, November 1995, p. 28.
16.　A discussion of the *Hilal* article can be found in *Defence Journal*, 21, May–June 1996.
17.　Brian Cloughley, *A History of the Pakistan Army: Wars and Insurrections*, Oxford University Press, Karachi, 2000, p. 361.
18.　Cohen, *The Pakistan Army*, pp. 55–74.
19.　Hamoodur Rehman Commission Report, The Supplementary Report. General Niazi, it should be said, denied the accusations.
20.　Sardar Muhammad Chaudhry, *The Ultimate Crime: Eyewitness to Power Games*, Qaumi Publishers, Lahore, 1997, p. 97.
21.　Cohen, *The Pakistan Army*, pp. 169–70.
22.　Quoted in Talat Aslam, 'The Changing Face of the Army', *Herald*, July 1989, p. 8.
23.　Zaffar Abbas, 'Pakistan Arrest Army Officers', BBC News, 31 August 2003.
24.　Zulfikar Ali, 'Musharraf Convicts' Plan to Appeal', 29 August 2005.

25. Syed Saleem Shahzad, 'Pakistan Foils Coup Plot', *Asia Times*, October 14 2006.
26. Captain (retd) Ayaz Amir, 'Soldiering On', *Herald*, November 1995, p. 37.
27. Brigadier (retd) Shaukat Qadir, interview with the author, February 2001.
28. Hasan-Askari Rizvi, *The Military and Politics in Pakistan: 1947–1986*, Progressive Publishers, Lahore, 1987, pp. 44–5 and 124–5.
29. Hamid, *Early Years*, p. 177.
30. Lieutenant General Jahan Dad Khan, *Pakistan: Leadership Challenges*, Oxford University Press, Karachi, 1999, p. 51.
31. *Hamoodur Rehman Commission Report*, chapter 5, *Dawn*, 18 January 2001, p. 21.
32. 'Retired Pak Generals Criticise Kargil Manoeuvre', Rediff On The Net, 18 July 1999, available on www.rediff.com/news/1999/jul/18pakgen.htm.
33. Interview with the author, February 1998.
34. Associated Press of Pakistan, 'Pakistan and India Finalize Consular Access Agreement', 20 May 2008.
35. 'Indian Army Chief Says Positions at Disputed Glacier Must be Authenticated', *Asian Age*, 27 December 2007.
36. Reuters, 'Pakistan Protests Indian Trek on Disputed Glacier', 17 September 2007.
37. Interview with the author, October 1999.
38. Star TV interview with General Musharraf, 28 January 2000.
39. Interview with the author, 7 October 2007.
40. Mohammed Ayub Khan, *Friends Not Masters: A Political Autobiography*, Oxford University Press, Karachi, 1967, pp. 186–91.
41. Khan, *Pakistan: Leadership Challenges*, p. 126.
42. G.W. Choudhury, *The Last Days of United Pakistan*, Oxford University Press, Karachi, 1993, p. 48.
43. Hamid Khan, *Constitutional and Political History of Pakistan*, Oxford University Press, Oxford, 2001, p. 60.
44. 'Q&A Pakistan Referendum', BBC News Online, http://news.bbc.co.uk/2/hi/south_asia/1958219.stm.
45. Hasan-Askari Rizvi, 'Civil Military Relations in Pakistan', *Herald*, May 1999, p. 40.
46. Azhar Abbas. 'The Creeping Coup', *Herald*, May 1998, p. 28.
47. Unless otherwise stated, the material on the army's economic interests is based on interviews with senior retired officers who wish to remain anonymous.
48. Ayesha Siddiqa, *Military Inc.: Inside Pakistan's Military Economy*, Pluto Press, London, 2007, p. 115.
49 Nawaz, *Crossed Swords*, p. 445.
50. Quoted in Siddiqa, *Military Inc.*, p. 15.
51. Nawaz, *Crossed Swords*, p. 446.
52. Tim Johnson, 'Pakistan Military Retreats from Musharraf's Influence', *McClatchy Newspapers*, 18 January 2008.
53. Siddiqa, *Military Inc.*
54. Mohammed Attiqur Rahman, *Our Defence Cause: An Analysis of Pakistan's Past and Future Military Role*, White Lion Publishers, London, 1976.
55. Roedad Khan, *Pakistan: A Dream Gone Sour*, Oxford University Press, Karachi, 1998, p. 43, quoting Altaf Gauhar, *Ayub Khan: Pakistan's First Military Ruler*, Lahore Sang-e-Meel Publications, 1994, p. 479.

CHAPTER EIGHT: THE MUSHARRAF YEARS

This account of the coup is largely drawn from my own eyewitness observations and contemporaneous interviews. It is also based on the transcript of all the (sometimes conflicting) evidence given in the trial of Nawaz Sharif. The full verdict reached by Judge Rehmat Hussain Jaffri used to be available on the Pakistani government website but has been removed. A fuller, more detailed account of what happened can be found in the first edition of this book.

1. This and all subsequent quotations involving air traffic control are taken from the transcript of the tapes recorded in the tower at the time. The court that tried Nawaz Sharif never heard the tapes, but the news magazine *The Herald* obtained them. Like the transcript of the trial (see opening note), this used to be accessible on the web but appears to have been removed.
2. Eyewitness account from *The Nation*, 13 October 1999.
3. 'Events', *Pakistan Defence News Bulletin*, 1–15 October 1999.
4. Musharraf's account, which follows, was published by the Associated Press of Pakistan, 11 November 2000.
5. Full text available on http://news.bbc.co.uk/1/hi/world/monitoring/473175.stm.
6. http://www.fas.org/news/pakistan/1999/991017-mushraf_speech.htm.
7. 'Full text of Musharraf's last address', http://www.paktribune.com/news/index.shtml?204631.
8. *The Friday Times*, Lahore, 27 April–3 May 2001.
9. 'NAB agrees to free Mansur ul-Haq, for Rs 457.5 million', *The News*, 1 January 2002.
10. Michael Peel and Farhan Bokhari, 'Doubts Cast on Zardari's Mental Health', *Financial Times*, 25 August 2008.
11. Author interviews, Islamabad, September 2008.
12. Luke Harding and Rory McCarthy, 'Special Report: Pakistan', *Guardian*, 16 May 2001.
13. Ishrat Husain, governor of the State Bank of Pakistan, 3 February 2005, http://www.bis.org/review/r050217g.pdf.
14. International Monetary Fund, *Pakistan*, IMF Country Reports no. 08/21, January 2008, p. 3.
15. International Monetary Fund, *Pakistan*, p. 3.
16. US Government Accountability Office, 'Securing, Stabilizing, and Developing Pakistan's Border Area with Pakistan', February 2009, p. 11.
17. Craig Cohen, *A Perilous Course: US Strategy and Assistance to Pakistan*, CSIS Report, August 2007, pp. 32–3.
18. Ibid.
19. Greg Miller, 'US Military Aid to Pakistan Misses its Al Qaeda Target', *Los Angeles Times*, 5 November 2007.
20. US Aid, 'Failing to Reach Target', BBC News, 16 May 2008.
21. Alan Kronstadt, *Pakistan–US Relations*, Congressional Research Service Report for Congress, 25 August 2008, p. CRS-99.
22. Kronstadt, *Pakistan–US Relations*, 25 August 2008, p. CRS-61.
23. Panel 1 of a hearing of the International Development and Foreign Assistance, Economic Affairs and International Environmental Protection Sub-Committee of the Senate Foreign Relations Committee. December 6, 2007.
24. Hearing, 16 January 2008, US.–Pakistan Relations: Assassination, Instability and the Future of U.S. Policy, Sub Committee on the Middle East and South Asia.
25. *CRS Report for Congress-Pakistan-US Relations*. Updated January 11. 2008 K Alan Kronstadt CRS-36
26. Glenn Kessler, 'Congress Sets Limits on Aid to Pakistan', *Washington Post*, 20 December 2007.
27. Panel 1 of a hearing of the International Development and Foreign Assistance, Economic Affairs and International Environmental Protection Sub-Committee of the Senate Foreign Relations Committee. December 6, 2007, evidence of Richard Boucher.
28. *Reform of Tax Administration in Pakistan*, Report of the Task Force on Reform of Tax Administration, 24 April 2001, p. 2.
29. 'Raising Tax Revenues', *Dawn*, 9 August 2001.

30. 'Shaukat Announces Tax Survey', *The News*, 5 August 2001.
31. *Reform of Tax Administration in Pakistan*, p. 91.
32. Interview with the author, January 2002.
33. *The News*, 28 August 2001.
34. International Monetary Fund, *Pakistan*, pp. 4 and 16.
35. Henri Lorie, 'A Growth Promoting Fiscal Policy for Pakistan', remarks at the pre-budget seminar of *The Nation* newspaper, Lahore, 16 May 2006.
36. Abdullah Yusuf, *Pakistan: Reform Process in Tax Administration*, 17th Tax Conference, Tokyo, October 2007.
37. See, for example, B. Raman, Director, Institute of Topical Studies, *General Pervez Musharraf: His Past and Present*, 1 July 1999, available on www.angelfire.com/al4/terror/musharraf.htm.
38. Joshua T. White, *Pakistan's Islamist Frontier: Islamic Politics and US Policy in Pakistan's North-West Frontier*, Religion & Security Monograph Series, no.1, Center on Faith & International Affairs, Arlington, VA, 2008, p. 36.
39. Interview with the author, November 1999.
40. Interview, BBC Urdu Service, November 1999.
41. Address to the nation by General Pervez Musharraf, 17 October 1999, available on http://findarticles.com/p/articles/mi_m2242/is_1669_286/ai_n13661903/pg_3.
42. 'Pakistan Senate Backs Rape Bill', BBC News, 23 November 2006.
43. 'Man on a Mission?', *The Herald*, July 2001, p. 34.
44. International Crisis Group, 'The State of Sectarianism in Pakistan', *Asia Report*, 95, 18 April 2005, p. 23.
45. Ibid., p. 14.
46. Ibid.
47. See Katja Riikonen, *Sectarianism: A Destructive Way of Dealing with Difference*, Pakistan Security Research Unit, March 2007.
48. 'Musharraf Wants at least 5 Years', *The News*, 21 January 2002.
49. Erik Eckholm, 'Pakistan Pledges to Bar any Groups Linked to Terror', *New York Times*, 13 January 2002.
50. Frederic Grare, Policy Brief 45. 'Pakistan: The Myth of an Islamist Peril', Carnegie Endowment for International Peace, February 2006.
51. Grare, Policy Brief 45. 'Pakistan: The Myth of an Islamist Peril', p. 5.
52. 'The Next Chapter. A Report of the Pakistan Policy Working Group', September 2008, p. 23.
53. For a plausible account of Taliban fighters moving through checkpoints, see 'Pakistan's Dangerous Double Game', *Newsweek*, 13 September 2008; see also Dexter Filkins, 'Right at the Edge', *New York Times*, 5 September 2008.
54. 'Militants Escape Control of Pakistan, Officials Say', *New York Times*, 15 January 2008.
55. A.H. Nayyar, 'Madrassa Education: Frozen in Time', in Pervez Hoodbhoy (ed.), *Education and the State: Fifty Years of Pakistan*, Oxford University Press, Karachi, 1998, p. 226.
56. Musharraf television interview with CNN, 30 September 2001.
57. *National Education Census Highlights*, Government of Pakistan, Ministry of Education Statistics Division, Federal Bureau of Statistics, Islamabad, 2006.
58. For a full discussion of the numbers see Christine Fair, *The Madrasah Challenge: Militancy and Religious Education in Pakistan*, United States Institute of Peace Studies, Washington, DC 2008, pp. 7 and 10.
59. Musharraf's Address to the Nation, Islamabad, 12 January 2002, http://www.pakistantv.tv/millat/president/1020200475758AMword%20file.pdf.
60. Alexander Evans, 'Understanding Madrasahs: How Threatening Are They?' *Foreign Affairs*, January/February 2007, vol. 85, no. 1, p. 10.
61. Paul Anderson, *Madrassas Hit by Sex Abuse Claims*, 10 December 2004, http://news.bbc.co.uk/2/hi/south_asia/4084951.stm.

62. Fox News, 30 May 2008, http://www.foxnews.com/story/0,2933,360925,00.html.
63. http://www.newsline.com.pk/NewsJuly2003/newsbeat6july.htm.
64. Fair, *The Madrasah Challenge*, p. 10.
65. Marc Sageman, *Understanding Terror Networks*, University of Pennsylvania Press, Philadelphia, 2004, p. 74.
66. Fair, *The Madrasah Challenge*, p. 10.
67. Musharraf's Address to the Nation, Islamabad, 12 January 2002, http://www.pakistantv.tv/millat/president/1020200475758AMword%20file.pdf.
68. Ibid.
69. Fair, *The Madrasah Challenge*, p. 84.
70. *National Education Census Highlights*, 2005.
71. Independent Evaluation Group, *Evaluation of the World Bank's Assistance to Basic Education in Pakistan: Pakistan Country Study*, World Bank, Washington, 2007, http://go.worldbank.org/VD7D7978I0.
72. http://hdrstats.undp.org/indicators/100.html.
73. I have formed a habit, whenever the opportunity arises, of dropping in on government schools unannounced. I have never yet found one in which all the staff have turned up for work.
74. International Crisis Group, 'Pakistan: Reforming the Education Sector', *Asia Report*, no. 84, Islamabad and Brussels, 7 October 2004, p. 17.
75. See Aamer Ahmed Khan, 'US Concern at Pakistan Textbooks', BBC News, Karachi, 19 August 2005, http://news.bbc.co.uk/2/hi/south_asia/4167260.
76. Quoted in International Crisis Group, *Pakistan: Reforming the Education Sector*, p. 17.
77. Pervez Hoodbhoy, 'Education Reform: Signs of Hope', *Chowk*, 12 February 2007, www.chowk.com/articles/11633.
78. http://www.9-11commission.gov/report/911Report.pdf, p. 369.
79. Quoted in International Crisis Group, *Pakistan: Reforming the Education Sector*, p. 1.
80. Cohen, *A Perilous Course*, pp. 32–3.

Bibliography

Books

New books, reports, etcetera, published since the second edition of *Pakistan: Eye of the Storm* are marked with *.

*Abbas, Hassan, *Pakistan's Drift into Extremism: Allah, the Army, and America's War on Terror*, M.E. Sharpe, New York, 2005.

Ahmad, Lt Colonel Syed Iqbal, *Balochistan: Its Strategic Importance*, Royal Book Company, Karachi, 1992.

Ahmed, Akbar S., *Jinnah, Pakistan and Islamic Identity: The Search for Saladin*, Routledge, London, 1997.

—— 'Tribes, Regional Pressures, and Nationhood', pp. 139–55 in Victoria Schofield (ed.), *Old Roads and New Highways: Fifty years of Pakistan*, Oxford University Press, Karachi, 1997.

Ahmed, Feroz, *Ethnicity and Politics in Pakistan*, Oxford University Press, Karachi, 1999.

Ahmed, Munir, *How We Got It: A True Story of the Pakistani Nuclear Programme*, Sham-Kay-Baad, Lahore, 1998.

Akbar, M.K., *Kargil: Cross Border Terrorism*, Mittal Publications, Delhi, 1999.

Akhund, Iqbal, *Trial and Error: The Advent and Eclipse of Benazir Bhutto*, Oxford University Press, Karachi, 2000.

Ali, Chaudri Muhammad, *The Emergence of Pakistan*, Research Society of Pakistan, Lahore, 10th impression, 1998.

Ali, Hamid, *Martial Law Orders and Regulations*, The Ideal Publishers, Karachi, 1980.

Ali, Tariq, *Can Pakistan Survive? The Death of a State*, Penguin, Harmondsworth, 1983.

Amin, Tahir, *Ethno-National Movements of Pakistan*, Institute of Policy Studies, Islamabad, 1993.

Arif, General K.M., *Working with Zia*, Oxford University Press, Karachi, 1996.

Aziz, K.K., *The Murder of History: A Critique of History Textbooks Used in Pakistan*, Vanguard, Lahore, 1993.

—— *The Making of Pakistan: A Study in Nationalism*, Sang-e-Meel Publications, Lahore, 1993.

Bahl, Major General Y. (ed.), *Kargil Blunder: Pakistan's Plight, India's Victory*, Manas Publications, Delhi, 2000.

Barth, Fredrik, *The Last Wali of Swat*, Columbia University Press, New York, 1985.

*Baruah, Amit, *Dateline Islamabad*, Penguin, Delhi, 2007.

Baxter, Craig and Kennedy, Charles H. (eds), *Pakistan 2000*, Oxford University Press, Karachi, 2000.

*Bhutto, Benazir, *Reconciliation: Islam, Democracy and the West*, Simon & Schuster, London, 2008 (hardback).

Bhutto, Zulfikar Ali, *The Myth of Independence*, Classic, Lahore, 1995.

—— *If I am Assassinated . . .*, Classic, Lahore, n.d.

Bose, Sumantra, *The Challenge in Kashmir: Democracy, Self-Determination and a Just Peace*, Sage, New Delhi, 1997.

Callard, Keith, *Pakistan: A Political Study*, George Allen & Unwin, Oxford, 1957.

Chaudhry, Sardar Muhammad, *The Ultimate Crime: Eyewitness to Power Games*, Qaumi Publishers, Lahore, 1999.

Chisti, Lt General Faiz Ali, *Betrayals of Another Kind*, Jang, Lahore, 1996.

Choudhury, G.W., *The Last Days of United Pakistan*, Oxford University Press, Karachi, 1993.

Cloughley, Brian, *A History of the Pakistan Army: Wars and Insurrections*, Oxford University Press, Karachi, 2000.

Cohen, Stephen, *The Pakistan Army*, Oxford University Press, Karachi, 1998.

*Cohen, Stephen Philip, *The Idea of Pakistan*, Brookings, Washington, DC, 2004.

Collins, Larry and Lapierre, Dominique, *Freedom at Midnight*, HarperCollins, London, 1997.

*Copley, Gregory R. and Purvis, A. Hussain, *The Defense and Foreign Affairs Handbook on Pakistan, Pakistan: The Global Strategic Lynchpin*, The International Strategic Studies Association, Alexandra, USA, November 2008.

*Corera, Gordon, *Shopping for Bombs: Nuclear Proliferation, Global Insecurity and the Rise and Fall of the A.Q. Khan Network*, Hurst & Co, London, 2006.

Dil, Anwar and Dil, Afia, *Bengali Language Movement to Bangladesh*, Ferozons, Lahore, 2000.

Duncan, Emma, *Breaking the Curfew: A Political Journey through Pakistan*, Arrow, London, 1989.

Durrani, Tehmina, *My Feudal Lord*, Corgi, London, 1994.

Embree, Ainslie T., *Pakistan's Western Borderlands*, Vikas, Delhi, 1985.

Feldman, Herbert, *The End and the Beginning, Pakistan 1969–1971*, Oxford University Press, Karachi, 1976.

French, Patrick, *Liberty or Death: India's Journey to Independence and Division*, HarperCollins, London, 1997.

Gjelstad, Jorn and Njolstad, Olav (eds), *Nuclear Rivalry and International Order*, Sage Publications, London, 1996.

Hamid, Major General S. Shahid, *Early Years of Pakistan*, Ferozons, Lahore, 1993.

*Haqqani, Husain, *Between Mosque and Military*, Carnegie Endowment for International Peace, New York, 2005.

Harrison, Selig S., *In Afghanistan's Shadow: Baluch Nationalism and Soviet Temptations*, Carnegie Endowment for International Peace, New York, 1981.

Hoodbhoy, Pervez (ed.), *Education and the State: Fifty Years of Pakistan*, Oxford University Press, Karachi, 1998.

Huntingdon, Samuel P., *The Clash of Civilisations and the Remaking of World Order*, Viking, India, 1996.

Hussain, Ijaz, *Kashmir Dispute: An International Law Perspective*, Quaid-e-Azam University, Rawalpindi, 1998.

Hussain, S. Shabbir and Kamran, Mujahid (eds), *Dr A.Q. Khan on Science and Education*, Sang-e-Meel Publications, Lahore, 1997.

*Hussain, Zahid, *Frontline Pakistan: The Struggle with Militant Islam*, I.B. Taurus, London, 2007.

Iqbal, Afzal, *The Islamisation of Pakistan*, Vanguard, Lahore, 1986.

Jacob, Lt General J.F.R., *Surrender at Dacca: Birth of a Nation*, Manohar Publishers, Delhi, 1997.

Jalalzai, Musa Khan, *Sectarianism in Pakistan*, A.H. Publishers, Lahore, 1992.

Jamal, Rashid, *Mohajirs of Pakistan: Plight, and Struggle for Survival*, Loh-e-Adab, Karachi, 1998.

Jha, Prem Shankar, *Kashmir 1947*, Oxford India Paperbacks, Oxford University Press, Delhi, 1998.

Khan, Hamid, *Constitutional and Political History of Pakistan*, Oxford University Press, Oxford, 2001.

Khan, Lt General Jahan Dad, *Pakistan: Leadership Challenges*, Oxford University Press, Karachi, 1999.

Khan, Mohammad Asghar, *Generals in Politics: Pakistan 1958–1982*, Vikas, Delhi, 1983.

Khan, Mohammad Ayub, *Friends Not Masters: A Political Autobiography*, Oxford University Press, Karachi, 1967.

Khan, Roedad, *Pakistan: A Dream Gone Sour*, Oxford University Press, Karachi, 1998.

Khan, Roedad (ed.), *The American Papers: Secret and Confidential Documents. India-Pakistan-Bangladesh, 1965–1973*, Oxford University Press, Karachi, 1999.

Khan, Brigadier (retd) Z.A., *The Way it Was*, Ahbab, Karachi, 1998.

Kissinger, Henry, *The White House Years*, Weidenfeld and Nicolson and Michael Joseph, London, 1979.

Kurin, Richard, 'A View from the Countryside', pp. 115–27 in Anita M. Weiss (ed.), *Islamic Reassertion in Pakistan*, Vanguard, Lahore, 1987.

Lamb, Alistair, *Kashmir: A Disputed Legacy 1846–1990*, Oxford University Press, Karachi, 1992.

Lamb, Christina, *Waiting for Allah: Pakistan's Struggle for Democracy*, Viking, Delhi, 1991.

*Levy, Adrian and Scott-Clark, Catherine, *Deception: Pakistan, the United States and the Global Nuclear Weapons Conspiracy*, Penguin, Delhi, 2007.

McGrath, Allen, *The Destruction of Pakistan's Democracy*, Oxford University Press, Karachi, 2000.

Malik, Iftikhar H., *State and Civil Society in Pakistan*, Macmillan, Basingstoke, 1997.

Malik, Brigadier S.K.,*The Quranic Concept of War*, Wajidalis, Lahore, 1979.

Malik, Zahid, *Dr A.Q. Khan and The Islamic Bomb*, Hurmat Publications, Islamabad, 1992.

Matinuddin, Kamal, *The Nuclearisation of South Asia*, Oxford University Press, Karachi, 2002.

Mazari, Sherbaz Khan, *A Journey to Disillusionment*, Oxford University Press, Karachi, 2000.

The Military Balance, 2000–2001, International Institute of Strategic Studies, Oxford University Press, London, 2000.

*Musharraf, Pervez, *In the Line of Fire: A Memoir*, Free Press, New York, 2006.

Nasr, Seyyed Vali Reza, 'State Society and the Crisis of National Identity', pp. 103–30 in Rasul Bakhsh Rais (ed.), *State Society and Democratic Change in Pakistan*, Oxford University Press, Karachi, 1997.

*Nawaz, Shuja, *Crossed Swords: Pakistan, Its Army and the Wars Within*, Oxford University Press, Oxford, 2008.

Nayyer, A.H., 'Madrasa Education', pp. 215–50 in Pervez Hoodboy (ed.), *Education and the State: Fifty Years of Pakistan*, Oxford University Press, Karachi, 1998.

Niazi, Lt General A.A.K., *The Betrayal of East Pakistan*, Oxford University Press, Karachi, 1999.

Niazi, Zamir, *Press in Chains*, Karachi Press Club, Karachi, 1986.

Noman, Omar, *Economic and Social Progress in Asia: Why Pakistan Did Not Become a Tiger*, Oxford University Press, Karachi, 1997.

Palit, Major General D.K. and Namboodiri, P.K.S., *Pakistan's Islamic Bomb*, Vikas, Delhi, 1979.

Perkovich, George, *India's Nuclear Bomb: The Impact on Global Proliferation*, University of California Press, Berkeley, CA, 1999.

Rabbani, Ata, *I Was the Quaid's ADC*, Oxford University Press, Karachi, 1996.

Rabbani, Ikram M., *A Comprehensive Book of Pakistan Studies*, Ch Ahmad Najib, Lahore, 1998.

Rafiushan, Kureishi, *The New Pakistan*, G. Bell and Sons, London, 1977.

Rahman, Lt General M. Attiqur, *Our Defence Cause*, White Lion Publishers, London, 1976.

—— *Back to the Pavilion*, Ardeshir Cowasjee, Karachi, 1989.

Rahman, Tariq, *Language and Politics in Pakistan*, Oxford University Press, Karachi, 1996.

Rais, Rasul Bakhsh (ed.), *State, Society and Democratic Change in Pakistan*, Oxford University Press, Karachi, 1997.

Rashid, Abbas and Shaheed, Farida, *Pakistan: Ethno-Politics and Contending Elites*, Discussion Paper No. 45, United Nations Research Institute for Social Development, June 1993, Geneva, available online at www.unrisd.org.

*Rashid, Ahmed, *Descent into Chaos: How the War Against Islamic Extremism is Being Lost in Pakistan, Afghanistan and Central Asia*, Allen Lane, London, 2008.

Raza, Rafi (ed.), *Pakistan in Perspective 1947–1997*, Oxford University Press, Karachi, 1997.

Rehman, Shahid ur, *Long Road to Chagai: Untold Story of Pakistan's Nuclear Quest*, Print Wise Publications, Islamabad, 1999.

—— *Who Owns Pakistan?*, Mr Books, Islamabad, 1999.

Riza, Major General (retd) Shaukat, *The Pakistan Army War 1965*, Services Book Club, Lahore, 1984.

—— *The Pakistan Army 1947–1949*, Services Book Club, Lahore, 1989.

—— *The Pakistan Army 1966–1971*, Army Education Press, Lahore, 1990.

Rizvi, Hasan-Askari, *The Military and Politics in Pakistan: 1947–1986*, Progressive Publishers, Lahore, 1987.

Salik, Siddiq, *Witness to Surrender*, Oxford University Press, Karachi, 1977.

Schneider, Barry R. and Dowdy, William L. (eds), *Pulling Back From the Nuclear Brink: Reducing and Countering Nuclear Threats*, Frank Cass, London, 1998.

Schofield, Victoria, *Kashmir in Conflict: India, Pakistan and the Unfinished Conflict*, I.B. Taurus, London, 2000.

Schofield, Victoria (ed.), *Old Roads and New Highways: Fifty Years of Pakistan*, Oxford University Press, Karachi, 1997.

*Shaikh, Farzana, *Making Sense of Pakistan*, Hurst & Co., London, 2009.

Sharma, Rajeev, *Pak Proxy War: A Story of the ISI, Bin Laden and Kargil*, Kaveri Books, Delhi, 1999.

*Siddiqa, Ayesha, *Military Inc. Inside Pakistan's Military Economy*, Pluto Press, London, 2007.

Singh, Karan, *Autobiography*, Oxford India Paperbacks, Oxford University Press, Delhi, 1994.

Sisson, Richard and Rose, Leo E., *War and Secession: Pakistan, India and the Creation of Bangladesh*, Oxford University Press, Karachi, 1990.

Spector, Leonard S. and Smith, Jacqueline, *Nuclear Ambitions: The Spread of Nuclear Weapons 1989–1990*, Farda Publishing Company, Karachi, 1992.

Syed, G.M., *A Case for Sindu Desh*, Sorath Publications, Bombay, 1985.

Talbot, Ian, *Pakistan: A Modern History*, Vanguard Books, Lahore, 1999.

*Talbott, Strobe, *Engaging India: Diplomacy, Democracy and the Bomb*, Brookings Institution Press, Washington, 2006.

Uzair, Mohammad, 'Foreign Aid and Indebtedness in Pakistan', in Mehrunnisa Ali (ed.), *Readings in Pakistan Foreign Policy 1971–1998*, Oxford University Press, Karachi, 2001, pp. 367–73.

Weiss, Anita M. (ed.), *Islamic Reassertion in Pakistan*, Vanguard, Lahore, 1987.

Weiss, Anita M. and Gilani, S. Zulfiqar (eds), *Power and Civil Society in Pakistan*, Oxford University Press, Karachi, 2001.

Weissman, Steve and Krosney, Herbert, *The Islamic Bomb: The Nuclear Threat to Israel and the Middle East*, Times Books, New York, 1983, 2nd edition.

*White, Joshua T., *Pakistan's Islamist Frontier: Islamic Politics and US Policy in Pakistan's North-West Frontier*. Religion & Security Monograph Series, no. 1, Center on Faith & International Affairs, Arlington, VA, 2008.

*Whitehead, Andrew, *A Mission in Kashmir*, Penguin, Delhi, 2007.

Wilder, Andrew R., *The Pakistani Voter: Electoral Politics and Voting Behaviour in the Punjab*, Oxford University Press, Karachi, 1999.

*Wirsing, Robert G., *Kashmir: In the Shadow of War*, M.E. Sharpe, New York, 2003.

Wolpert, Stanley, *Zulfi Bhutto of Pakistan: His Life and Times*, Oxford University Press, New York, 1993.

—— *Jinnah of Pakistan*, Oxford University Press, New York, 1994.

Zaheer, Hasan, *The Separation of East Pakistan: The Rise and Realization of Bengali Muslim Nationalism*, Oxford University Press, Karachi, 1995.

—— *The Rawalpindi Conspiracy 1951*, Oxford University Press, Karachi, 1998.

Zaidi, S. Akbar, *Issues in Pakistan's Economy*, Oxford University Press, Karachi, 1999.

Zaidi, S. Akbar (ed.), *Regional Imbalances and the National Question in Pakistan*, Vanguard, Lahore, 1992.

Ziring, Lawrence, *Pakistan in the Twentieth Century: A Political History*, Oxford University Press, Karachi, 1998.

Journals and Reports

2001 Report on Foreign Terrorist Organizations, US Department of State, available on www.state.gov/s/ct/rls/rpt/fto/2001/5258.htm.

Abbasi, Major General Zahir ul Islam, 'Maj. Gen. Abbasi's Intended Address to the Nation', *Defence Journal* 21, May–June 1996, 53–4.

Ali, Syed Akhtar, 'Towards a Safe and Stable Nuclear Environment in South Asia: Options, Choices and Constraints for Pakistan', *National Development and Security,* 'Special on Nuclear', 8:2, November 1999, 1–26, published by the Foundation for Research on International Environment, National Development and Security, Rawalpindi, Pakistan.

Amnesty International, *Pakistan: Human Rights in Karachi*, ASA 33/01/96, February 1996.

Anand, Vinod, *India's Response to the Kargil Aggression*, IDSA, www.idsa-india.org.

Annual Report on Military Expenditures, US State Department, 1998 and 1999, now available on www.state.gov.

Anon., 'Nuclear South Asia: Opportunities and Challenges for Pakistan', *Air War College Journal*, 1999, 19–37.

Boisard, Dr Marcel A., 'Islamic Conduct of Hostilities and the Protection of the Victims of Armed Conflicts', *Defence Journal* 5:1–2, January–February 1979, 9–19.

Bokhari, E.A.S., 'India-Pakistan: The Nuclear Option', *Defence Journal* 2:3, March 1998, 49–52.

Carnegie Endowment for International Peace, 'Non-Proliferation', fact sheet, 15 April 1999.

Country Report on Human Rights Practices, 1998, US Department of State, available on 222.usis.usemb.se/human/human1998/India.html.

Country Report on Human Rights Practices, 1995–2000, US Department of State, available on www.state.gov/www/global/human_rights/hrp_reports_mainhp.html.

Economic Survey 2000–2001, government of Pakistan, published by the Economic Advisers Wing, Finance Division, Islamabad.

'Events', *Pakistan Defence News Bulletin*, 1–15 October 1999.

Executive Summary of the Kargil Review Committee Report, available on www.fas.org/news/india/2000/25indi1.htm.

Gallup Poll, May 1985 and April 2000, Gallup Pakistan, Islamabad.

Gregory, Shaun, 'Nuclear Command and Control in South Asia', *Strategic Issues* 3, March 2000, entitled 'The Nuclear Debate', published by The Institute of Strategic Studies, Islamabad.

Hamoodur Rehman Commission Report, Dawn, 8 January–1 February 2001. A version of the report is also available on www.dawn.com/report/hrc.

Human Rights Commission of Pakistan, *State of Human Rights in 1997*, Lahore, 1998.

—— *State of Human Rights in 1998*, Lahore 1999.

Jaffri, Judge Rehmat Hussain, verdict on the trial of Nawaz Sharif, SPL. Case No. 385/1999, available on http://pak.gov.pk/public/govt/reports/vtext/htm.

Kapur, Ashok, 'Western Biases', *Bulletin of the Atomic Sciences* 51:1, January/February 1995, available on www.bullatomsci.org/issues.1995/jf95/jf95/Kapur.html.

Khan, Munir Ahmed, 'Nuclearisation of South Asia and its Regional and Global Implications', *Institute of Regional Studies*, Islamabad, 1998.

Musharraf, Pervez, *Address to the Nation, 12 October 1999*, available on http://news/bbc.co.uk/hi/english/worldmonitoring/newsid-473000/473175.stm.

—— *Address to the Nation, 17 October 1999*, available on www.pak.gov.pk/public/president-adress-19-09-01.htm.

—— '12 January 2002, Speech Highlights', available on http://news.bbc.co.uk/hi/English/world/south_asia/newsid_1757000/1757251.stm.

National Intelligence Council, *Global Trends 2015: A Dialogue About the Future with Nongovernment Experts*, Washington, 2000.

Reform of Tax Administration in Pakistan, *Report on the Task Forces on Reform of Tax Administration*, 21 April 2001.

Siddiqi, Brigadier (retd) Abdul Rahman, 'Army and Islam: An Appraisal', *Defence Journal* 21, May–June 1996, 3–11.

*Sultan-i-Rome, 'Swat: A Critical Analysis', *Institute of Peace and Conflict Studies*, India, January 2009.

United Nations Development Programme, *Human Development Report 2001*, Oxford University Press, New York, 2001.

World Military Expenditures and Arms Transfers 1995–1997, US Arms Control and Disarmament Agency, Washington, DC, 1996–1998, available on www.state.gov/www/global/arms/98_amiexroc.html and www.state.gov/www/global/arms/99_amiextoc.html.

Zaman, Muhammad Qasim, 'Sectarianism in Pakistan: The Radicalisation of Shi' e and Sunni Identities', *Modern Asian Studies* 32: 3, 1998, 689–716.

Index